Adobe

After Effects® 6.5
STUDIO TECHNIQUES

Mark Christiansen

Adobe

Adobe After Effects 6.5 Studio Techniques

Mark Christiansen

This Adobe Press book is published by Peachpit. For information on Adobe Press books, contact:

Peachpit
1249 Eighth Street
Berkeley, CA 94710
(510) 524-2178
Fax: (510) 524-2221
http://www.adobepress.com

To report errors, please send a note to errata@peachpit.com
Peachpit Press is a division of Pearson Education

Adobe Press Editor: Kelly Ryer
Development and Copy Editor: Linda Laflamme
Production Editor: Connie Jeung-Mills
Technical Editor: Stu Maschwitz
Proofreader: Haig MacGregor
Compositor: Kim Scott
Indexer: Jack Lewis
Cover design: Aren Howell
Cover illustration: Nathan Clement

Notice of Rights

Notice of Liability

Trademarks

ISBN 0-321-31620-7

9 8 7 6 5 4 3 2 1

Printed and bound in the United States of America

Contents at a Glance

Contents

Section II Effects Compositing Essentials

About the Authors

Mark Christiansen has created visual effects and animations for feature films, television, computer games, and an array of companies in and around the San Francisco Bay Area, his native home. Recent feature film effects credits at The Orphanage include *The Day After Tomorrow* and *Spy Kids 3-D*. His studio, Christiansen Creative, produces effects, motion graphics, and written content. His independent directing work has been featured at film festivals including the 2004 Los Angeles International Short Film Festival.

He is the coauthor of *After Effects 5.5 Magic* with Nathan Moody and a contributing editor for *DV Magazine*. He has been a guest speaker at NAB, DV Expo, and GDC. Mark was officially the "number one beta tester" for After Effects 6.0, on which he also consulted directly for Adobe as a technical writer.

Mark's career began in the art department at LucasArts Entertainment, where his work directing the innovative (yet ultimately obscure) *Behind the Magic* was honored with *Entertainment Weekly*'s pick of Number 1 of 1998 for Multimedia (a category that disappeared altogether the following year). He also pioneered LucasArts' short-lived inquest into live-action video, single-handedly compositing over 100 shots in After Effects for *Rebel Assault II*.

Mark is a graduate of Pomona College. He and his wife have two amazing kids.

 **Stu Maschwitz** is a director, visual effects supervisor, renowned technologist, and founding partner of The Orphanage, where his credits include mind-bending effects for award-winning commercials, as well as such feature films as *Sin City*, *Spy Kids 3-D*, and *The Adventures of Shark Boy and Lava Girl in 3-D*, which is currently in production. An innovator in filmmaking technology, he is also the creator of The Orphanage's Magic Bullet software. Prior to joining up with his fellow co-conspirators to start The Orphanage, Stu spent five years at George Lucas' Industrial Light + Magic, supervising all of the space battle sequences on *Star Wars, Episode One: The Phantom Menace* and contributing visual effects to such blockbusters as *Twister*, *Men in Black*, and *Mission: Impossible*.

 **Brendan Bolles'** roundabout path to digital imaging passed through summers at camp, stage acting, physics classes, and Mac user groups. He now works for The Orphanage as a visual effects artist and software developer, recently completing shots for *Hellboy* and *Sin City* using After Effects and eLin, a set of plug-ins he helped create. His other independent software projects are available at www.fnordware.com.

Acknowledgments

Many people deserve thanks for helping with this book, and I hope none will be forgotten here, but without the influence of Stu Maschwitz, who also contributed the final chapter, I would never have attempted it.

Stu offered his support and the resources of The Orphanage, where I had done a lot of my best work, and followed through with dozens of email exchanges at all hours on a variety of related topics that were a constant head-check on my understanding of compositing and After Effects. That's one reason his name recurs throughout this book. The other reason is that he's a flat-out knowledgeable and influential guy. Stu has written clearly and cogently (and often hilariously) about the most geeky and arcane aspects of effects compositing.

I'm also very grateful to Brendan Bolles for gamely jumping in to contribute a nifty chapter on film and high dynamic range compositing. The best writing comes from clear thinking, and Brendan came through on both counts despite his grueling production schedule on a Super Bowl commercial that wouldn't quit.

Thanks to all of my past clients who gave me the firsthand experience that went into this book, and in particular to the people who helped secure elements or final shots for use in this book's figures despite no benefit to themselves: Rama Dunayevich and Marc Sadeghi at The Orphanage, Coral Petretti at ABC Photography, Tim Fink of Tim Fink Productions, Gary Jaeger and Cameron Baxter at Core Studio, Jonathan Barson at The Foundry UK, Fred Lewis at Moving Media, and Matthew Ward and the wacky goofiness that is markandmatty.com.

To the people at Adobe who've made After Effects what it is, in particular Dave Simons, Dan Wilk, Erica Schisler, and Steve Kilisky, and to some of the developers who've helped me understand it better over the years, including Michael Natkin and Chris Prosser.

Thanks to the companies that contributed to the book's CD: Julie Hill at Artbeats, Peder Norrby, who *is* Trapcode, Russ Andersson of Andersson Technologies, Sean Safreed of Red Giant Software, and Philipp Spöth of Frischluft. These were my choices for inclusion because they all provide something vital to effects compositing in After Effects.

Other people who were helpful e-mailing their feedback on various topics include Bruno Nicoletti at the Foundry UK, Alex Czetwertynski at Disciple Films Paris, Jance Allen and Aaron Rhodes at The Orphanage, Don Shay at *Cinefex Magazine*, and Matt Silverman at Phoenix Editorial.

Thanks to Peachpit, to Marjorie Baer and Kelly Ryer, as well as Karen Reichstein and Rebecca Ross, for getting things kicked off, to Linda Laflamme for being a dedicated, supportive, and thorough editor on the opposite end of the continent, and to Connie Jeung-Mills for all the help getting the figures and layout into the form you see them here.

A special thanks to the people who offered help during the dark days when I was sure there was no way I was going to finish this book, especially my childhood friend and former editor at *DV Magazine*, Jim Feeley. Thanks to my former students at the Academy of Art and to *The Day After Tomorrow* compositing crew at The Orphanage. Helping experienced compositors as well as novice students work with After Effects for the first time offered a lot of insight that went into this book.

A huge expression of gratitude to the people of Bali and our hosts on the writing sabbatical that kicked off this effort, Jade and Mali Hyde. With all of the visual and cultural splendor that is featured in this book, the people are Bali's greatest resource, and I will always associate this project with their warmth, generosity, and extraordinary resourcefulness and creativity.

Finally, thanks to my mom, who remains always supportive and loving, and my father, who told me—much too late to make any difference—how grueling and tedious he found writing his own textbook several years ago.

I

Introduction

Adobe® After Effects® 6.5

Version 6.5.1 Professional

© 1992–2004 Adobe Systems Incorporated. All Rights Reserved.
See the patent and legal notice in the about box.

6.5.1.7
QuickTime installed
11% used of 1021 MB
378 Plug-ins

Mark Christiansen
Christiansen Creative

Adobe

Patent & Legal Notices

If you aren't fired with enthusiasm, you will be fired with enthusiasm.

—Vince Lombardi

Introduction

Why This Book?

After Effects 6.5 Studio Techniques has a different focus than any other After Effects book: creating realistic visual effects. Other After Effects books focus predominantly on motion graphics, touching only briefly on topics that make up the core of visual effects.

Not only is this the first After Effects book to deal specifically with visual effects, but it is one of the few to discuss the creation of visual effects in detail, period. As I wrote, I wondered why. Why, with visual effects such a mature industry, do so few books describe exactly how to do effects that appear all the time, effects that no longer comprise someone's trade secret?

I was reminded of a similar code of silence in a bygone era of magic, nearly a century ago. Not movie magic but practical magic, the kind promoted at the Magic Castle, which is headquartered, coincidentally enough, in Hollywood.

The Cult of Magic

Back in the early days of magic, before you could go to your local bookstore or magic shop and buy a copy of David Pogue's *Magic for Dummies* (Hungry Minds), magic was a dark art practiced by masters sequestered in private clubs and learned by a handful of apprentices. The roots of the word "magic" refer to the Magi, the members of the Zoroastrian priesthood. I don't suppose it gets much more sequestered than that.

NOTES

One of the great novels of the decade is Michael Chabon's *The Amazing Adventures of Kavalier and Clay* (Random House). If you enjoy stories about magic in the days of Houdini, stories about the birth of comics, or just an extremely well-written novel, I highly recommend this Pulitzer Prize winner.

Visual effects, those skillful re-creations of reality, have been an art form since the beginning of filmmaking; just watch 1900's *Trip to the Moon* by George Meliés (**Figure I.1**). In fact, the earliest films capitalized on two phenomena above all others: the startling realism of the medium and the ability to make up scenes that were impossible to create any other way.

But until the 1990s, special effects post-production for movies was a craft known only to a few hundred practitioners worldwide, and the dark art of its practices (often photo-chemical, sometimes crude, sometimes sophisticated, almost always labor-intensive and fraught with treacherously little room for error) was largely known only to them, passed on in a guild-like fashion to those few apprentices who found their way to this strange specialization (**Figure I.3**).

Enter the color desktop computer, then Adobe Photoshop, then After Effects, and suddenly anyone with a few thousand bucks for equipment, or access to borrow it, could have a go at creating a visual effects shot. And have a go people did, creating visionary low-budget videos (as well as hundreds of *Star Wars* tribute films) and growing the professional visual effects community exponentially.

Figure I.1 *Trip to the Moon* is sometimes called the first visual effects film.

The earliest public motion picture display by the Lumière brothers (**Figure I.2**) reputedly included footage of a train pulling into a station that had the poor naive audience diving to the floor in panic, believing a real train was headed their way. Louis Lumière evidently grew quickly tired of this spectacle, famously declaring a short time later, "The cinema is an invention without a future."

Figure I.3 A torture device? Only according to your point of view. An optical printer such as this one was the sole means of compositing film prior to the digital age.

Figure I.2 The Lumière borthers. Louis Lumière famously declared, "The cinema is an invention without a future."

A 2004 survey by an Adobe product manager turned up some *250* Hollywood features that had relied on After Effects. Stu Maschwitz, author of Chapter 15, "Learning to See," led the Rebel Mac group at Industrial Light + Magic for several years in the 1990s; their use of After Effects on big-budget, Academy-nominated effects films was largely unpublicized, mostly due to the perception (even among film studios) that only "big iron" was up to work of that caliber.

Yet the old cultish attitudes in many ways prevailed. Sure, lots of kids proved that they could produce a convincing lightsaber battle on the family computer, but try to learn how to create an elaborate effects shot by reading up on it and you got smoke, mirrors, vagaries, and what has quickly become a cliché of *Cinefex* magazine (once the source for all kinds of nitty-gritty details): the use of "proprietary software." Visual effects work might as well have been magic because it seemed to be made up of a bunch of exacting techniques crafted by super-geniuses and jealously guarded as trade secrets.

After Effects 6.5 Studio Techniques aims to demystify the realm of visual effects, focusing on the skill of re-creating reality with After Effects, of fooling viewers into thinking they are seeing a shot that was taken with a camera all at once.

Think of this book as a basic magic manual, teaching you the visual effects equivalents of hiding a card or palming a coin. If your goal is to be the David Blaine of compositing, you must master the basics that come up again and again, those effects that are often a key part of the most original and fantastic movie sequences.

Truly Challenging

Ironically, visual effects artists themselves often fail to notice how complicated it is to craft a shot; until you step back a little bit, all you notice is that you spent long days of hard work making subtle corrections to dozens of takes of a few seconds of film. The individual steps now seem almost unremarkable and trivial, but a complex shot might consist of thousands of such steps, many of which were at some point surprising and revelatory to each of us.

Also, each visual effects shot seems to be unique, and in many ways, it is. Explaining the exact steps to create one shot may be of little use when it comes time to create the next one. Some bread-and-butter effects, however, are done at every studio and are no one's trade secret. These come up all the time, sometimes as a component of a larger and more complex shot, sometimes as the main focus of a simple shot. Every compositing artist should know how to do them.

This book is about those kinds of effects; ultimately, it is about the process of building them up to create a shot that is greater than the sum of its parts and fools the eye of the viewer.

All visual effects can be broken down into comprehensible components (although, to comprehend some of the components might very well also require an understanding of wave dynamics or Fourier transforms). Moreover, very few (even simple) effects can be called complete without being broken down much further than the novice artist typically wants to go with them.

This brings us to the keys to creating the best visual effects, those that are often pretty close to invisible and call no attention to themselves whatsoever. They do not detract from the story, but enhance it, and only later on do you wonder, "How the heck did they do that?"

The Keys

You do it by following some simple guidelines—simple, yet so important in delineating your success or failure as an effects compositor. The keys are

▶ **Get reference.** You can't re-create what you can't see clearly and in great detail. Great artists recognize many features of the world that the untrained eye fails to see.

▶ **Simpler is often better.** Effects compositing is complicated enough without overcomplicating it with convoluted processes and needless extra steps. A robust effects pipeline is typically made up of the simplest available solutions, and it's usually worth the extra effort

NOTES

The willingness to go beyond the one-button solution and break apart a shot into adjustable components is what will make your shots stand out. Otherwise you're just relying on luck to overcome laziness.

to simplify your workflow however you can. Occam's Razor, which states that the simplest solution or explanation is often the best one, applies in spades here.

▶ **Break it down.** This, more than anything else, addresses the biggest error made by beginners: They try to solve problems using a single solution, applied globally to the whole shot or one of its elements. For example, beginning artists tend not to look at individual color channels when matching foreground and background colors. As Chapter 5, "Color and Light: Adjusting and Matching," lays out, you must be willing to examine the individual red, green, and blue channels and adjust them separately to match overall color effectively. And if this advice applies to something so fundamental as color matching, you'd better believe it applies to more complex effects.

▶ **It's not good enough.** This sounds discouraging, doesn't it? What you must take away is the spirit, rather than the literal truth of this statement, and always strive for the best result possible.

If you let your guard down and settle for "good enough," someone's going to say it…

"That Looks Fake"

Can't you just hear that flat condemnation, uttered with no subtlety or restraint by the teenage kid sitting behind you at the multiplex? That kid is sometimes wrong (I've heard this label slapped on a shot that I knew had no visual effects), but you can hardly argue with the sentiment if your goal is to fool the skeptical viewer.

A little bit of that petulant teen lives in all of us. Ideally the statement will evolve to "That looks fake because…" with you able to complete the phrase using your eyes, your observations of the world and those of your colleagues, and information from a source like this book.

A somewhat more civilized version of that rude teenager shows up at dailies on a feature film effects project, but with the title of Visual Effects Supervisor. Here's how dailies generally go: At the start of a workday, a bunch of people get some coffee, go into a dark screening room, watch a shot more times in a minute or two than the average audience will watch it in a lifetime (unless of course it's a shot from *Star Wars*), and you are told why it doesn't look right. It sounds like a harsh way to start the day, but actually, this is absolutely where the real process of doing great work is rooted.

Relentless dissatisfaction is one of the keys to successful visual effects. Try not to confuse it with actual discouragement, no matter how harsh your own (or someone else's) criticism. If it doesn't look right to you, it doesn't mean you're a bad artist; it simply means you have the taste and discrimination to know the difference (a wise statement I first heard from my former colleague Paul Topolos, now at Pixar).

What Compositing Can (and Can't) Do

The type of full visual effects pipeline used to produce a big-budget feature film contains many roles and specializations; depending on your point of view and on the shot in question, the compositor's role can be the most crucial or the most denigrated. Typically, with the possible exception of a colorist, the compositor is the last one to touch the shot before it goes in the movie, so it's an important job if only for that reason.

To a large extent, a composite is only as good as the sum of its elements. The best compositors have a reputation for producing gold out of dross, building a great-looking shot despite poorly shot plates and slap-dash 3D elements. But compositors still need elements to do their work, and poorly shot or created elements typically lead to an equally poor result.

If you're still learning how to composite, you may be creating all of your elements yourself. That's great, because compositors benefit from understanding the disciplines that feed into the shot. For example, it's essential that you understand how the camera gathers images so you can mimic the reality created by a camera. If you're comfortable as a 3D animator, those skills will help you navigate the 3D capabilities of After Effects, and you will learn how much time you can save fine-tuning your shots in 2D rather than tweaking them endlessly in numerous 3D renders.

As a compositor, you have to know about these other disciplines, because to some extent you're re-creating their results from scratch, and you have far more room to cheat and make up your own rules. A cameraman cannot go further than the limits of what a camera can do, but you can. And one dirty secret is that sometimes you must cheat actual reality to make your shot believable.

About This Book

After Effects 6.5 Studio Techniques will help you toward more believable shots in many ways, but it is not intended to help you create your first After Effects project. It is the textbook that I didn't have when I taught the course Introduction to Visual Effects at the Academy of Art University in San Francisco. My students were familiar with how to use After Effects but had not yet put it to work finishing shots.

If you're new to After Effects, first spend some time with its excellent documentation or check out one of the many books available to help beginners learn to use After Effects, such as *After Effects 6.5 for Windows and Macintosh: Visual QuickPro Guide* (Anthony Bolante, Peachpit Press), *Adobe After Effects 6 Hands-On Training* (Lynda Weinman, Peachpit Press), and *Adobe After Effects 6.0 Classroom in a Book* (Adobe Press).

If, however, you're moderately comfortable with After Effects, or with compositing in general, and you want to take your visual effects work to the next level, read on. This book was written for you.

After Effects 6.5 Studio Techniques is organized into three sections:

▶ **Section I, "Working Foundations,"** reviews fundamentals of After Effects, in the context of helping you to work smarter and more efficiently. You'll explore how to make the best use of the program's core features and how to optimize your workflow. Even if you already are an experienced After Effects artist, skim this section for tips and tricks you might not have known or have forgotten.

▶ **Section II, "Effects Compositing Essentials,"** focuses on the core techniques required for effects compositing: color matching, keying, rotoscoping, motion tracking, and emulating the camera. For example, you'll delve deeply into how the Levels effect and Keylight contribute to the essential work of visual effects. This section also tackles a couple of topics that most other books consider too complicated for average users: the use of expressions and how to work with film source and high dynamic range compositing

▶ **Section III, "Creative Explorations,"** demonstrates actual effects and looks at the phenomena you might wish to re-create, taking observations of how these things look in the natural world. Most importantly, you'll learn how to apply that understanding to your shot.

What you won't find in these sections are menu-by-menu descriptions of the interface or step-by-step tutorials that walk you through projects with little connection to real-world visual effects needs.

Understanding Is Preferable to Knowledge

The goal of *After Effects 6.5 Studio Techniques* is to help you understand how the world within After Effects works and how it corresponds to the physical world you are attempting to re-create.

Your goal should be to apply what you learn here to your own shots and continue to expand your knowledge. By understanding how things work, not by mimicking prearranged steps, you will truly learn to do this work on your own. Compositing is the methodical buildup of individual component steps, steps that recur in unique combinations on each individual shot and project. This book offers advice on those steps. Putting them all together for your individual shot is up to you.

If You've Used Other Compositing Programs

After Effects 6.5 Studio Techniques partly grew from my being "The After Effects Guy" on various projects. On *The Day After Tomorrow*, for example, I joined a team of veteran freelance compositors at The Orphanage, few of whom had ever used After Effects. They were far more experienced with Apple's Shake, Digital Domain's Nuke, and Discreet's Flame. My role was not only to complete my own shots but also to help debug their problems using After Effects, freeing the compositing supervisor's time.

This double duty helped me gain a perspective on what is confusing about After Effects to people who otherwise understand compositing well. Believe it or not, compositing programs do not vary as much in their fundamental workflow as, say, 3D animation programs do. Although After Effects appears to operate completely differently than Shake, Nuke, Flame, and other node-based applications, the fundamental differences are relatively few. To summarize, they are

▶ **Render order in After Effects is established on the timeline and via pre-composing.** The clearest distinction between After Effects and its node-based brethren is its lack of a tree/node interface. Open Project Flowchart view and you see that, under the hood, After Effects tracks rendering order works the same way as these other applications (**Figure I.4**). After Effects, however, doesn't let you interact this way. (See Chapter 2, "The Timeline," and Chapter 4, "Optimizing the Pipeline.")

▶ **Transforms, effects, and masks become part of a layer and render in a set order.** In After Effects, layers have properties that belong only to them. To an After Effects user, the Shake method of applying a transform to a clip, rather than simply animating a layer's Position property, is a little hard to get used to (**Figure I.5**). On the other hand, as is explained in Chapter 4, After Effects sometimes enforces a specific order in which certain properties render, and you need to know what that is.

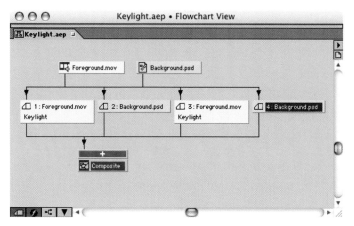

Figure I.4 Project Flowchart view is perhaps the most unrecognizable After Effects view.

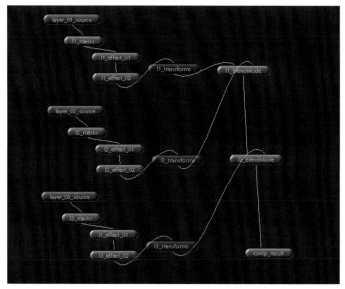

Figure I.5 A Shake node flow re-creates the set order (masks, effects, transforms, and finally blending modes) in After Effects for a three-layer composite. (Image courtesy of Stu Maschwitz.)

▶ **After Effects, like other Adobe applications, tends to think in terms of four channels: red, green, blue, and alpha (or transparency).** This is a subtle one, but the distinction plays out as soon as you start creating selections for layers (see Chapter 3, "Selections: The Key to Compositing"). Node-based applications tend to encourage you to think of mattes as luminance data, which they are. Like Photoshop, however, After Effects retains through its pipeline the persistent idea of a fourth color channel, the alpha channel, which controls transparency. You will have more success working with After Effects if you are willing to work on building alpha channels rather than combinations of luminance data for transparency.

▶ **After Effects works always in straight alpha mode, and it handles the conversion from straight to pre-multiplied alpha internally.** Not only does After Effects have a persistent idea of an alpha channel, but internally, it is always working with that alpha in straight mode. Chapter 3 covers the few provisions that are given to deal explicitly with pre-multiplication inside of After Effects.

▶ **There is, alas, no direct equivalent in After Effects to macros.** If you've never used an application like Shake, you don't know what you're missing. If you've gone far enough with the node-based application to write your own macros, however, After Effects may leave you scratching your head. It offers little in the way of direct pixel calculation and no way to batch process images via a script. The workarounds typically involve effect plug-ins and pre-composing.

▶ **Temporal and spatial settings tend to be more absolute in After Effects.** Many differences between After Effects and the node-based applications contain both benefits and pitfalls. If you need to carefully manage timing and spatial data (animation), the After Effects timeline offers huge advantages. On the other hand, all layers contain spatial and timing information relative to their composition. In other words, if you create a cool effect on the adjustment layer of a video resolution comp, and then copy the adjustment layer to a longer film-resolution comp, the layer won't cover the whole frame, nor will it last the duration of the new comp. This is something you don't typically have to think about in a node-based application.

▶ **After Effects lacks support for floating-point linear calculations and high dynamic range images.** It's pretty difficult to get used to, but the fact is, the world of high-end compositing has changed dramatically in the last few years around a new model. If you've never worked in a linearized floating-point pipeline with the capability of handling overbright pixels, you may not even be aware of all the compromises you end up having to make to get the light in your scenes to behave naturally. High dynamic range images and a floating-point, linearized pipeline are the waves of the future, but the future is here today for After Effects users in the form of a plug-in set known as eLin. (See Chapter 11, "Issues Specific to Film and HDR Images.")

Of these differences, some are arbitrary, most are a mixed bag of advantages and drawbacks, and a couple of them are constantly used by the competition as a metaphorical stick with which to beat After Effects. The two that come up the most are the handling of pre-composing and the lack of macros.

This book attempts to shed light on these and other areas of After Effects that are not explicitly dealt with in its user interface or documentation. The truth is that Shake, Nuke, and others require that you understand their own issues, such as managing pre-multiplication in your pipeline, to master them. After Effects spares you details that as a casual user, you might never need to know about, but that as a professional user you should understand thoroughly. This book is here to help.

What's On the CD

If you want to find out more about some of the plug-ins and software mentioned in this book, look no further than its CD-ROM. For example, the disc includes demos of

▶ Adobe After Effects 6.5

▶ Andersson Technologies' SynthEyes (3D tracking software)

▶ Plug-ins from Trapcode, including Particular and Lux

▶ Red Giant Software's Primatte, Magic Bullet, Knoll Light Factory, Composite Wizard, and eLin

You'll also find footage from Artbeats with which you can experiment and practice your techniques. Artbeats is a great source for stock clips of all types. Finally, there are a few example files to help you deconstruct some of the more complicated techniques.

The Bottom Line

Just like the debates about which operating system is best, debates about which compositing software is tops are largely meaningless—especially when you consider the number of first-rate, big-budget, movie effects extravaganzas that were created on three or four different platforms, with half a dozen 2D and 3D programs. If the proof of the pudding is in the eating, the consistent quality of effects in such films as *The Day After Tomorrow*, which used a variety of programs and effects houses, should show that it is the *artists* not the tools who make the biggest difference.

I like using After Effects, because I have come to think in the same way the software lays out my shots; it's no longer work, it's instinct. The goal of this book is to help you reach that point as well.

If you have comments or questions you'd like to share with me, please e-mail them to AEStudioTechniques@gmail.com.

SECTION I

Working Foundations

1

The Effects Toolset

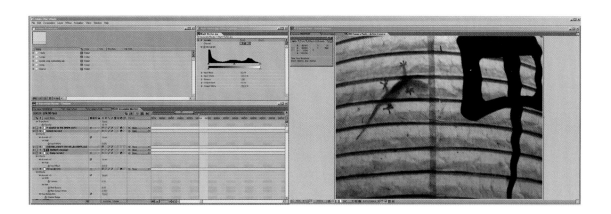

Good surfing is power, speed, and flow. The rest of it doesn't matter to me at all.

—Gary Elkerton, Australian surfer

The Effects Toolset

After Effects is, above all, a visual problem-solving tool. It is complete and logical in its ability to help you solve visual effects problems—so complete that many advanced users feel as though they are thinking with it, using the program's interface and workflow to dissect and analyze tricky situations.

Not everyone reaches that point, however, and experienced artists, especially those used to working in other applications, can miss the core logic of how things operate in After Effects. Others become frustrated stumbling through specific steps in the user interface, not knowing that their needs have been anticipated and that a better alternative is readily available.

This first chapter, then, is a tour through the user interface as a whole, pointing out specific opportunities for you to take full advantage of the best working methods available to you in After Effects.

We're not, in fact, starting at the very beginning (although I've heard it's a very good place to start). I assume that you've used After Effects before—perhaps just a few times, perhaps hundreds—and you've sensed that there are options you're missing and better ways to work. This chapter will provide some strong suggestions as to how you can make your use of the application lucid and efficient, and how to overcome some of the stumbling blocks that seem to trip up many users, beginning and advanced alike.

True, there is no single "best" approach, and After Effects offers many different ways to accomplish a task. In the end, work the way that is most comfortable and effective for you. For now, however, consider the options as they are

TIP

If you feel this book is beginning at too advanced a level for you, check out *After Effects Classroom in a Book* (Adobe Press) and *After Effects Visual QuickPro Guide* (Peachpit Press), two excellent beginner's resources.

laid out for you in this chapter, and throughout Section I of this book.

I find great pleasure in streamlining processes, in accomplishing tasks with the fewest steps possible. In over a decade of using After Effects, I have developed my own set of approaches that I find not only most efficient but also most pleasing to use. There is something truly energizing about having banged your head against what you perceived to be a flaw in the way software is designed, only to find out that there is a different approach available that anticipates your needs perfectly. Even if you consider yourself an experienced user, therefore, I encourage you to look through this chapter and the rest of Section I to see if there's anything you've been missing.

Preparing Your Workspace

For better or worse, the After Effects 6.5 user interface—like all of the versions that preceded it—is heavily based on palettes and menus. When you open After Effects for the first time, the interface itself doesn't tell you a whole lot about how to work with the program (**Figure 1.1**); you see an empty Project window and a few palettes (Tools, Info, Audio, Time Controls, and Effects and Presets, to be precise).

What you don't see are the areas of the program—the Timeline, Composition, and Layer windows, not to mention the Effect Controls window and Render Queue—where you will do most of your work. (Meanwhile, you could have a ten-year feature film career using After Effects and never once use the Audio palette.)

Also, if you're on a Mac, you may see other open programs or your desktop in the background; on Windows, you should see only a gray background field (and if you have two monitors, you'll see the field and any windows on only one of them when you begin). What happens next is that you begin the sequential work of creating a shot in After Effects—moving from the Project window to the Composition window and timeline, applying effects, masks, and so

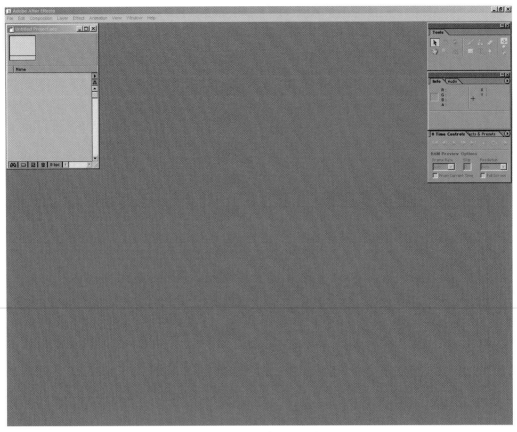

Figure 1.1 The default After Effects user interface implies little, if anything, about how you use it.

on, and rendering the result. You open lots of windows and palettes (**Figure 1.2**), move them around as needed, and maybe start to feel like you're spending as much time moving things around as you are getting work done.

None of the many windows and palettes has a default position, and if you go around to ten different artists' desks, you'll see these tools splayed out differently on each monitor. With too little screen real estate—and even with two monitors there never seems to be enough—it can quickly become a bit of a mess, really. There is no perfect, universal solution to this problem, but there are steps that you can take to introduce balance and flow to the interface.

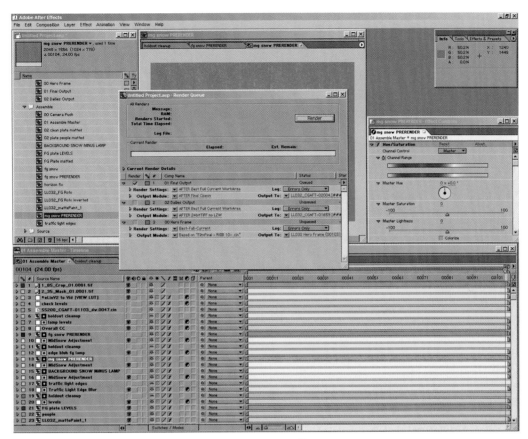

Figure 1.2 By the time you're ready to render a complex shot, After Effects may look more like this—assuming you're being tidy!

Setting (and Resetting) Your Workspace

Workspaces are an underused feature in After Effects. Everyone knows that you can use the Tab key in Adobe applications to make palettes appear and disappear, but not so many people know that you can make all of your windows snap into place so that the palettes that you *actually need* remain visible. Some users dislike and avoid this feature before they get very far with it, partly because if you don't take the necessary steps to set it up the way you like it, it's not so helpful.

NOTES

The other default options, Two Comp Views and Four Comp Views, are intended for use with the 3D features of After Effects to view a 3D scene from more than one point of view.

TIP

How do you get rid of a tab that shares a palette with a tab you want to keep? Simple: Click and drag the unwanted tab away from its palette, which automatically creates a new palette window with just that tab. Now click the X button at the top to close it.

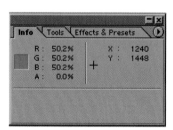

Figure 1.4 For the most part, you can be perfectly happy with this single, three-tabbed palette, with Info forward most of the time you are working.

Under the Window menu, choose Workspace; you'll see it offers three default workspaces and the ability to save more of your own. If you haven't set a workspace before and your screen has become a bit of a mess, you can always choose Window > Workspace > One Comp View to reset the location of your windows and palettes to their defaults (**Figure 1.3**).

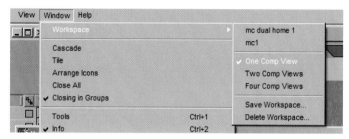

Figure 1.3 One Comp View is like a panic button for resetting your UI if things get too far out of hand.

In most cases, however, you want to do better than that, and the way to improve things is to set your own workspace. This means that you set all of the windows and views the way you are likely to want them most of the time, according to the following guidelines, and save this layout as a custom workspace of your own. Here's how:

▶ **Consolidate palettes.** In most cases you don't even need Audio, and Time Controls is not so essential either once you have it set the way you want it and know the shortcut for creating a RAM preview (the 0 key on your numeric keypad). I recommend pulling the Info tab off of the palette with Audio, and dragging Tools and Effects & Presets to that same palette (**Figure 1.4**). If you prefer, make Info the only palette in your workspace, and activate the other palettes as needed using shortcuts (**Ctrl/Cmd+1** through **Ctrl/Cmd+9**, listed in order in the Window menu).

▶ **Open, resize, and position your most frequently used windows.** The Project window is always open but not always used; most of your work is done in the Timeline, Composition, Layer, and Effects Control windows, so open all of these. With an empty project open, create a composition that is the size you normally work at. Add a solid to that composition and apply any effect to that solid—now you have the windows you need to position. Give prominence to the Composition window because that's where your focus is; note that your choice of magnification will be recorded as part of the workspace. Now leave as much space as possible for the timeline. Position the Effects Control window and palettes adjacent to the Composition window (**Figure 1.5**).

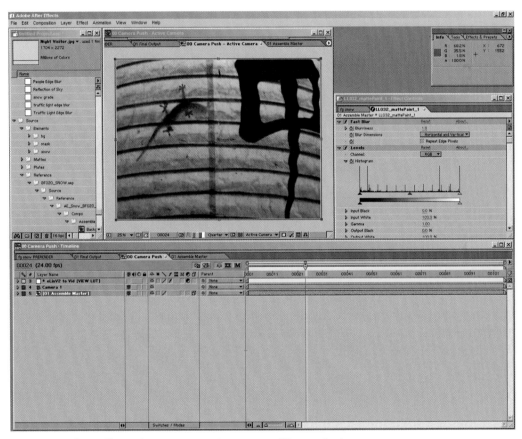

Figure 1.5 Working at film resolution on one monitor means you'll be zooming in and out of this UI setup. This workspace provides a clean default to return to when you need to see all of the palettes necessary to properly edit the composition.

TIP

Workspaces can get you out of tight spots; if some portion of your user interface seems to be missing, it may have moved to an area of the display where you can no longer click and drag it out, particularly on Windows. This doesn't happen often, but when it does, switching to a saved or default workspace is about the only solution.

▶ **Save your new workspace.** Choose Window > Workspace > Save Workspace, give your workspace a name, and then click OK. The name now appears in the Workspace menu, and you can return to that layout anytime your user interface needs to be cleaned up.

One more step you should consider is turning off Auto Resize for the Effects Control window (toggle it off from the window's wing menu). I find a fixed length and position preferable to a window that resizes itself to cover other windows. While you're at it, you can turn off Animation Presets for a less-cluttered UI (**Figure 1.6**).

Create as many workspaces as you need—one with a dominant timeline, another with a dominant Composition window, and variations for one- or two-monitor setups if you have that option.

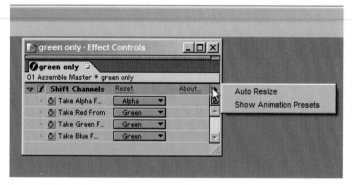

Figure 1.6 For a clean, consistent user interface, turn both of these options off.

A Second Monitor Is Useful

Adding a second monitor is a little luxury you might consider affording yourself if you budget your own equipment (and you might request it if you don't, considering how inexpensive it typically is). You can use it for user interface elements only and keep the Composition window on your main screen. **Figure 1.7** shows the kind of layout possible with a two-monitor setup. Generally, one monitor is your carefully calibrated master monitor on which your

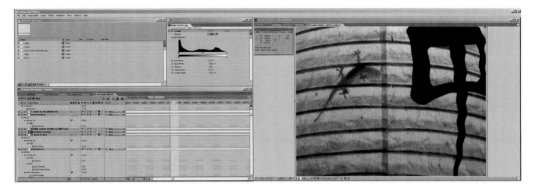

Figure 1.7 Ahh, room to breathe thanks to two monitors.

color and intensity are carefully adjusted, while the other monitor can be any old monitor you have around, holding only your timeline, Project window and other informational palettes.

Most professional laptops will drive a second monitor right out of the box, and with desktop computers it may mean only adding a video card or changing settings on the one you have. Because the monitor doesn't have to be spectacular, you can go for an inexpensive, even small one (and gamers are an excellent source for cheap, late model display cards because they upgrade theirs constantly). Where I live, used CRT monitors are often offered for free as everyone switches to flat panel displays.

Setting Preferences and Project Settings

While you're getting your workspace more comfortable, take some time to optimize your Preferences and Project Settings for the way *you* work—not the way the default settings thought you would probably work. Specifically, you may want to make these adjustments right off the bat:

▶ **Preferences > General:** The default is 20. Somehow, at this level, I occasionally run out of undos, whereas if it's set somewhere between 30 and 50, I never notice the limit. Setting it to the maximum value of 99 won't bring the application to a grinding halt, but it may shorten the amount of time available in RAM previews.

NOTES

Beware that you can get into certain kinds of trouble with a two-monitor setup on Windows, particularly if the two monitors are not the same size. For example, you must stretch the main After Effects window to cover both monitors, which means you can end up with inaccessible areas of the window if the two monitors are not the same pixel aspect). Furthermore, the application sometimes will snap back to occupying only one monitor— for example, if it is minimized—yet there will still be hidden contents of the project in the no-longer-visible area. Luckily, in all such cases, resetting your workspace will allow you a clear view and a fresh start.

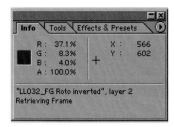

Figure 1.8 You are missing out on very helpful information—showing what After Effects is doing at any given moment while creating a preview frame in the lower half of the Info palette—if you leave this preference at default.

▶ **Preferences > Display:** Check on Show Rendering in Progress in Info Palette & Flowchart. This is absolutely one of the Info palette's most useful features: It allows you to see what After Effects is doing anytime you are waiting for a frame to update (**Figure 1.8**).

▶ **Preferences > Display:** Go ahead, set Disable Thumbnails in Project Window. If you never look at the thumbnails at the top of the Project window, you might as well disable the feature. Otherwise, be prepared for situations in which you wait for it to update. If you're working on film resolution files, for example, you can expect delays while you wait for those updating thumbnail images.

▶ **Preferences > User Interface Colors:** You may wish to darken the UI using the User Interface Brightness slider (**Figure 1.9**). In the same dialog, consider turning on Cycle Mask Colors so that multiple masks applied to a layer automatically have different colors.

▶ **Preferences > Memory & Cache:** If you can dedicate a disk with the default 2 GB (or more) of free space, check Enable Disk Cache. This adds swap space for After Effects beyond what is available in your physical memory (RAM). Any part of the pipeline that would take longer to re-render than recover will be stored in the

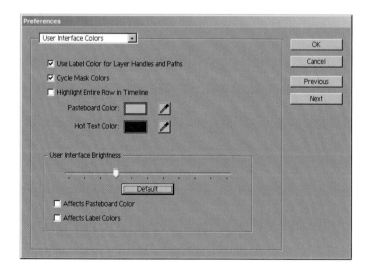

Figure 1.9 On my machine, the After Effects user interface is more pleasing to the eye about two shades darker than the default. On a Mac, which does not let you set system user interface colors, you may even want to go further.

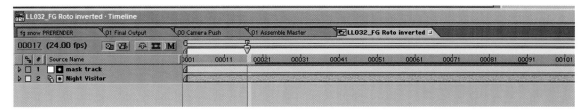

Figure 1.10 You know Enable Disk Cache is working when you see a blue line in your Timeline window.

cache (**Figure 1.10**). More on this in the "Caching and Previewing" section of this chapter.

▶ **File > Project Settings (Ctrl+Alt+Shift+K/Cmd+Option+ Shift+K):** Yes, there are yet more preferences on a project-by-project basis (**Figure 1.11**). If you're going to be working on film projects, change the Timecode Base to 24 fps. It's also standard practice to work in Frames rather than Timecode, so check that. Color depth can be toggled in the Project window (and is explained in depth in Chapter 11, "Issues Specific to Film and HDR Images").

To restore Preferences to their defaults, hold down **Alt+Ctrl+Shift/Option+Cmd+Shift** immediately after launching After Effects, and click OK on the prompt.

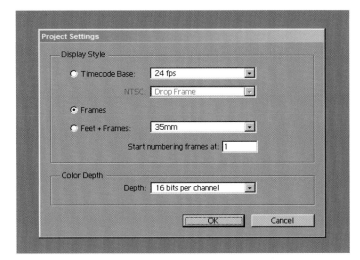

Figure 1.11 Project Settings are an extension of preferences. They are located in a different part of the UI (under the File menu) because of the potential that they must change on a project-to-project basis. Some users, of course, will always use the same Project Settings.

Digging in Deep: Editing the Prefs File

My top recommendation of a preference to change isn't even found in the After Effects user interface. You must locate the Preferences file itself and edit it. The name of the file is Adobe After Effects 6.5 Prefs.txt, and you generally can find it in the C:\ Documents and Settings\"username"\Application Data\Adobe\After Effects\Prefs folder (Windows) or Users/"username"/Library/Preferences (Mac). You can also just search on the filename.

Open the file with a text editing program that doesn't add headers, such as Notepad for Windows or Textedit for Macs; avoid Microsoft Word for this purpose. Search for Drop Footage At Time Zero. Now change the number that follows the equals sign from 00 to 01. Touch nothing else, save, and quit. Any footage you add to a composition now automatically starts at the beginning of the comp rather than the current time.

This can get you out of all kinds of unforeseen difficulty with effects work; you won't see layers suddenly and unexpectedly pop on in the middle of a composition, and you're saved the trouble of dragging them to the beginning of the composition.

Maybe someday this will even be the default, who knows?

Figure 1.12 As a minimum, it's helpful to keep pre-comps and source files in their own separate folders, so that only the composition that is being rendered appears at the root level of the Project window. The Solids folder is created automatically as soon as you add a solid.

Elegant UI Usage

There are many different ways to use After Effects, and typically there is more than one way to solve even the simplest visual effects problem. Nevertheless, not all approaches are created equal.

Here, then, are some overall tips and opinions as to how to work quickly and effortlessly in After Effects. Setting up the UI properly, as you just did, is a good start, but now you need to look at specific interactions that come up all of the time.

Project Window Organization

There are many compelling reasons for keeping a well-organized Project window, and they sound a lot like the reasons for keeping a well-organized hard drive. You create individual folders for individual types of items and organize them hierarchically. Why bother?

▶ To avoid frustration and wasted time when you go looking for an item in your project.

▶ To help someone else if they ever have to open and make sense of your project.

▶ To help you think through and organize the steps of your composition. In a complex project, a well-organized Project window can actually help you do this.

1. Say that a simple project uses some source footage, a main composition, a couple of pre-comps, some reference footage, and at least one solid layer. For this project, I would propose the organization shown in **Figure 1.12** as a minimum; each type of item resides in its own folder. You can quickly see the location of the key composition—the one where all the work is—as well as where its main components reside. No one would have trouble digging right into this project, even if they were completely unfamiliar with it.

2. On larger and more ambitious projects, you may want to create a project template that anticipates a certain workflow, so that many anticipated items beyond the main composition are easy to find. Chapter 4, "Optimizing the Pipeline," outlines an example of such a template and discusses working with multiple compositions.

Context-Clicking (and Keyboard Shortcuts)

Throughout this book you will see references to *context-clicking* on interface items. I would call it right-clicking, but, even at this late date, the Mac does not ship with a multi-button mouse (although every Mac-based artist I know has one). Therefore, on the Mac, to get the same effect without a right mouse button, you must hold down the Control key while clicking.

After Effects does not let you take your hands off the mouse very often; many important operations are not possible with keyboard shortcuts alone. Although I highly advocate learning and using keyboard shortcuts wherever possible, and offer effective keyboard shortcuts throughout the book, I advocate context-clicking just as strongly because it is such a good fit with an interface that has the mouse always in your hand, engaged in the process.

Between keyboard shortcuts and context menus, I practically never visit the menu bar in After Effects. The amount of mouse dragging and clicking I've saved might not stretch from my studio to the moon, but if I lost this workflow, I would be much less happy.

I actively encourage you to choose context clicking and shortcuts over the menu bar whenever possible. There are dozens of context menus available, too many to discuss in detail without boring the pants off of you. **Figure 1.13** displays a couple of the menus I use all of the time in the Project and Timeline windows.

Keeping Sources Linked

If you've been using After Effects for any amount of time, you understand that it is a nondestructive application that edits pointers to source files but has no way of editing those files directly. Therefore, it's very rare that any After Effects project is an island unto itself on your hard drive or server; to operate properly it also requires the presence of source footage files.

It's all very well to keep a well organized project, but what if you have a constant problem with source footage files becoming unlinked? This problem arises particularly when

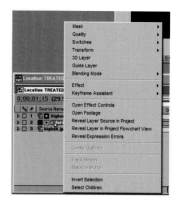

Figure 1.13 Context menus are everywhere and very effective. Context-click the tab of your Timeline window, and you will see very different selections than if you context-click a layer in that window. And depending on whether that layer is a camera, a solid, or footage, you will see different options, as well.

you move a project from one location on your drive to another, to another drive, or to another computer or server altogether.

Should a footage item become unlinked and you know where the source is located, or you can search for it on your drive, the solution is simple: Just choose your favorite method to bring up the Replace Footage File dialog:

▶ Double-click the missing footage item in the Project window

▶ Context-click the missing footage, choose Replace Footage, and then choose File

▶ Highlight the missing footage, and press **Ctrl+H/ Cmd+H**

In the Replace Footage File dialog, navigate to and choose the missing footage item (**Figure 1.14**).

If you receive a warning on opening a project that a file or files are missing, but you don't know which ones (sometimes a project is too big or complex to spot them easily), try clicking on the little binoculars icon at the bottom of your Project window (**Figure 1.15**). Leave the text field blank and check the Find Missing Footage box; After Effects will search through your project for items that have become unlinked. If you have more than one, repeat this process and After Effects will search for each missing item in turn. It's not sophisticated, but it works. If you want to search for a specific file instead, simply clear the check box and type the filename in the text field.

TIP

If you want to reload footage because it was updated in the background after you opened your project, choose Reload Footage from the context menu (**Ctrl+Alt+L/Cmd+Option+L**). After Effects avoids, where possible, re-reading a file on your drive or server, caching it instead. This command refreshes the cache.

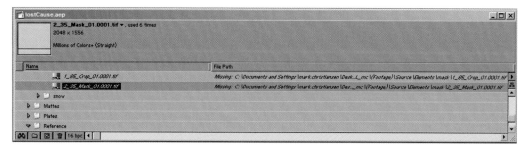

Figure 1.14 Missing footage appears with small color bar icons. In the File Path column, After Effects also displays the path where the file was expected to be, which can help when searching on your drive or network for a missing, unlinked file.

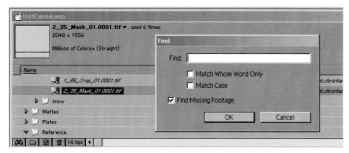

Figure 1.15 Click the binoculars icon at the lower left of the Project window and then check Find Missing Footage, entering nothing in the Find field. After Effects will look for unlinked files in your project.

If all of your source files are missing, there is probably a better option than relinking each item individually. If all of the files are contained in one source folder (or one of only a few), after you link the first missing file After Effects may surprise you with the message that it has found and relinked others: The program automatically searches for other missing items in folders to which you relink. (For advice on guarding against the need to relink, see the section "Collect Files.")

If for some reason a file refuses to relink (the item you are attempting to select is gray and cannot be highlighted in the dialog), After Effects is somehow not recognizing that footage as the format that it should be. There are a few potential reasons for this, but the most common is simply moving a project from Mac to Windows, or vice versa. The most common solution is to add a missing three-character extension to the file (for example, .jpg for a JPEG file). Note that this problem is not limited to Windows; when the headers are stripped from a file by transferring it via FTP or e-mail, OS X will fail to recognize it until the extension is restored. Get in the habit of always naming files with these extensions; unfortunately, some applications (such as Apple's Final Cut Pro) do not actively support this practice.

If the file still won't relink even with the proper extension, it may have become corrupted or it may be one of the file types that does not work equally well on Mac and Windows. For example, Mac PICT files don't work well on Windows.

To avoid this, use formats that are universally understood on all platforms: TIFF, TGA, PNG, or JPEG. (For more on choosing formats, see the section "Footage and Composition Settings.")

Collect Files

Of course, a better approach is to avoid having to relink files at all, and you do have some elegant options for preparing After Effects projects and their source files to be moved or backed up. The old-fashioned way was to place the After Effects project in a master directory and all of its source files in subdirectories because this is how the program automatically searches for linked files (using relative, rather than absolute files paths). If you don't want to organize your files this way, however, consider the Collect Files alternative, which does this for you automatically.

Located in the File menu, the Collect Files command was originally designed to support the Watch Folder command, which enables you to render an After Effects project on several machines (see Chapter 4). If you leave all the default settings for Collect Files and click the Collect button, you can select the location for creating a new folder that contains a copy of the project and all of its source files (**Figure 1.16**).

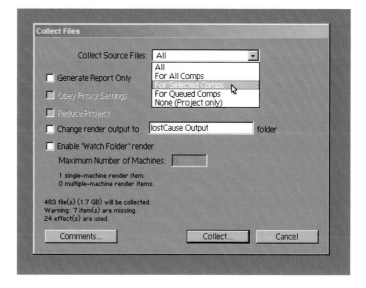

Figure 1.16 The Collect Files dialog includes several options. It's useful to select the final rendering composition prior to activating Collect Files if the project is complete—that way you don't collect files you don't need. In the lower left is a summary of what will be collected, what is missing, and how many effects are employed.

This is incredibly useful for transporting or archiving After Effects projects and their source files, a "no file left behind" policy for your workflow. To streamline even further, you can reduce your project down to only the files that are used in existing compositions. Instead of leaving Collect Source Files set to All, choose a subset of files—only those used in comps in this project or in comps in the Render Queue, for example. Or you can select a composition prior to choosing Collect Files and reduce the project to only the files used in that one composition.

Reduce Project

Reduce Project is available as a command under the File menu, in addition to being part of the Collect Files process, so you can engage its services at any time to clean up a project. With a composition selected, choose Reduce Project; After Effects removes all of the source files in the project that are not used in that comp (**Figure 1.17**). After Effects even lets you know (in a dialog box) how many files it removed and reminds you of the ability to undo this process.

But wait, that's not all. Just above Reduce Project in the File menu are a couple of other highly useful tools for cleaning up your project: Consolidate All Footage and Remove Unused Footage. Consolidate All Footage looks for two or more instances of the same source file and combines them, choosing the first instance, top to bottom, in the Project window to replace all other instances (**Figure 1.18**). Remove Unused Footage does exactly as it says, ridding your project of all footage that is not included in any composition.

Figure 1.17 Do not be alarmed. After Effects is only reminding you that Reduce Project will delete items from the project. Click OK and then double-check to make sure you really had the comp you wanted selected.

Editing and Replacing Source

Perhaps you are working away in After Effects and notice something you want to change about a piece of source material that you created or edited in another application. There is a shortcut for opening that file in the program that created it (according to its file tag): **Ctrl+E/Cmd+E**. You then make your edits in the other application and save the result. After Effects checks to see if the file has been updated (by looking at the modification date, so remember to save) and imports the result.

This very convenient feature doesn't always work properly, however, particularly when dealing with a multi-image source (either an image sequence or a multiple layer Photoshop or Illustrator file). Many users, myself included, have instead become used to context-clicking the item in the Project window and selecting Reveal in Explorer/Reveal in Finder, then opening and editing the image, saving it, and coming back to After Effects to reload it, one layer of the file at a time, if necessary.

Figure 1.18 A similar warning appears when you choose File > Consolidate Footage, which looks for duplicate instances of the same source file in the project and chooses the first of these from top to bottom to represent all instances.

Alas, Consolidate All Footage does not eliminate solids clutter—the presence of several identical solids in the Solids folder of your project. After Effects assumes that you are keeping each instance unique so as not to inadvertently edit them all by changing one (despite also offering a check box in the Solid Footage Settings dialog to Affect All Layers that Use This Solid).

Footage and Composition Settings

Why devote a section to footage and composition settings if After Effects does its best to automate them and stay out of your way? Because by trying to make your life easier, After Effects is inadvertently making it more difficult: Shielding you from the details contributes to user ignorance of them. And you need to understand these details, so you can get them right from the start. A misinterpreted alpha channel, nonsquare pixel footage interpreted as square, undetected scan lines, and similar issues will leave you fighting an up-hill battle if you don't make the proper settings before you ever start putting together a composition.

Although the automatic settings in After Effect are great most of the time, it pays to understand how they work for those times you need to do some manual tweaking. Take a closer look.

Interpreting Footage

This book generally eschews the practice of taking you menu by menu through After Effects. Sometimes, however, the UI perfectly encapsulates a set of production challenges. The Interpret Footage dialog, then, is like a section-by-section checklist of all that can go wrong when you import footage: misinterpreted Alpha, incorrect Frame Rate, misadjusted Fields and Pulldown settings, incorrect Pixel Aspect Ratio. To bring up the Interpret Footage dialog, select some footage in the Project window and press **Ctrl+F/Cmd+F** or context-click and select Interpret Footage > Main.

Alpha

Alpha settings are more complicated than you might think when it comes to compositing; most After Effects users have no idea just how complicated, in fact. **Figure 1.19** shows the common symptoms of a misinterpreted alpha channel.

For the time being, I offer a couple pointers and reminders:

▶ If you're unclear about which type of alpha channel you're working with, click Guess in the Interpretation dialog that shows up when you import footage with alpha. This will typically get the setting right.

▶ Under Preferences > Import is a setting for how you want After Effects to handle footage that comes in with an alpha channel. Beware of setting this to anything besides Ask User until you are certain you know what you are doing with alpha channels and that circumstances aren't likely to change without you noticing.

Figure 1.19 It's easy to distinguish a good (right) from a bad alpha channel (left). Note the grey area in the cockpit canopy and the black line around the misinterpreted version (left). In this case, the image had a premultiplied alpha, and the black data in the edges is the result of misinterpreting it as straight.

For a more in-depth discussion of alpha channels and how they operate in the After Effects pipeline, see Chapter 3, "Selections: The Key to Compositing."

Frame Rate

The clearest symptom of an incorrectly set frame rate is footage that does not play smoothly in a composition with the target frame rate. Interpreting frame rate properly is an issue only when you import image sequences, which, of course, is the most common way that you will import moving footage in a visual effects setting. Image sequences are preferred to formats such as QuickTime (.mov) or Windows Media (.avi) in a production setting because

▶ If something goes wrong with a rendered image sequence, only the missing frames need to be replaced. With a movie file, the whole file typically has to be discarded and replaced, potentially costing hours of render time.

▶ Movie file formats are not as universally recognized and standardized across various platforms and programs as still image formats. QuickTime is the most robust and flexible of the moving image formats, yet many Windows-based programs do not even natively support it.

Therefore, when importing still image sequences to use as moving footage, remember

▶ Just because you've set your Project Settings to the proper frame rate (say, 24 fps for a feature film project), your image sequences may still import at 30 fps by default. You can change this default setting under Preferences > Import.

▶ You can assign whatever frame rate you like to a footage sequence if you determine the default setting is not correct.

▶ Just because an imported moving image file (such as QuickTime) has its own frame rate does not mean you cannot override this rate as needed by checking Assume This Frame Rate and entering a value. Be certain, however, that this is really what you want to do; typically, it is only a correction for outputs that were set incorrectly in another application.

Keep in mind that you can highlight any clip in your Project window and see its current frame rate, along with other default settings, displayed at the top of the window (**Figure 1.20**).

Fields, Pulldown, PAR

As creators of digital movie clips, we all look forward to the day when interlaced footage is a thing of the past. In the meantime, you must guard against symptoms such as those depicted in **Figure 1.21.** The best way to avoid field artifacts in moving footage is by making sure your Field setting matches that of your incoming footage; Separate Fields unweaves the two fields embedded in a single frame to be two separate frames, allowing you to transform them without creating a complete mess.

For DV footage, this process is automated and After Effects knows what to do by default. For other formats, you need to know not only whether your footage is coming in with fields but also whether the upper or lower field is first. Furthermore, with film footage you may have to deal with pulldown.

Figure 1.20 To find useful information about any file in the Project window, highlight the file and look at the top of the window. You'll find frame rate, duration, color depth, pixel aspect, and how many times the clip is used in the project. To see and select specific comps in which it is used, click the little arrow at the end of the file name.

Figure 1.21 The foreground pickup truck spells trouble if you're planning on doing much more than a simple color correction; fields were not removed for this clip. If you see a problem like this, check your footage interpret settings immediately.

Digital Source Formats

After Effects is capable of importing and exporting a wide array of footage formats, yet only a small subset of these recur typically in visual effects production. Here are some of the most popular raster image formats and their advantages (for a summary, see **Table 1.1**):

▶ **TIFF (.tif):** In many ways the most flexible of formats, with the possible exception of PNG, TIFF is longstanding enough to be supported by most applications. It can be compressed effectively (and losslessly) by enabling LZW compression, which looks for recurring instances and patterns in the image and encodes them. Although 16-bit support is not native to After Effects, it is available via a free third-party plug-in (for more on this see Chapter 11).

▶ **Targa (.tga):** This format has the dual advantages of being universal to most computer graphics applications and offering lossless RLE (run length encoding) compression, which looks for sets of identical pixels that can be losslessly grouped together (such as a solid color in the background or alpha channel).

▶ **PNG (.png):** In many ways the most misunderstood of formats, PNG natively supports images of 8 or 16 bits per channel in Photoshop, and it often does the most effective job of losslessly keeping files sizes small. Because PNG has a reputation as a Web-oriented format, users sometimes mistakenly assume that it adds lossy compression, as is the case with JPEG files.

▶ **Cineon (.cin):** A common format for transferring digitized film images, this format works in nonlinear, 10-bit color and is discussed in greater detail in Chapter 11.

▶ **Photoshop (.psd):** Although a universally supported format with many built-in extras, such as support for individual layer transparency, these files can be huge, as Photoshop offers no lossless compression options.

▶ **Open EXR (.exr):** This is an advanced format for use solely with high dynamic range imaging (HDRI), source that has been taken in bit depths higher than linear 16 bit. Moreover, it is not supported natively by After Effects but requires a special plug-in. If this all sounds like gobbledygook but you still want to learn more, have a look at Chapter 11.

TABLE 1.1 Raster Image Formats and Their Advantages

FORMAT	BIT DEPTH	LOSSLESS COMPRESSION	ALPHA CHANNEL
TIFF	8 or 16 bit	Y	Y
TGA	8 bit	Y	Y
PNG	8 or 16 bit	Y	Y
CIN	10 bit		
PSD	8 or 16 bit		Y (multiple via layers)
EXR (non-native)	16 bit, 32 bit (floating point)	Y	

So which format should you use? I would give TIFF the edge for 8-bit images, but use PNG for 16-bit images, because the file sizes are losslessly so much smaller. Cineon is the only choice for 10-bit log files, and there's nothing particularly wrong with Targa (except perhaps slow run length encoding) or Photoshop (except the huge file sizes).

Adobe Formats

After Effects supports some special features for dealing with files created by other Adobe applications. For effects work, the most handy one is support for multilayer Photoshop images, including layer names, transfer modes, and transparency settings.

To take advantage of this feature, import the Photoshop source as a composition, which leaves all of the properties of each individual layer editable in After Effects. The alternative is to import only a single layer or to flatten all layers and import the entire file as one image.

The ability to import a Photoshop file as a composition means you can set up a shot as a Photoshop still and import it with everything already in place. This is particularly useful with matte paintings that include separate elements, such as multiple planes of depth.

NOTES

Be sure to note that 8 bit means 8 bits per channel, for a total 24 bits in an RGB image or 32 bits in an RGBA image. Targa includes a 16-bit option that actually means 16 bits total, or 5 per channel plus 1. Avoid this.

Figure 1.22 Dragging a source background clip to the highlighted icon at the bottom of the Project window creates a new composition with the clip's duration, pixel dimensions, pixel aspect, and frame rate. It's a reasonably foolproof way to set up a new composition if you are working with a master background clip.

If you don't need the elements ready to go as layers of a composition, however, I would forego this option because it makes editing and updating the source trickier. Each layer becomes a separate element that must be updated separately, and it's wasted effort if you're never editing the associated composition.

Composition Settings

There are two relatively sure-fire methods for ensuring that your composition settings are exactly as they should be:

▶ Use a prebuilt project template that includes compositions whose settings are already correct.

▶ Create new compositions by dragging a clip to the Create a New Composition icon and using only clips whose settings match the target output size and frame rate (**Figure 1.22**).

The crucial settings to get correct in the Composition Settings window are the pixel dimensions, Pixel Aspect Ratio, Frame Rate, and Duration. (Actually, even Duration is negotiable so long as it is not too short.) If you're working with a footage format that isn't accurately described in any of the Preset options and you're going to be using this format again and again, then by all means create your own Preset setting by clicking on the small icon adjacent to the Preset pull-down menu, the icon that looks like a little floppy disk (**Figure 1.23**).

And what of that other tab, labeled Advanced in the Composition Settings dialog? It pertains to specific options for dealing with time and space (see Chapter 4) and for working with motion blur and 3D (see Chapter 9, "Virtual Cinematography").

Previewing Like a Pro

Nothing sets you apart as a visual effects pro more than the way you examine footage. I had a tax accountant years ago who dealt solely with artists, who encouraged me to write off my VCR (this was before DVDs were common currency) and any movies I rented. She told me that the IRS had no idea of the way that effects people look at movies—back

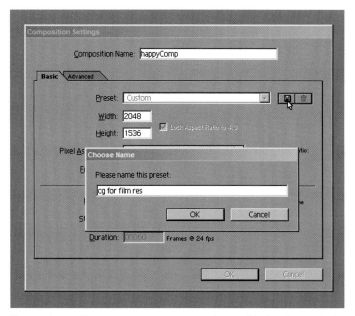

Figure 1.23 Feel free to create your own preset if none of the listed ones match one that you will be using continually for your project.

and forth over the same section, frame by frame, and so on—nor the wear and tear it puts on video equipment.

Obviously, the way you look at a clip in After Effects is much different than the way your audience will look at it once it's in the finished movie. So to get to the heart of the matter: How exactly does a professional work with footage in After Effects? This section offers some of the habits of highly effective compositors, so to speak.

The strategies outlined here are particularly helpful when working with such large format footage as 2 K film plates (film resolution footage measuring approximately 2000 pixels horizontally), but they're not bad habits for speeding you along regardless of format (or the speed of your workstation).

Resolution and Quality

After Effects 6.5 finally made it standard for any new layers in a composition to be set to Best quality in the timeline (with a check box for the setting in Preferences > General). Long ago, in the era of truly slow desktop computers,

Figure 1.24 It's usually good to keep the resolution (highlighted, right) matched to the current magnification setting (highlighted, left); that way, you don't overrender for the view you're using, given how typical it is to work with film resolution footage at 50% until it's time to render.

NOTES

The Auto-Zoom When Resolution Changes setting found in Preferences > Display enables you to use the keyboard shortcuts to change resolution, and the Composition window zooms in or out so that the Magnification setting matches resolution. I find this useful only in cases where I'm doing a lot of zooming in and out to check details followed by short previews, such as when pulling a color key or rotoscoping.

Draft quality was an effective hedge against slow previews, but in this day and age there are far more effective ways to manage preview speed without creating inaccurate previews, as Draft quality does. In other words, don't use it, because the potential pitfalls generally are not outweighed by the benefits.

There are several other effective ways to speed up previews and interactivity without ever resorting to Draft quality:

▶ Change Resolution/Down Sample Factor to Half; or in extreme cases, change it to Quarter

▶ Preview a Region of Interest (ROI)

▶ Change the way controls update using Preview settings and the Option key (for more on this, see the section "Caching and Previewing")

▶ Enable the Caps Lock key to prevent further updates to rendered views; use only in cases of extreme slowdown

Most production monitors do not themselves have a horizontal resolution of 2000 pixels—even 23-inch CRT monitors make you squint at this resolution—but artists tend to use this to their advantage by leaving the footage at 50% magnification and Half resolution (**Figure 1.24**). There is a preference that will keep magnification locked to resolution, but most users don't like it because it causes the View window to pop in and out suddenly.

This setup allows four times as much data to fill a RAM preview, and preview renders are created in a fraction—sometimes one half or, in extreme cases, one tenth—of the time required for Full resolution, which is reserved for cases in which it is necessary to zoom in and look closely, and for final render preparation.

To quickly change the display resolution in the Composition window, use the keyboard shortcuts shown in **Table 1.2**.

Zooming and navigating around footage at first seems the same as in other Adobe applications: Hold down the spacebar or activate the Hand tool (H) to move its position around in the window. Use **Ctrl+=/Cmd+=** or the Zoom tool (**Z**) to zoom in, and use **Ctrl+-/Cmd+-** or the Zoom tool with the Alt/Option key pressed to zoom out. Note, however, that there is a significant difference in the two methods of zooming in and out—the keyboard shortcut causes the Composition (or Layer) window to scale up or down relative to the size of the format area. To keep your windows the same size and only zoom the footage, use the comma and period keys as zoom shortcuts instead.

TABLE 1.2 Keyboard Commands for Changing Display Resolution

Resolution	Keyboard shortcut
Full	Ctrl+J/Cmd+J
Half	Ctrl+Shift+J/Cmd+Shift+J
Quarter	Ctrl+Shift+Alt+J/Cmd+Shift+Option+J

Reducing Things Further

When you really need to look at something at full resolution in full motion, consider whether you need to see the full frame or just some area of it, as is often the case. In such a situation, use the Region of Interest (ROI) tool (**Figure 1.25**).

Figure 1.25 Activating the Region of Interest is like cropping your composition. In fact, there is even a Crop Comp to Region of Interest command in the Composition menu, should you decide you like what you see. You save much of the render time involved for other parts of the frame, and all of the preview storage.

Figure 1.26 Live Update is activated by this switch in the timeline; it is active by default. When it is active, the Composition and Layer windows update in real time, as you adjust sliders. Holding down Alt/Option as you adjust a slider prevents the views from updating. If Live Update is not activated, then holding down Alt/Option updates the view (the functionality is reversed).

Clicking the ROI tool turns your cursor into a set of crosshairs that you use to define the rectangular region you wish to isolate. Now as you preview, only the layer data that you need to render is calculated, and only this area of the screen buffers into physical memory, lengthening the temporal capacity of RAM previews (detailed further in "Caching and Previewing").

Maintaining Interactivity

One major gotcha in After Effects occurs in heavily render-intensive projects that need a lot of tweaking (say, fine adjustments of effect controls). The problem is that, as the processor becomes heavily loaded updating the frame display, UI interaction itself is slowed down—so much so in some cases that dragging a slider or a layer position becomes stuttery and noninteractive.

In some cases, deactivating Live Update is enough to prevent the problem (**Figure 1.26**). If you're working with high-resolution footage, you probably want this toggled off so that waiting for updates does not drive you crazy. Holding down the Alt/Option key as you make adjustments in the UI causes the Live Update setting to toggle; some users prefer to leave Live Update on and to hold down Alt/Option when needing to freeze the update.

In extreme cases, the panic button is the Caps Lock key. Activating this key (**Figure 1.27**) prevents any further updates to any rendered displays until it is deactivated. I have worked on productions where the server load was so heavy that it was necessary to work "blind" with Caps Lock active for several consecutive edits before being brave enough to reactivate the update and take a little break while the frame updated. Ah, the good old bad old days (which continue to this day, given the number of facilities that insist on leaving all source files on a remote server connected via gigabit Ethernet, and given how completely slammed those servers can become).

Caching and Previewing

One key to getting the best performance possible out of After Effects is to get the application to cache as much

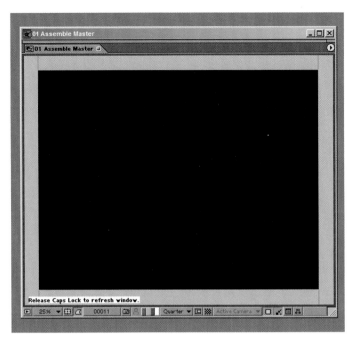

Figure 1.27 Desperate times call for desperate measures. Pressing the Caps Lock key prevents view windows from updating and draws a big red border with a reminder in the corner that it's on.

of your footage as possible into physical memory. This is something that After Effects does automatically, whether you are simply navigating from frame to frame (Page Up and Page Down keys) or loading frames into memory for a RAM preview (0 on your numeric keypad).

You can optimize the caching, however. For example, you can extend the amount of space available to the cache to physical media (a high-speed local drive) by enabling Disk Cache in Preferences > Memory & Cache. This locks away a portion of your drive for use only by After Effects. Just as green areas at the top of your Timeline window indicate frames that have been cached to RAM, blue areas have been cached to the Disk Cache. In most cases, even setting this to the default 2 GB (2000 MB) size greatly extends your caching capability without occupying needed disk space (because you shouldn't be filling your drives to more than 90% of capacity anyhow, and even modest machines have tens if not hundreds of gigabytes of space these days).

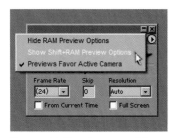

Figure 1.28 The wing menu of the Time Controls palette contains the menu options for revealing the RAM Preview and Shift+RAM Preview options.

If RAM previews are still slowing you down by taking too long to render and refined motion is not critical to your preview, you can take advantage of the option to skip frames in RAM preview. This is accessible only via the Time Controls palette, which I usually leave closed other than to adjust the number of frames skipped. Under the wing menu of that palette, choose Show Shift+RAM Preview Options if they're not already visible (**Figure 1.28**). To preview every other frame, saving half the render time, set Skip to 1 (or set it to 4 to render only every fifth frame, and so on). The shortcut to access Shift+RAM Preview is, naturally enough, **Shift+0** (again, on the numeric keypad).

Setting the Preview Region

By default, the RAM Preview feature caches and previews all frames in the work area, starting with the first. This is not always what you want. One alternative is to check the box in Time Controls to preview From Current Time. With this setting, the Work Area is ignored and the preview begins wherever the time needle is, continuing to the end of the composition.

You can also change the Work Area to limit your preview timing, but this is a pain—unless you use shortcuts. Specifically, **Ctrl+Alt+B**/**Cmd+Option+B** sets the Work Area to the length of any highlighted layer, and double-clicking on the hash marks at the center of the Work Area bar resets it to the length of the composition. It's not perfect, as editing the Work Area for a RAM preview can inadvertently cause the wrong frames to render, but it's often handy.

What's Your Background?

For a lot of effects work, setting a custom background while you work with foreground layers only can be useful. You probably already know that you can change the background color to anything you want (use the keyboard shortcut **Ctrl+Shift+B**/**Cmd+Shift+B** or choose Background Color in the Composition menu). No doubt you also know about the toggle at the bottom of the Composition window to display the Transparency Grid (familiar to Photoshop users).

Sometimes that's not enough, however, which is one area where *guide layers*, new to After Effects 6.5, become handy. If you want to insert background plate footage into a nested foreground composition without it ever appearing in any subsequent comps or in the final render, try this: Add the background layer at the bottom of the timeline, then context-click (or go to the Layer menu) and choose Guide Layer (**Figure 1.29**). You just made this layer into a special kind of layer that will show up only when you preview the composition—not when you render it, nor when you insert it in another comp.

This allows you to create custom backgrounds for the sole purpose of previewing, as well. For example, a gradient can help reveal qualities that are difficult to spot against a solid color or the Transparency Grid, particularly when you're refining a matte. Apply the Ramp effect to a solid, then toggle on Guide Layer and you have a perfect preview background (**Figure 1.30**).

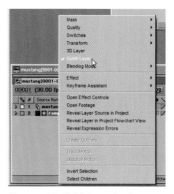

Figure 1.29 Guide Layer has been set for the background layer, evident by the small aqua-colored icon that appears beside the layer name.

Figure 1.30 You can often get a much better view as you work in a subcomposition with a gradient background (left), rather than a solid color or a checkerboard. Guide Layer prevents the gradient from appearing in any subsequent comp or render; here it is nested into a main comp that shows only a checkerboard background (right).

Changing the Channel

Another way in which you will want to continually check your work is by studying footage one color channel at a time or by looking only at the alpha channel. Those four little color rectangles at the bottom of the Composition window are there for this purpose, and a line in the color of the channel you've chosen helpfully appears around the edge of the window when one of them is toggled on (**Figure 1.31**). The corresponding keyboard shortcuts—**Alt/Option+1** through **Alt/Option+4**—accomplish the same end.

Unfortunately, After Effects does not allow you to display a RAM preview in individual channel mode. You can work around this by pressing the spacebar to preview instead, in which case whatever channel is active will remain so. Unfortunately, your preview speed may be much slower. You could also set an adjustment layer at the top layer of the timeline with the Shift Channels effect applied and

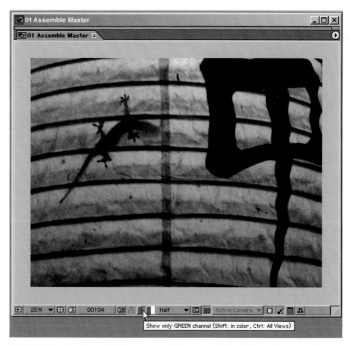

Figure 1.31 The thin green line around the edge of the Composition window indicates that only the green channel is displayed.

set all channels to the desired preview channel (**Figure 1.32**). Assuming that you don't want this adjustment layer to render, you can set it, too, to be a guide layer. Most of the time, this won't be necessary. If you ever complain that you can't preview a single channel at full-speed, however, remember this simple work-around. It will work for any preview-only effect you wish to set.

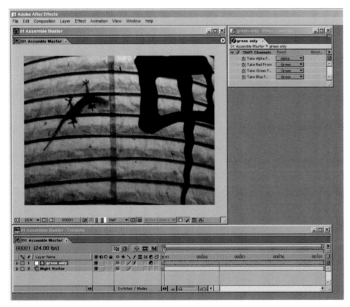

Figure 1.32 The same result, displaying only the green channel, but this time using the Shift Channels effect applied to an adjustment layer, which is also set as a guide layer. This allows you to preview a channel at full speed, without having to worry that the effect will remain active when you render.

A Useful Effects Palette

There's an old joke among effects artists working in After Effects that virtually any visual effect can be accomplished with just two effects: Levels and Fast Blur. This is, of course, a major exaggeration (I would want at least half a dozen!), but it makes a couple of important points about After Effects and its users:

▶ Most users will never use the majority of effects in the Effect menu. Many effects, in fact, are there only to support old, otherwise outdated projects created in previous versions of After Effects.

Figure 1.33 Wondering how many different blur options you have available? Type blur in the Contains field and find out. It may not be this many, as some here are from third-parties. This display is in Alphabetical mode (chosen from the wing menu, top right).

Hardly anyone uses the third available view, Explorer folders/Finder folders. These allow you to organize your plug-ins however you like them where they are stored, in your Plug-ins folder, and see them that way in the Effects & Presets palette. By the time most users are confident enough to sort plug-ins this way, however, they've already adapted to the default organization.

▶ After Effects artists get a bad rap in the visual effects community for always wanting an effect plug-in to do for them what can actually be done with the core tools, if the artist knows how the effect is achieved.

Meanwhile, there's a big problem with the Effect menu and the Effects & Presets palette: the categories. They're ancient, often nonintuitive, and each category contains a mishmash of constantly used and rarely to never used effects. The Adjust menu has Levels, the single most-used effect in the program, right above Photo Filter, a Photoshop rip-off better suited to still images. You can colorize footage with Hue/Saturation (from that same category) or with Tint, Change to Color, or Colorama from the Image Control menu.

Luckily, there are alternatives. For one thing, you don't ever have to use the Effect menu. The Effects & Presets palette has options for displaying effects without their categories (**Figure 1.33**). Once you know what you're looking for, listing effects in alphabetical order and searching for them in the palette's text field can speed things along a bit. You then apply the selected effect by double-clicking it (if the target layer is selected) or by dragging it to the target layer in the Timeline window (or to its Effect Controls window).

Types of Effects

You may have noticed those little icons that appear next to the effect names in the Effects & Presets palette. There are four main types: 8- and 16-bit effects, Animation Presets, and Audio. You may not be working at 16-bit depth yet, but it is worth noting which effects are 16-bit ready; for the most part, those are the core After Effects plug-ins, the ones you'll consider using first and most often. Note that these effects are capable of supporting 16 bits, but they don't require that you work at that setting. Chapter 12 contains more about the difference between 8- and 16-bit depths and how to work with them.

Using the wing menu you can specify which type of effect you want to see (**Figure 1.34**). For example, you can show only 16-bit effects, or you can see the contents of an Animation Preset (what it actually does, step by step). Beware if you set this option, however, because you may find yourself looking for an effect that is unexpectedly missing from the palette.

Animation Presets

Formerly known as Effects Favorites, Animation Presets are particularly useful when you're working with a team and sharing standardized practices. You can recognize an Animation Preset in your system by its .ffx file suffix.

In the Effect Controls window or the timeline, select whatever effects and properties you want to save and choose Animation > Save Animation Preset. You can save the preset wherever you like, but for it to show up in the Effects & Presets palette automatically, save it to the Presets folder (the default choice for After Effects). In a studio situation, you can roll a preset out to a number of users by placing it in this folder for them. The next time they restart After Effects or update the palette (using the Refresh List command in the wing menu), the preset appears, ready for use.

Other Effects Tips

The wing menu of the Effect Controls window contains two options that interfere with a clean and consistent UI, so I turn them off (by default they are on). Auto Resize messes up the effort made by setting workspaces, making the effects window an arbitrary length, and Show Animation Presets leaves an extra little pull-down menu at the top of each effect instance that, frankly, rarely gets used.

There are a few different ways to adjust individual effects settings, depending on the type of setting. For the majority of them, which include a blue numerical setting, you can click and drag directly on the number, dragging left or right to decrease or increase it, respectively. And there are even the following refinements:

▶ Hold down shift while dragging and the number increments by ten times its normal amount

▶ Hold down **Ctrl+Alt** (**Cmd+Option**) and the increments are one-tenth the normal amount

Figure 1.34 The Effects & Presets wing menu includes options for sorting effects alphabetically, for showing or hiding presets and their contents, and for showing only 16-bit-per-channel effects, highlighted here.

TIP

I rarely save Animation Presets with keyframes on them, because keyframes vary with the timing of the shot. When possible, I use expressions that advance with time instead (detailed in Chapter 10, "Expressions").

TIP

New in version 6.5 of After Effects is the Increment and Save feature (**Ctrl+Alt+Shift+S/ Cmd+Option+Shift+S**). This saves a new version of your project with a forward incrementing number at the end of the project name. If no number was present in the original project name, After Effects adds one. It's a good habit to use this feature every time you're about to try something major, new, and potentially destructive in an effects shot.

These same shortcuts work in the timeline as well, where applied effects can be revealed by highlighting a layer and pressing **E** on the keyboard. (More on optimal usage of the timeline follows in the next chapter.)

Render Queue: Flight Check

The Render Queue itself is not terribly puzzling, but like many other key portions of the After Effects UI it contains a few features that many users miss, and a few gotchas that hit them from time to time.

There are two key sections for each Render Queue item: Render Settings and Output Module. You can click on each to adjust settings, but I find that almost immediately you will want to get into the habit of choosing a preset, or template, from the pull-down menu. And in the altogether likely case that one does not already exist, you choose the selection at the bottom of each menu: Make Template.

Why make a template for each render? Render Settings tends to be standardized across a project, and you likely will use one of just a few output modules throughout the duration of the project. So why waste time thinking about settings each time you render, when that only leads to a higher likelihood of careless errors (which are, probably more than anything else, the bane of a compositor's existence)?

Placing an Item in the Queue

After Effects is flexible about how you add an item to the Render Queue. You have a choice of two keyboard shortcuts: **Ctrl+M/Cmd+M** and the one I always tend to use, **Ctrl+Shift+/ (Cmd+Shift+/** for those of you on Macs). You can also select a number of items in the Project window and drag them to the Render Queue. If you drag footage without a comp to the Render Queue, After Effects makes a default comp for you to render the footage as-is, which can be handy for quick format conversions.

The output path you choose for the first of your active Render Queue items becomes the default for the rest of them, which is handy until you find yourself rendering lots of image sequences, because each of those typically needs its own folder to keep things well organized.

Render Settings: Your Manual Overrides

There's probably one set of parameters from the Render Settings dialog that you will prefer throughout your project; in fact, on a film or high-definition project, Best is probably pretty much that group, whether you are outputting still image sequences or movies.

Mostly the Render Settings dialog contains manual overrides for the settings in your composition itself (**Figure 1.35**). The window is divided into three sections:

▶ The Composition area (top) has a series of settings that optionally override the Quality, Resolution, and Disk Cache settings, as well as the layer-by-layer Proxy, Effects, Solo, and Guide Layer toggles. The Best setting assumes you want to use all of these as they were designed, with Quality forced to Best and Resolution at Full. There is a school of thought (of which I've never been a member) that says you should default Effects to All On. The idea here is not to present yourself with any unexpected gotchas, but forcing on all effects turns on an effect you meant to delete at least as often as it toggles on an effect you accidentally turned off.

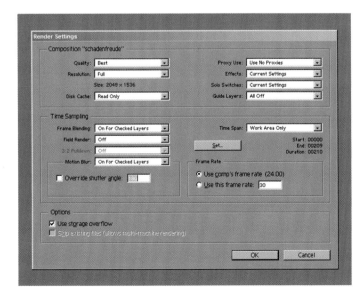

Figure 1.35 The Render Settings dialog has three sections: overrides for the composition settings (top), specific time sampling overrides and settings (center), and two extra options for where and how files are rendered (bottom).

▶ The Time Sampling section (center) contains settings that override decisions that exist in the composition itself: the Frame Blending and Motion Blur toggles, plus the Shutter Angle setting for motion blur. Field Render and 3:2 Pulldown pertain only to preparing the comp for broadcast video output; on projects you will either use them all the time or not at all for final output. The Time Span setting comes into play in situations where you need to re-render some portion of your total comp (otherwise, Work Area or Length of Comp should be preferable).

▶ The Options section (bottom) contains precisely two mutually exclusive options: If you check Use Storage Overflow then the overflow volumes that you can specify in Preferences > Output come into play (**Figure 1.36**). If the first one fills up, the second is used, and so on. If you do not check this option, you can let After Effects look in the destination folder and skip any files that it finds whose output names match files already in that folder. This is designed specifically for the Watch Folder option, but you can use it in any case where you are creating an image sequence and have some, but not all, of the rendered images already completed.

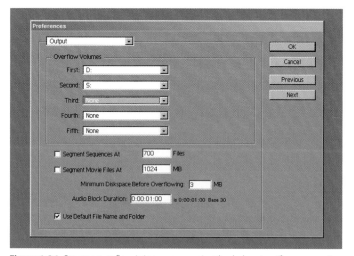

Figure 1.36 Storage overflow is insurance against bad planning; if you run out of space on the primary rendering drive, the volumes specified in this Preference dialog can be set to handle the overflow. With ample disk space, you should not need this, but it's preferable to a failed overnight render.

The way to use Render Settings overall is as a checklist of all the things you need to think about to get your output footage to look the way you want. It may work to simply use Best settings and walk away, or you may be reminded of something specific that needs to be custom set.

Output Modules: As Many as You Need

Throughout the course of your After Effects career you will probably create a large number of Output Module templates. The settings themselves are not so tricky if you know what you're after: Once you've chosen a format, and set the appropriate options (under Video Output), you have the additional options of stretching or cropping the output, and adding audio.

Note that Output Module appears after Render Settings, item by item. This is with good reason: As you will see in detail in Chapter 4, the order in the user interface shows the rendering order, and so Render Settings are applied to the render prior to the application of the Output Module settings.

This becomes important, for example, when scaling output: To scale down a clip and retain the highest quality, you will in most cases want to apply the scaling as a Stretch setting in the Output Module rather than a Resolution setting in the Render Settings (unless speeding up the render is more important than quality, in which case the inverse advice applies).

There are several elegant problem-solving tools embedded in the Output Module setup, some of which many users tend to miss. Among the most significant are

▶ You are allowed more than one Output Module per Render Queue item (**Figure 1.37**).

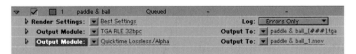

Figure 1.37 So many users—and not just beginners, by any means—fail to notice that you can add multiple Output Modules to a single render queue item, via Composition > Add Output Module. This can be an immense timesaver, as several versions of a render can be created in one pass (for example, one at full resolution stills and a Web-compressed version).

▶ You can change the Output Module of all of your Render Queue items by selecting the Output Module (rather than the Render Queue item itself) of the first item and then Shift-selecting the Output Module (again, rather than the item itself) of the last item (**Figure 1.38**).

▶ You can start numbering an image sequence from any number you like (**Figure 1.39**).

Figure 1.38 Oh no, I have to change all those? Fear not, you can select any number of consecutive Output Modules to change them, but don't select the render queue items themselves. Instead, select the first Output Module in the group and Shift-select the last, then change any of the selected ones and they all follow.

- ▶ Stretching and cropping your output is often a quick, elegant solution to an otherwise thorny rendering problem.

- ▶ Included in the Output Module Settings, and also hidden under the twirl-down arrow (**Figure 1.40**) is an extra option, to perform one of three Post-Render Actions to import or replace the composition that was the source of the render. Chapter 4 contains more about how to use these.

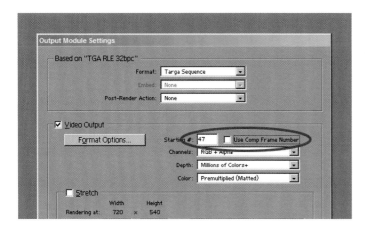

Figure 1.39 To custom-number your frame sequence, clear Use Comp Frame Number and enter your own. This one is easy to miss, so it is highlighted here.

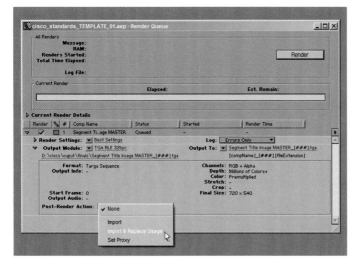

Figure 1.40 Post-Render Actions save you steps, if you intend to view your render in After Effects (Import) or replace a pre-comp with the render permanently (Import & Replace Usage) or just temporarily (Set Proxy).

▶ The shorthand for creating a numbered image sequence is simple if you follow the rules: After Effects replaces the string [###] within the overall output name with a three digit sequential number. The number of # characters in this string corresponds to the amount of digits in the sequential number; if you want extra padding, add extra # characters.

Paying attention to the options available with Output Modules and taking the time to customize and apply presets that you can use again and again are big parts of getting optimum output out of After Effects.

Optimizing Output Settings

Here are some general guidelines for the output settings (Render Settings and Output Modules) that you can use in specific situations:

▶ **Lossless output:** Interframe compression (QuickTime with Animation/Most) is acceptable for movie files, lossless encoding (TGA with RLE, TIFF with LZW, or PNG) and for still images.

▶ **Low-loss output:** QuickTime with Photo-JPEG at 70% is ideal for creating test renders that are relatively small at full resolution yet show little in the way of compression artifacts.

▶ **Web review:** This is a fast-changing area. At this writing, QuickTime with MPEG-4 files offer some of the best results, but your mileage may vary.

▶ **DV/HDV:** If working with these or other compressed source formats, remember that they recompress prerenders, so make all of your edits to the source file and render once!

Obviously, there is much more to choosing your output settings than I've covered here; I only intended to help you get started. In many cases, the settings you need to use will be dictated by your delivery format or by what is needed by the next person after you in the production pipeline.

Study Footage Like a Pro

If you've never had your work reviewed in dailies at an effects studio, your first time in that setting may be a bit of a shock. Seasoned visual effects supervisors miss nothing, and in some cases they do not even need to see a clip twice to tell you what needs to change—even if it is only 40 frames long. In other cases, your shot will loop on and on for several minutes while the whole team gangs up on it, picking it apart.

Typically, however, footage is examined in dailies the same way that you want to look at it in After Effects, but in After Effects, you have a huge advantage—extra tools at your disposal to show you what is going on, and no surly supervisor sitting near you!

Throughout the book, and in your work, as you preview your shot you are encouraged to

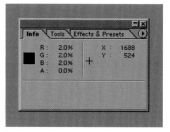

Figure 1.41 Whoops! You thought your background level was pure black, but a glance at the Info palette while your cursor is over the background shows that it is actually 2% grey, which can cause problems further down the line.

▶ Check your Info palette (**Figure 1.41**)

▶ Loop and rock and roll previews (**Figure 1.42**)

▶ Zoom in and take a close look

▶ Examine footage channel by channel

▶ "Slam" your levels to see your work in extreme contrast; this is the practice of temporarily (via a top level Adjustment Layer) applying high-contrast to your composition to make sure that blacks, midtones, and highlights still match (introduced in Chapter 5)

▶ Keep looking for the thing you cannot initially see, and remain critical of the result (without being unfair to yourself)

▶ Expect that you will make careless errors; many final takes are lost to this factor. Effects compositing is a little like computer programming: a series of exacting decisions, where one careless error can invalidate the whole effort.

Figure 1.42 The three available settings for looping previews are highlighted in blue: loop (the default, top), ping-pong (center), or play through once (bottom); toggle these by clicking on the icon.

If I were teaching you this subject in person, I would remind you of these practices constantly; because doing that throughout a book isn't practical (and could get downright annoying), I encourage you to remind yourself. You will reap the benefits: a shot that is final in fewer takes, thanks to few careless mistakes, resulting in a pleased effects team who lauds your efforts and awards you with trickier, even more impressive shots (and an occasional break).

2

The Timeline

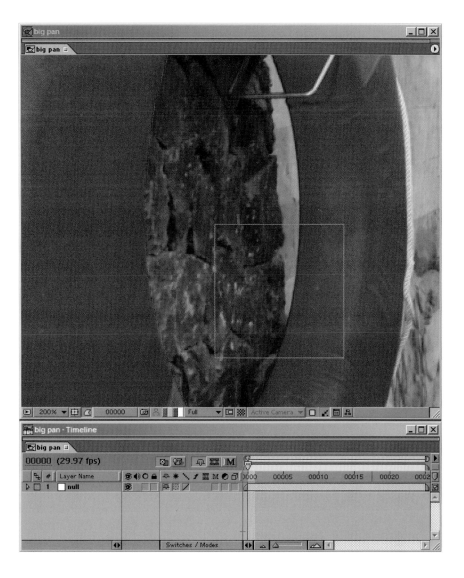

I've been a long time coming, and I'll be a long time gone. You've got your whole life to do something, and that's not very long.

—Ani Difranco (American singer, songwriter, and guitarist)

The Timeline

The timeline is After Effects' killer application. It is the reason above all others that After Effects is equally effective for motion graphics or visual effects work. Node-based compositors make it easy to see render order, but they can make coordinating the timing of events more difficult.

With the timeline, you always know how layers and their keyframes relate in time. Some would argue that render order is more significant than timing for visual effects work. Of course, both are significant, but once you get the hang of managing the timeline well, render order is no longer such a problem.

The Timeline window is also a relatively user-friendly part of the application, albeit one packed with hidden powers. By unlocking those powers and mastering them, you can streamline your workflow a great deal, setting the stage for more advanced work.

One major source of hidden powers is the timeline's set of shortcuts: A lot of what you can accomplish in the timeline can be accomplished more efficiently and effectively with keyboard shortcuts and context menus. My feeling is that these are not extras to be learned once you're a veteran, but small productivity enhancers that you can learn gradually all the time, enhancers that collectively give you a lot of extra momentum and confidence as an After Effects artist.

Organization

Customization is what the timeline is all about; as you work with it, you constantly change not only its contents but your view of it. Thus a good number of the tips offered in this chapter are workflow improvements (views and shortcuts) designed to speed you on your way.

The Timeline window's top-level customizable views are its columns. Right-clicking on any column heading shows a menu list containing all of the possible views; you would never work with all of them revealed, because it's pointless; there are much better organized ways to keep these displayed to get you quickly to what you need to edit.

Column Views

Context-click on any of the column headings and you can reveal or conceal all the different types of columns available in After Effects. Don't bother revealing them all—several are only occasionally useful, and After Effects provides you with a better way of finding them in context.

Figure 2.1 shows a typical minimal column setup that still gives you instant access to all of the columns, from which you can toggle in one step to each of the columns that don't currently display. From there, you have several options:

▶ **Switches/Modes:** If only Switches or Modes (not both) is displayed, the label Switches/Modes appears at the bottom of that column (**Figure 2.2**). You can click on that to toggle from one to the other (or use the **F4** function key). I tend to find that I get the switches the

Figure 2.1 You don't need to vary your view much from the default to have it about as streamlined as you can get. Here, the Parent column is hidden but all columns other than Parent and Comment are available in a single left-click or via a shortcut.

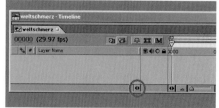

Figure 2.2 Reveal or conceal the Switches/Modes column quickly for extra horizontal space with this toggle.

way I want them (more about that later) and then re-main in Modes view so that I can easily see where I have used track mattes and transfer modes. You can alterna-tively keep both columns visible, but it's a space hog. If you temporarily want neither column to display, click the little double-sided arrow at the bottom-right corner of the Source/Layer Name column.

▶ **Layer/Source:** Another toggle awaits you at the top of the Layer Name column. This is the one column that is grayed out in the context menu because hiding it would be utterly confusing, but if you left-click on its column heading, you can toggle from Layer Name to Source Name. Source Name is the name of the file (in the Project window), but Layer Name can be any name you want to assign to that layer (by selecting it, press-ing the Enter/Return key on your keyboard—don't press Enter on the numeric keypad—and typing in a name). Many users are more careful about layer names than about source names, for example using the same source repeatedly and naming each individual instance (**Figure 2.3**).

▶ **AV Features/Keys:** There is no reason ever to choose Keys from the context menu, as long as you have the Switches column open. Keys appear below AV Features for a given layer when you twirl down the Keys arrow.

▶ **Time Stretch:** Similarly, there is no reason ever to choose In, Out, Duration, or Stretch from the context menu, because you can reveal all of them with the little double-sided arrow at the bottom right of the columns. You will rarely (if ever) use any of these anyhow; the only useful edit to perform here is to time-reverse a layer, giving it a stripy appearance (discussed later, in the "Playing with Time Itself" section); any other changes to timing should be done with Time Remap-ping (detailed later in this chapter).

▶ **Parent:** The Parent column is often left on in the many compositions that use no parenting, which wastes horizontal space. Context-click on it, and choose Hide This at the top of the column if you're not using it (**Figure 2.4**).

Figure 2.3 Give multiple itera-tions of the same source individual layer names to make them easy to distinguish.

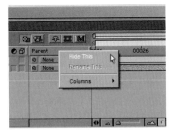

Figure 2.4 Here's another quick way to get some horizontal space when you're not using the parenting hierarchy.

▶ **Minimalism:** If you really want the minimal UI experience, you can even hide AV Features and access those features by context-clicking layers instead, but I don't recommend it; that column takes up very little horizontal space, doubles as a holder for Keys, and is just plain useful as it is. The same goes for the Label and # columns.

With unused columns hidden, you'll have more space for the columns you need most.

Comments and Color

Ever try to make sense of someone else's project? Chaos, right? Make it easy on your coworkers: Color code your layers and use plenty of comments. Choosing a distinct color for each layer can provide intuitive visual clues. It can even help you as you work. How you handle colors is really up to you; **Figure 2.5** shows an example of a timeline with several layers that are color coded by type.

The Comments column is probably the most neglected, yet it enables you to say a few words about the purpose and use of a layer, which is especially useful when creating templates. But even better than enabling the Comments column is to add a layer marker. Press the * key on your numeric keypad, then double-click the layer marker, and enter text in the comment field. Unlike the Comments column, which requires quite a bit of that precious horizontal space and might quickly get turned off, layer marker text is written right over the layer bar itself, so you have as much horizontal space as the layer has.

TIP

Pay no attention to the other options in the Marker dialog; the Chapter and Web Links fields work only when you are writing to a medium that supports them, such as QuickTime or SWF. It's a nifty feature, but you're likely never to use it.

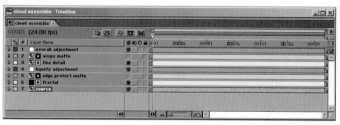

Figure 2.5 A unique color has been assigned to each type of layer (and to the composition itself), making it easy to quickly distinguish between them.

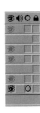

Figure 2.6 You probably already use the Solo switch, engaged here for the bottom layer; remember that leaving a layer solo in a subcomposition will display it that way in the main comp, a common gotcha.

Figure 2.7 Hey, why are those layers numbered 1, 3, 4, 6, 7? The track matte layers have been set to shy and hidden by enabling the Shy toggle at the top of the timeline (highlighted). Very useful for showing only the layers you're still adjusting, but don't forget about those hidden layers.

Solo, Lock, and Shy

Three toggles on the A/V and Switches columns pertain to how layers are edited and viewed as you work, and because I've seen users who should know better miss or forget them, I'm including a quick refresher.

The small circular icon in the A/V Features (**Figure 2.6**) column is the Solo switch. After Effects decided not to copy Photoshop this time around, so Alt/Option-clicking on the layer eyeball does not solo it—this switch does. The reason for doing it this way is that too many of your layer visibility options in After Effects are permanent in nature to have them inadvertently toggling on and off. Solo a layer and you see only it; send a comp with a layer toggled solo, and the Solo Switches menu in Render Settings determines whether it renders that way.

The Lock toggle is really great in situations where you are certain you no longer want to inadvertently edit a layer (or you want to signal to other users of the project not to edit it). You can't even select a layer that is locked.

Shy is trickier to new users; toggle a layer to shy and nothing happens until you also activate the Shy toggle for the whole composition (**Figure 2.7**). Then suddenly, the shy layers disappear from view in the timeline, although they will still be visible in the comp itself, if they were previously. This is a way to temporarily reduce clutter in your timeline, but beware—if you're left scratching your head as to where that layer went, when you can plainly see it's still there, take a close look at the Index numbers: If they are no longer in sequential order, then the missing number belongs to a layer that is now shy.

Navigation and Shortcuts

More than any other window in After Effects, the Timeline window is *the* place where keyboard shortcuts—lots of them—come into play. There's a heck of a lot you can do in the timeline via either a single keyboard shortcut or a single click of the mouse, where a beginner would use several clicks of the mouse.

Time Navigation

Most users learn time navigation shortcuts right away, while others are content simply to drag the time needle around all of the time, a policy I oppose on the grounds that it quickly becomes tedious. Here are a few handy navigation shortcuts:

▶ The **Home**, **End**, **Page Up**, and **Page Down** keys correspond to moving to the first frame, the last frame, one frame backward, and one frame forward. **Shift+Page Up** and **Shift+Page Down** skip ten frames backward or forward, respectively. Press **Shift+Home** or **Shift+End**, and you are taken to the In and Out points of the work area.

▶ Click on the blue time status at the upper left of the timeline to open the Go To Time dialog (press **Ctrl+G/Cmd+G**). Here, you can enter a new time. There's no need to add punctuation, so 1000 is ten seconds in Seconds mode or frame 1000 in Frames mode.

▶ To navigate an arbitrary but precise number of frames or seconds (say, 48 frames after the current time), in the Go To Time dialog, replace the current time with your increment, in the format +48, click OK, and After Effects calculates the increment for you.

But here's a gotcha: If you need to navigate backward in time 48 frames, you can't simply enter −48 in the Go To Time dialog. If you do, you're transported to negative 48 (frames or seconds, either of which probably moves the time needle right off the timeline). Instead, you must use the format +−48; that's right, you're adding a negative number, not subtracting. It's weird, but it works (**Figure 2.8**).

Making Layers Behave

The timeline becomes a liability for effects work when layers inadvertently pop on or off because they started at a frame other than zero or are pre-comps that are too short for the master comp. This one burned me on *The Day After Tomorrow*, where a bit of haze added to a window at 3% opacity—too low to see clearly when previewing on my

Figure 2.8 Setting this value to −48 would set the current time to that negative frame value, probably not what you want. But entering +−48 adds an offset of −48 frames, which might very well be useful.

TIP

The add-a-negative method for offsetting values works in many number fields in the program. For example, you can subtract 30 degrees to Rotation by entering +−30, and you can multiply or divide as well, using the * and / symbols, respectively. This won't work, however, in certain number fields outside the timeline, such as those in the Composition Settings dialog, where it would occasionally be quite useful.

monitor—abruptly shut off two-thirds of the way through a film-out of the shot. For this reason, some users prefer to make all of their comps longer (in duration) than they ever expect to need, and manage them with the Work Area.

To add a layer to a composition, you have many options for dragging and dropping. The one I like best for an existing comp is to drag the source to the layer position where you want it. For a new comp, drag it to the Create a New Composition icon. The keyboard shortcut **Ctrl+/** (**Cmd+/**) drops the footage into the top layer of the active composition.

If you skipped Chapter 1, "The Effects Toolset," you missed a major tip for making layers behave for visual effects work—editing your Preferences file itself so that all layers that are added to the timeline come in at frame zero on the timeline. Here are some other useful tips and shortcuts:

▶ Set the current frame to be the beginning or end of the Work Area by pressing **J** or **K**, respectively.

▶ Navigate to the beginning or end frame of the Work Area by pressing **Shift+Home** or **Shift+End**, respectively.

▶ To reset the Work Area to the length of the composition, double-click its center hash marks; to set it to the exact length of the currently active layer, press **Ctrl+Alt+B/Cmd+Option+B**.

▶ Select a layer by clicking on it (the old-fashioned way), or enter the layer's index number with the numeric keypad (the cool way).

▶ To select an adjacent layer without touching the mouse, use **Ctrl+Up Arrow** (**Cmd+Up Arrow**) to select the next layer up, and **Down Arrow** the next layer down.

▶ Add the **Alt** (**Option**) key and you can move the layer up or down in the stack, which you can also do with **Ctrl+]** and **Ctrl+[**. **Ctrl+Shift+]** moves a layer to the top of the stack and **Ctrl+Shift+[** moves it to the bottom.

TIP

That all saves quite a bit of unnecessary clicking and dragging, but what about the annoying fact that the Work Area controls which frames are rendered to RAM preview and, by default, which frames render? The Work Area's dual influence is another good reason to use a project template (as advised in Chapter 1). If you have a final "Render Me" composition that contains all of the settings for the final render, including the correct framing of pixel aspect and time, you never have to worry about managing these settings to get a clean render every time.

▶ Every once in a great while you will need to invert the layers you have selected: Context-click on a layer, and choose Invert Selection. Locked layers will not be selected by this method, but shy layers will.

▶ Duplicate any layer using **Ctrl+D** (**Cmd+D**). If you duplicate a layer and its track matte, they retain proper orientation in the copy.

▶ If you need a layer to straddle another layer in the stack or you need an effect that you can't disable to end at a certain frame, you can split the layer (**Ctrl+Shift+D**/ **Cmd+Shift+D**). Plus you can set a preference for whether split layers are created above or below the original layer (for example, Preferences > General > Create Split Layers Above Original Layer).

▶ To move a layer's In point to the current time, use the [key, or press] to move the Out point. Add the **Alt** (**Option**) key, and you're trimming the layer to the current time.

▶ If you click and drag over a trimmed layer's white space, you see a double-ended arrow cursor between two lines that indicates you are "slipping and sliding" the layer, changing the In and Out points of the source footage while leaving them the same in the timeline.

Often, you may add elements to your composition that are a different size or pixel aspect, yet which are meant to fill the frame (or fill it on the vertical or horizontal axis). No need to break open the Scale controls and guess. We come now to one of my favorite sets of shortcuts in After Effects: the "fit to fill" shortcuts.

The standard fit to fill, **Ctrl+Alt+F** (**Cmd+Option+F**) is dangerous in that it will not lock the aspect ratio of your layer, stretching the X and Y scale individually so that each is identical to that of the comp itself.

More useful, and just plain cooler, are the shortcuts for fit to fill on a single axis, X or Y, because they do lock the aspect ratio of the nondominant axis. For fit to fill on X only, the shortcut is **Ctrl+Alt+Shift+H** (**Cmd+Option+Shift+H**), and for the Y axis twist your fingers around **Ctrl+Alt+Shift+G** (**Cmd+Option+Shift+G**).

These choices of letters might seem a little obtuse until you note that they are adjacent to F on the keyboard; your visual memory picks up that they are close cousins to the regular F fit to fill command.

Timeline View Options

Now that I've barraged you with useful shortcuts, what about interacting with the view of the timeline itself? I'll assume you're familiar with the process of setting keyframes and move right on to some controls for zooming in and out of keyframe data:

▶ The **;** key toggles between a view that's fully zoomed in on the current frame and the whole timeline view.

Figure 2.9 Unless you have a mouse with a scroll wheel, this click-and-drag interface at the bottom of the Timeline window is probably the fastest method of zooming in and out.

▶ The slider at the bottom of the timeline is handy for zooming in and out more selectively (**Figure 2.9**).

▶ If you have a mouse with a scroll wheel, there's a cooler option: Not only can you scroll up and down the layer stack, and Shift-scroll left and right in a zoomed in timeline view, but Alt-scrolling (Option-scrolling) dynamically zooms you in and out of time. All of these operate simply by having the cursor positioned over the Timeline window.

TIP

The scroll wheel also zooms in and out of footage view windows when the cursor is placed over them.

Your time needle is actually capable of going where your Timeline window cannot: to time frames that are below the first frame of the composition or beyond the last frame. This needle disappearing act typically happens after you navigate the timeline in the Layer window and then return to the Composition or Timeline window. Have no fear, clicking where you want the time needle to be or using any of the time shortcuts will save you.

You can, of course, view the timeline without seeing the associated Composition window; it's just tricky to unlink the two because making it easy would be confusing to beginning users. If you Alt/Option-click on the box to close the Composition tab, you close the Composition view while the Timeline tab stays active. This "headless" timeline is useful for making adjustments in one timeline while seeing the results in another comp (**Figure 2.10**). I'll cover this more in Chapter 4. If you need to bring back the Composition view for your timeline, click the Comp button at the right edge of the timeline (**Figure 2.11**).

Just above the Comp button is the comp marker bin, where you can click and drag out a marker to a point on your timeline. Markers are numbered sequentially, and you can also add whichever number you like at any time (even when a RAM preview is up) by pressing Shift and one of the numbers at the top of your keyboard (*not* the numeric keypad this time). These aren't quite as cool as layer markers (which you can add at any time with the asterisk key) because you can't label them, but they're sometimes useful anyhow. Holding down the Shift key as you drag the time needle snaps the needle to any comp or layer markers that are present.

Replacing Layers

Sometimes you need to replace the source of a layer with an alternate take or a different element in the Project window. You can easily do this by highlighting the layer to be replaced in the timeline and holding down the Alt (Option) key while dragging the new source to the timeline. An even easier method is to select both the existing layer and the new source and then press **Ctrl+Alt+/ (Cmd+Option+/)**.

All of the settings from the previous layer, along with any applied effects, translate to the new layer automatically. Beware if you are replacing with source of a different size or aspect, as the mask and transform values may only be appropriate to the predecessor.

While we're on the subject, what do you do to neutralize a layer that is taking up a disproportionate amount of render time? I recommend that you not replace it in this manner; Chapter 4 covers some much more elegant methods for assigning proxies and pre-rendering embedded compositions.

Figure 2.10 There's an easier way to preview one comp while continuing to adjust another related one, or several others. Activate the Always Preview This View toggle in the lower left corner of the Composition window. Now, whenever you set RAM Preview, that's the view that will load and play.

Figure 2.11 Clicking the Comp button reveals the Composition window for the current timeline; this is helpful if you have closed the comp view while leaving the timeline open.

TIP

If your replaced layer has a time that mismatches with the previous source and there's no simple fix such as extending the end point, see the section called "Playing with Time Itself" later in this chapter.

Transforms

Twirl down any layer in the timeline, and you find the Transform controls. On a typical layer, transforms are spatial data related to Position and its cousins Anchor Point, Scale, Rotation, and, um, Opacity. Opacity isn't really spatial transform data, but Adobe decided to sort of grandfather it in here as an essential layer property; transforms has a snappier ring to it, evidently.

▶ The keyboard shortcuts to reveal individual transforms are the first letter of each type: **P**, **A**, **S**, **R**, and, um, **T**—Opacity is the oddball again, because O is already in use as the Out point of the Work Area (mentioned above).

▶ To reveal additional properties, hold down **Shift** when typing the letter shortcut.

A *property* in After Effects is a data channel that you can find under a twirled-down layer. Typically the channel can be animated and has a stopwatch icon beside it which, when clicked, sets the first keyframe at the current time.

That's simple enough. But there are, in fact, many different ways to animate a property in After Effects. How many can you think of? As an example, if you wanted to move a layer 200 pixels along the X axis over 24 frames, after setting the first keyframe and moving the time needle forward 24 frames, you could

▶ Drag the layer to the new position in the Composition window (with the Shift key held down to constrain it to one axis)

▶ **Shift+Right Arrow** 20 times to move the layer exactly 200 pixels

▶ Enter the new value by highlighting the X Position numerical value and typing in the new number

▶ Use rub text to drag on the X Position numerical value, dragging to the right until it was 200 pixels higher (and to move faster, holding down Shift to increment it by ten pixels)

▶ Enter a numerical offset by highlighting the X Position numerical value and typing +200

▶ Copy the new Position keyframe from another layer or another point in time (if there were a keyframe with the needed Position value) and paste it to this layer at this time

And that's just an example of some of the things you could do with an added Position keyframe. There are options for causing the animation without setting a new Position value. You could also get that layer to transform 200 pixels over 24 frames by

▶ Offsetting the anchor point in the opposite direction (negative 200 pixel X value) and keyframe that over 24 frames

▶ Enabling 3D for the layer, adding a 50mm camera, and animating it moving 200 pixels, again in the negative X direction

▶ Parenting the layer to another layer that has the transform

▶ Replacing the layer with a composition that contains the layer and transform

▶ Assigning an expression to the Position channel that performs the animation without keyframes

If that's not crazy enough, you could even

▶ Apply the Transform effect to the layer and animate the effect's Position value

▶ Animate in real time via the cursor using Motion Sketch (I did say crazy)

▶ Paste in a path (from a Mask or a Path from Photoshop or Illustrator) to the Position channel, adjusting timing as needed (this method defaults to creating a two-second animation)—again, crazy, but possible

The last two sets of options, in particular, are obviously designed for situations more complicated than the one I set up. Parenting is useful when several layers should all transform in the same manner, and expressions let you link just a single property or create one from scratch. The Transform effect exists for one reason only: to allow you to change the order in which Transforms occur. Normally, they occur before all effects, but this plug-in lets them

NOTES

My point is not that you need to be able to rattle off this list to qualify for a job in a production situation. The point is that there are many approaches to a given problem in a program like After Effects, and the more of them you know, the more prepared you'll be for whatever comes your way.

TIP

When using rub text in either the Timeline or Effect Controls window, holding down **Shift** while dragging increments at ten times the normal amount, while holding down **Ctrl+Alt** (**Cmd+Option**) increments at one tenth the normal amount. The "normal amount" is often, but not always, 1 for any given property; it depends on the slider range, which you can edit by context-clicking on the value and choosing Edit Value.

occur after an effect is applied as well, without the need to pre-compose.

Note that there are even many ways to enter values while animating: You can click and drag using the Selection tool (shortcut: **V**), the Pan Behind tool to move the anchor point (shortcut: **Y**), or the Rotate tool (shortcut: **W**, which the official documentation even points out is for "wotate"). But you can also work directly with the values found in the timeline, and you can do so by entering values or using the rub text feature.

Working with Keyframes

The After Effects keyframe interface is fairly highly evolved, meaning you can create quite complex animations in After Effects. I mastered keyframes in After Effects by matchmoving shots in After Effects 2.0, before there was any tracker. If you feel like you need a refresher of the basics of keyframes, they are well detailed in the documentation. Press **F1** to launch After Effects Help in a Web browser and choose Animating Layers for solid, basic information on transforms and keyframes. If you want to know all the nuances of the various types of keyframes available, choose Fine-tuning Animation. In this chapter, I will focus only on the issues that come up all the time for effects compositors.

Temporal Data and Eases

The most common way that keyframes are used in an effects situation is to say, about a given value, "I want it to be this value at this point in the shot, and this value here." By default, After Effects sets linear temporal transitions; in other words, you travel from keyframe A to keyframe B at a steady rate, then from keyframe B to keyframe C at a separate but still steady rate.

Many basic animations are greatly aided by adding eases. Experienced animators and anthropologists alike will tell you how rare it is that anything in nature proceeds in a linear fashion; nature is full of arcs and curves. A classic example of this is a camera push: In most cases, with a real camera operator, a push would start and stop gently, moving at a steady rate only at the middle of the transition.

Easy Ease

A quick way to deal with easing is to apply the Easy Ease keyframe assistants. To apply them, context-click on a keyframe. Now, look under the Keyframe Assistant submenu, or use the keyboard shortcuts. Clicking **F9** applies Bezier interpolation, creating eases in and out of a keyframe, while **Shift+F9** creates an ease into the keyframe only, and **Ctrl+Shift+F9** (**Cmd+Shift+F9**) creates an ease out. For the camera push example, you would ease out of the first frame and ease in to the final frame, and you would add an ease in both directions if there were any keyframes in the middle (for example, if the speed of the push changed at some point).

To see the result, twirl down the property to which the eases were applied. **Figures 2.13a** and **b** show the difference between a default linear camera push and one to which eases have been applied. The keyframes have changed from linear to Bezier type, and rate of motion is described by a curve instead of a straight line.

Flips and Flops

That's all very well, but how do I flop a shot? Unlike many other compositing and editing applications, After Effects has little in the way of dedicated transform effects, so searching in the Effects palette for flop is not going to help you. For those unfamiliar with the term, to flop a shot is to invert it horizontally, on its Y axis (as opposed to flipping a shot upside down on its X axis). To flop, you toggle Constrain Proportions off and set the X value to −100 (**Figure 2.12**).

Figure 2.12 To flop a shot, be sure to uncheck Constrain Proportions before setting the X value to −100%.

Figure 2.13a With no eases, the Speed: Position graph is flat, moving at a steady rate of 34.72 pixels/sec.

Figure 2.13b Add eases and it arcs from 0 (at the beginning and end of the move) to 52 pixels/sec (at the center peak of the ease).

Holds

You must set Hold keyframes deliberately, by context-clicking on the keyframe and choosing Toggle Hold Keyframe from the menu or by using the shortcut **Ctrl+Alt+H** (**Cmd+Shift+H**). A Hold keyframe's value does not to interpolate to the next keyframe, which is indicated by the square appearance of the right side of the keyframe.

If you need a layer to reposition over time with no transitions (no keyframe in-betweening whatsoever) begin by setting the first frame as a Hold keyframe; all keyframes that follow it in time will be Hold keyframes, signaled by their completely square appearance (**Figure 2.14**).

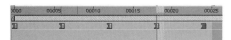

Figure 2.14 A series of Bezier keyframes have been converted to Hold keyframes, evident by the square shape at the right of each keyframe and the speed of 0.0.

Keep holds in mind as a problem solver any time you see unwanted in-between information creep into an animation, which can particularly happen with Position animations.

Spatial Data and Curves

Effects compositors are rarely, if ever, called upon to perform complex animations, but eventually your project may require it, and the keyframe interface of After Effects has long been one of its strengths. Rather than teach you to be a great animator in After Effects, though, I prefer to keep it simple and focus on what you need to know to keyframe effectively and to avoid common pitfalls.

When keyframing Position (or Anchor Point) data, there are in fact two ways you can adjust keyframes: temporally (on the timeline) and spatially (in the Composition window). To illustrate this, I'm going to use the most classic bare bones animation the world has ever known: the bouncing ball (**Figures 2.15** to **2.18**). This example will show you (rather than just tell you) what you need to know about adjusting spatial keyframes.

You'll probably never have to bounce a ball to create a realistic effect, so what can you possibly learn from the example? Let's recap:

Figure 2.15 Under Preferences > General (**Ctrl+Alt+;** or **Cmd+Option+;**) the option Default Spatial Interpolation to Linear is off by default, producing this result when you create three or more position keys. After Effects also applies an automatic Bezier shape to any point that falls between two other points—the opposite of what you want for a bouncing ball.

Figure 2.16 Click the check box for Default Spatial Interpolation to Linear, restart After Effects, and you get this result: three keyframes that are linear in both time and position. Often this is they way you want moves to go, but it does not create the realistic arcs of a bouncing ball.

Figure 2.17 Hold down the Ctrl/Cmd key while clicking the middle keyframe to activate its Bezier handles, then Ctrl/Cmd-click on one of the handles to "break" them, enabling you to form the V-shape shown here, which naturally causes curved arcs to and from the bounce point.

▶ If your keyframes aren't cornering sharply at transition points, check Preferences > General and, if necessary, turn on Default Spatial Interpolation to Linear. For the most part, this setting is more intuitive and useful in the work you'll do, but do watch out for the opposite problem: transition points that are too abrupt.

▶ Either way, you can take control of the shape of your motion path in the Composition window, using the same shortcuts for adjusting Beziers as with the Pen tool (described in detail in the next chapter).

▶ Realistic motion often requires a combination of shaping the motion path Beziers and adding eases to keyframes; you can perform the two actions independently on any given keyframe.

So, even though there is an infinite variety of position animations available to you in After Effects, they will all be done with the basic constraints covered here. True, it can get a little trickier in 3D, but mostly it's just trickier to see what you are doing; the basic rules and constraints remain the same, with each Position keyframe having three basic transition types: Linear, Automatic Bezier, and Custom Bezier Shapes.

Figure 2.18 Finally, temporal eases create a more realistic variation in motion speed. Selecting the first and last frame and pressing **F9** causes eases to those frames and an effective acceleration in and out of the keyframe in between them. Look closely. The dots are spaced further apart (traveling faster) at the bottom and closer together at the top, where the eases are.

Copying and Pasting Trickery

There's a bit of a gotcha possible when copying and pasting keyframe data. The key is to recognize which item is active when you copy and which is active when you paste.

By default, After Effects does its best to help you work this out. If you copy keyframes from a particular property, then simply paste them to another layer, After Effects pastes them to that layer's corresponding property. If that property doesn't exist, because it comes from an effect that isn't applied on the target layer, After Effects adds the effect containing the property to the target layer, but with only the property that you copied.

However, you can also apply keyframes from one property to another similar property. For example, if you want to apply a 2D Position keyframe to the position of an effect, such as the Flare Center position of a Lens Flare effect, you can do so, but only by selecting the Flare Center property in the timeline before pasting.

That's still pretty logical. Where people get screwed up is by not noticing, for example, that an effect in the Effect Controls window is active and forward when they attempt to copy and paste a whole layer. **Figure 2.19** shows a classic example, where a layer does not have its properties twirled down, and so it's easy to miss that the Effect Controls window is forward and has an effect highlighted, so that's what gets copied, instead of the whole layer.

Bottom line: If strange things happen when you copy and paste, immediately undo and try the copy operation again, selecting exactly the thing you want to copy and copying it with no intervening steps. Because even if the logic of how copy and paste works seems obvious, you can still get tripped if you don't pay attention. When something stops making sense in After Effects, there is almost always a good reason traceable to something you've just done (and can undo). This is more than you can say for much graphics software.

Figure 2.19 A classic example where you can get tricked: Five separate items are highlighted: the source comp in the Project window, the target layer, the Curves effect (in both the Timeline and Effect Controls windows), and the layer itself in the Composition window. If I click Delete, which item disappears? Hint: Check which menu bar is not grayed out. Further hint: The Effect Controls window.

Velocity and Value Graphs

Twirl down properties that have keyframes with numerical values, and you'll reveal graphs that are useful for fine-tuning transitions, going beyond what is possible with just keyframe assistants, such as Easy Ease. You only have to understand what these graphs are trying to show you.

Figures 2.20a, b, and **c** show the timeline of the bouncing ball example, this time with linear keyframes, with automated eases (courtesy Easy Ease, **F9**), and with eases accentuated manually, the result of adjusting the curve handles. You will mostly use the Velocity graph to fine-tune eases. The easiest way to do this, especially if you're not yet at home with this graph, is to start with an Easy Ease adjustment. Draw the handles out further from the keyframe to extend the ease, or move them in closer to shorten it.

The main thing to understand about the Velocity graph is that it is shows you the rate of change in keyframe values; the Value graph shows the change of the values themselves. The other important thing to understand, which applies

TIP

Take care not to extend handles so far that they overlap; this can cause curves to spike and buckle, leading to sudden jumps in the animation. If you see something strange while previewing, look for a sudden sharp jolt in the graph and back the handles off to smooth it.

Figures 2.20a, b, and c These three
timelines show a progression, from
a default linear animation (2.20a), to
adding eases to all keyframes (2.20b),
and finally to toggling the middle
keyframe back to a linear keyframe by
Ctrl/Cmd-clicking on it and hand-ad-
justing the other eases, to accentuate
the first and moderate the second
(2.20c). Do not feel the need to follow
these as a "recipe for a bouncing ball."
Rather, they exemplify a progression
of how you can use curves to refine an
animation, and what that looks like.

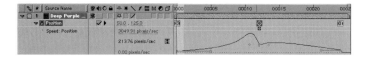

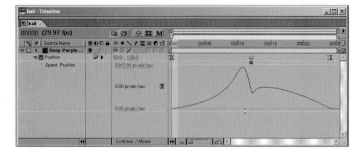

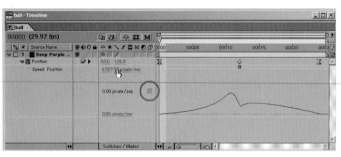

to both of these graphs, is that they show relative values;
200% velocity makes a steep slope if the surrounding values are smaller, but is dwarfed by an added 600% velocity
change.

You can drag the lower boundary of the graph view to
enlarge it and adjust the viewable range by editing the upper and lower values, in blue. Checking the box next to the
current rate resets the graph view.

CLOSE-UP

Roving Keyframes

Say you need an animation to follow an exact path,
hitting precise points, but you want the animation
to progress steadily, with no variation in the rate
of travel. This is the situation for which Roving keyframes were devised. **Figure 2.21** shows a before
and after view of roving keyframes being applied
to the finished bouncing ball animation; the path
of the animation is identical, but the keyframes are
now evenly spaced. This won't come up often, but if
it does, Roving keyframes will be very useful.

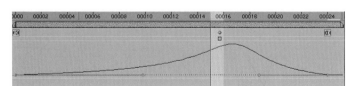

Figure 2.21 The middle keyframe was set to rove (by turning off the tiny toggle
below the keyframe) and is now positioned in between frames 15 and 16; the
keyframe's interpolation setting is no longer taken into account, and it moves to
keep the curve created by the other keyframes smooth and steady.

Über-mastery

With a wink at Friedrich Nietzsche, who theorized the *über-mensch* (the overman or superman) and no doubt would be proud, I'll now focus in on the shortcuts that will make you a rapid-fire animator in the Timeline window. This section is not only about the überkey, possibly the most useful timeline shortcut of all, but about taking control of keyframe data in general with useful shortcuts and tips.

The überkey comes in two delicious flavors: **U** and **UU**. Highlight a layer that contains keyframe data but has no keyframes revealed, and press **U** on your keyboard. All of the properties with keyframes are revealed. Press **U** again, and they are all concealed.

But wait, there's more. Now highlight a layer with no keyframes whatsoever and press UU on your keyboard (two Us in quick succession). All of the properties that are set at any value other than their default, including those with keyframes, are revealed (**Figure 2.22**).

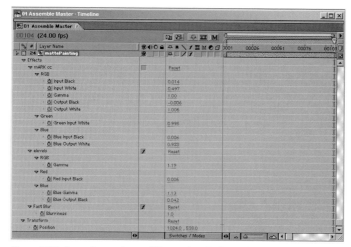

Figure 2.22 Sometimes a layer will have a lot of values adjusted to transforms and effects but no keyframes whatsoever. Pressing UU with the layer highlighted reveals everything that is not set at the default value for a given layer. It's very handy.

To reveal only the applied effects on a layer, use the **E** key. Or, if the über-key reveals effects and transforms and you want the transforms only, use **Shift+E** to toggle the revealed effects.

The utility of the U shortcut is obvious: It's a quick way to get at keyframes to edit them or to find an animation that you suspect is hiding somewhere. But **UU**—now that is a full-on problem solving tool. It allows you to quickly investigate what has been edited on a given layer, helpful when troubleshooting your own layer settings, and priceless when investigating someone else's. Highlight all of the layers in your comp, press **UU**, and you have before you all of the edits that have been made to all of the layer properties. Fabulous.

Dissecting a Project

Suppose you've been handed someone else's project and have to make sense of it; two tools will help you more than any others.

For a broad overview of the project setup, you can enable the Project Flowchart view; look under the Window menu or use the shortcut **Ctrl+F11/Cmd+F11**. This is it—the node interface option in After Effects (**Figure 2.23**), similar but far less interactive than the process trees at the heart of competing applications such as Apple's Shake, Eyeon's Digital Fusion, and Digital Domain's Nuke.

This view allows you to see how the objects in your project have been used and how they interrelate. The toggles at the lower left of the window show layers and effects, but these muddy the waters somewhat on a project of any complexity; for a project overview, toggle them off. The most intuitive view that fits well on a monitor seems to be Left to Right, which you can choose via the pull-down menu at the lower left of the menu. Whether you choose straight or angled lines is up to you, but you can clean up the view by choosing one of them with the Alt/Option key pressed.

Click on the plus signs at the left of each comp, and you can see the component source files. This is step one in dissecting the project: Understand what is used where.

Step two is to open the individual comp; you can double-click to open it directly from the flowchart. Turn off the

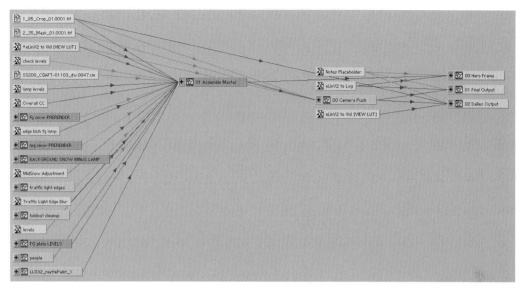

Figure 2.23 What node-based compositing application is this? Why, the decidedly non-nodal After Effects. You cannot interact with this view much, but along with being an occasionally handy way to dissect an unfamiliar project, this view shows that all compositing applications are nodal, when you get right down to it.

Shy toggle at the top if it's on, highlight all of the layers, and press **UU** to reveal all properties that have been altered on all layers. Now preview the composition, stopping at any frame where you have questions and investigating which settings and animations apply to that point in time. If there is a nested composition, you can open it and investigate that in the same manner.

The most effective way to do this is to start with the top-level compositions, the ones that are not contained in other compositions, and work your way backward. While I wouldn't call this process speedy, if you approach it in this logical manner, it will diminish the sense of "Where am I?" that can come over users who come to After Effects used to a more node-based approach. It also opens new comps on tabs that array to the right of the currently open comp, helping keep the tabs in visual order.

Keyframe Navigation and Selection

Although every other shortcut pales in comparison with the überkey, there are several other highly useful shortcuts for dealing with keyframe:

▶ Navigate backward and forward, respectively, through all visible keyframes (and layer markers, and Work Area boundaries) with the **J** and **K** keys. These shortcuts include all revealed keyframes, so if you want to navigate from keyframe to keyframe in one channel only, you might choose instead to click the arrows that appear under A/V Features (also known as the Keys column). Or you can reveal only those keyframes; hidden keyframes are skipped by this shortcut.

▶ Select all of the keyframes for a property by clicking on that property's name.

▶ Select all previous or all following keyframes by context-clicking on the keyframe in the timeline and choosing the respective option from the menu (**Figure 2.24**). The context menu even offers an option for selecting equal keyframes, those with an identical value.

▶ Don't use Ctrl/Cmd to multiselect nonadjacent keyframes, although this works everywhere else in the application. Ctrl/Cmd-clicking on keyframes converts them to Auto Bezier mode. Shift-clicking accomplishes what you're after. You can, of course, drag a box around a subset of keyframes to select them or Shift-drag to deselect them.

▶ Use **Alt/Option+Shift+**the shortcut corresponding to the property (**P**, **A**, **S**, **R**, or **T**) to set a keyframe for a Transform property. This is a more obscure one, but it will save you at least one click each time you use it.

▶ Set a keyframe at the current frame for an effect from the Effect Controls window by clicking on its stopwatch there, instead of revealing it in the timeline.

Keep these tips in mind, and your keyframe edits should be rapid and painless.

Figure 2.24 Three handy and easily missed options for selecting previous, following, and equal keyframes for a given property.

Keyframe Offsets

To offset the values of multiple keyframes by the same amount, use rub text. If instead you edit one of the values, all of the keyframes will be set to that value—not what you want. Here are a few more tips for working with multiple keyframes:

▶ Nudge selected keyframes (one or many) forward or backward in time using **Alt+Right/Left Arrow** (**Option+Right/Left Arrow**), respectively.

▶ Deselect keyframes only using **Shift+F2**. Select all visible keyframes (without selecting their layers) using **Ctrl+Alt+A** (**Cmd+Option+A**); this is useful for deleting a bunch of keyframes but leaving the layers.

▶ Delete a bunch of keyframes, and the value of the first keyframe remains; turn off the stopwatch to clear them, and the current value remains.

▶ Scale the timing of a set of keyframes by selecting the keyframes to be scaled in time and Alt/Option-clicking and dragging on a keyframe at either end of the selected set, stretching it out to whatever time you need. This method can cause intermediate keyframes to fall in between frames, but After Effects is still able to work with them and maintains the proportionality between the keyframes perfectly.

There is no easy way to scale an animation spatially, but I can offer a method if you ever really need to do it:

1. Copy a set of Position keyframes, and paste it into the Mask Shape property of an existing or new mask.

2. Scale the mask.

3. Copy the Mask Shape, and paste the data into an empty Position channel.

The new animation automatically will be two seconds long with roving keyframes, making the cases in which this is useful even rarer.

But what the heck, maybe you can impress someone at a party with this trick—that is, if you invite other After Effects nerds to your parties.

Animation Offsets

The two most common ways to offset a transform animation—to have a layer change its position, rotation, and scale from a point other than its center—are intuitive, easy to use, and well documented. In an individual layer, move the anchor point from the center to a specific point in the frame, typically using the Pan Behind tool (keyboard shortcut: **Y**). Details on that are in the "Editing the Anchor Point" section.

You can center several layers around a single layer by parenting them to that layer. The children take on all of the transforms of the parent layer (not Opacity, which, remember, isn't a real transform) plus whatever offsets they already have.

The number one piece of advice when setting an anchor point or a parent-child relationship is to do so *before* animating, if at all possible, because the only places where this gets tricky have to do with editing the anchor point or the parent-child relationship when Transform keyframes are already in place. The problem is that these settings work as offsets, and can change the current Position frame, messing up the animation as a whole.

The development team is consistent in their design of extra animation features: You can activate the features without changing what is already set up in the composition. So when you change an anchor point position, for example, After Effects performs an offset to the position of the layer in the exact opposite direction so that the layer maintains the same apparent position. And when you parent a layer to another layer, you are setting the default relationship between the parent and child at the frame where you parent; nothing changes in the Composition window on that frame.

That's nice and clear. But reset an offset anchor point in the middle of a Position animation, and the Position keyframe where you reset it changes. Or undo parenting at a frame other than the one where you set it, and its Position value changes, but it appears to remain in the same place. Weird.

NOTES

After Effects has a "prime directive" with animation settings: At the default, setting them should not change the appearance of the current frame. This holds when toggling layers between 2D and 3D, adding or removing parenting, moving the anchor point with the Pan Behind tool, and applying most effects.

You can override this default behavior, moving the anchor point or undoing parenting without changing the Position value in either case, by holding down the Alt (Option) key as you make the change.

Editing the Anchor Point

There are a bunch of ways to edit the anchor point position, and the effect on existing Position data varies with each method.

The most straightforward method is to edit the anchor point with the Pan Behind tool (**Y**) right in the Composition window; doing so causes Position to offset to maintain its current appearance. For a similar result, if you edit the anchor point numbers in the timeline, it is like holding down the Alt (Option) key using the above methods: The Position data does not change.

If you want to edit animated anchor point data, you may have a difficult time in the Composition window. Activate the Layer window, and under the View pull-down, change the default of Masks to Anchor Point Path (**Figure 2.25**).

Editing the Parent Hierarchy

When setting up (or, if necessary, dismantling) a parent-child relationship, you have a choice of methods. You can choose the target parent layer from the pull-down menu in the Parent column of the timeline. Or, you can use the pickwhip control next to the pull-down menu, clicking and dragging from the pickwhip icon of the child layer to the target parent layer. If you have several layers selected and want to parent them all to a single layer, either method will set them all to the same parent.

Parenting does an effective job of sticking even when you change layer order or you duplicate or rename the parent. You can select all of the children of a parent layer by choosing Select Children from the bottom of the context menu. You can remove parenting from all selected layers by choosing None from the pull-down menu.

Figure 2.25 Masks, rather than the anchor point path, appear in the Layer window by default. Change that with this menu at the bottom of the Layer window.

Nulls and the Parenting Cure

Keep parenting in mind whenever you are trying to solve a problem that involves individualizing transforms. A prime example is the lack of separate transform channels in After Effects.

Position, Anchor Point, and Scale properties share a single keyframe for all three channels. Animators who are used to being able to keyframe these as separate channels sometimes find this a bit of a drag. There is a way to solve this problem with expressions sliders, but I'll leave that aside in favor of one that's easier to set up: a null axis hierarchy.

Null objects are quite useful, invisible, nonrendering layers that occupy only a single point in space, although they are based on layers with dimensions that show up in the Composition window (**Figure 2.26**). You can create a null by context-clicking an empty space in the Timeline window and choosing New > Null Object (you can choose it from the Layer menu, as well).

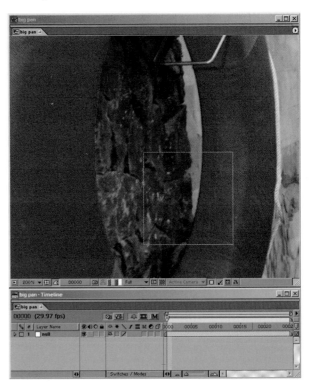

Figure 2.26 A null object in After Effects looks like the outline of a 100-by-100-pixel layer, but cannot show up in renders. The reason for showing the outline is to give you something to easily recognize and grab.

Consider an example of creating a hierarchy for 2D Position. This addresses a concern some animators have with After Effects: that it does not provide the ability to keyframe transforms on separate axes individually.

Figure 2.27 shows the basic setup, in which two nulls are created, one called X and the other Y; the layer is parented to Y, which is then parented to X. Ideally there would be a way to now lock the second (Y) Position value in X, and the first (X) value in Y, but there's not, so you must remember to adjust only the X Position value in X and the Y Position value in Y. If it's important to you to stagger keyframes between the two values, however, this is an effective workaround.

Except for one thing: After Effects 6.5 has no curve editor, nowhere to see the animation data from two distinct channels together. So visually coordinating this edit may turn out to be a hassle. As a matter of full disclosure, I will add that I have rarely ever needed to set things up this way; I tend either to anticipate the problem by animating in a certain order to avoid it, or to use expressions to tie each animation channel to a slider (described in Chapter 10, "Expressions").

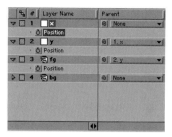

Figure 2.27 You may never need to animate a layer on separate axes, but it's a good example of how a parent hierarchy can help you out. The foreground (fg) layer is parented to the Y control, which is in turn parented to the X control. The idea is to animate only the X Position value of X and only the Y Position value of Y, so that the timing of each channel can vary (which it cannot with standard keyframes).

Motion Blur

Motion blur plays into many of the more advanced illusions you can create with After Effects, but it is fundamentally quite simple. If a layer animates at a sufficiently high velocity, and the Motion Blur toggle is enabled, for it and for the composition containing it, then for free you get this great illusion that the elements blur to match the apparent motion of the scene.

Motion blur is an artifact of motion occurring while a camera shutter is open. It is not something that you encounter with your naked eye, yet it looks very natural when you see it on film or video. It is a complement to your eye's persistence of vision that helps your eye to accept the low frame rate of film (or video). It also looks quite pretty even in still photos, which is part of the reason that efforts to eliminate motion blur from a sampled image have tended to fall flat.

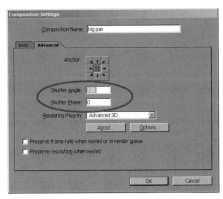

Figure 2.28 The Shutter Angle and Shutter Phase settings on the Advanced tab of the Composition Settings dialog control the appearance of motion blur.

The Virtual Camera Shutter

With a real, physical camera, there is a good reason for how long the shutter is open: Along with the aperture setting, it controls how much light is passed on to the film or video pickup. Low-lit scenes tend to be blurrier as a result of the shutter remaining open longer to gather more light. Other scenes may deliberately be shot with a slow shutter (and the aperture closed down to compensate) just to get some nice, streaky blur.

After Effects is unconcerned with light gathering and does not emulate the differing amount of light that would pass through a lens with a high or low shutter angle setting (nor when adjusting the Aperture setting on a 3D camera, discussed in Chapter 9, "Virtual Cinematography"). Therefore, you only get the desirable part—the blur itself.

The thing that some users don't realize is that After Effects gives you control over how long and when the camera shutter is open via the Composition Settings dialog's Advanced tab (**Figure 2.28**). Or, more typically, users encounter these settings without really understanding them.

The Shutter Angle setting controls how long the shutter is open; a higher number means more blur. The Shutter Phase controls when, during a given frame, the shutter opens; at the default of 0, the shutter opens at the moment in time when the frame begins. See the section "What the Settings Mean" for an explanation of why you'd ever want it any other way.

What the Settings Mean

A physical film camera typically has an angled shutter that can open in a circular fashion anywhere between a few degrees and a full 360 degrees (an electronic shutter does not behave the same, but never mind about that in this context). Theoretically, 360 degrees would provide the maximum amount of blur a shot could have.

After Effects, however, cheats by offering you double the blur overhead of a fully open shutter. The maximum setting for Shutter Angle in the Composition Settings dialog is 720, an impossibility in the real world (because a fully open shutter only has 360 degrees, or a full circle, to reveal).

A camera report may help you adjust this setting, although it's often good enough to carefully eyeball it by zooming in on an area where your background and foreground element both have blur and matching them (**Figures 2.29a and b**). If you do have a camera report and it gives you the shutter speed, you can calculate the Shutter Angle setting with the following formula:

shutter speed = 1 / frame rate * (360 / shutter angle)

This isn't as gnarly as it looks, but if you hate looking at formulas, try thinking about the relationship this way: If your camera shoots at 24 frames per second, but Shutter

Figures 2:29a and b In 2.29a, the default Shutter Angle setting of 180 degrees is too heavy for this white solid masked over the front hubcap, which has been tracked to match the shot motion. In 2.29b, Shutter Angle was cut down by 50% to 90 degrees. In this case, there was no camera report to guide the decisions; they are based on blur that can be observed on the rest of the moving truck.

Angle is set at 180 degrees, then the camera is exposing half the total time of each frame (180/360 = ½), or 1/48 of a second. If your camera report tells you that the exposure was 1/96 of a second, the Shutter Angle setting should be 90 degrees.

The Shutter Phase setting determines when the shutter opens; in other words, the blur doesn't have to start at the beginning of the frame, the shutter could open between frames. Here's the trick: the Shutter Phase is meaningful as a fraction of the Shutter Angle.

In other words, a setting of 0 means the motion blur starts at the beginning of the given current frame. A –90 setting with a 180 Shutter Angle equates the blur starting –0.5 frames before the frame or in between this frame and the previous one. This setting is often used with motion tracking, where you are matching the middle of a motion-blurred target (not one end of it).

Consider a Shutter Phase setting of –50% of the Shutter Angle when working with motion-tracked plate (background) footage; otherwise, leave it at 0. The amount of blur won't change, only the timing of it.

When Blur Is Needed Where None Exists

Motion blur is cool and automatic, if you animated the layer to receive the blur in After Effects. However, if the element comes in already animated but without sufficient blur—as can happen with 3D elements or when a scene is retimed to be faster—you need a different solution, because After Effects has no motion to sample to generate blur.

The painful way to deal with this is to apply directional blur to the elements in question. The problem is that that natural motion blur is rarely unidirectional.

In such cases, and when there's no possibility of reshooting or re-rendering, it's worth considering an investment in Real Smart Motion Blur by RE:Vision Effects (www.revisionfx.com). This plug-in can sample motion from other layers and enhance the amount of blur created by that motion. It's render intensive and can require some tweaking, but it can be just the thing for such situations. A demo version is available on the book's CD-ROM.

Ricochet

One place a −50% Shutter Phase setting is used is when tracking in an object that ricochets, such as a bouncing ball, so that you can see the motion in both directions at the frame of impact. The thing is that this effect doesn't work by default in After Effects 6.5, because it averages the surround frames (**Figure 2.30a**). You have to trick it into making the V-shape of the ricochet by adding a very slight rotation to the ricochet layer. This forces After Effects into sampling all of the frames necessary to create the ricochet (**Figure 2.30b**).

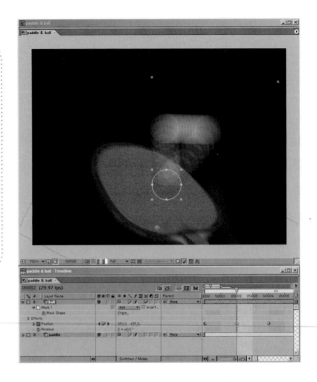

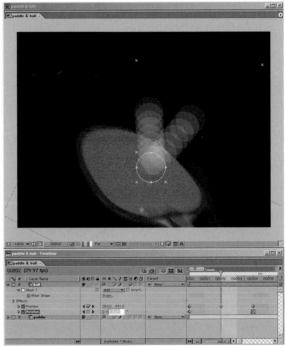

Figures 2.30a and b These two images should look the same, but you have to force After Effects into getting the result in 2.30b by adding a slight bit of rotation. The other key is setting the Shutter Phase to −50% of the Shutter Angle, which causes the motion blur to be sampled right at the middle of the motion.

Playing with Time Itself

After Effects has the advantage of being quite flexible when working with time. Ordinary video applications are quite rigid about locking you down to a single frame rate, and they're rather stilted about how they let you retime footage or mix and match speeds and timing.

After Effects offers quite a few options; it's mostly a question of choosing the right approach for the given situation. Because it's not always obvious how to handle situations in which source footage needs retiming, it's worth looking at the overall approach to time in After Effects and the ways in which timing can be edited, highlighting which are useful and for what situations.

Absolute (Not Relative) Time

The thing to understand about how After Effects thinks about time is that, internally, it thinks in absolute terms, in seconds (not in frames that change in absolute time according to how many of them there are per second). If it were instead calculating time as number of frames total, or frames per second, it would have difficulty if you were to change the frame rate, but actually, at the deepest level, it doesn't care what the frame rate is; After Effects lets you worry about that, while it continues to think in terms of total time measured in seconds.

What does that mean? In real terms, it means that you can change the frame rate of any comp on the fly and the keyframes and other timing information will stay the same in seconds: The timing will not change even though the frames play back at a faster (or slower) rate. The keyframes won't even be nudged to the nearest frame; they will rest between frames, if necessary, to hold the same position in seconds. You can't place them between frames manually, mind you; it only occurs in service to absolute time (**Figure 2.31**).

Figure 2.31 This composition was changed from 29.97 fps to 24 fps. All frames following the first one now fall in between whole frames, and After Effects averages the data accordingly.

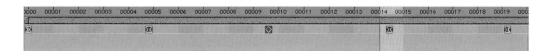

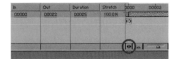

Figure 2.32 The double arrow (high-lighted) reveals and conceals the Time Stretch features.

Figure 2.33 You can set an alternate Duration or Stretch Factor in the Time Stretch dialog. Here you can also specify the pivot point for the stretch by choosing whether the In point, Out point, or current time is held in place.

The same goes for footage (or a composition) that comes into a composition with an alternate frame rate; After Effects simply looks for the current frame in absolute time, whether it started at the same exact moment in time or not.

Time Stretching

Sometimes you need to change the duration and speed of an incoming clip or subcomp; perhaps you need it longer and slower to cover the duration of the shot, or maybe it must be shorter and run faster to complete sooner. Your solution in both situations is the Time Stretch feature, provided you don't need the frame rate to change in the course of the shot (in which case only Time Remapping will do).

There are several ways to activate stretch, depending on how you want to set it up. Click on that little double-sided arrow along the bottom, between the columns and the Zoom slider (**Figure 2.32**). This reveals four columns that show the four basic ways you can set Time Stretch for a layer. You can stretch by

▶ Setting a different In or Out point: **Ctrl+Shift+comma** (**Cmd+Shift+comma**) stretches the In point to the current frame, **Ctrl+Alt+comma** (**Cmd+Option+comma**) stretches the Out point to the current time

▶ Changing the duration of the layer

▶ Changing the stretch value from 100% to an alternate value

Click on the Duration or Stretch value to bring up the Time Stretch dialog (**Figure 2.33**).

Note that stretching a layer does not cause any keyframes applied to that layer to stretch as well; you can highlight a set of keyframes and Alt/Option-drag on the keyframe at one end of the set to stretch keyframes as needed, or you can pre-compose the clip prior to time stretching, guaranteeing that all of the animation stays lined up.

Frame Blending

There is, of course, a downside to lengthening a source clip (and to a lesser extent, to shortening it); frames repeat or skip, and unless the stretch value is an even multiplication or a division of 100% (say, 50% or 200%), the repeating or skipping occurs in irregular increments, potentially causing a herky-jerky motion.

Enable Frame Blending for the layer and the composition, and After Effects averages the frames together. This works not only on layers with time stretching but with any footage that comes in at a frame rate other than that of the composition.

There's only one problem: To say that After Effects "averages" adjoining frames to create the Frame Blending effect is really too generous; it actually just overlays them, making them appear blurrier than at 100%. Although, at Best quality, After Effects averages as many as five adjacent frames in each direction, it's not enough to prevent a disconcerting variation between blurry and sharp images at irregular frame rates.

So, use this feature only in cases where it doesn't count for much; where the element itself will help conceal the trick. For example, use it for something already soft in appearance, such as smoke or clouds.

Time Reversal

You can reverse the timing of a layer with a simple shortcut: Highlight the layer, and press **Ctrl+Alt+R** (**Cmd+Option+R**) to set the Stretch value to –100%. The layer takes on a stripy appearance to remind you that its time has been set in reverse motion (**Figure 2.34**).

There are some bizarre side effects of doing this, however, which may lead you to prefer using Time Remapping to achieve this effect (more on this soon) or to drop the time-reversed clip into a composition of its own. The first thing you notice is that the layer jumps in time, so that the layer now begins where the last frame had been. Moreover, everything to do with that layer is reversed: the In and Out shortcuts are inverted, keyframes appear at the end of each frame, making them look offset from the time needle, and moving forward in time in the Layer window moves you backward in the composition.

When Frame Blending Won't Do

When it's critical to retain as much detail and accuracy in your footage as possible but frame blending is causing its trademark blurriness, you may want to consider another plug-in: Twixtor from RE:Vision Effects.

This plug-in transcends frame blending, sampling adjacent frames to realistically synthesize new ones by warping and extrapolating frames from the original sequence. Rather than simply blending adjacent frames, Twixtor tracks and calculates motion for each individual pixel. For a demo version, go to www.revisionfx.com.

Figure 2.34 The candy-striping is a clear indication that the Stretch value is negative. Keyframes no longer align with the beginning of the frame, a potential gotcha if you're adding animation.

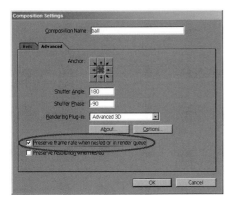

Figure 2.35 If you need a subcomposition to run at a different rate than the master composition, checking the highlighted box in the subcomp will prevent After Effects from resampling keyframes at the master comp's rate.

Time Stretching an Animated Composition

If you apply Time Stretch (or Time Remapping) to a composition, After Effects, by default, goes back to that composition's animation and recalculates its frame rate, slicing any keyframe animations to fit the new rate instead of adhering to the old one.

Be aware, therefore, that the frame values on any given frame will be different unless the underlying time values match. After Effects does not round off to the nearest whole frame; again, it looks at where the animation is in absolute time, even if that means it's between frames in the subcomposition.

You can override this behavior and force After Effects to round off, however. On the Advanced tab of the Composition Settings window of the *nested* comp, toggle on Preserve Frame Rate When Nested or in Render Queue (**Figure 2.35**) to force After Effects to look at only whole frame increments in the underlying composition. This would be a way to show footage at a film frame rate (24 fps) in a composition designed for NTSC television (29.97 fps). You may never need this feature, but knowing it's there and how After Effects otherwise handles precomposed animations is helpful.

Time Remapping

You can do away with the Time Stretch feature set altogether if you are comfortable working with Time Remapping instead. This feature may require a bit of work to wrap your head around, but once you understand it, it has fewer pitfalls than with Time Stretch.

The philosophy behind Time Remapping is elusively simple: Time has a value, just like any other property, which means you can keyframe it, ease in and out of it, loop and ping-pong it, and do all of the other things you can do with any other keyframe data.

Figures 2.36a, b, and **c** show sample timelines that contain typical uses for Time Remapping in an effects situation. The presumption is that you're not going completely nuts rolling footage back and forth, ramping the frame rate up and down, although you can; I'm just considering the deep exploration of this ability to be off-limits for realistic effects work.

You can set Time Remapping by selecting it under the Layer menu or using the shortcut (**Ctrl+Alt+T**/ **Cmd+Option+T**). This sets and reveals two keyframes at the beginning and end of the layer (not the In and Out points, if they've been edited).

If you've set different In or Out points from the default to the layer being time remapped, then a logical first step is to set Time Remapping keyframes at the In and Out points, then delete the default ones.

Time remapped layers have a potentially infinite duration. When you apply time remapping to a layer whose duration is shorter than that of the composition, the layer automatically becomes the duration of the comp, filling the extra frames by holding on the final time remapped keyframe value.

TIP

Beware that if you apply Time Remapping to a source layer that is longer than the composition in which you're applying it, there are two keyframes assigned every time you activate this feature, and the second one hides somewhere off the end of the timeline. Set a new keyframe at the (visible) end of the composition, click the Time Remap property title to highlight all three keyframes, Shift-click the first two to deselect them, and then press Delete to get rid of that hidden final one.

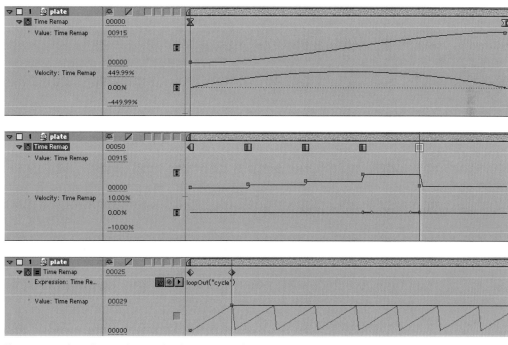

Figures 2.36a, b, and c Simple, everyday things you can do with Time Remapping: speed up the source with eases (shown in 2.36a as Value and Velocity curves), progress through a series of stills selected from the moving clip using Hold keyframes (2.36b), and loop the source using a simple expression (2.36c).

Figure 2.37 This is what a still frame taken from the first frame of a moving clip looks like; You know it's the first frame of the source not because that's where the keyframe lies (it could be anywhere on the layer, because there's just one), but because the value is set to 00000.

Still from a Moving Image

Believe it or not, the simplest way to create a still in After Effects from a moving image clip is to set Time Remapping to that clip with just a single key-frame (**Figure 2.37**). The value of that keyframe is the time at which the desired frame appears in the source clip. It doesn't even matter where on the timeline the one keyframe appears, as long as it is the only one applied.

To reverse a clip using Time Remapping, highlight all keyframes by clicking on the Time Remap property name. Next, context-click one of the highlighted keyframes, and select Keyframe Assistant > Time-Reverse Keyframes.

Time remapping can take awhile to get used to in complex situations, but because this book is concerned more with simulating realism than with stylized artistry, I'll use Time Remapping mostly for eases, holds, loops (discussed in Chapter 10), and the occasional time reversal. If you find yourself in deeper, the same principles apply; you just have to track them more closely.

In Conclusion

This chapter aimed to unlock some of the elegance and logic behind the After Effects timeline. Not everything is straightforward to the first-time user, but lots of short-cuts can help you around what might initially seem to be tedious or exacting edits.

If the information seems overwhelming, remember that most of the advice is tied to specific situations in which it may come in handy. Don't try to memorize every shortcut or tip, but do keep the working scenarios in mind. You then can refer back to the related advice as needed, when those circumstances present themselves.

3

Selections:
The Key to Compositing

I'm fixing a hole where the rain gets in
And stops my mind from wandering
Where it will go.

—John Lennon and Paul McCartney

Selections: The Key to Compositing

A particle physicist works with atoms, a baker and a banker both work with dough, and a compositor works with selections—lots and lots of selections.

If compositing were simply a question of taking pristine, perfect foreground source A and overlaying it onto perfectly matching background plate B, there wouldn't even be a compositor in the effects process; an editor could accomplish the job before lunchtime.

Compositors break images apart and reassemble them, all in motion. Often, it is one element, one frame, or one area of a shot that needs special attention. By the clever use of selections, a compositor can save fellow artists and camera operators, taking control of whatever part of the source footage is necessary.

In this chapter, we'll look at the foundation techniques that define how a layer merges with those behind it. Then Section II, "Effects Compositing Essentials," will focus on particular ways to refine selections, creating high-contrast mattes, and pulling keys from blue-screen footage.

The Many Ways to Create Selections

After Effects offers a number of ways to create selections, yet far fewer than exist in Photoshop. Why? To Photoshop's advantage, its selection tools need work only with still images. This is a much simpler problem, believe it or not, than selection tools for moving images, which must deliver consistent results across the changing array of frames which make up a single clip.

So what are the After Effects methods for creating selections? Take a look.

Pull a Matte

You may think that pulling a matte refers to keying out the blue or green from an effects film shoot (**Figure 3.1**). True enough, but there are other types of mattes too. Even more common than blue-screen keys are high-contrast, or *hi-con*, *mattes*. You create these by maximizing the contrast of a particular channel or area of the image. There are other types of mattes possible as well, such as the elusive *difference matte*. Chapter 6, "Color Keying," discusses pulling mattes in depth.

Use an Existing Alpha Channel

Using an existing alpha channel sounds like a no-brainer, right? The source footage was created with an alpha channel (typically in a 3D animation program); just bring it in as is (**Figure 3.2**). No worries, done deal, right?

That's theoretically true, except that After Effects mostly conceals an issue that is quite explicit in other similar software packages (such as Apple's Shake): the interpretation of the alpha channel. Is the edge premultiplied or not, and

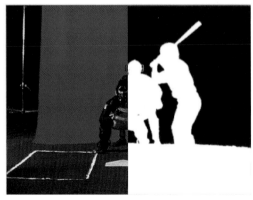

Figure 3.1 This split-screen image shows a blue-screen shoot (left) and the resulting matte. (All baseball images courtesy of Tim Fink Productions.)

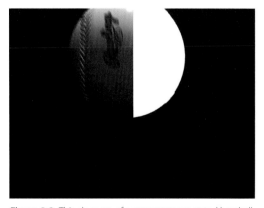

Figure 3.2 This close-up of a computer-generated baseball is split into color (left) and alpha channels.

what do you do in either case? The questions are raised not only when you import the initial image (as you do in After Effects) but also when applying effects to layers with an alpha.

How does After Effects get around this, and is it a good or a bad thing for compositors? For the answer, see the "Alpha Channels and Premultiplication" section later in this chapter.

Create a Mask (or Several)

A mask, by contrast, is a vector shape that determines the opaque and transparent areas of an image (**Figure 3.3**). Masks are generally created by hand, although After Effects does include a provision to generate them automatically by examining the raster data of an image. You can use the Layer > Create Outlines command, but typically it's not too useful for anything besides stylized motion graphics effects.

This chapter focuses instead on the basics of creating and combining masks. You can find a follow-up discussion in Chapter 7, "Rotoscoping and Paint," which focuses specifically on rotoscoping, the art of animating selections over time.

Use Blending Modes Instead

It's even possible to composite without selections at all, instead using blending modes (Add, Multiply, Screen) to combine color channels mathematically, pixel by pixel, in ways that mimic how light and shadow play out in the world (**Figure 3.4**). You can also use selections combined with blending modes to get the best of both worlds.

This chapter goes over the modes that are relevant to effects compositing and gets into the nitty-gritty of what these blending modes are actually doing to the pixel data as they combine it.

Use an Effect

Many effects can be used to create transparency effects or to refine the ones you have. Section II discusses these in detail.

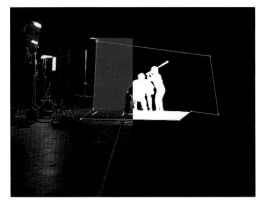

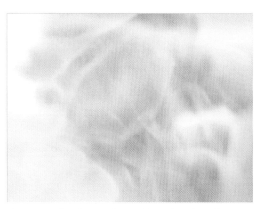

Figure 3.3 In this split-screen view, you can see the garbage matte mask that was added to remove areas of the stage that didn't have a blue screen.

Figure 3.4 Blending modes are the preferred way for compositing elements that are composed of light rather than matter, such as fire.

Combine Techniques

As mentioned with blending modes, there is no reason to think that you're barred from combining these techniques, using a garbage matte to clean up a color key or a hi-con matte to enhance the effect of a blending mode. This is very common in advanced effects work, where no two shots are exactly the same and where a single frame or clip can require a variety of approaches.

So What's the Big Deal?

The real skills here are knowing which approach to apply for a given situation, knowing how to apply it, and knowing when to try something else, either to enhance or to replace what you already have. None of these techniques or approaches is particularly sophisticated by itself, but applying them properly requires a clear vision of what the shot needs and how to supply it.

Compositing: Science and Nature

What exactly is happening in a simple A over B composite? You're just laying one image over another, right? Nothing to it—was obvious from the first time you used Photoshop, right?

For most people, the basic compositing operation is a completely intuitive process that is rarely questioned, but to deal with the crucial part of an A over B composite—the edge detail of layer A—it helps to know what is going on, not only in the world of software, but in the real world as well. The two worlds do not operate the same, but it is the job of the digital world to re-create, as faithfully as possible, what is happening in the natural world.

Bitmap Alpha

A *bitmap selection channel* is one in which each pixel is either fully opaque or fully transparent. This is the type of selection you get if you use, say, the Magic Wand tool in Photoshop. You can feature or blur the resulting edge, but the default selection has no semi-transparent pixels.

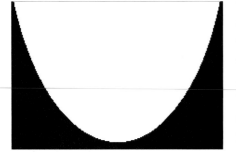

Figure 3.5 Using 400% magnification, you can see clearly how ugly a curved or angled shape is if it can be described by only bitmap pixels, pixels that are either fully off or fully on.

This type of selection has its place—say, isolating pixels of one particular color range to change them—but it is not how nature works. A bitmap cannot describe a curve or angle smoothly, and even a straight line with no edge transparency looks unnatural in an image whose goal is realism (**Figure 3.5**).

Feathered Alpha

But although it's easy enough to see that a bitmap edge does not occur in nature, it's hard to imagine that a *feathered alpha* does occur—hard objects don't have semi-transparent edges, do they? Of course not. Look at the edge of this page, or anything in the foreground of your field of vision. Do you see semi-transparent edge areas? No.

Not exactly, anyhow. It so happens that semi-transparent edge pixels are the best approximation we have digitally for nature (**Figure 3.6**), because they solve two problems in translating the world of objects to the world of pixels:

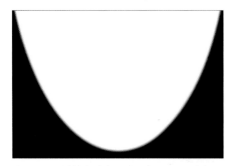

Figure 3.6 Ahh, that's better. With a proper alpha channel and a one-pixel feather adjustment, even at 400%, the edge does a much better job of describing a smooth, soft curve.

▶ They come closer to describing organic curves.

▶ They approximate the physics of light as it bends around objects.

Say what? The first point is easy enough to see and appreciate, but the second one is a doozy, an observation that can be traced back a century to Einstein's *annus mirabilus*, in which he demonstrated how mass and light are inter-related. Light is bent—slightly—by any amount of mass that it passes. The greater the mass, the higher the amount of bending, right up to the extreme of black holes from which light cannot escape. With most objects, your eye sees a slight, subtle effect.

You can study this effect close-up in a digital photo with no compositing whatsoever (**Figures 3.7a, b,** and **c**). In the digital image, you can see areas at the edge of objects that become a wash of color combining the foreground and background. This is caused by the influence of the mass of that object itself on the light (color) coming from behind it.

Opacity

But we're not done with the surprises connected to basic image combination; the way that Opacity edits work in After Effects often takes people by surprise as well, although they can work with it for years without coming face to face with what is counterintuitive about it.

Say you have two identical layers, no alpha/transparency information for either layer. Set each layer to 50% Opacity, and the result should look exactly like either one of the layers at 100%, right?

Wrong (**Figure 3.8**)! If you've ever heard of Zeno's Paradox, that's something like how opacity is calculated in After Effects, but for good reason.

Geek Alert: The Compositing Formula

When you layer a raster image with semi-transparent alpha over an opaque background image, here's what happens: The foreground pixel values are multiplied by the percentage of transparency, which, if not fully opaque, reduces their value. The background pixels are multiplied by the percentage of opacity (the inverse of opacity), and the two values are added together to produce the composite. Expressed as a formula, it looks like

$$(Fg * A) + ((1-A)*Bg) = Comp$$

With real RGB pixel data of R: 185, G: 144, B: 207 in the foreground and R: 80, G: 94, B: 47 in the background, calculating one edge pixel only might look like

$$[(185, 144, 207) \times .6] + [.4 \times (80, 94, 47)] = (143, 124, 143)$$

The result is a weighted blend between the brightness of the foreground and the darker background.

Other effects compositing programs, such as Shake, do not take this operation quite as much for granted the way that After Effects and Photoshop do. You can't simply drag one image over another in a layer stack, you must apply an Over function to create this interaction. Is there a difference? Not until you add to the discussion the operations that go along with an Over, in particular premultiplication, which is detailed later in this chapter.

Figures 3.7a, b, and c Consider a simple digital photo that is not composited (3.7a). When you look closely, you can see that there is a natural softness around the contour of the head despite that it is in sharp focus (3.7b). The effect is even more evident at 400%, if you compare the sharpness (albeit pixilated) of the detail in the fur to the softness of the edge (3.7c). (Images courtesy of Matt Silverman.)

Figure 3.8 Two white solid layers sit one on the other, each at 50%, yet they do not add up to 100% (full) opacity. They add up to 75%, hence the 25% visibility of the checkerboard background.

NOTES

Zeno's Paradox goes something like this: Suppose I wish to cross the room. First, of course, I must cover half the distance. Then, I must cover half the remaining distance. Then, I must cover half the remaining distance. Then I must cover half the remaining distance, and so on forever. The consequence is that I can never get to the other side of the room.

Zeno was evidently violating the bounds of common sense with his observation. But a lead developer on the After Effects team once described the program's opacity calculations similarly: Imagine you have a light which is 1. You now have half the light showing through ($0.5 * 1 = 0.5$). Put a 50% transparent object in front of that. Half of the light shows through ($0.5 * 0.5 = 0.25$), and so on.

Hence, and invoking Zeno's Paradox, After Effects is mimicking how transparency behaves in the real world, which you can try yourself using sheets of vellum or other semi-transparent paper. (This is extra credit, of course!)

Alpha Channels and Premultiplication

Clearly, you don't need to be able to write out the compositing formula to composite, any more than you need to be able to design a car in order to drive one. After Effects helps you by shielding this formula and many other mathematical portions of the compositing operations from your view.

Ignorance is not always bliss, however, when it comes to premultiplication, which After Effects also shields from view when you build a composition. Like Photoshop, After Effects uses non-premultiplied data for the compositing operation, yet it never explicitly tells you (or even lets you find out) how an image is premultiplied and unmultiplied in the image pipeline.

Fortunately, After Effects does an effective job of managing premultiplication under normal circumstances—fortunate because managing it yourself is a tedious process. You just need to know how things can go wrong, the symptoms that show you that something has gone wrong, and what to do to set it right.

Premultiplication Illustrated

Premultiplication exists for one reason only: so that source images look nice, with realistic, anti-aliased edges, *before they've been composited.*

That's right, we have premultiplication just so that a matted object looks right against a black background when it comes out of, say, your 3D animation program. All premultiplication does is composite the foreground against the background, so that the edges and transparency blend as well into that solid color (typically black) as they would against the final background.

It's not the alpha channel that distinguishes a premultiplied from a straight alpha image, it is the color channels. When you ask After Effects to "guess" how to interpret the footage (on import, by choosing Guess in the Interpret Footage dialog, or using **Ctrl+F/Cmd+F**), it looks for a solid color background with edge pixels that seem to have had that color multiplied into them.

What does it mean to have the background multiplied into the edge pixels? Revisit "Geek Alert: The Compositing Formula," but imagine the background value to be 0,0,0. There's your answer. The effect is to darken semi-transparent edge pixels if the background is black, to lighten them if it's white, and to really wreak havoc with them if it's any other color.

The close-ups in **Figures 3.9a** and **b** show a section of the same foreground image with the alpha interpreted properly and with it misinterpreted. A misinterpreted alpha either fails to remove the background color from the edge pixels, or removes color that should actually be present.

Figures 3.9a and b Motion Blur clearly reveals the sins of improper premultiply settings. Although there are dark areas in the blur of the properly interpreted foreground, they are consistent with the dark areas of the plane itself (3.9a). The improperly interpreted version has dark matting all around it, including in the areas of the canopy that should be translucent, and around the blur of the propeller (3.9b). You suspect it's wrong simply because it looks bad around the edges.

NOTES

Most computer-generated images are premultiplied, unless the artist takes specific steps to counteract the process. The Video Output section of the Output Module Settings for items in the Render Queue includes a pull-down to specify whether you render with Straight or Premultiplied alpha; by default, it is set to Premultiplied (**Figure 3.10**).

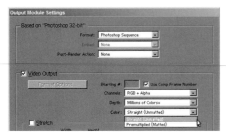

Figure 3.10 The cursor points at the Color selection, determining whether After Effects renders footage with straight or premultiplied alpha.

Why should you care about premultiplication? First of all, because incorrectly managing your alpha channels can cause undesirable fringe artifacts. But just as important, you may find yourself in a situation where those artifacts seem to be presenting themselves although you've carefully managed the process; suddenly your composited elements have black edges around them. Your job depends on getting to the bottom of this. There are two basic ways it can happen:

▶ An alpha channel is misinterpreted on import (see "Getting it Right on Import")

▶ A matte is added within a composition and premultiplication isn't accounted for (see "Solving the Problem Internally")

Unfortunately, users who aren't confident enough to trace the underlying problem often end up resorting to all sorts of strange machinations to try to get rid of the black edge; re-rendering the element against a different color, choking the alpha matte even though it comes from a 3D program and is accurate, and possibly even more frightening and desperate maneuvers.

Getting It Right on Import

Most people's ace in the hole if they don't really understand pre-multiplication is the Guess feature that sits next to the premultiplication settings in the Footage Settings dialog. There is also a preference that determines what happens when footage is imported with an alpha channel; if this is set to anything other than Ask User (the default) you may be importing files with alpha channels without knowing what is happening (**Figure 3.11**).

Is Guess ever wrong? Yes, it can be, if the factors it expects in a premultiplied alpha are there in a straight image, or vice versa. Thus it is best not to automate this process, if only so that you're able to hear the beep. In the case of a premultiplied image, After Effects attempts to guess not only the setting but also the color of the background; generally this will be black or white, but watch out for situations where an artist has become creative and rendered against canary yellow or powder blue. For that reason,

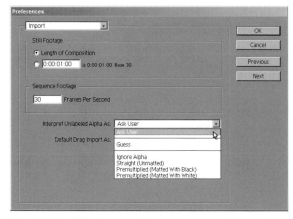

Figure 3.11 By default, the import preferences are set to ask the user how to interpret an alpha channel, which is a good thing, generally speaking, as a check against errors. If you're not sure about the appropriate setting, you can click on the Guess button, which typically can determine the type of channel. If it cannot guess confidently, it beeps.

there is an eyedropper adjacent to the Matted with Color setting (**Figure 3.11**). When in doubt, look at your footage without the alpha applied: If you see a solid background that is neither pure black or white and After Effects isn't detecting it, use the eyedropper.

Fundamentally, though, as an effects compositor you need to be able to examine your images and spot the symptoms of a misinterpreted alpha: dark or bright fringing in the semi-opaque edges of your foreground.

Solving the Problem Internally

The really gnarly fact is that premultiplication errors can be introduced within the After Effects pipeline. Usually this happens when you apply a selection as a track matte

TIP

To see footage that was imported with a premultiplied alpha displayed in straight alpha mode (with edge transparency removed) use this shortcut in the Layer/Composition window: **Alt+Shift+4** (**Option+Shift+4**).

to footage (described in more detail toward the end of this chapter), and After Effects, of course, doesn't anticipate premultiplication. If the sequence was rendered with premultiplication but the alpha channel was created on a separate pass, as a separate file, for example, you would apply that alpha using a track matte. After Effects would have no idea that the image was premultiplied, however, because the color channels came in through the back door, as it were, without an alpha.

If you see fringing in your edges and need to solve it internally in After Effects, there is a tool to help: the Remove Color Matting effect (**Figures 3.12a** and **b**). This effect has one setting only, for background color, because all it does is apply the unpremultiply calculation (the antidote to premultiplication) in the same manner that it would be applied in the Footage Settings.

NOTES

Remove Color Matting will not work properly on a layer with a track matte; because this is the main situation in which it's useful, be sure to pre-compose the layer and its track matte prior to applying Channel > Remove Color Matting.

Masks

Although hand-created and animated for the most part, masks open up all kinds of possibilities in After Effects. Masks are the principal method for defining transparency regions in a clip without regard to actual pixels, because they are vector shapes. This section lays down the basics for smart use of masks.

Typical Mask Workflow

There are three tools for creating masks: two shape tools and the Pen. To activate the Rectangular Mask tool, use the

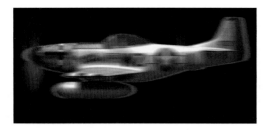
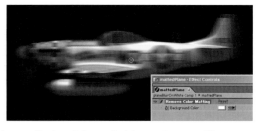

Figures 3.12a and b In 3.12a, the plane against the white background had an alpha applied via a track matte without premultiplication removed, revealing white fringing, which is clear here against the black. With the color set to pure white, the Remove Color Matting effect corrects the problem (3.12b), but only once the color and track matte layers have been pre-composed.

keyboard shortcut **Q**; press **Q** again to toggle the tool to the Elliptical Mask tool. If your mask doesn't conform well to a rectangle or an ellipse, you can draw it point by point with the Pen tool (**G**).

Whether you draw the mask in the Composition window or the Layer window is up to you. It is somewhere between difficult and impossible to draw or see a mask accurately in the Composition window if, say, the layer was offset and rotated in 3D space, but if you want to see the layer over its background, you need to have the Composition window open. With enough monitor space, an ideal compromise is to keep both windows open side by side, working in the Layer window and watching the Composition window for live updates.

Remember that your target shape doesn't have to be an ellipse to benefit from starting by drawing an ellipse. Indeed, if the shape calls for a perfectly circular curve on one side, you might do well to draw an ellipse (holding down Shift to make it perfectly circular) and then editing other sides of it with the Pen tool.

When drawing a rectangle or ellipse

▶ Double-click the Mask tool (in the Tools palette) to set the boundaries of the mask to match those of the layer.

▶ Use **Shift** to constrain the shape and **Ctrl/Cmd** to draw the shape from the center rather than from a corner.

▶ Try the Mask Shape dialog if you need to set the boundaries to exact dimensions and can't do it visually. Although this dialog's use is quite limited, you access it by clicking the underlined word "Shape" under Mask options (highlight the layer and click **M** to reveal it).

▶ Double-click a point on the shape to activate Free Transform mode, which enables you to offset, rotate, or scale the entire mask shape (**Figure 3.13**). As always, hold down **Shift** to keep the scale proportional, snap the rotation to 45 degree increments, or constrain movement to one axis.

TIP

If you need other common primitive shapes—a rectangle with rounded corners, a hexagon, or the like—you're best off drawing the shape in Adobe Illustrator, then copying and pasting it. This, however, will not work unless the preferences in Illustrator are set properly. Under the File Handling & Clipboard preference, choose AICB with Preserve Paths checked. This is not the default. You can also select and copy paths in Photoshop for use as masks.

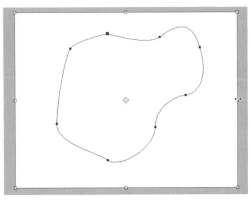 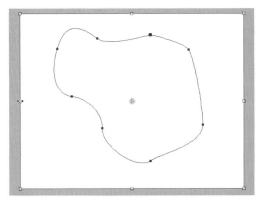

Figure 3.13 Flipping a custom mask symmetrically on one axis is no easy trick in After Effects. Holding down the Shift key scales both axes proportionally, which is not usually what you want. Instead, with View > Show Grid enabled and View Snap to Grid turned on, double-click the Rectangular Mask tool to create a mask that is the size of the layer. Select both masks in the timeline, and double-click a point on one of the masks to set the Free Transform tool. Now drag the handles at either side of the image and swap their positions, deleting the layer-sized mask when you're done.

Highlighting a layer with a mask and pressing the **M** key twice in rapid succession reveals the full Mask options for that layer. Some tips for those are

▶ Feather is set for the entire mask and operates in both directions (to the inside and outside of the mask shape); there is no way around these defaults. All kinds of lighting, smoke, and glow effects can begin with a masked solid that is heavily feathered. In other words, the feather setting is approximately half the width of the mask at its narrowest crossing, meaning the masked solid is now a big soft gradient (**Figure 3.14**).

▶ Pressing the **F** key reveals only the Mask Feather property in the timeline.

▶ A hidden gem is Mask Expansion: You can use it to expand or, with a negative value, to contract the mask area. This has all sorts of uses, including creating an edge mask using one mask duplicated into two, each with a Mask Expansion value that is the inverse of the other, and the inner mask subtracted from the outer.

Keyboard shortcuts are a big part of eliminating a lot of the fuss and bother that comes with masking in After Effects.

Figure 3.14 The Feather of this mask is set roughly equal to its radius, creating a big, diffuse gradient in the shape of the mask (in this case, elliptical), useful for many types of lighting effects.

Drawing Bezier Masks

By default, the Pen tool draws Bezier curves, and in After Effects you can do everything you need to create a mask by keeping the Pen tool active throughout the mask edit.

I sometimes draw a Bezier mask first as straight lines only, clicking to place points at key transitions and corners. Once I've completed the basic mask shape, with the Pen tool still active, I can go back point by point and edit the shape, because I have instant access to all of the mask shortcuts:

▶ Clicking on a point with the Pen tool active deletes it.

▶ Clicking on a segment between points with the Pen tool active adds a point.

▶ Alt/Option-clicking on a point with the Pen tool enables the Convert Vertex tool: Apply it to a point with no handles, and you can drag out to create handles. Apply it to a point with handles, and you cancel the handles.

▶ Clicking on a Bezier handle with the Pen tool breaks the center point of the Bezier, enabling you to adjust the handles individually; Alt/Option-clicking on a handle restores a linear connection between the handles.

▶ Context-clicking on the mask shape with the Pen tool (or the Selection tool, for that matter) enables the

TIP

As with most selectable UI elements in After Effects, pressing **F2** or **Ctrl+Shift+A (Cmd+Shift+A)** deselects the active mask. This is handy when you're done drawing one mask and want to create the next one without switching tools.

context menu of options for that mask, including all of its settings on the timeline, the ability to specify a First Vertex, and Motion Blur settings for the mask, which can be unlocked from the layer itself.

Only when you want to double-click to free transform the entire mask is it necessary to switch to the Selection tool, which you can do either by pressing **V** or by holding down Ctrl/Cmd while you double-click a vertex. The **Ctrl/Cmd** key toggles back and forth between the Pen and Selection tools, regardless of which one is currently active.

Combining Multiple Masks

By default, all masks are drawn in Add mode, meaning that the contents of the mask are added to the layer selection, and the area outside all of the masks is excluded. There are other options for combining them, however; the five primary mask modes are

▶ **Add:** The default mode; adds the density (luminance) values to the image as a whole, including masks higher in the stack (**Figure 3.15**)

▶ **Subtract:** Subtracts density (luminance) values from masks higher in the stack or from the image as a whole if no other masks precede it (**Figure 3.16**)

▶ **Intersect:** Combines only the areas of the density that overlap with masks higher in the stack (**Figure 3.17**)

▶ **Difference:** Subtracts overlapping areas. (**Figure 3.18**)

▶ **None:** Has no effect on the image whatsoever; it can be useful as a placeholder or for effects that use masks (**Figure 3.19**)

Particularly when rotoscoping (masking an animated shape) it is very wise to take advantage of using multiple masks, for one simple reason: The more points you have to keep track of on a given frame, the more likely you'll have to add a keyframe and the more likely you'll lose track of a point. With multiple masks there is far more forgiveness for small errors and fewer keyframes per mask are needed to complete the job. This topic is explored in greater detail in Chapter 7, "Rotoscoping and Paint."

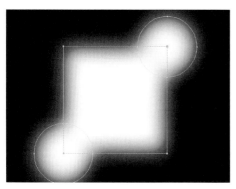

Figure 3.15 In Add mode, the luminance values of the overlapping masks are combined, increasing the masked area.

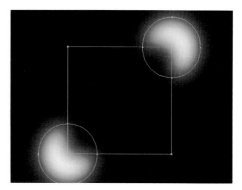

Figure 3.16 Subtract mode is the inverse of Add mode.

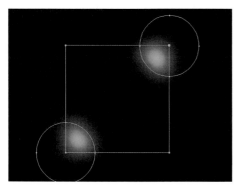

Figure 3.17 Intersect mode adds only the overlapping areas of opacity.

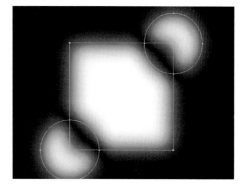

Figure 3.18 The inverse of Intersect, Difference mode subtracts overlapping areas.

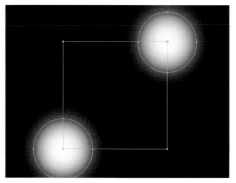

Figure 3.19 In None mode, the mask is effectively switched off.

Figures 3.20a and b With a lighten (3.20a) or a darken (3.20b) mask, the transparency values are chosen either from the mask set to this mode or those overlapping it, depending on which has the lighter (higher) or darker (lower) values.

Managing Density

When combining masks that have semi-transparent areas, either because the opacity of the masks is less than 100% or, as in the examples shown here, because the edges are heavily feathered, you may not always want the densities to have a completely linear relationship in the overlapping areas. That's when Lighten and Darken modes come into play.

Figures 3.20a and **b** show the result of using each of these modes; they prevent mask densities from building up the way that they do with the other modes. No pixel within the combined masks will have a value that is not already represented in one of the overlapping masks; either the lighter or the darker of the two will be represented.

Keep these in mind when combining multiple feathered or semi-transparent masks. Remember that mask modes apply to the layers above them, so these modes should be applied as each overlapping mask is added, not to the top mask in the stack.

Managing Multiple Masks

A few features in After Effects exist specifically to help you manage multiple masks in a single layer.

One is Cycle Mask Colors, which is tucked away in the User Interface Colors section of Preferences. When Cycle Mask Colors is off, your masks are created in the same color (the mask itself and its swatch in the timeline) each time. To change it, you click the swatch. With Cycle Mask Colors checked on, which I recommend, the mask colors vary on their own.

Also, when editing overlapping masks, you may find it helpful to use the context menu to lock and hide other masks. Context-click on the mask, and choose Lock Other Masks; now you can edit the active mask only. Context-click again, and choose Hide Locked Masks; this time your view is uncluttered as well.

TIP

Don't forget that you can name masks by highlighting them in the timeline, pressing Return, and typing in a new name. The names don't come along when you copy and paste the layers, unfortunately, but they're still useful.

Putting Masks in Motion

Putting masks in motion for visual effects work is also known as *rotoscoping*, which is covered in greater depth in Chapter 7. There are all kinds of uses for masks, however, and that chapter is fairly specialized, so here is an overview of some things to pay attention to when putting a mask in motion.

Interpolation Basics

You can set a temporal ease on a mask keyframe, but you have no corresponding spatial curves with masks. Each point travels in a straight line to its position in the following keyframe.

This means that to precisely mask an object traveling in an arc, you need to set a lot more keyframes than for an object traveling in a single direction.

The real bummer about mask keyframes is that you can't select a group of them and translate the mask; as soon as you move, rotate, or scale it, your selection snaps to the current keyframe only.

There is a workaround. You can duplicate the layer being masked and use it as an alpha track matte for an unmasked source of the same layer, in which case you're free to transform (or even motion track) the duplicate using the normal layer transforms. It's not a perfect solution by any means, but it is often useful and hardly anyone thinks of it.

Moving, Copying, Pasting, and Masks

You can freely copy mask shapes from one source (a different mask, a different keyframe in the same mask animation, Illustrator, or Photoshop) and paste them into an existing mask channel. You just have to follow some rather strict rules that depend on the situation:

▶ **With no keyframes involved in the source or target:** Selecting the mask itself and pasting it to another layer automatically applies it as-is to a new mask or to any mask that is selected.

Bug Alert, or Not?

Does a bug still count as a bug if the development team knows about it and has decided to leave it as-is to be backward-compatible? I'll let you be the judge. Say there's one part of an overlaid element that you want to mask and reduce to partial opacity, say 50%.

You create a mask for the area to be dialed back, set it to Subtract, and set Mask Opacity to 50%. But instead of the anticipated result, displaying the layer at full opacity and the masked area at 50%, the masked area is subtracted 100% and the rest of the layer displays at 50% opacity!

This is the identical result to applying the same mask in Add mode with Invert checked, only in that case the behavior is at least anticipated.

The workaround is to add a mask at the top of the stack, giving the mask the dimensions of the entire layer (double-click the Rectangular Mask tool). The Subtract mask will now work properly relative to this first mask, set to Add mode.

▶ **Source mask has Mask Shape keyframes, but target has none:** Highlighting the mask (not the specific keyframes) and pasting creates a new mask as if pasting from time 0. Highlighting any or all Mask Shape keyframes pastes a new mask with keyframes starting at the current time.

▶ **Target layer has masks with or without keyframes:** To paste Mask Shape keyframes into a particular mask at a particular time, highlight the target mask before pasting. Highlighting the target Mask Shape property highlights any keyframes and replaces them (not usually what you want).

In all cases, if the target layer is a different size or dimension from the source, the mask stretches to maintain its relationship to the layer boundaries.

In many situations, pasting Mask Shape keyframes blindly in this manner is not what you're after, but a rather obscure feature in the Layer window *will* help you. The Target pull-down along the bottom of the window has a unique function: When you choose an existing mask as the target, you can start drawing a new mask anywhere in frame and it will replace the shape in the target mask layer (**Figure 3.21**).

First Vertex

When pasting in shapes or radically changing the existing mask by adding and deleting points, you may run into the issue of how the points line up. Hidden away in the mask context menu, and available only with a single vertex of the mask selected, is the Set First Vertex command. If you are having problems with mask points twisting around to a

The Smart Mask Interpolation tool (available via a palette found in the Window menu) is designed to smooth transitions between two radically different shapes. It's useful for stylized motion graphics of detailed masks transitioning from one to the next, but less useful for effects masking and rotoscoping because it's a bit too automated. The result, while sometimes pleasing, doesn't usually obviate the need to more carefully keyframe an accurate mask transition.

Figure 3.21 This pull-down menu at the bottom of the Layer window makes it easy for you to create a mask shape from scratch, replacing the shape in the target mask. If the target mask has keyframes, After Effects creates a new keyframe wherever you draw in a new shape for that mask.

mismatched point during an interpolation, setting the First Vertex to two points that definitely correspond should help straighten things out. It also can be necessary for effects that rely on mask shapes, such as the Reshape tool (described in Chapter 7).

Blending Modes: The Real Deal

After Effects includes 34 blending modes, each created with a specific purpose (**Figure 3.22**). For effects work, however, the majority of them are not particularly recommended. In fact, traditional optical compositing would effectively include only two of them: Add and Multiply.

So that's it? Use these two or none at all? Not quite—I'll point out a few other useful modes as well. Once you understand how your options work, you can make informed compositing decisions, rather than lazily playing Go Fish by trying one mode after the other until you see something you kind of like.

The mathematical descriptions of blending use values normalized to 1; in other words, the full range of pixel values is 0 to 1 instead of 0 to 255, as it typically appears in your color controls. A medium gray on any channel is 0.5 instead of 128, pure white is 1, and pure black is 0 (**Figure 3.23**). This makes it much simpler to show the calculations that are actually used to create the blended pixels, because the internal math typically is based this way. For information about overbright values, which have a value greater than 1, see Chapter 11, "Issues Specific to Film and HDR Images."

Figure 3.23 The Info palette can display pixel values in several different modes, including decimal values, shown here with the cursor over a medium gray. The values are normalized to a maximum luminance value of 1.0 and a minimum of 0.0, which make calculations more straightforward than 0 to 255, the standard 8-bit range. Select a color mode for the Info palette via its wing menu; whatever mode you select is thereafter also used by the Adobe color picker.

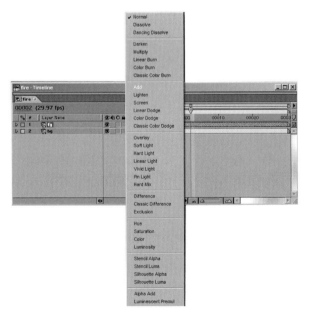

Figure 3.22 You have 34 blending modes, but how many will you really use?

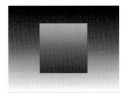

Figure 3.24 Compare **Figures 3.25** through **3.30** to this one, which shows a masked section of a gradient over its exact inverse. Blending here is set to Normal.

Remember, blending modes are all based on mathematical operations for combining pixels in the layer containing the given blending mode and the pixels behind it—either below it in the stack, if all the layers are 2D, or positioned behind it in 3D space, if all the layers are 3D.

To help you understand what the various blending modes are doing, **Figures 3.24** through **3.30** show you what happens when a masked gradient is blended with its exact inverse. Remember that color operations are fundamentally no different than grayscale, except that they happen via three channels instead of one.

Figure 3.25 The same combination with Add mode applied to the masked foreground area, which becomes full white as each pixel in the background is added to its inverse in the foreground.

Figure 3.26 Screening results in combined pixels that are not as bright as with Add, but which are combined in a similarly linear manner resulting in a flat color.

Figure 3.27 Multiplying a value with its inverse causes it to be zero or full black. This is like having the two gradients on two separate pieces of film and laying one over the other, making the combination darker because less light passes through the denser (darker) areas.

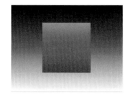

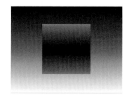

Figure 3.28 Overlay is a combination of Screen and Multiply; areas of the background below 50% brightness are multiplied, those above 50% are screened.

Figure 3.29 The inverse of Overlay: This time areas of the foreground below 50% brightness are multiplied, those above 50% are screened.

Figure 3.30 Difference bases the luminance of the foreground pixels on the amount of difference between the foreground and background source. In this case, pixels along the vertical center have no difference and are black, with the difference increasing as pixels move toward the upper and lower edges.

Add and Screen

Add and Screen modes both brighten the image. Screen typically yields a subtler effect than Add, which results in brighter values overall.

Add mode is every bit as simple as it sounds; the formula is

$$newPixel = A + B$$

where A is a pixel from the foreground layer and B is a background pixel (although they are obviously interchangeable in this formula). The result is clipped at 1 for normal 8- and 16-bit pixels; any pixels that add up to a value of more than 1 take the value of 1, full white.

This mode is used a lot; it brightens the overall image, but black in the foreground becomes transparent, effectively adding a value of 0 to the background. It is useful for laying fire and explosion elements shot in negative space (against black) into a scene, adding noise or grain to an element, or any other element that is made up of light and texture (**Figures 3.31a**, **b**, and **c**).

Screen mode has an influence similar to Add mode's, but via a slightly different formula. The pixel values are inverted, multiplied together, and the result is inverted:

$$newPixel = 1-((1-A) * (1-B))$$

Note that with this formula, fully white pixels stay white, fully black pixels stay black, but a mid-range pixel (0.5) takes on a brighter value (0.75), just not as bright as would be with Add (1).

NOTES

What is the difference between Add and Linear Dodge? The name! Open Photoshop and you'll notice it contains no blending mode called Add. Apparently Photoshop lacks the legal rights to use this term, hence Linear Dodge, which exists in After Effects only to match Photoshop.

NOTES

Because Screen depends on no values being greater than 1, do not use it in a floating-point image pipeline that includes the possibility of pixel values over 1, such as eLin (Chapter 11).

Figures 3.31a, b, and c Add mode takes the source foreground element, the fire shot against a black background shown in 3.31a, and adds its pixel values channel by channel to the background (3.31b), causing the pure black pixels to disappear completely (3.31c).

Figure 3.32 Using Screen on an element brings it in more softly; notice there's less brightness in the areas of overlapping fire. A similar effect could be achieved using Add plus a Levels correction to the foreground to reduce its Output White value.

Figure 3.33 Dark smoke (actually a grayscale fractal noise pattern with no alpha channel) is multiplied over the background, darkening the areas that are dark in either the foreground or background further.

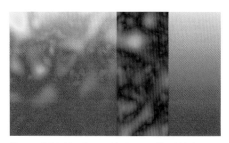

Figure 3.34 Overlay and its inverse, Hard Light, are useful for combining color and texture. Here, an instant lava lamp texture was created using the components shown at the right: a solid with Fractal Noise applied set to Overlay mode on top of a red-to-yellow gradient.

You use Screen much like Add. Screen is most useful in situations where Add would blow out the highlights too much—glints, flares, glow passes, and so on (**Figure 3.32**).

Multiply

Multiply is another mode that is as simple as it sounds; it uses the formula

$$newPixel = A * B$$

This would seem to make the values much higher until you recollect that we are dealing only with values between 0 and 1. Multiplying them together, therefore, actually has the effect of reducing midrange pixels and darkening an image overall, although pixels that are full white in both images remain full white.

In optical compositing (the way this was all done before we had computers) the equivalent of multiply was layering two images, one over the other, combining their densities such that the dark areas of one image held out light from the other image.

Multiply literally has the inverse effect of Screen mode, darkening the midrange values of one image with another. It is useful in cases where you have dark tones that you want to include in an image without replacing the lighter tones as much, for example to layer in texture, shadow, or dark fog to a background (**Figure 3.33**).

Overlay and the Light Modes

Overlay uses the bottom layer to determine whether to screen or multiply. If the top layer is lighter than 50%, it is screened. Below 50%, it is multiplied. Hard Light does the same, only using the top layer to determine whether to screen or multiply, so the two are inverse effects. Reversing layer order and swapping Overlay for Hard Light yields an identical result.

These modes, along with Linear and Vivid Light, can be most useful for combining a layer that is predominantly color with another layer that is predominantly luminance, or contrast detail (**Figure 3.34**). This is how you create textures; for example, a lot of the lava texturing in the Level 4 sequence of *Spy Kids 3–D* was created by combining a hand-painted color heat map with moving fractal noise patterns using Hard Light.

This type of usage is fine, but don't start fishing in the various Light modes when combining images. They don't work with overbright levels (explored in Chapter 11), and this method of adjusting images is a warning sign that you haven't thought things through in terms of what you're trying to do.

Figure 3.35 Setting a deep-blue-colored solid to Color mode and overlaying it on the plate footage has the effect of tinting the colors in the image blue. Subtler uses of this mode are explored in Chapter 12, "Working with Light."

Difference

Difference is a subtraction mode that inverts a pixel in the background according to how bright the foreground pixel is. There is one very specific use for Difference that is never rendered: You can line up two identical layers using this mode. When all of the pixels line up properly, layer details disappear.

HSB and Color Modes

The Hue, Saturation, and Brightness modes each combine the given value from the foreground layer with the other two from the background layer. Saturation applies the foreground saturation to the background hue and luminance values, Hue combines the foreground hue with the background saturation and luminance, and Brightness uses the foreground luminance in combination with the hue and saturation of the background.

Color takes both the hue and saturation of the top layer, using only the luminance from the underlying background (**Figure 3.35**).

Keep these modes in mind as a shortcut to channel operations in which you might want the color from a foreground combined with the detail (luminance) of the existing background.

Stencil and Silhouette

The Stencil and Silhouette blending modes apply transparency information to all of the layers below them in the composition. The Stencil modes use the light pixels, and

Silhouette the dark pixels, of either the Alpha or Luminance values to determine the areas that remain visible in the layers below the current layer.

You should keep these in mind for that rare occasion where they save you extra setup work.

Alpha Add and Luminescent Premultiply

Alpha Add and Luminescent Premultiply are special-case blending modes that affect semi-transparent edge pixels only.

Have you ever tried matting a layer with an alpha channel over the same layer with the alpha channel inverted? **Figures 3.36a** through **d** show the typical result: a semi-opaque line tracing the edge of the alpha, where the pixels remain semi-transparent because they are blended together in the same manner as semi-opaque layers. Alpha Add adds the actual values of the alpha pixels without compensating for the opacity effect, so two 50% opaque pixels become 100% opaque.

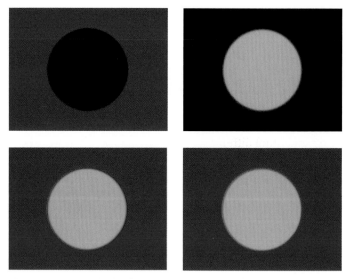

Figures 3.36a through d (left to right) Laying a matted object over a background with the inverse matte seems as though it should result in a fully opaque image (3.36a, b). Instead, edge pixels become semi-transparent (3.36c). Alpha Add does just what the title implies, adding the alpha values together so that inverse mattes total up to 100% throughout the image (3.36d).

Why would you combine a layer with itself, inverting the alpha? You probably wouldn't. But you might combine two layers with overlapping transparency that should work this way—for example, two parts of the same layer.

Luminescent Premultiply is an alternative method of removing premultiplication from source footage, retaining bright values that would otherwise be clipped. Premultiplication over black causes all semi-transparent pixels to become darker; removing the black values while adding transparency, which is what removing premultiplication does, can cause them to appear dimmer than they should. This is useful for bright overlaid elements that come in with alpha channels and premultiplication, such as flares and explosions; you can set the footage to interpret as Straight on import and use this mode instead of Normal to overlay the element. It's another trick to keep in your arsenal should you ever see the symptoms (dim translucent elements) for which it is recommended.

Track Mattes

Track mattes are the primary method by which you can use the alpha or luminance information of one layer to set the transparency of another layer (**Figure 3.37**). This is actually the normal way to apply a matte channel in many compositing applications, which don't have the concept of the alpha channel so firmly integrated into the overall pipeline as After Effects.

The perceptual difference between an alpha channel and a track matte isn't, for the most part, too difficult to grasp. In both cases, you have pixels with a value (in 8-bit color space) between 0 and 255, whether they are color or grayscale alpha pixels. That any image would be interchangeable with the alpha channel shouldn't be too shocking; even if you're using the luminance of a full-color image, After Effects simply averages the 0 to 255 value of the three color channels into one value. The principle doesn't even change in 16-bit color—it's just the same range of values, with finer increments, being sampled.

Figure 3.37 A basic alpha track matte setup: The alpha of layer 1 is set as the alpha of layer 2 via the highlighted pull-down menu. The small icons just to the left of the layer names help remind you that this relationship has been set up, and which is the color layer and which is the matte.

You set a track matte by placing the layer that contains the transparency data directly above its target layer in the timeline and choosing one of the four options from the Track Matte pull-down menu:

▶ **Alpha Matte:** Uses the alpha channel of the track matte layer as if it were the alpha of the underlying target layer

▶ **Alpha Inverted Matte:** Does the same as Alpha Matte but inverts the result, so that the lighter areas of the alpha are transparent and the darker areas are opaque

▶ **Luma Matte:** Uses the luminance data of the track matte layer (the relative brightness of the red, green, and blue channels combined) as if it were the alpha of the underlying target layer

▶ **Luma Inverted Matte:** Does the same as Luma Matte but inverts the result, so that the lighter areas of the alpha are transparent and the darker areas are opaque

By default, the source layer for the track matte (the upper of the two) has its visibility turned off when you set the track matte, which is almost always what you want. This sets the track matte with a single click to the Track Matte pull-down menu. If you need to adjust the source after setting it, you can always temporarily turn it back on; just remember to turn it back off when you're finished.

Why They're Useful

Track mattes are not the only way to apply alpha or luminance data to the transparency of a layer, but they're the clearest and most straightforward way. They help you out of a lot of jams in which creating a selection via other means would be inconvenient or in which mask or matte features constrain you.

For example, it's not possible to track a mask in After Effects. But it is possible to apply the mask to a track matte instead, and then to track that layer (instead of the mask itself). Chapter 8, "Effective Motion Tracking," discusses this in detail.

In Chapter 6 you will learn of the many ways to pull a key, including hi-con mattes. Some of these methods apply their results directly to the alpha channel of the target layer, but others cannot. Additionally, specific operations such as blue-screen keying can change the color of the source (automatically removing blue spill from the foreground); applying the key via a track matte to a duplicate clean source instead is an effective workaround if you want the matte but not the despill.

Why They're Occasionally Tricky

Unlike with parented layers (described in Chapter 2, "The Timeline"), selecting a track matte layer does not lock it to the current layer. In fact, setting a track matte means that no matter which layer is next higher in the stack, that layer is the source of the matte. Thus, accidentally moving a layer in between a layer and its track matte can cause easily solvable but, nonetheless, disastrous results.

When you duplicate a layer with a track matte activated (**Ctrl+D**/**Cmd+D**), After Effects automatically duplicates it above the matte layer or two layers above the current layer. If you duplicate the matte layer at the same time, the duplicate will also move up two layers, so that all layers preserve their proper track mattes (**Figure 3.38**). That's good. What's bad is if you forget to duplicate both layers, because the track matte remains active in the duplicate layer, even if it has been duplicated to the top of the stack, and you can't see that it's active.

Figure 3.38 Selecting and duplicating the layers from **Figure 3.37** creates two new layers that leapfrog above the previous layers to maintain the proper color/matte relationship in the source and duplicate layers.

If the layer to which the track matte is applied already has an alpha channel, then the new selection area created by the track matte will be opaque only in the areas that are opaque in both mattes. So applying a track matte in this situation is like making a subselection of the current selection.

Render Order

Also tricky to work out with track mattes is the render order: Sometimes adjustments and effects that you apply to the matte layer are applied to the target matte, and sometimes you must first pre-compose to get the applied effects and adjustments.

And what happens if you apply a track matte to a track matte? It's actually hard to say; sometimes it will work, sometimes not. The user interface does not prohibit this behavior so you can try it, but a better idea is probably to pre-compose the first instance of track matting and apply the second track matte to that nested composition.

The next chapter, "Optimizing the Pipeline," looks in depth at solving issues related to render order, and you'll begin to use After Effects as a visual problem-solving tool for these issues.

4

Optimizing the Pipeline

Build a system that even a fool can use and only a fool will want to use it.

— George Bernard Shaw

Optimizing the Pipeline

This chapter examines the flow of data through After Effects in specific detail. I realize that might not sound utterly gripping, but once you learn to efficiently use the features that affect the order and conditions in which things happen, After Effects can help you work faster and solve thorny problems.

Your mission, should you choose to accept it, is two-fold. At times, you must be the After Effects version of a master chef—someone who knows what has to be finished before something else can be started, and what can be prepped and considered "done" before it's time to serve the final result. At other times, you must think like a programmer. You have to isolate and "debug" elements of your project when the result doesn't look anything like what was planned. This chapter helps you reach both goals.

In the big picture, the keys to mastering the After Effects data pipeline are

▶ Understanding how to use multiple compositions

▶ Knowing when to pre-compose

▶ Optimizing your rendering time

This chapter will help you get After Effects running closer to real time, so that you're less likely to give your client the lame excuse that your shot is late because After Effects is still rendering. Efficient rendering, however, depends on well-organized compositions and plenty of advanced planning.

Navigating Multiple Compositions

When working with a complicated project, you can easily lose track of how things are organized. This section will show you

▶ The benefits of designing and perhaps standardizing a project template with your specific project in mind

▶ Simple methods for keeping your comps laid out so that you can visually remember their order

▶ Shortcuts that can help you when you've lost track of something

These tips have come in very handy when I've found myself working with artists who understood compositing quite well, but were nonetheless wrestling with tracking down and solving problems in After Effects.

Project Template Benefits

If you're working on your own, you're basically free to organize your projects however you like, just as if you live alone, you're free not to clean your apartment. Successful collaborative projects at studios, however, make use of project templates that specify where different types of items live in the Project window.

Figure 4.1 shows a typical project template containing multiple compositions. It's a simplified version of a comp template used at The Orphanage for feature film work. Considering the days or even weeks that can be involved doing multiple takes of a visual effects shot, a template like this can be a lifesaver. Here are some of the template's useful attributes:

▶ The Master comps are numbered so that they show up in order at the top of a list (sorted by name) in the Project window.

▶ The Final Output comp is preset to the exact format and length specified for it to be filmed out for the movie. No work whatsoever occurs in this comp; previews are not done here, so its work area does not change, and no effects, animations, or expressions are created here that might inadvertently be left off at render time.

Figure 4.1 Here's a top-level look at the organization of an unpopulated composition template that could be used on a feature film effects shot. There are two basic categories of folders (Source and Comps), and numbered, pre-configured compositions listed in correct render order.

▶ There is a locked placeholder layer at the top of various comps reminding you how to use them.

▶ Helpful guide layers, such as masks for different formats and preset adjustment layers with Levels set to high contrast (for checking black and white level matches), are placed in ahead of time (**Figure 4.2**).

▶ A Source folder is organized with preset compositions to hold elements, such as the background plate, as well as reference items. These comps, rather than the footage items themselves, are used thereafter in the project. Like the Final Output comp, this seems to prevent careless errors that can occur when footage is replaced.

▶ Standardized organization means that anyone, a supervisor or someone coming in to help clean up, can much more quickly recognize where the elements of the project reside.

You can take this idea as far as you want. The basic concepts of a Master comp, source comps, and a render comp seems useful on just about any shot to which you will be devoting more than a couple of hours of work, but a template can include a lot more than that. The Orphanage designs a custom template AEP file for each film production, and the template alone can be 4 MB before any work has been added, including custom expressions, camera rigs, log/linear conversions, and recurring effects setups.

Figure 4.2 The default Assemble Master composition has preset layers specified by the supervisor. These include two nonrendering layers, one an eLin LUT, the other a Levels check. There is a color correction that is specified not to be edited, as well as pre-populated plate and background layers.

Working with Tabs

Because After Effects does not include a tree/node interface, it is incumbent upon you, the artist, to keep your windows organized in a way that makes sense to you. If you've ever found yourself hunting around for a particular comp's tab in the Timeline window, here are a couple of suggestions.

First of all, you may have too many tabs open. It can be helpful to close the entire Timeline window and start over: Reopen your master composition. Alt/Option-double-click on the subcomp you want to work on, and if the specific composition you want is three or four layers deep, keep going until you've reached that one. Now your reopened tabs follow, right to left, the basic render order.

If you need to see two timelines at once, it is possible to drag a tab out of the Timeline window, effectively creating a second Timeline window. If, alternatively, you want to see only the results of work you're doing in a subcomp of the Master comp, remember that Alt/Option-clicking the box to close a Timeline tab leaves the Composition window open (and vice versa). Or, if it's only at preview time that you want to see the Master comp, remember the Always Preview This View toggle at the lower left of the Composition window.

Where Am I?

We all lose our bearings sometimes. For that reason, context menu shortcuts in the Timeline window enable you to select a layer and reveal it, either in the Project window or in Project Flowchart view. Unfortunately, there is no context menu item to reveal the current comp in the Project window. But you can reveal any of its component layers.

Although you can use the Project Flowchart view to map out an existing project, I find it more helpful to keep the Project window as clearly and hierarchically organized as is usefully possible, thereby continuing in the spirit of the templates. This might sound about as much fun as keeping

TIP

To move from tab to tab quickly, hold down the **Shift+period** or **Shift+comma** (you can remember them as the > and < keys) to navigate you forward or backward through a set of open comp tabs.

TIP

If you're adjusting properties in the Timeline window and nothing seems to be happening, it may be that you've closed the Composition window but left the timeline open. Far more likely, however, is that you have a Layer window open and have mistaken it for the Composition window.

Debugging a Shot

Compositing is not unlike computer programming in that a complicated shot is made up of a series of individual decisions, any one of which can affect the whole. If you ever find yourself needing to troubleshoot a complicated shot, in which some unidentified variable seems to have crept in uninvited, you can attack the problem beginning from the Master comp. Solo layers one by one until you find the culprit, and if it's a comp, Alt/Option-double-click to open it, and repeat the process, until you've isolated the culprit and nailed it.

your room clean, but if you think in terms of helping someone new to your project to understand it, you may find that you help yourself as well. For example, if you want to refer back to that project in a few months' time, you effectively are that other artist arriving at the project completely cold.

Descriptive Names

It's rather obvious, but you can help yourself a lot by using descriptive names for your compositions. For example, if you want to keep track of composition order, you can number the master comp 00, the first nested comp 01, and so on, using descriptive names after the numbers, for example 00_master and so on. Some After Effects veterans joke that leaving the name of a composition at the default Comp 1 is a firing offense.

Pre-Composing and Nesting

Pre-composing is sometimes regarded as a kludgy, ill-conceived solution to render order problems. I couldn't disagree more. To me, it is one of the most effective ways to solve problems and optimize projects in After Effects, provided you plan things out a little.

Just to get our terms straight, *pre-composing* is the action of selecting a set of layers in a composition and assigning them to a new subcomp. Closely related to this is composition *nesting*, the action of placing one already created composition inside of another.

Typically, you pre-compose by selecting the layers of a composition that can and should be grouped together and choosing Pre-compose from the Layer menu. (You can also use the keyboard shortcut **Ctrl+Shift+C/Cmd+Shift+C.**) You are given two options: to leave attributes where they are or to move them into the new composition. One of the options is often grayed out for reasons that are clearly explained in the fine print of the dialog box (**Figure 4.3**). If you're wondering what constitutes an attribute that would be pre-composed, it's pretty much anything that you've edited on the layer: an effect, a mask, paint strokes, or even layer In and Out points.

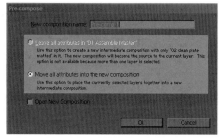

Figure 4.3 If you ever need a reminder of what will happen when you choose either of the two basic pre-compose options, the dialog spells it out for you in detail. In this case, the first option is grayed out because two layers have been selected for the pre-composition. Two layers cannot share basic settings such as Transforms, so those settings must go to the new comp.

Why Do It?

Depending on who you ask, pre-composing is either the solution to most problems in After Effects or one of the most annoying things that you have to do in the program.

So why not just work in one big happy composition? The advantages of doing so would seem to be many. All of the properties and keyframes that you would want remain right there in front of you, you never have to go digging into some subcomp to fix a Levels setting, and there's no difficulty keeping track of composition order.

To wax poetic about it for a moment, there are almost as many reasons to pre-compose as the day is long. Here are a few of the most common:

▶ **To keep two layers in sync:** If you ever find yourself making the same adjustments to two different layers in the same comp, that may be a signal that those layers now comprise an element and you need to pre-compose.

▶ **As a fix for render order problems:** Sometimes it is simply not possible to make one render action occur prior to another without pre-composing. For example, if you want to mask a layer after applying effects to it, you must apply the effects to a pre-composition and then mask that.

▶ **To keep the Master comp tidy:** This one should be self-explanatory. A Master composition with six well-organized elements is far more useful than one with 47 disparate elements (**Figure 4.4**).

▶ **To reuse an element:** If you've used a set of layers to create an element that you think might be used again or that your client might want to change globally in several locations, it makes a huge amount of sense to nest these layers as a composition. That way, to reuse the element, you need only drop it into a new timeline.

▶ **Because an element or a set of layers is essentially done:** This, in case you didn't know it, is your big picture goal. If you can finish some part of your shot, particularly if it's a render-intensive portion, pre-composing that part gives you the option of pre-rendering it.

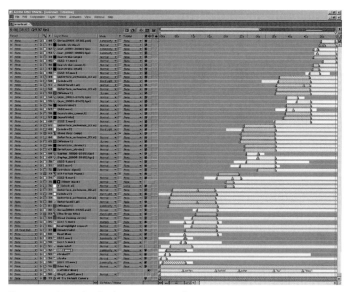

Figure 4.4 Never let this happen to one of your compositions.

NOTES

For years, Discreet's Flame and In-ferno seem to have cornered mind share in terms of perceived speed and power. This is not entirely unde-served, but what many people fail to notice is that these applications are not truly real time; they still require time to render. Inferno art-ists often conceal this requirement by rendering in the background or requiring that elements come in already rendered—often having been created, somewhat ironically, in After Effects.

If you're already comfortable with the idea of pre-composing, the last point is probably the most important for you to keep in mind. As you'll see later in this chapter, there are huge advantages to changing your mentality from that of an artist who wants to keep all options open, to that of an artist who understands the benefits of finishing an element, if only for the time being.

Options and Gotchas

Pre-composing a single layer using the Leave All Attributes option is relatively straightforward. Most of the time, how-ever, you will pre-compose multiple layers using the Move All Attributes option, a route that is more fraught with peril if you don't pay attention. Typical gotchas associated with this process include:

▶ Changes in layer duration and offset as they appear in the timeline.

▶ The need to pre-compose some attributes, but not all.

▶ The inability to easily undo pre-compositions later on.

▶ Difficulty coordinating blending modes and 3D settings.

▶ Confusion about recursion: When do motion blur, frame blending, and collapsed transformation switches affect nested comps?

Take a closer look at each of these situations, as well as some useful strategies for working with them.

Layer Duration Confusion

Figure 4.5 demonstrates the layer duration problem: Pre-composing a set of layers that are not the same duration as the source composition puts them in a new composition whose duration matches that of the source composition, but not that of the layers. The result is that the pre-composition layer includes empty frames at the top or tail of the shot.

You can trim the layer to match the original edits, but there's a better option. This works best if you have Synchronize Time of All Related Items checked in General Preferences (**Figure 4.6**):

1. In the pre-comp, move the time needle to the first frame that contains any data.

2. Select all the layers, and with the Shift key held down move them so that that first frame lines up as the first frame of the composition.

3. With the time needle still where the layers originally began, return to the main comp.

4. Press the [key to realign the first frame of the composition at the correct point.

Figure 4.5 What's up with all the empty space before and after the layers? Pre-composing using the second option creates a new comp with the exact time settings as the source, even if all of the layers begin much later in time than frame 0.

Figure 4.6 This preference is the key to realigning layers in a pre-composition easily.

123

If you like, you can trim the tail as well by going into the subcomp, putting the time needle on the last frame that contains any data, then returning to the Master comp and pressing **Alt+]** (**Option+]**) to trim the layer.

The Missing Option

There are, of course, situations in which the two options in the Pre-compose dialog don't cover everything you need. What if you want to move some but not all attributes into a new composition? Unfortunately, there is no automated solution for such a situation and all its variables.

NOTES

Unlike earlier versions, After Effects 6.5 and beyond allow you to use the Cut command with effects. Cut and Paste now work the same with effects as with everything else.

The best way to handle this is probably to choose the Move All Attributes option, check the Open New Composition box, and then cut any attributes that belong in the Master composition, pasting them there. Or, if you're pre-composing one layer only, you can do it the other way around: Leave the attributes in the Master comp, and then cut and paste the ones you want into the subcomp.

Data Pass Through

CLOSE-UP

Undoing a Pre-Composition

If you set a pre-comp and then change your mind immediately, you can, of course, undo the action. A problem emerges, however, when you progress further with your project and decide that pre-composing was a bad idea. In that case, the only option is to cut the layers from the pre-comp and carefully paste them back into the Master comp, taking care that layer order is preserved and that such basic properties as Transforms remain correct.

Finally, how do you know if 3D position data or blending modes of a layer in the subcomp will be preserved and appear correctly in the Master comp? Or, if you turn on motion blur or frame blending on the subcomp layer in the Master comp, how do you know those elements you animated in the subcomp, or even in a subcomp of a subcomp, are going to take on those settings? To manage these situations properly, you should be aware of a couple of settings.

For motion blur and frame blending, the key is the Switches Affect Nested Comps check box in General Preferences. With this checked (as it is by default), turning on these features in the Master comp turns them on in any affected subcomps as well. Unless you specify otherwise in the Render Settings, this is also how this situation is handled when rendering.

Passing through 3D position data and blending modes, on the other hand, is a question of enabling the Collapse

Transformations toggle for any comp layer (**Figure 4.7**). Turning this option on causes these properties to behave as if the pre-composed layers were still in the Master comp; turning it off prevents them from interacting with the Master comp.

The Cool Way Time Is Nested

After Effects is less rigid than many digital video applications when it comes to working with time. You are not forced to have all of the compositions in a given project use the same frame rate, and changing the frame rate of an existing composition is handled rather gracefully, with all of the keyframes retaining their positions relative to overall time.

That doesn't mean you can be sloppy, of course, it just means you have options. Artists familiar with other applications often forget to pay attention to frame rate settings when

▶ Importing an image sequence

▶ Creating a new composition from scratch

▶ Embedding a composition with a given frame rate into another with a different frame rate

In the third instance, by default, After Effects does its best to stretch or compress the frame rate of the embedded composition to match that of the Master composition. Sometimes, however, that's not what you want, which is when you need to examine options on the Advanced tab of the Composition Settings dialog.

The Advanced Tab

The Composition Settings dialog's Advanced tab contains a hodgepodge of extras that can come in handy. For example, Anchor Grid specifies how a composition is cropped if you adjust its pixel dimensions downward on the Basic tab. Shutter Angle and Shutter Phase affect motion blur (see Chapter 9, "Virtual Cinematography"). As for the rendering plug-in, you will almost certainly always leave it at the default setting of Advanced 3D (**Figure 4.8**).

Figure 4.7 As the tool tip alludes, this switch beside the cursor has two roles (and two names). In a nested composition, it is a Collapse Transformations toggle. Enable it, and blending modes and 3D positions from the nested comp are passed through. (Its other role, Continuously Rasterize, applies to such vector layers as Adobe Illustrator files only.)

NOTES

Users of older versions of After Effects may recall that applying a mask or an effect to the layer that also had Collapse Transformations enabled was impossible. This limitation no longer exists.

CLOSE-UP

Collapsing New Blenders

One limitation of turning on Collapse Transformations is that you're thereafter prevented from setting a blending mode on the collapsed layer. The blending mode menu shows only a – symbol.

The workaround is to apply an effect to the layer that does nothing or that is even turned off. This forces After Effects to render the collapsed layer (making it what the Adobe developers call a *parenthesized* comp), a side benefit of which is that blending modes become available.

The downside is that 3D layers are no longer passed through. But this workaround is helpful when you wish to pre-compose for the purpose of scaling.

Figure 4.8 Rare is the occasion when you would not use the default Advanced 3D rendering plug-in, and at this writing no developer outside of Adobe has offered one. The Options button allows you to control the resolution of the shadow map; keep it in mind if your shadows need refinement.

CLOSE-UP

Maladjusted

There are only a couple of things to watch out for with adjustment layers. Primarily, you must keep in mind that their timing and Transform properties still apply.

In other words, make sure that your adjustment layer starts at the first frame of the comp and extends to the last frame of the comp (or the start and end frames of the portion for which you need it), otherwise its effects will pop on and off unexpectedly. And if you set any transforms to the adjustment layer, make sure you mean for them to be there, as the boundaries of these layers are still respected in the rendering process.

Figure 4.9 You can convert any layer, except a camera, to an adjustment layer by toggling this switch. Creating a new adjustment layer simply creates a white solid the size of the comp with this switch toggled on.

And then there are the two Preserve check boxes. Preserve Frame Rate maintains the frame rate of the current composition no matter what the frame rate settings of anywhere you place it—into any other composition or into the Render Queue with given frame rate settings. So if you've keyframed a simple cycle animation that runs at just 4 frames per second, and then place that composition into a 24 fps comp, After Effects will not try to stretch that composition across the higher frame rate. It maintains the effect of 4 fps. The situation doesn't come up a lot, but when it does, knowing Preserve Frame Rate is useful.

Ditto the Preserve Resolution When Nested option: Typically, if an element is scaled down in a pre-comp and the composition is scaled up in the Master comp, you will want After Effects to treat these two opposing scales as one operation so that no data loss occurs. However, if you want the data in the subcomp to appear as if it were scaled up from a lower-resolution element, toggle on Preserve Resolution When Nested.

Adjustment and Guide Layers

As you may already know, versions 6.0 and 6.5 of After Effects introduced two new layer forms—adjustment layers and guide layers—that are easy to use and seem simple enough on the surface. Each has vitally useful applications, however, that might not occur to you immediately. They deserve a second look.

Adjustment Layers

Any layer in your timeline can become an adjustment layer. An *adjustment layer* is itself invisible, but the effects applied to it affect all layers below it in the stack. This an elegant, profound feature too often overlooked, perhaps because it is fundamentally so simple, yet it can be employed for many uses.

To convert a layer to an adjustment layer, toggle the feature in the Switches column (**Figure 4.9**). The best approach, however, is usually to create a new layer specified as an adjustment layer from the get-go. Simply add a solid set to the size and duration of the comp, and toggle it to be an adjustment layer.

That's easy enough. So what's so cool? What can you do with Adjustment layers that you can't with normal effects?

For one thing, you can dial them back using Opacity. An effective quick fix, this is the equivalent of a dissolve operation in a node-based compositing application. Most effects do not include the ability to be dialed back, even though it makes intuitive sense to do so. For example, you colorize footage with the Hue/Saturation effect. You are then asked to dial back the color 50%. What could be simpler than setting the Opacity for an adjustment layer with this effect to 50%?

You can also matte or mask adjustment layers, delineating specific areas for the layer's effects. This often enables you to avoid pre-composing, which would otherwise be the only way to apply an effect to selected layers of a composition. Instead, you only need a track matte layer that contains the necessary transparency information; it could be a separate composition containing only those layers (**Figure 4.10**).

NOTES

Effects that normally apply to the alpha channel do not apply to adjustment layers. This is consistent with the general rule about these layers: They affect layers below them only and contain no image data.

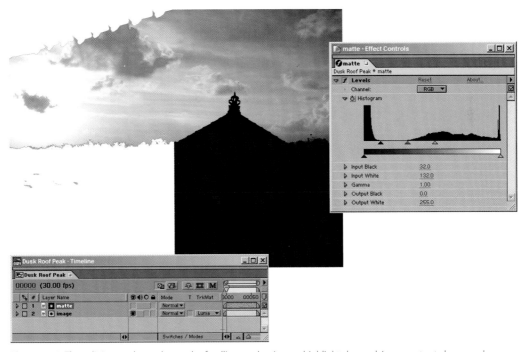

Figure 4.10 The split image shows the result of pulling out luminance highlights by applying a contrasty layer as a luma matte of itself and adjusting Levels on the matte layer to get the right density. This technique is also effective for pulling out the highlights of a layer to emphasize, colorize, or soften and bloom them.

Guide Layers

Like adjustment layers, *guide layers* are normal layers that have been toggled to behave differently. In this case, guide layers appear in the current composition but disappear in any compositions into which their original comp is nested. They, therefore, remain invisible in the final render (unless you specify otherwise).

The most common use for this feature is when you want to see an element against the final background footage in a subcomp, but you don't want to have to worry about whether you'll remember to turn off the background when you're done using it.

You can toggle any type of layer into a guide layer either by context-clicking it or by choosing Guide Layer from the Layer menu. Within the current comp, you'll notice no difference (**Figure 4.11**). You can still apply effects to this layer or have other layers refer to it, and it is fully visible. Nest this composition in another composition, however, and the guide layer disappears. If you decide you want guide layers to appear at render time, there is an option to do so in the Render Settings.

TIP

Guide layers are not just for temporary backgrounds. For example, throughout this book I suggest that you add an adjustment layer to slam the contrast of your comp, helping you to see whether foreground and background levels match. Because this is an effect that you would never want to see in the final render, these test adjustment layers are prime candidates to be guide layers.

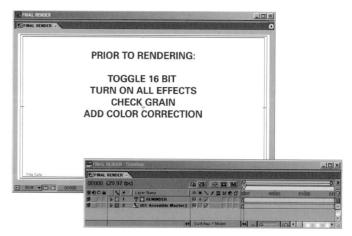

Figure 4.11 Don't let your take be ruined by careless errors! Setting a checklist as a guide layer that blocks your render comp guarantees that it won't show up in your final render, but helps you to remember what to double-check. This is just one of the many creative uses for guide layers.

Understanding Rendering Order

To truly master After Effects and become an expert compositor, you must understand the order in which actions occur. For example, you need to know whether a mask is applied before an effect and whether an effect is applied to a track matte. You need to understand the render pipeline.

For the most part the render pipeline is plainly visible in the timeline and follows consistent rules:

▶ 2D layers are calculated from bottom to top of the layer stack

▶ Masks, effects, transforms, paint, and type are calculated from top to bottom (as shown by twirling down layer properties)

▶ 3D layers are calculated based on their distance from the camera; coplanar 3D layers use stacking order just like 2D layers (but this setup can introduce errors and should be avoided)

Let's recap that for a moment. In a 2D composition, After Effects starts with the bottom layer, calculates any adjustments to it in the order properties are shown, then calculates adjustments to the layer above it, composites the two of them together, and so on up to the top layer of the stack. If you want to know what order is used to calculate layer properties, you need only reveal them in the timeline (**Figure 4.12**).

This, then, adds an extra advantage to adjustment layers. They behave just like other 2D layers in the stack, so that they are always rendered after all calculations on layers below them are completed. Effects within layers, on the other hand, always calculate prior to transforms.

And what about track mattes? Track mattes (and blending modes) are calculated after all of the other layer properties (masks, effects, and transforms) have been calculated. Of course, before track mattes are applied, their own mask, effect, and transform data is applied to them. Therefore, it should not be necessary to pre-render a track matte in order to see these edits affect the matte.

Figure 4.12 Just because After Effects lacks a tree/node interface doesn't mean you can't easily see the render order; it's laid out for you in the Timeline window. Layer properties render in top to bottom order (shown here, Motion Trackers, then Masks, Effects, and finally Transforms).

NOTES

Behind the scenes, After Effects is often being much more clever about what to calculate and what not to calculate in order to optimize rendering speed. Thus portions of a layer at the bottom of the stack that are not visible (because they are covered, masked, or otherwise obscured in layers above them) often will not be calculated. The only way you'll ever know is if your render seems faster than expected.

TIP

The Transform effect gives you an alternative method to transform a layer prior to adding a given effect; it allows you to select when transforms occur relative to specific effects, all chosen by you.

129

As I mentioned in the previous chapter, you are taking your chances if you try to apply two consecutive track mattes (in other words, you apply a track matte to a track matte). Sometimes the method works, and the UI does not specifically prohibit you from doing it; however, it's inconsistent. I recommend pre-composing instead. Better safe than sorry.

Optimizing Projects

I sometimes surprise directors and effects supervisors with the speed and interactivity I squeeze out of After Effects, even at full 2K film resolution. Here's my secret: As I work, I organize portions of my master comp that I consider finished into their own subcomps, and if they require any render cycles at all, I pre-render them.

It's astonishing to me how many veteran compositing artists waste redundant rendering time by failing to commit to their own decisions, especially given how easy it is to make changes if you've guessed wrong. For example, on effects shots that begin with a blue-screen key, but develop into very complex shots, artists often fail to pre-render the keying results for fear that they might need to tweak them later. This can add several seconds to an individual frame update and minutes or even hours to a film-resolution render. Every time you want to see the result of a new color correction, you end up waiting for your keyer to redo its work.

After Effects does have a RAM cache (which is further optimized with each major upgrade of the application) to keep track of what has not changed when you make adjustments and avoid unnecessary re-rendering. This is a great feature, but you should not rely on it solely to make your workflow speedier.

Post-Render Options

Happily, the After Effects UI anticipates that you may want to pre-render nested compositions and use the rendered output, without eliminating your ability to go back and change your mind. Tucked away in the Render Queue window, but easily visible if you twirl down the arrow next to Output Module (**Figure 4.13**), is a menu of three post-render actions. After the render is complete, you can choose

▶ **Import:** Imports the result

▶ **Import & Replace Usage:** Does not eliminate the source comp from the project; only takes its place (or that of any other item you specify) in the project

▶ **Set Proxy:** Makes the rendered output a proxy (temporary substitute) of the source comp (or of any other item you specify)

If you choose either of the latter two options, a pickwhip icon appears adjacent to the menu. Click and drag from this icon to whatever item in the Project window you wish to replace. By default, the comp that you're rendering is replaced.

What if you choose Import & Replace Usage and need to change your mind later? It's not actually such a big deal, assuming you haven't lost track of the original comp. To change usage back to the comp instead of the rendered footage, hold down the Alt key (Option key) as you drag and drop the comp over the footage in the Project window; this replaces its usage throughout the project. Doing the same type of drag and drop into a Timeline window replaces only the individual instance, which is useful in other cases.

If your intention is only to make your work speed faster, but you anticipate re-rendering everything from scratch when you're ready to create the final render, use proxies.

Proxies

Any visual item in your Project window can be set to include proxy footage. A *proxy* is an image file or sequence on your drive that stands in for an item in your project. Its pixel dimensions, color space, compression, and even its length can differ from the item it's replacing; for example, you could use a low-resolution, JPEG-compressed still image as a stand-in for a full-resolution, moving image background.

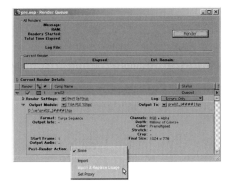

Figure 4.13 Twirl down the arrow beside the Output Module settings for a Render Queue item and you reveal options to perform actions following the render. The last two options are particularly useful for speeding up future renders, if you apply them to sub-compositions and render those.

Figure 4.14 The black square to the left of a footage or comp item in the Project window indicates that a proxy is enabled; a hollow square would indicate a proxy was attached but not currently active. Both items are listed at the top of the Project window, the active one in bold. Rendering with Use Comp Proxies Only would cause the proxy to be used instead of re-rendering the comp in this case.

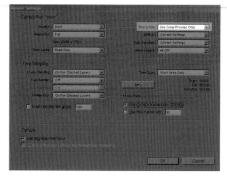

Figure 4.15 Use Comp Proxies Only offers you the best of both worlds with proxies. Source footage can have low-resolution stand-ins that do not appear in the final render, while source compositions have fully rendered stand-ins that save gobs of rendering time thereafter.

Figure 4.14 shows what an item with a proxy looks like in the Project window. Even though the scale of the proxy is different from that of the source item, transform settings within the comps that use this item remain the same whether the proxy is enabled or not. That's the beauty of it.

The "official" use of proxies seems to be as a low-resolution image or clip to stand in for one that is high resolution. However, the feature is also useful for pre-rendering compositions. The Use Comp Proxies Only option (**Figure 4.15**) is included for just such a case: pre-rendering compositions at full resolution to be used as final elements. The source composition is not blown away by this action; it remains in place but no longer expends rendering resources.

Proxies are relatively easy to blow away if no longer wanted. Select the items, and from the item's context menu in the Project window (or the File menu) choose Set Proxy > None (or simply choose to use no proxies at render time).

Network Renders

A single machine can only do so much to render an After Effects project. If your studio is large enough to have a network with more than one or two machines, it would behoove you to look into network rendering, in which all available machines are used to render a shot simultaneously.

There are two basic options for network rendering. The built-in solution is the Watch Folder command. It instructs After Effects to look in a specific place for projects that need to be rendered and to collaborate on rendering them. This works reasonably well on small, intimate networks; the main downside to it is that it has to be set up manually on each machine that will run it. This becomes impractical in a facility with a *render farm*, a rack of servers dedicated only to rendering, none of which typically has even a dedicated mouse or monitor (and all of which ideally sit in an air-conditioned little room). On a feature film project, the facility might have hundreds of these.

In such a case, consider going to the extra expense and effort to invest in a third-party rendering solution that takes advantage of After Effects' command-line rendering capabilities, such as Rush Render Queue (http://seriss. com/rush/). These programs run scripts that manage the process of rendering an After Effects project on many machines (**Figure 4.16**). They include a user interface that includes everything you need to intelligently manage a complex set of renders. They can deal with complicated situations, such as machines becoming unavailable or going down during a render.

However, implementing such a system is not quite as simple as buying a box of software off the shelf and installing it. It requires the skills of a system administrator or equivalent technical expert. Most network facilities have such a person on staff, and many advanced After Effects users are capable of setting this up.

If you want to start with a Watch Folder render, however, and aren't certain how to do it, the online documentation provided by Adobe is complete and helpful. The help topic "Rendering" on the "Network: Using a Watch Folder" page includes everything you need to know, so there's no reason to reiterate it here.

Onward to Effects

You've reached the end of Section I and should now have a firm grasp on how to wring the most out of After Effects. Equipped with a toolbox full of shortcuts, you're ready to focus more specifically on the art of visual effects. Section II, "Effects Compositing Essentials," will teach you the techniques, and Section III, "Creative Explorations," will show you how they work in specific effects situations.

Let's get started.

Figure 4.16 That's not the Render Queue! Rush Render Queue may not be pretty, but it's pretty sophisticated; This Submit panel allows you to specify which CPUs on your render farm will pick up the render, at what priority, how many of them to use to divide the job, and how much time to give each of them to try rendering it before you bail out and go to the next. At big studios, this is indispensable.

Effects Compositing Essentials

5

Color and Light: Adjusting and Matching

I cannot pretend to be impartial about the colors. I rejoice with the brilliant ones, and am genuinely sorry for the poor browns.

—Winston Churchill

Color and Light: Adjusting and Matching

What is the pinnacle, the *sunnum bonum,* or (don't speak Latin?) the ultimate achievement of compositing? Pulling the perfect matte? Creating a convincing effect seemingly from nothing? Leaving the last doughnut at dailies for the effects supervisor? Those are all significant, but they pale in comparison with the ability to authoritatively and conclusively adjust and match the color of a foreground to a background.

Without this skill, you will not have earned the privilege of the compositor to be the last one to touch the shot before it goes into the edit. No matter how good your source elements are, they'll never appear to have been shot all at once by a real camera.

With this skill, however, you can begin to perform magic, injecting life, clarity, and drama into standard (or even substandard) 3D output, adequately (or even poorly) shot footage, and flat, monochromatic stills, drawing the audience's attention exactly where the director wants it to go, and seamlessly matching the other shots in the sequence.

This sounds like pure art, doesn't it? It's something that requires a good eye, an ineffable skill that can't be taught? Actually, no. It's a skill that you can learn even if you have no feel for adjusting images—indeed, even if you consider yourself color blind.

And what is the latest, greatest toolset for this lofty job? Most of the time, you're going to use Levels. In some cases,

Curves is a preferable alternative (although plenty of talented After Effects artists never touch Curves), and Hue/Saturation remains indispensable for certain situations in which Levels and Curves are too cumbersome. You may use the rest of the tools in other situations, but for effects work the no frills approach of using these tools still seems to be the one that endures, and with good reason: These tools are stable and fast, and they will get the job done every time—once you know how to use them.

This may, nevertheless, leave you with some thorny questions:

▶ Why are we still using the same old tools, found in Photoshop since even before After Effects existed, when there seem to be so many cool new ones in 6.5, such as Color Finesse and Auto Color?

▶ Shouldn't I use Brightness & Contrast, or Shadow and Highlight when those are exactly what I want to adjust?

▶ What do you mean I can adjust Levels even if I'm color blind?

This chapter holds the answers. You will begin by looking at how to effectively adjust a standalone source clip, focusing on optimizing brightness and contrast, as well as the more mysterious gamma. You'll then move into matching a foreground layer to the optimized background, and take your adjustment skills into all three color channels to balance color as needed.

More specialized color adjustments are discussed later in the book, in Chapter 12, "Working with Light."

Optimizing Plate Levels

No doubt you've tried to make a good image look better or, at the very least, tried to make a poorly shot image look acceptable. Even if you're beyond using that time-honored method of flailing around with the controls until arbitrarily arriving at a marginally acceptable result, take some time to review the basic tools of the trade and how to use them.

We're going to start by balancing brightness and contrast of the *plate* footage. The term "plate" stretches back to the earliest days of optical compositing and refers to the source footage, typically the background onto which foreground elements will be composited. A related term, "*clean plate*," refers to the background with any moving foreground elements removed, something we'll look at creating later in the book.

Matching footage is absolute, right or wrong, but optimizing footage is relative. What constitutes an optimized clip? Let's look at what is typically "wrong" with source footage levels and the usual methods for correcting them.

Adjusting Brightness and Contrast with Levels

Levels is your tool for optimizing black and white levels; in other words, you use Levels to adjust brightness and contrast. You'll soon see why it's much preferable to the Brightness & Contrast effect for this purpose, and later in the chapter I'll show you some further uses for Levels and its Histogram palette.

TIP

An often overlooked feature of Levels, Alpha Channel mode allows you to directly adjust brightness, contrast, and gamma of the grayscale transparency channel, saving you from having to make a separate track matte to make these adjustments.

Figure 5.1 shows the Levels control and the clip to which it was applied, starting with the default settings. The Levels effect consists of the histogram and five individual controls, each of which can be applied either to the full RGB image or to individual red, green, blue, or alpha channels by selecting them using the Channel menu at the top. For now, we'll focus on the relatively uncomplicated technique of adjusting brightness and contrast in overall RGB, the default Channel setting.

The basic function of the histogram is to help your assessment of whether the changes you are making are liable to help or harm the image. There is no one typical or ideal histogram—they can vary as much as the images themselves (**Figure 5.2**). Below the histogram is a black to white gradient, showing where each part of the histogram falls on the luminance scale.

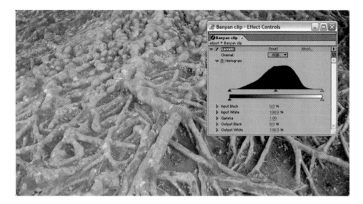

Figure 5.1 Possibly the most used "effect" in After Effects, the Levels adjustment control consists of a histogram and five basic controls per channel; the controls are usually accessed using the triangles on the histogram, with corresponding numerical/slider controls below. The default settings are shown here.

Figure 5.2 The same basic subject will have a variety of histograms depending on lighting conditions. There is no such thing as a "good" histogram, although alongside their images these histograms can tell you quite a bit about how much contrast and range of color is already present, and what might need correction.

Although I've just said no one histogram is ideal, there's a simple trick for optimizing brightness and contrast using Levels. Look at the top and bottom end of the histogram—the highest and lowest points where there is any data whatsoever—and bracket them with the triangle controls for Input Black and Input White. By bracket them, I mean move these controls in so each sits just outside its corresponding end of the histogram (**Figure 5.3**). The result stretches values closer to the top or bottom of the dynamic range, as you can see by applying a second histogram (**Figure 5.4**).

Figure 5.3 When you bring the triangle controls corresponding to Input Black and Input White in to bracket the histogram, the change in percentages can be seen numerically below.

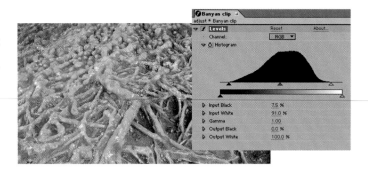

Figure 5.4 Adding a second Levels effect just to view its histogram reveals what has happened as a result of the prior adjustment; the histogram looks similar but now extends to each end of the contrast spectrum. The stripes are quantization, showing that values have been stretched. Although not severe in this case, they are a by-product of working in 8-bit color.

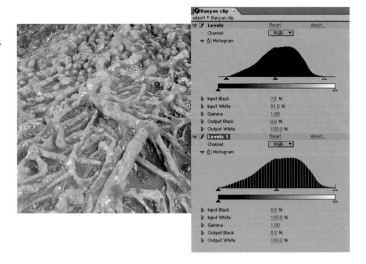

It is generally advisable not to move Input Black above the lowest black or Input White below the highest white value when optimizing an image. This is known as *crushing* the blacks (or whites), and once that detail has been crushed, it cannot be brought back subsequently. Low blacks all turn to pure black, light colors blow out to white. Unless you're working in linearized color space with overbright values (if you're unsure, that means you're not, but you can check Chapter 11, "Issues Specific to Film and HDR Images," for the lowdown), you don't get the organic roll-off common to overlit film images. Many a stylized look calls for this effect, but generally speaking and until you really know what you're doing, this is bad form (**Figure 5.5**).

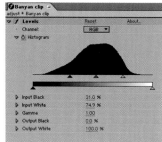

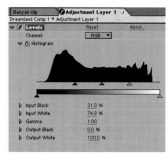

Figure 5.5 The same Levels adjustment, crushing the blacks and blowing out the highlights, can bring a rich dramatic quality to one clip, while totally ruining another. Note in the histogram how much more of the image is affected by this adjustment in the lower example, including most of the lower range and all of the highlight variation.

Same Difference: Levels (Individual Controls)

Adjacent to one another under the Adjust section of the Effects menu (or palette) are two versions of the same effect: Levels and Levels (Individual Controls).

Do not fret: Both of these effects accomplish the same basic task using the same basic controls, arranged differently. The main difference is that if you set keyframes for Levels, After Effects lumps together all of your adjustments into one keyframe setting. The values are then inaccessible to expressions and cannot be individually reset.

Therefore you should consider using Levels (Individual Controls) if

▶ You need to animate individual Levels adjustments.
▶ You want to drive a Levels value using an expression or to use a Levels value to drive an expression.
▶ You like being able to right-click on each slider value to reset it.

The number of cases in which the above criteria hold true is likely to be very few. On the other hand, you will get the same result with the same settings in either effect, so it's largely up to you which one you choose. Most people simply use Levels for most situations.

Therefore, because your source footage is dynamic and the dynamic range can vary from frame to frame, it is a good idea to leave headroom for the whites and foot room for the blacks. Generally speaking, you can use the inside corners of the adjustment triangles to line up with the edge of the image data (as in **Figure 5.3**). This is a reliable way to adjust the Input Black. The Input White level will need more headroom if something exceptionally bright—such as a sun glint, flare, or fire—comes into frame.

Black and white are not at all equivalent, in terms of how your eye sees them. Blown-out whites are not pretty and are usually a sign of overexposed digital footage, but your eye is much more sensitive to subtle gradations of low black levels. These low, rich blacks account for much of what makes film look filmic, and they can contain a surprising amount of detail, none of which, unfortunately, would be apparent on the printed page.

So what about the Output Black and Output White controls? These have the effect of raising the blackest black and lowering the whitest white, respectively, toward gray, which lowers the dynamic range and the contrast of the image (**Figure 5.6**).

Figure 5.6 Output Black and Output White can help with a particular look (here the scenery appears misty and hazy), but they will come into play more in the Matching section.

Reading the Histogram

You now know the basics of what to look for on a histogram when optimizing an image's brightness and contrast. Now take a look at some potentially unhealthy symptoms that a histogram can help you recognize.

The Levels histogram shows only incoming image data, not the results of any Levels adjustments. Unlike Photoshop CS, After Effects does not have a Histogram palette for constantly monitoring current image levels, but you do have the option to see the results of one Levels adjustment by applying a second Levels effect. This is not a typical thing to do, mostly because people don't like the extra effect sitting in the pipeline, but it can certainly be useful as a temporary check if you think something might be amiss.

Applied to a backlit shot adjusted to bring out foreground highlights, the resulting histogram reveals a couple of new wrinkles (**Figure 5.7**). At the top end of the histogram the levels increase right up to the top white, ending in a spike. This may indicate that the white data has been crushed slightly, forcing too many whites to pure white and destroying image detail.

At the other end of the scale is the result of the Gamma adjustment: a series of spikes rising out of the lower values like protruding hash marks. The Gamma value has been

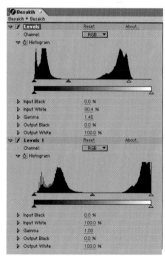

Figure 5.7 In the first instance of Levels, Gamma has been raised and the Input White brought in to enhance detail in the dark areas of the foreground. The second instance has no adjustments and is applied only to see the result of the first adjustment in a second histogram.

X Marks the Histogram

If you are working with Levels and find at some point that the histogram is no longer displaying data, but instead has an x shape across it, this simply means that the data in the image may have changed without the histogram automatically updating. You wouldn't want Levels to be updating its histogram all the time; the background polling of data could slow the application to a crawl.

The simplest way to let After Effects know that you want to update the histogram before making any changes is to toggle the Levels effect off, then back on. The data is polled when the effect is first switched on.

raised, moving the midpoint closer to black to raise mid-range brightness. That means that you effectively stretched the levels below the midpoint, causing them to *posterize* slightly, to clump up at regular intervals.

In this case, the spikes are not a worry because they occur among a healthy amount of surrounding data—there are no empty gaps between the spikes, there is a curve of data across the range. In more extreme cases of posterization in which there is no data in between the spikes whatsoever, you will see the result of too much level adjusting in the form of *banding*. (**Figure 5.8**)

Banding is the result of limits associated with working in 8-bit color, and After Effects offers a ready-made solution: 16-bit color mode, which you can access by Alt-clicking (Option-clicking) on the bit-depth identifier along the bottom of the Project window (**Figure 5.9**). For more on what 16-bit color is and how it can be used with other technologies, such as floating-point linearized color, see Chapter 11.

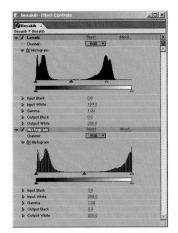

Figure 5.8 Attempting to bring out the foreground highlights with too much Input White adjustment instead of Gamma blows out the sky and heavily quantizes the resulting image. The histogram of a second Levels effect shows quantization and clipped levels, and banding is apparent in the sky. Adjusting Gamma is a better approach.

Figure 5.9 An entire project can be toggled from the default 8-bit color mode to 16-bit mode by Alt-clicking (Option-clicking) on this toggle in the Project window.

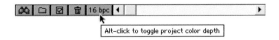

Why Not Use Brightness & Contrast?

I just had you try an adjustment of brightness and contrast on an image and entirely ignored the effect called Brightness & Contrast. Are we just too good for that effect? In a word, yes. The reason why is easily seen with the image you just optimized.

Brightness & Contrast has two sliders, and I'll give you three guesses what each of them controls. The Contrast control, if set to a value higher than 0.0, causes the values above middle gray to move closer to white and those below the midpoint to move closer to black. Set it to a value below 0.0, and it takes all pixels closer to gray. The Brightness control, unlike Gamma, adjusts all pixel values in the image at once, and identically.

So what's the problem? The example image was typical in that it did not need black and white levels enhanced to the same extent. In fact, it did not need input black levels enhanced at all, as you could see from the histogram. Cranking up the Contrast control to get more detail into the whites would, in this case, crush the blacks—forcing more of them to pure black. And then if you attempted to bring them back by raising the Brightness value, you would quickly have blown out the detail in the sky completely (**Figure 5.10**). Maddening.

Figure 5.10 Oh, what a tangled web we weave when first we apply Brightness & Contrast. Something's gotta give: Increasing Contrast crushes the blacks, and raising Brightness blows out the sky, as you see here. There is no good reason to use this tool.

Geek Alert:
What Is Gamma, Anyway?

It would be so nice simply to say, "gamma is the midpoint of your color range" and leave it at that. The more accurate the discussion of gamma becomes, the more obscure and mathematical it gets. There are plenty of artists out there who understand gamma intuitively and are able to work with it without knowing the math behind it or the way the eye sees color midtones. That's fine, but if you'd like to broaden your understanding, read on.

The idea with gamma adjustment is to take the midpoint of color values and shift it without affecting the black or white points. This is done by taking a pixel value and raising it to the power of the gamma value, then inverting the value. The formula looks like this

$$newPixel = pixel^{(1/gamma)}$$

You're probably used to thinking of pixel values as being 0 to 255, but this formula works only if they are *normalized* to 1. In other words, all 255 values occur between 0 and 1, so 0 is 0, 255 is 1, and 128 is .5—which is the "normal" way the math is done behind the scenes.

Why does it work this way? Because of the magic of logarithms: Any number to the power of 0 is 0, any number to the power of 1 is itself, and raising a fractional value (less than 1) to a higher and higher power makes it closer and closer to 0. This value is then inverted, or subtracted from 1, so that the higher the gamma, the closer the value gets to 1 or pure white. The real "magic" of logarithms is that the values are described on a curve, hence a *gamma curve*.

Hmmm, was that simple? If not, look ahead to the Curves discussion for a visual example.

The other big problem with Brightness & Contrast is the linearity of it—the fact that all pixels are affected equally by the controls. The ability to create a nice roll-off in complex Brightness & Contrast settings is where Curves stands out.

Gamma Adjustments: Levels and Curves

Gamma, the midrange of the image levels, is a more subjective adjustment: Generally you can think of it as giving more reach to adjustments you may have already made to brightness and contrast, making the image more brilliant or darker without changing the white and black points.

You can adjust gamma in Levels, but, in most cases, the histogram won't really help you decide where a gamma adjustment is needed as much as the image itself. By moving the midpoint in Levels to the left, you are raising gamma, effectively putting more values in the image above the midpoint; moving it to the right has the opposite effect (**Figure 5.11**).

How do you know when to stop? In my first professional color correction job, my supervisor told me that he had to see it go too far before he knew how much to dial it back. And that's always remained my basic approach with the sliders.

The Subtlety of Curves

I consider Curves preferable to Levels for correcting gamma, because

▶ Curves can be used to gently roll-off adjustments, giving a gentler, more organic curve to the corrections they introduce.

▶ You can use Curves to introduce more than one gamma adjustment to a single image or to restrict the gamma adjustment to just one part of the image's dynamic range.

▶ You can often nail an image adjustment with a single well-placed point in Curves, when deriving the equivalent adjustment using Levels would require coordinated adjustment of three separate controls.

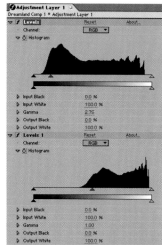

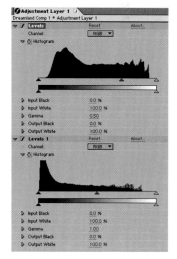

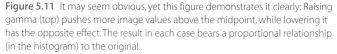

Figure 5.11 It may seem obvious, yet this figure demonstrates it clearly: Raising gamma (top) pushes more image values above the midpoint, while lowering it has the opposite effect. The result in each case bears a proportional relationship (in the histogram) to the original.

It's also worth understanding Curves controls because they are a common shorthand for color adjustments in visual effects work; this control recurs not only in all of the other effects compositing packages but also in more sophisticated tools within After Effects, such as Color Finesse (discussed briefly later in this chapter).

Curves does, however, have a couple of drawbacks, compared with Levels:

▶ It's not initially intuitive how to use Curves, and on any team there will probably be people who aren't as comfortable with Curves as with Levels.

▶ Unlike Photoshop, After Effects doesn't offer an eyedropper for placing sampled values on a curve, nor does it attach a numerical value to the points you create. In other words, it's a purely visual control that is difficult to standardize.

▶ Without a histogram, you can miss obvious clues as to what your image needs.

Nonetheless, the benefits far outweigh the disadvantages, if you're patient enough to gain the necessary skills to use Curves, so I'm going to try to rocket you to comfort with this powerful effect in this section.

By default, Curves displays a grid with a line extending diagonally from lower left to upper right. There is a Channel selector at the top, set by default to RGB as in Levels, and there are some controls on the right to help with drawing, saving, and recalling certain types of curves.

Figure 5.12 shows some basic Curves adjustments and their effect on images, as well as on a linear gradient, and the equivalent Levels settings. This is the best way I could conceive to show what is happening with Curves, and it's the kind of thing you can try easily on your own, using the Ramp effect to create a gradient if you want a neutral palette on which to see the result of the changes. Î would even go so far as to say that performing these kind of scientific explorations into how these tools work is one of the things that will separate you from the mass of artists who work more haphazardly.

More interesting than these basic adjustments (which are included only to give you a clear idea of what Curves is doing) are the types of adjustments that only Curves allows you to do—or at least do easily. I came to realize that most of the adjustments I make with Curves fall into a few distinct types that I use over and over, and so those are summarized here.

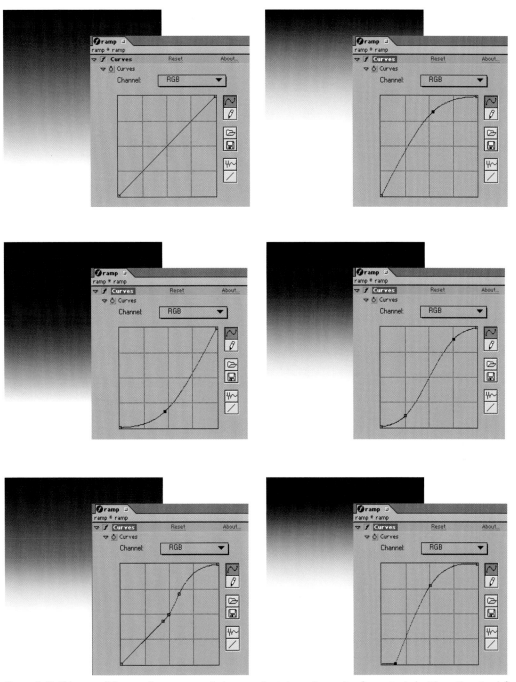

Figure 5.12 This array of Curves adjustments applied to a gradient shows the results of some typical settings. From top-left to bottom-right: The default gradient and Curves setting, an increase in gamma, a decrease in gamma, an increase in brightness and contrast, raised gamma in the highlights only, and raised gamma with clamped black values.

The most basic adjustment is to simply raise or lower the gamma with Curves, by adding a point at the middle of the RGB curve and then moving it upwards or downwards. **Figure 5.13** shows the result of each adjustment. Interestingly, this produces a vastly different result from raising or lowering the Gamma control in Levels, and the exact effect of the adjustment is impossible to recreate without Curves' ability to gently roll off the adjustment (**Figure 5.14**).

Take this idea further, and you can weight the adjustment to the high or low values of the image, pushing a nice roll-off into an image that might have appeared rather low in contrast (**Figure 5.15**). Combine high and low adjustments and you have the classic S-curve adjustment, which is universally understood to enhance brightness and contrast, but which additionally has the benefit of introducing

Figure 5.13 Two equally valid gamma adjustments using the Curves control. Dramatically lit footage particularly benefits from the roll-off possible in the highlights and shadows.

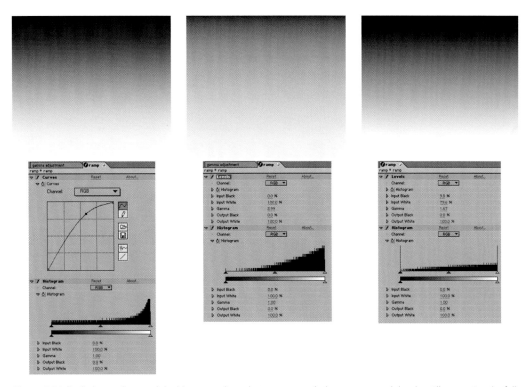

Figure 5.14 Both the gradient and the histogram show that you can push the gamma much harder, still preserving the full range of contrast, with Curves than with Levels, where you face a choice between losing highlights and shadows or crushing them.

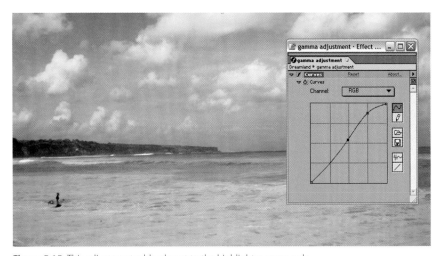

Figure 5.15 This adjustment adds a boost to the highlight gamma only.

roll-offs into the highlights and shadows (**Figure 5.16**). Keep in mind that you want to aim the curve to travel directly through the midpoint of your Curves grid if you don't wish to affect gamma.

Some images need a gamma adjustment only to one end of the range—for example, a boost to the darker pixels, below the midpoint, that doesn't alter the black point and doesn't brighten the white values. Here you are required to add three points (**Figure 5.17**):

▶ One to hold the midpoint

▶ One to boost the low values

▶ One to flatten the curve above the midpoint

I find I'm usually able to complete a Curves setting by adding between one and three points to my color curve. More than three points seems to do something not very organic—for want of a better expression—to the image. My method is usually to add a single point and then to add a second or third as needed.

Just for Color: Hue/Saturation

Third in the troika of primary image adjustment tools is Hue/Saturation. This one has many individualized uses:

▶ Colorizing images that were created as grayscale or monochrome

▶ Shifting the overall hue of an image

▶ De-emphasizing, or knocking out, an individual color channel

▶ Desaturating an image or adding saturation (the tool's most common use)

All of these uses will come into play when you learn about creating monochrome elements, such as smoke, from scratch in Chapters 12 to 14.

The Hue/Saturation control allows you to do something you can't do with Levels or Curves, which is to directly control the hue, saturation, and brightness of an image. The HSB color model is merely a different way of looking at the

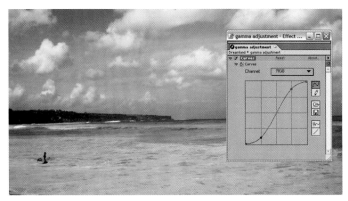

Figure 5.16 The classic S-curve adjustment: The midpoint remains the same, but contrast is boosted.

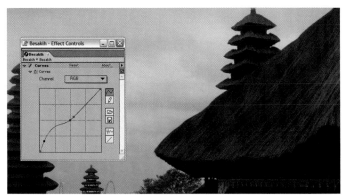

Figure 5.17 A solution for backlighting: Adding a mini-boost to the darker levels while leaving the lighter levels flat preserves the detail in the sky and brings out detail in the foreground that was previously missing.

same color data as exists in the RGB model used by Levels and Curves. All good color pickers, including the Apple and Adobe pickers, handle RGB and HSB as two different modes that use three values to describe any given color, which is the correct way to conceptualize it.

In other words, you could arrive at the same color adjustments using Levels and Curves, but Hue/Saturation gives you direct access to a couple of key color attributes that are otherwise difficult to get at.

For example, you can adjust the overall saturation of the image, or even the saturation of individual color channels. Desaturating an image means moving the red, green, and blue values closer together, reducing the relative intensity of the strongest of them. Why attempt this using three separate channels of red, green, and blue when a single slider will do it?

Desaturating an image slightly—lowering the Saturation value somewhere between 5 and 20—can be an effective way to make an image adjustment come together quickly (**Figure 5.18**). This is a case where understanding your delivery medium is essential, as film is more tolerant and friendly to saturated images than television.

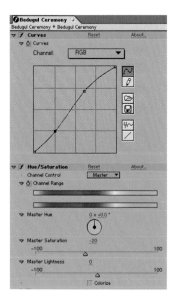

Figure 5.18 For footage that is already saturated with color, even a subtle boost to the gamma can cause saturation to go over the top. There's no easy way to control this with RGB controls, such as Levels and Curves, but moving over to the HSB model allows you to single out Saturation and dial it back.

The other quick fix that Hue/Saturation affords you is a shift to the hue of the overall image or of one or more of its individual channels. The Channel Control menu for Hue/Saturation includes not only the red, green, and blue channels but also their chromatic opposites of cyan, magenta, and yellow. When you're working in RGB color, these secondary colors are in direct opposition, so that, for example, lowering blue gamma effectively raises the yellow gamma, and vice versa.

But in the HSB model all six are singled out individually, which means that if a given channel is too bright or over-saturated, you can dial back its Brightness and Saturation levels, or you can shift its Hue toward the part of the spectrum where you want it (**Figures 6.19** and **6.20**).

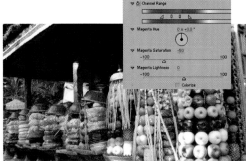

Figure 5.19 Sometimes one color channel comes in much too strong, and you can get away with isolating that channel—in this case, magenta—and knocking its Saturation back heavily. Go too far, however, and you may not notice artifacts such as areas that have lost too much saturation (see closeup).

The Perils of Automation

Skynet may have become self-aware at 2:14 a.m. August 29, 1997, but that doesn't mean that in the early twenty-first century you should be relying on the computer to make your decisions for you.

New with After Effects 6.5 is a trio of automated adjustment tools: Auto Color, Auto Contrast, and Auto Levels. Apply any of these to your footage, and you'll immediately see a result without adjusting anything—the benefit of a tool with "auto" in the title.

There are a couple of obvious problems with using these tools. One is that, although they can instantly give your image a nice kick, the adjustments are "black box" in nature, based on an engineer's educated guess of how your image should look. Also, because these plug-ins rely on sampled data and you can't specify a single frame to sample, the adjustments will, by their very nature, shift over time—not usually a desirable side-effect.

There is also a hidden problem. The sampling takes more processing power than you might think; even on a fast machine these effects can add several seconds per frame on broadcast-quality footage (to say nothing of HD or higher). So these plug-ins don't really even save you time, once you factor in how much longer your renders will take.

Therefore, the only use that I can see for these plug-ins is as idea generators. If you're stuck trying to nail an image adjustment, go ahead and apply one of them. If you like the result, take a snapshot of it and then go about matching it using the controls and matching techniques discussed in this chapter.

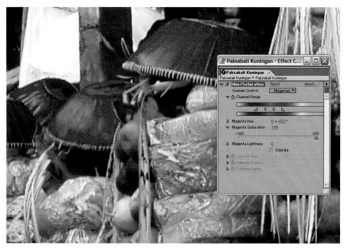

Figure 5.20 When in doubt about the amount of color in a given channel, try boosting its Saturation to 100%, blowing it out—this makes the presence of that tone in pixels very easy to spot.

Alternative Color Tools and Techniques

I've largely limited the discussion here to The Big Three color tools—Levels, Curves, and Hue/Saturation—for a couple of reasons. For one thing, they are the common currency of color correction, not only in After Effects but also Photoshop. The other main reason is that any other technique you might use would not obviate the need to somehow involve these tools and techniques.

The truth is that there are lots of ways to adjust the color levels of an image. Some alternatives for achieving a specific look—layering in a color solid, matting an image with itself, and more—are discussed in Section III of this book, and the next chapter will get into methods for making very specific color matches.

Even using what was covered in this chapter, there are more alternatives. For example, you can apply these basic color correctors using an adjustment layer rather than directly to your footage. This gives you the added advantage of being able to dial back the correction by varying the opacity of the adjustment layer.

Color Matching

You've examined the tools; now it's time to move on to the bread and butter of compositing: matching foreground and background images.

Melding images together and eliminating all clues that they came from separate sources is as much science as art. Up to this point we've focused on optimizing source footage, which is a more relative and artistic practice. Once the background has been properly graded, however, matching the foreground using the same tools is much more straightforward. The process obeys such strict rules that you can do it with no artist's eye at all. Assuming the background has already been color-graded, you even can satisfactorily complete a shot on a monitor that is nowhere near correctly calibrated.

How is that possible?

As with so many things in visual effects work, the answer is really a question of correctly breaking down the problem. In this case, the job of matching one image to another obeys rules that can be observed channel by channel, independent of the final, full-color result.

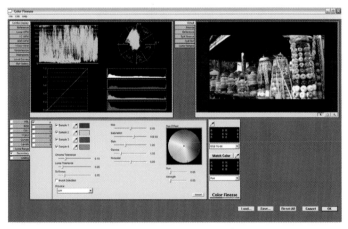

Figure 5.21 Do the controls in Color Finesse seem familiar? They certainly should. Although snazzier looking, they are fundamentally based on the tools covered in depth thus far in the chapter.

Color Finesse

The Color Finesse tool set is elegant and full featured, but I'm considering it out of scope for this book for a couple of reasons.

First, its core features are based on the same principles as the tools I've outlined: histograms, such as those in Levels, Curves, and Hue/Saturation adjustments (see **Figure 5.21**). You have no business working in Color Finesse, therefore, if you don't understand how to get a similar result from the core tools.

Second, I don't like the fact that Color Finesse runs in its own user interface; for example, you have to open a second application to do color correction. I find this cumbersome for use in the effects pipeline and even less stable than sticking with the core tools.

For some situations, however, you will definitely want to check out Color Finesse on your own, and look through its 60-page manual. I love the fact that it lets you isolate secondary color ranges and adjust only them. When I need a quick color fix, this method is much faster than taking the trouble to create a mask for a layer so I can adjust just some subset of the full image. I also think that it could be the tool you want if your only job is conforming the color of an entire edited piece, a job that often goes to dedicated colorists and Inferno operators.

Just make sure you've mastered the core tools first.

Of course, effective compositing is not simply a question of making colors match; in many cases that is only the first step. You must also obey rules you will understand from having done the kind of careful observing of nature described in the previous chapter. And even if your colors are correctly matched, if you haven't interpreted your edges properly (Chapter 3) or pulled a good matte (Chapter 6), or if such essential elements as lighting (Chapter 12), the camera view (Chapter 9), or motion (Chapter 8) are mismatched, your composite will not succeed.

These same basic techniques will work for other situations in which your job is to match footage precisely—for example, color correcting a sequence to match a hero shot, a process also known as *color timing*.

The Fundamental Technique

Integrating a foreground element into the color space of a background scene breaks down into three steps:

1. Match brightness and contrast as if the images were grayscale, using Levels. When matching the black and white points, pay attention to atmospheric conditions. Matching the midtones, however, may not always be necessary or even possible.

2. Using Levels, match the brightness and contrast of individual color channels as needed.

3. Note any fundamental mismatch problems that remain and ascertain whether they are related to color matching or some other issue, such as the edges, matte, lighting, camera view, and so on.

This approach, although not complicated or even particularly sexy, can take you to places your naked eye doesn't readily want you to go when looking at color. Yet, when you see the results, you realize that nature beats logic every time.

Start with a simple example: inserting a 3D element lit for daylight into a daylight scene. As you can see in **Figure 5.22**, the two elements are close enough in color range that a lazy or hurried compositor might be tempted to move on without adjusting the foreground.

Figure 5.22 An unadjusted foreground is slapped over the background.

With only a few minutes of effort, you can do a world better. Make sure the Info palette is somewhere that you can see it, and for now, choose Percent (0-100) in that palette's wing menu to have your values line up with the ones discussed here. You are free to choose any of the color modes in this menu; I advocate this one only for the purpose of standardizing the discussion.

This particular scene is a good beginner-level example of this technique because it is full of elements that would be monochromatic under white light. The background is dominated by concrete, which is generally flat, colorless gray, and the foreground element is an aircraft with a silver body that is lit from the top with white light with dark shadows underneath.

Begin by looking for suitable black and white points to use as references in the background and foreground. In this case, the shadow areas under the archways in the background, and underneath the wing of the foreground plane, are just what's needed for black points—they are not the very darkest elements in the scene, but they contain a similar mixture of reflected light and shadow cast onto similar surfaces, and you can expect them to fairly nearly match. For highlights, you happily have the top of the bus shelter to use for a background white point, and the top silver areas of the plane's tail in the foreground are lit brightly enough to contain pure white pixels at this point.

Figure 5.23 shows the targeted shadow and highlight regions and their corresponding readings in the Info palette. The shadow levels in the foreground are lower (darker) than those in the background, while the background shadows have slightly more red in them, giving the background a warmth that the unadjusted foreground lacks. The top of the plane and the top of the bus shelter both contain levels at 100%, or pure white; the blue readings on the bus shelter, which are a few percentage points lower, give it a more yellow appearance.

To correct for these mismatches, apply Levels to the foreground and move the Output Black slider up to about

Figure 5.23 The target highlight and shadow areas are outlined in yellow; levels corresponding to each highlight are displayed in the adjacent Info palette.

7.5%. This raises the level of the blackest black in the image, lowering the contrast, something we didn't expect to do when optimizing images earlier in the chapter.

Having aligned the contrast levels, it's time to correct for the differences in color. Remember the red levels in the background shadows are higher than blue or green, which is a clue that you should now switch the Composition window to the red channel (click on the red marker at the bottom of the window or use the **Alt+1/Option+1** shortcut). A thin red line around the outside of the display reminds you that you are looking only at red levels, and you can zoom in to an area that shows both of the regions you're comparing (**Figure 5.24**).

Now you can see clearly that the black levels in the red channel are still too low in the foreground, so raise them to match. Switch the Channel pop-up in Levels to Red, and raise Red Output Black slightly to about 3.5%. You can move your cursor from foreground to background and look at the Info palette to check whether you have it right, but the great thing about this method is that your eye usually gets variations in luminance correct when looking at a grayscale image.

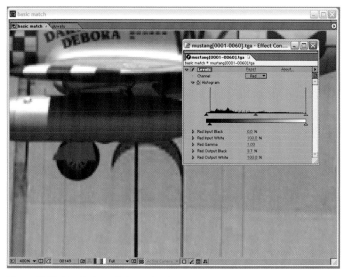

Figure 5.24 Match the red channel only.

The human eye is more sensitive to green than red and blue. Often, when you look at a shot channel by channel, you will see the strongest brightness and contrast in the green channel. For that reason, a sensible approach to matching color may be to get the overall match in the ballpark so that the green channels match perfectly, and then adjust the other two channels to make green work. That way, you run less risk of misadjusting the overall brightness and contrast of your footage.

Now for the whites. Because the background highlights have slightly less blue in them, switch to the blue channel (clicking the blue marker at the bottom of the Composition window or use **Alt+3/Option+3**). Pull back slightly to where you can see the top of the bus shelter and the back of the plane. Switching Levels to the blue channel, lower the Blue Output White setting a few percentage points to match the lower blue reading in the background. Back in RGB mode (**Alt+3/Option+3** toggles back from blue to RGB), the highlights on the plane take on a more sunlit, yellow quality. It's subtle, but it seems right.

What about the midtones? In this case, they're taking care of themselves because both the foreground and background are reasonably well balanced and your corrections are mild.

Figure 5.25 shows the result, with the same regions targeted previously, but with the levels corrected. To add an extra bit of realism, I also turned on motion blur, without yet bothering to precisely match it (something you will learn more about in Chapter 8, "Effective Motion Tracking"). You see that the plane is now more acceptably part of the scene. Work on this composite isn't done either; besides

Figure 5.25 This is a better match; motion blur helps sell the color adjustment as well.

matching the blur, you could add some sun glints on the plane as it passes, similar to those on the taxi. On the other hand, you can tell that you don't need to bother adding a pilot to the cockpit; the blur on the plane is too much to even notice that the pilot is missing.

Depth Cueing

The first example was fairly elementary with lots of good reference in the background, corresponding levels in the foreground, and no variables in the environment—no particulate matter in the air, for example. Now let's complicate matters.

One of the most common phenomena noticeable in the world at large is what happens to objects at a great distance (provided they are here on our planet, anyhow). Particulate matter in the air—not just pollution and fog, but even normal water condensation in otherwise pristine climates—causes objects in the distance to lose contrast and to take on some of the atmosphere color.

Figure 5.26 shows this phenomenon in full effect. Examine the airplane landing in the background, and the land around it. The darkest black levels are a medium gray, while the rooftops visible in the foreground at the bottom of the frame are as dark as any of the shadow areas in the previous shot.

Now say you want to insert that same airplane into this shot—not as far away as the plane landing in the distance, but not as close as those rooftops. Drop the plane in and scale it down to about 20%, and you'll see that in spite of its size, the depth cueing—the indications to your eye of its scale—are all wrong because of its contrast levels (**Figure 5.27**).

You want the black levels somewhere between those of the plane in the distance and the rooftops in the foreground. You have foreground black level reference (the rooftops) but no white levels. From the black levels in the foreground, you can see that there is not much of a color shift occurring in the shot overall; the blacks are fairly monochromatic, with RGB values within a percentage or two of one another, all around 20%.

All kinds of studies show how taking a break once in a while helps your concentration and lets you stay healthy by stretching your body, but in this case there is a more specific use for turning away from your monitor for a minute or two. When you come back, even to a labored shot, you regain an immediate impression that can save you a lot of noodling. The process outlined in this section is designed to remove many variables to color correction, but it's still a question of whether the final shot looks right or not.

Figure 5.26 The unadjusted background plate is not pretty, but it is hazy and realistic.

Figure 5.27 At this point, we appear to have a toy airplane from another shot.

When Reference Is Missing Something

There will be times when your background is missing the clues that simplify this work. In particular, your background may not have anything in it that would be pure white under normal lighting conditions. In extreme cases, you may have to guess what the color of an object in your background would be if you took a close-up shot of it under normal lighting conditions. Things may also be happening in your background, such as a cloud passing overhead, that should not be occurring in the foreground.

In such cases, you have to do your best knowing the basic rules about how light behaves (outlined here and in Section III).

There is one situation where you will have to use scientific fact instead of reference, unless your background was shot from a spaceship. In outer space, outside of the Earth's atmosphere, there is very little particulate matter (other than the occasional cloud of flying debris) and no atmosphere, so items in the distance tend to retain their full contrast.

On other planets, however, the same rules as Earth's will apply, assuming the planet in question has some kind of atmosphere.

In the background, however, everything starts turning cyan. Black and white levels in the background have nearly 10% less red than green or blue.

To place the plane in the mid-ground, you're going to take the levels toward, but not quite as far as, those of the background. First, working in RGB, raise Output Black about 30% and lower Output White around 85% to bring the blacks above 40% and the whites into the 80% range. The Info palette reveals that the corresponding levels in the far background are in the mid-50% range for blacks and the mid-70% area for highlights, so you've approached those levels without going quite that far.

Now if you toggle among the red, green, and blue channels in the Composition window, you'll notice that the red channel is slightly darker overall than the other two, accounting for the overall cyan quality of the image. Here is a clear case for the use of gamma—specifically, lowering the Red Gamma value to about 0.85, darkening the red midtones and taking the overall layer more toward cyan.

Just for fun, a second plane is added in the distance, as if it was chasing the plane that is landing, its levels matched to the source plane exactly. **Figure 5.28** shows both planes added to the background footage.

Figure 5.28 Here distance cueing has been corrected.

Gamma Slamming

Maybe you've seen an old movie on television—my favorite example is *Return of the Jedi* (before the re-release)—in which you see black levels that you really shouldn't be seeing. *Jedi* was made prior to the digital age, and some of the optical composites worked fine on film, but when they went to video, subtleties in the black levels that weren't previously evident suddenly became glaringly obvious. For example, some ugly garbage mattes around the inside of the Emperor's hood looked black on film, but look astonishingly bad on video.

Don't let this happen to you! Now that you know how to match levels, put them to the test by *slamming the gamma* of the image. To do this, you need to make a couple of adjustment layers. I usually call one slam up and the other slam down, as in the examples. Be sure that both of these are guide layers so that they have no possibility of showing up in your final render.

To slam up, apply Curves with the gamma raised significantly (**Figure 5.29**). This exposes any areas of the image that might have been too dark to distinguish on your

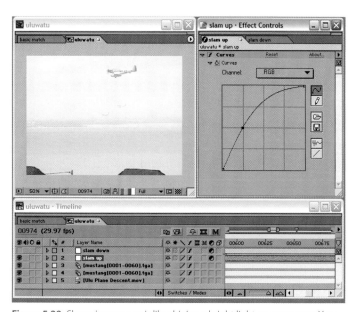

Figure 5.29 Slamming gamma is like shining a bright light on your scene. Your black and midtone levels should still match when seen this way.

monitor; if the blacks still match with the gamma slammed up, you're in good shape.

Similarly, and somewhat less crucial, you can slam down by lowering the gamma and bringing the highlights more into the midrange (**Figure 5.30**). All you're doing with these slams is stretching values that may be difficult for you to distinguish into a range that is easy for you to see.

This method is useful anywhere that there is a danger of subtle discrepancies of contrast; you can use it to examine a color key, as you'll learn in the next chapter, or a more extreme change of scene lighting.

Extra Credit

This chapter has covered some of the basics for adjusting and matching footage. Obviously there are exceptional situations, some of which occur all of the time: changes in lighting during the shot, backlighting, interactive light and shadow. There are even cases in which you can, to some degree, relight a shot in After Effects, introducing light direction, exchanging day for night, and so on. These topics and more are covered in depth in Chapter 12.

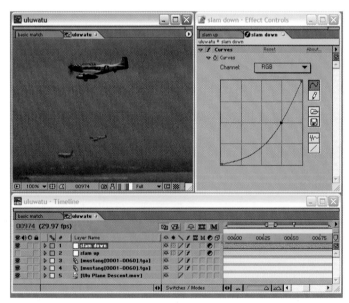

Figure 5.30 If in doubt about the highlights in your footage, you can also slam the gamma downward.

6

Color Keying

Juxtaposing a person with an environment that is boundless, collating him with a countless number of people passing by close to him and far away, relating a person to the whole world, that is the meaning of cinema.

— Andrei Tarkovsky (Russian film director)

Color Keying

Color keying is the big lie that somehow manages to kinda, sorta reflect the truth. Someday perhaps, when we have cameras that can perform full 3D scene reconstruction—not just what the lens lays down in a two-dimensional image, but a scan of the full spatial and temporal information of the scene—we'll laugh about the old days when we used to send actors out on to a mostly empty stage of saturated blue or green, in some cases completely psyching out their performance (it's been compared to "acting in a void" or "acting in the desert"), so that later, the color could stand in for transparency.

Meanwhile, as they have for over half a century, blue screens (and their digital-era cousins, green screens) remain the state of the art for situations in which you want to shoot figures—usually actors—in one setting and composite them into another.

The process goes by many names: color keying, blue screening, green screening, pulling a matte, color differencing, and even chroma keying, a term more likely to conjure the image of a weather forecaster on your local news, waving her hands to make the clouds clear out over Columbus—or just Bill Murray in *Groundhog Day*.

This chapter will discuss not only color keying with blue- and green-screen footage but also all cases in which pixel values (color, luminance, saturation, and so on) stand in for transparency, allowing compositors to effectively separate foreground from background based on channel levels. You will learn how to create several types of keys using

NOTES

Novices often ask if a background has to be blue or green to be keyed. The answer is no. It just happens that, because blue and green are primary colors not dominant in human skin tones (unlike the third additive primary, red), they are well positioned to be clearly differentiated from the foreground colors, which generally will not be in as pure a tonal range but made of up values from all three color channels.

techniques that create luminance information that is then applied to the alpha channel of a layer (or layers). The black areas will be transparent, the white areas opaque, and the gray areas gradations of semi-opacity.

Good Habits and Best Practices

Before I get into detail about specific keying methods and when to use them, I want to mention some useful bits of advice that apply no matter which technique you choose:

▶ **Get used to soloing your foreground against a brightly colored background as you work in After Effects.** This will generally mean setting the background of the composition (**Ctrl+Shift+B/Cmd+Shift+B**) to a saturated yellow, red, orange, or purple (**Figure 6.1**). Choose a color that is

NOTES

In many ways this chapter follows on directly from Chapter 3, "Selections: The Key to Compositing," which covered many of the fundamentals in creating selections and discussed what constitutes a good matte. In this chapter, and the one following, we move beyond the fundamentals.

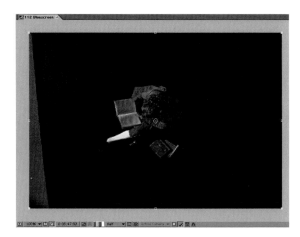

Figure 6.1 Your choice of background influences what you see. Against the default black, almost no detail is visible. With the checkerboard turned on, you can begin to see some flaws with the shadow. These flaws become clearer with a bright, solid, contrasting background. (Newton source images courtesy of Tim Fink Productions.)

distinct from both the foreground you are keying and the shot's existing background. If the foreground is going to be matted into a dark scene, you can use a dark shade, but in most cases you'll want it fairly bright to contrast with your foreground, showing any holes in the matte, or edge problems and noise in the background (**Figure 6.2**).

▶ **When isolating a foreground, protect edge detail at all costs.** Unless you're in a situation where your edges won't show up clearly, the game here is basically the same whatever tool you use: Solidify the opaque areas of the foreground, erase the background areas, but don't overdo either or your edge will suffer. Pushing edge pixels too far makes crunchy, chewy mattes (**Figure 6.3**).

▶ **Keep it simple, and don't be afraid to start over.** Particularly with the more sophisticated keyers, such as Primatte and Keylight, there are enough variables that you can easily overadjust your image to the point where you can't bring back detail that is already lost, try as you might, because too many different adjustments are fighting one another. As with rotoscoping (Chapter 7,

Figure 6.2 The keyed layer can be soloed at any time, revealing it against the background of your choice.

Figure 6.3 Attempts to firm up the edges of the shadow result in a matte so crunchy, you'd think it was still set to Draft quality.

"Rotoscoping and Paint"), there is something very Zen about keying: You can only explain so much before intuition and common sense about what you're dealing with have to kick in, or you'll fight endlessly with your shot. This is one case where throwing in the towel and starting over can save you an hour or two.

▶ **Get used to zooming in and looking hard for problems.** Don't spend all of your time on a single frame of the shot, and if possible, find a difficult frame to start on—one that has motion blur or one in which a little gust caught the character's wispy hair. That way you'll avoid nasty surprises after a lot of hard work. Also, even when you're on a single frame, use different methods to keep looking around the frame. Keep the Info window prominent as you scan around the background, noting whether the alpha values of the background are truly at zero, zoom in and out, and flip between the alpha and color channels (**Figure 6.4**).

▶ **Be prepared to combine multiple passes.** This is probably the most important step that too many artists try to skip, thinking it's simpler to get everything in one pass. One common misconception with keying is that it's an

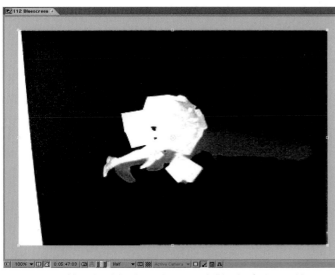

Figure 6.4 Enabling the alpha channel can reveal all kinds of other problems. The settings here are the same as in **Figure 6.1**.

173

automated process: You click a couple of buttons, and you're done. That can be true, on the rare occasions when the source footage is perfectly shot for keying. Even on a big-budget blockbuster, however, this happens only on the most straightforward of medium close-ups. In many cases, it is useful to create a core matte whose foreground is 100% opaque before refining the edges on a second pass. I'll describe this is in detail later in the Keylight section.

With these basics in mind, read on to learn about the various strengths of your keying options. I also urge you to revisit this list of best practices when it comes time to apply a key to your own shot, especially if you're new to keying.

Linear Keyers and Hi-Con Mattes

There are, of course, cases in which edge detail is not so critical, because you don't need to completely isolate an element: For example, you are matting it over itself, creating a *high-contrast*, or *hi-con, matte*. For cases where you just need to specify one area of a clip to adjust it, *linear keyers* will often do the trick.

I'm starting with these before bringing out the big guns of keying for a couple of reasons. Linear keyers are simpler to use and are useful in a wide variety of cases, beyond just blue- and green-screen shots. They contain fundamentals that carry forward into the more specialized keyers, such as Keylight, which is designed specifically to deal with blue and green screens.

Linear keyers differ from dedicated matte tools in that they do not do any kind of differencing of one channel or set of values against another (which is the key to blue and green screens); they are based merely on defining a range within a set of values.

The most useful linear keyers are

▶ Extract

▶ Linear Color Key

When, Exactly, Are Linear Keyers Useful?

Situations in which you'd want to separate levels in a single channel or by average the levels of multiple channels include

▶ Isolating a color range for the purpose of correcting it to a different color.

▶ Using garbage mattes and holdout mattes (defined later in this chapter).

▶ Matting elements that were shot over pure blackness or a close approximation. For example, fire is usually shot not on a blue-screen stage but outdoors at night or in a dark studio against a black background.

▶ Matting an element with itself to hold out specific portions of the element for enhancement. For example, you duplicate a layer and matte its highlights to add a bloom effect to enhance them (see Chapter 12, "Working with Light").

The keyers to be avoided are

▶ Luma Key

▶ Color Key

Color Key and Luma Key have no softness in their thresh-olding and should be filed under "never use." The means for grading edges provided by these keyers is a kludge; they offer Edge Thin and Edge Feather, which are crude methods for choking, spreading, and blurring the matte. Essentially they are *binary keyers*. They create pixels that are either transparent or opaque; the semitransparency is added afterward with no respect whatsoever to the source data. Linear Color Key is always a better option than Color Key; set to black or white, it can be used to generate lumi-nance mattes (as does Extract).

Linear Color Key and Extract

Although both are linear keyers, Linear Color Key and Extract excel in different areas. Extract is the most use-ful tool for luminance keying, using the black and white points of an image or any of its individual channels. Linear Color Key is more appropriate in cases in which you want to isolate a particular color or chrominance range.

Extract uses histograms to help isolate the black and white cut-off points for your matte and then grades the thresh-olds with black and white softness settings. Furthermore, you can easily use it for more than just luminance, as it of-fers a pull-down menu to access histogram controls for all four color channels (red, green, blue, and alpha).

Keep in mind that even when you're luma keying, one of the three color channels may be more suitable than overall luminance, which is just an average of the three. Green is often (but by no means always) the brightest and most contrasty channel, and blue tends to be the noisiest (**Figures 6.5a**, **b**, and **c**). If you are using full RGB for your luma key instead of a single channel, keep in mind that the luminance values are actually weighted.

All Channels Are Not Created Equal

If you set an RGB image as a luma matte, the red, green, and blue channels are averaged together to determine the luminance of the overall image. But they are not weighted evenly.

Compare **Figure 6.6** with **Figure 6.5c**, and you will note that the background of the averaged result is far less bright than the blue channel of the same image. The three channels are weighted according to how the eye sees them: Red at 29%, Green at 59%, and Blue at 12% luminance. This topic is explored in greater depth in Chapter 12, in the section on "Creating a Look with Color."

If you find yourself wanting to use one particular channel as a luma matte, use the Shift Channels effect (**Figure 6.7**).

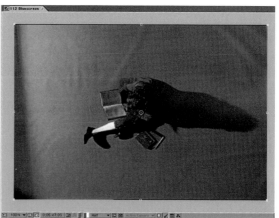

Figures 6.5a, b, and c You'll get different results from each of the three channels. In this case, blue (6.5c) is the brightest, because the blue screen is the dominant object in the image. It also contains the most noise, however, despite the fact that the footage was transferred from film with no compression.

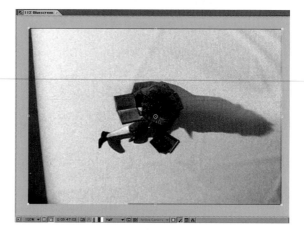

Figure 6.6 If this were an exact average of the gray-scale versions of the channels shown in **Figures 6.5a**, **b**, and **c**, the background would be brighter due to the brightness of the blue channel. But to mimic how the eye sees color, the averaging weights the three channels according to how the eye sees them, and the eye is far less sensitive to blue than green.

Linear Color Key offers direct selection of a key color using an eyedropper tool. The default color is blue—ironic because a basic blue-screen key is exactly what you shouldn't do with this tool. The other odd thing about the defaults is the 10% Matching Softness setting, which is arbitrary and gives a rather loose range of matched tones. I often end up with settings closer to 1%.

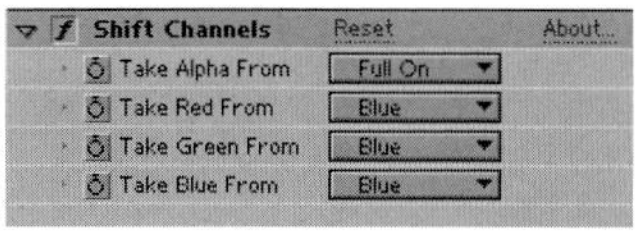

Note that there are, in fact, three eyedropper tools between the thumbnail images in the Linear Color Key effect. The top one replicates the Key Color eyedropper, and the other two add and subtract from the Matching Tolerance. You can click the eyedroppers on either of the adjacent thumbnail images, or if these are too small, you can open the Layer window and choose the effect in its View pulldown, using the eyedropper there (**Figure 6.8**). Do not try using these eyedroppers directly in the Composition window in a comp with multiple layers—the result may be odd.

Figure 6.7 Here the Shift Channels effect uses Blue for all channels save the Alpha, which is set to Full On.

Figure 6.8 The eyedropper tools of the Linear Color Key can be used in the Composition or Layer windows to select and refine the color range. This tool is useful for non-primary color matting; in this case, a maroon color is selected.

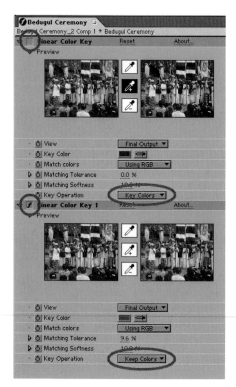

Figure 6.9 Two instances of Linear Color Key, the first set to Key Colors, the second set to Keep Colors. The key controls for setting up the second instance are highlighted: The first instance has been temporarily disabled so the full color of the image can be sampled for the color to be brought back in the second instance. Once setup is complete, all instances must be once again enabled.

Luma Mattes

A confession: I often use track mattes (detailed in Chapter 3) and a duplicate of my layer, instead of luminance keys applied directly to the layer. What I like about track mattes is that I can use Levels, a tool I know inside and out, and which gives me refined control of ranges on all channels, to refine transparency. Other artists may consider this approach more cumbersome, preferring to work with a single layer and an effect.

You can match the color using RGB, Hue, or Chroma values. In most cases, RGB will do the trick, but the best idea in unusual situations is probably to try each one before you start fine-tuning the controls. You can adjust the Tolerance, which specifies how close the colors have to be to the chosen value to be fully matted, and Softness, which then grades the threshold, softening the edges according to how close the color values are to the target range.

The default setting for the Key Operation is to Key Colors, which is straightforward enough. You might think, therefore, that the other option, Keep Colors, would simply invert the result. In fact, Keep Colors was designed with a separate purpose in mind, that of using Linear Color Key multiple times. If your first instance of the effect eliminates something you want to bring back, you have the opportunity to do so by adding a second instance of the effect targeting the color you want to bring back and set to Keep Colors. To set the second instance, you must first deselect the Effect option for the first instance, temporarily disabling it so you can set the color to keep (**Figure 6.9**).

Difference Mattes

The concept of a *difference matte* sounds simple: Frame two shots identically, one of them with your foreground subject present, the other with no foreground subject (commonly called a *clean plate*). Now, let the computer compare the two images and remove everything that matches between them, leaving only the foreground subject.

Unfortunately, there are all sorts of criteria that preclude this from actually working very well, specifically

▶ Both shots likely need to be locked off or motion stabilized, and even then it is common for there to be an offset that precludes a clean key.

▶ The foreground element probably is not completely devoid of whatever is in the background; low luminance areas, in particular, are prone to appear as background to the Difference Matte effect.

▶ Even such subtleties as grain and slight changes of lighting can cause a mismatch to two otherwise identical shots. Raising the Blur Before Difference setting helps correct for this, but by introducing inaccuracy.

You can gauge the challenges for yourself using any locked-off shot with movement in it, ideally one in which a character enters the frame. Lock off a frame of the source shot; you can apply Time Remap and use a single keyframe with the time of the clean plate shot. Turn off visibility of that layer, and apply Difference Matte to the other layer. Viewing final output, adjust Tolerance and Softness to try to get the key you're after. If the result has noise in it, try raising the Blur Before Difference value.

Figure 6.10 shows many of the problems with a difference matte by itself. It's not a terrible way to isolate something if the edge is not critical, but it cannot compare with more sophisticated methods for removing a solid color background.

Figure 6.10 This would seem to be a perfect scenario for using a Difference Matte effect. A locked-off camera was used to shoot a clean-plate image of the set as well as the action, and the two line up perfectly. Like Luma Key, however, this effect has no threshold controls, so you're pretty much stuck with whatever you are able to get by dialing in the Tolerance. Softness and Blur controls only make the matte less accurate.

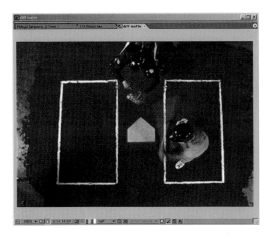

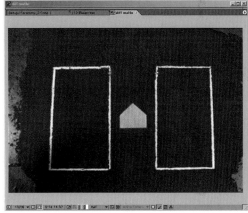

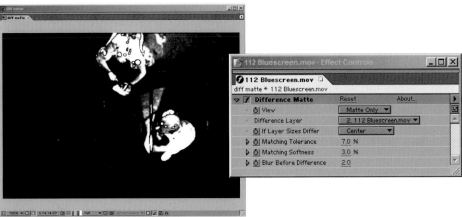

Blue-Screen and Green-Screen Keying

It used to be that if you wanted to go beyond the rather pedestrian Color Difference Key in After Effects you had to invest in a third-party keyer, and for a few years you had two choices: Ultimatte for After Effects (now AdvantEdge, Ultimate Corporation) and Primatte Keyer (Red Giant Software, formerly Pinnacle Systems, and before that, Puffin Designs).

Then with version 6.0, Adobe licensed a custom version of Keylight, a third well-known software keyer popular among Shake users, for After Effects Professional. It is still bundled with After Effects 6.5 Professional. Use of the other keyers has by no means disappeared. Personally I'm still a fan of Primatte for film keying, simply because I've been using it for so many years, and Ultimatte was a breakthrough when it was first released.

Primatte is particularly valuable for situations in which preserving transparency and edge detail is critical, because it allows direct selection of edge colors to be included and excluded from the key. Keylight allows direct selection only once—when picking the initial color to be keyed. But Keylight has other particular strengths, such as the ability to work with poorly lit mattes, and I have known fewer users to become frustrated with it than with Primatte. Therefore, I will focus on Keylight.

Keylight is useful in many keying situations, not just studio-optimized blue- or green- screen shots. For example, you can use Keylight for removal of a murky blue sky (**Figure 6.11**). You would not want to use Keylight when pulling a luminance key, however, or when simply trying to isolate a certain color range within the shot.

So when do you use Keylight? When your footage was shot against a uniform, saturated color background and when preserving edges is of utmost importance—in other words, most typically (but not exclusively) when working with footage that was specifically shot to be keyed, against a screen of blue or green.

NOTES

When I refer to Color Difference Key as pedestrian, I speak as someone who matted a feature's worth of footage with it, back before there were alternatives in After Effects. Its methodology is tried and true and can be replicated using channel math and Levels controls. In fact, the same basic methodology was used on some of the earliest digital composites in such blockbuster films as *Terminator 2*, and it's based on the optical compositing method that is as old as color film compositing itself.

Figure 6.11 In one pass, with no adjustments other than selecting the sky color, Keylight does a fairly effective job of knocking out the background even around the motion blurred bird in flight. The sky is nowhere near a perfect blue screen in this case, other than it's uniformity: blue saturation is around 50% and only about double the amount of red.

General Methodology: Keying

No two artists follow the exact same steps to key a complex shot, and no two complex shots are the same, but from all the variations you can distill a rough order of common steps for pulling a good matte, regardless of which tools you use. In the next section I'll show you how to apply some of these steps specifically using Keylight.

Don't worry about details until you get to the next section. For now, the basic steps, no matter what keyer you use, are

1. Garbage matte any areas of the background that can easily be masked out. By easily I mean, without needing to articulate the matte and animating individual mask points or without masking the whole shot—unless it's really a gnarly one—for more than about 20 minutes (**Figure 6.12**).

NOTES

The gauntlet I'm throwing down is that you make a habit of breaking down your footage into separate passes. The first pass can be a hard "core" matte that fills any holes you might have in your foreground without regard to the edge, the second is an overlaid edge matte to focus on edge detail only, without having to worry about those holes. Extra passes would be masked out to work on specific problem areas.

Figure 6.12 The quick-and-dirty garbage matte is your friend for eliminating unwanted parts of the stage.

2. Attempt a first pass key quickly, keeping this matte on the loose side, keeping as much edge detail as possible, with the idea that you'll be refining it later. Preview this at full resolution, in full motion, against a bright primary color. In rare cases, you will be done at this step.

3. Examine the alpha channel. Switch to a view that clearly displays the alpha channel (Keylight has several ways of doing this). Note any obvious holes in the foreground or areas of the background that have failed to key out, note any noise where the foreground or background areas should be solid (**Figure 6.13**), and move on to Step 4.

If things look too noisy and chaotic in the alpha channel or too clamped down on the edges, consider these strategies:

▶ Start over and try again from scratch with the basic key.

▶ Apply noise reduction to the foreground image and start over (there is a section called "Noise Suppression" later in this chapter).

▶ Use articulated or tracked garbage/holdout mattes to isolate one problem portion of the footage (discussed in the section called "Fixing Typical Problems").

Figure 6.13 A quick diagnosis of Keylight's first pass at this shot: A separate matte will be required to key out the underside of the leg, where there is evidently substantial reflected blue. The shadows will require separate mattes of their own if they are to be included in the key. The hair may have to be separated to retain softness and detail.

4. Decision time about separating the core and edge mattes. If your foreground has transparent areas that should be opaque and closing them in affects the edges adversely, duplicate the foreground and solo the duplicated layer. Push the settings further to create a hard core matte, and choke it far enough in that it does not affect the edges of the other foreground layer whatsoever.

5. Refine the edge. Focusing now on the edge matte, zoom in on a challenging area of the foreground edge (200% to 400%), and refine the key to try to accommodate it, using strategies outlined in the following sections. Challenging areas of the foreground whose edges you may need to carefully preserve include

   ▶ Fine detail such as hair

   ▶ Motion blurred foreground elements

   ▶ Cast shadows

   Watch out for, and consider rotoscoping, foreground features that can threaten an effective key, such as

   ▶ Reflective areas

   ▶ Edge areas whose levels closely match those of the background

   ▶ Non-contrasting foreground and background areas (in poorly lit regions of the shot)

6. Preview the shot in full motion. Again, note holes and noise, and now work on strategies (outlined in the "Fixing Typical Problems" section) to overcome these problems. Approaches you may employ at this stage are

   ▶ Using masks to create holdout mattes, either for the purpose of keying them individually or rotoscoping them out of the shot (**Figure 6.14**)

   ▶ Holding out the matte edge only, for the purpose of refining or blurring it (see the section called "Edge Matting" later in this chapter)

Figure 6.14 This is the step too many artists aren't willing to take. Most of the problems with keying this figure stem from the fact that he's seated on the floor, but that is also to your advantage, because he's not going to move much. Therefore, you could create holdout masks for separate areas to key, working individually on the body and the shadow-casting areas. In a closeup, it can be helpful to mask the hair, refining that separately.

That's the general approach with any keyer; the point I want to hammer home here is that trying to key a clip in a single pass is often too lazy an approach that, ironically, results in more work as you struggle to make all areas of your shot accommodate unified settings.

Using Keylight

Now take a look at some specifics when working with Keylight.

The very most important of the Keylight parameters, in all cases, is the Screen Colour selection (Keylight reveals its UK origins with that u). Choose wisely, and you have a shot at getting your footage to key in one pass. Choose poorly, and you'll be fighting an uphill battle from here onward. More about what this selection does appears in "The Inner Workings of Keylight," later in this chapter.

In the best case scenario, after creating any basic garbage mattes as usual, your steps will be

1. Use the eyedropper to sample a pixel in your background that you believe is roughly the median of the background. The view defaults to Final Result, so you can immediately examine the result of this one choice. (Remember to set your background to a bright color and solo the layer.)

2. If you think there is any chance of getting a better initial result, switch to the alpha channel (**Alt+4/ Option+4**), reset Keylight (do *not* undo) or switch the view to Source, and select again. Repeat again if you like. Now you have as many as three attempts saved in your undo buffer. If you're getting a pretty good result, you can accept a loose matte, but if not, look for the one that seems to have eliminated the most unwanted background (**Figures 6.15a**, **b**, and **c**). If necessary, examine the alpha channel of the soloed layer (**Alt+4/ Option+4**).

NOTES

Why not take snapshots of each attempt? You can (**Shift+F5** to **F8** to take snapshots, hold down **F5** to **F8** to see them), but the method described holds each pass in your undo buffer; the idea is to be able to recover the one you like.

Figures 6.15a, b, and c Even with source footage as well shot as this (6.15a), you will get very different initial results depending on whether you use the eyedropper to sample color at the low-lit edges (6.15b) or in the well-lit center of the image (6.15c). Zooming in on the wispy hair over a bright color shows the difference clearly: You want that extra detail, but you don't want that matte line along the arm. (Source image courtesy of The Foundry UK.)

Figure 6.16 Moving forward with the matte from Figure 6.15c, Status view shows lots of gray areas, with semitransparent pixels, in the background, but not many on the foreground figure other than where you want them (in the hair). This is a good initial result.

Now, as needed, you look for areas that could use refining:

1. Switch the view to Status in the View pull-down menu. This reveals the pixels that are fully opaque as white, those that are fully transparent as black, and those that are in-between as gray (**Figure 6.16**). It's like an exaggerated version of a normal alpha channel view. Try Screen Balance at settings of 5.0, the default 50.0, and 95.0, and choose whichever one yields improvement (more on this in the next section).

2. If there are gray semitransparent pixels in your background, boost the Screen Strength setting until the gray is mostly gone in Status view. Try to preserve any gray that is at the edges of your foreground. If gray remains in the background, but away from the edges of your figure such that you can easily garbage matte it, do that (**Figures 6.17a**, **b**, and **c**) if you want to preserve maximum edge detail, or if it's not costly to do so, tighten the matte at this point by raising screen strength.

The footage used in **Figures 6.15** through **6.17** was nearly perfectly shot, and although the footage includes flowing hair, which is a challenge, it does not include the floor, which is usually more of a challenge. The final step for this image is to raise the Despill Bias and with it, the Alpha Bias, which affects the matte, so recheck Status for holes. Raising it slightly reduces the blue matte line on the arm. In this ideal scenario, you

Figures 6.17a, b, and c Screen Strength has been raised to remove the gray. At this point it's an artistic decision whether to go with the loose matte (6.17a) and garbage matte out the noise in the corner, which doesn't affect the edge, or go for the tighter matte (6.17b), which still gives a very good result with lots of wispy hair preserved (6.17c).

are done without ever having gone beyond the first five controls at the heart of Keylight (**Figure 6.18**).

At the opposite extreme is the nightmare scenario of Newton seated directly on the blue stage in his white stockings, whose Status setting with a high Screen Strength boost reveals quite a few more problems (**Figure 6.19**).

If your shot also now contains some unwanted transparent areas in the foreground area—gray pixels amongst the white in Status view—this is an opportunity to shortcut the process by creating one or several core mattes. The Newton example is complicated by the shadows on the floor, so concentrate first only on the main body holdout area (from **Figure 6.14**).

3. Duplicate the layer with Keylight applied, so that the initial settings are now held by two layers, and solo the duplicate. You can rename the new layer core and the original layer edge. Press **F3** to make sure the core Keylight effect is displayed in the Effect controls—you don't want to adjust the wrong one!

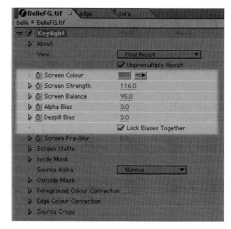

Figure 6.18 These controls make up the core of Keylight. Everything else is there only to compensate for footage that was not well lit, shot, recorded, or transferred.

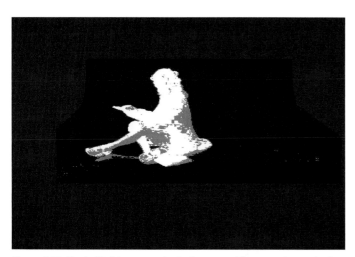

Figure 6.19 Ouch. All of those grays in the foreground figure are the result of reflected blue, due to the actor being seated on the floor. Why didn't Newton pack a picnic blanket?

4. On the core layer and still in Status view, twirl down the Screen Matte parameters. Adjust the Clip White value down until you start to see a matte that consists of entirely black pixels in the background, fully white pixels in the foreground, and gray pixels at the edges of the foreground. You may see some green coloration appear as well, which indicates pixels that had some of the background color in them that Keylight will replace (**Figure 6.20**). If areas of gray have reappeared in the background, raise Clip Black to eliminate them.

5. Choke the core matte. Turn on soloing for the edge matte as well, set both to Final Result, and toggle the core matte on and off in RGB and Alpha view. You will probably notice that it changes the appearance of the edge, thickening it in an undesirable way. Use the Screen Grow/Shrink control in Keylight to shrink the matte (using positive values) until you can toggle the core matte on and off and see no effect on the edges whatsoever; only the holes fill in. Be liberal here: Make sure that your core matte has no edge data in it anywhere; it's not atypical to have a setting of 2.0 or more.

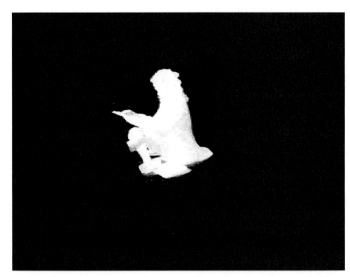

Figure 6.20 Even with the problematic shadow and leg areas held out, the figure's torso requires a fairly heavy Clip White adjustment, resulting in a lot of green areas. These are warning you that the color in these areas may be contaminated by the background, which can be remedied with the Replace Colour control.

6. Preview the clip in motion over the bright background. Note any problems you see with the edges; the next section focuses on methods to refine them.

At this point, you should have succeeded in eliminating any holes in your foreground. If you divided your image into separate holdout areas, as in the Newton example, you repeat the same process for setting up a core and edge matte for those layers. From that point, all the work left to do is on your edges alone, which is where you want to be able to focus your efforts.

Understanding and Optimizing Keylight

If you carefully followed the instructions in the previous section, your composite is now either closer to looking good or has an obvious problem. If you think it's looking good, focus in on a few details, and note if there are any problems with the following in your full motion preview:

▶ Hair detail: Are all of the "wispies" coming through?

▶ Motion blur or, in unusual cases with a defocus, lens blur: Do blurred objects appear chunky or noisy, or do they partially disappear?

▶ Screen contamination areas: Are there any remaining holes in the foreground?

▶ Shadows: Are they keying as desired?

You are, of course, free to find niggling problems of your own and share them with your friends (**Figures 6.21a** through **d**).

Alternatively, there may be something fundamentally wrong with your matte, including

▶ Ill-defined foreground/background separation or semitransparency throughout the foreground or background

▶ Crunchy, chewy, chattery edges

▶ Other noise in the matte

▶ Edge fringing or an overly choked matte

▶ Errors in the spill suppression

Figure 6.21a through d Fun challenges you may encounter when pulling a color key include wispy hair (6.21a), motion blur (6.21b), contamination of foreground elements by the background color (6.21c), and shadows (6.21d).

Keylight anticipates all of these issues, offering specific tools and techniques to address them. Before you delve into those (which I'm saving for the "Focusing In" section) take a look under the hood at how Keylight actually works.

The Inner Workings of Keylight

A few decisions are the key to Keylight, and most of the other controls compensate for how effectively you made those few decisions. This section offers a glimpse into the inner workings of Keylight, which will greatly aid your intuition when pulling a matte.

The core of Keylight involves generating the *screen matte*, and the most essential step is choosing the screen color. From that one color choice, Keylight makes nonlinear comparisons between its saturation and hue and each pixel, as detailed in **Table 6.1**.

TABLE 6.1 How Keylight Makes Its Key Decisions

COMPARED TO SCREEN COLOR, PIXEL IS	KEYLIGHT WILL
Of a different hue	Consider it foreground, make it opaque
Of a similar hue and more saturated	Key it out completely, making it transparent
Of a similar hue, but less saturated	Subtract a mathematically weighted amount of the screen color and make it semitransparent

The main lesson of Table 6.1 is that a healthy background color is of a reasonably high saturation level and of a distinct hue.

Those sound like vague criteria, not easily met—and it's true, they are somewhat vague. That's why Keylight adds the Screen Strength, Screen Balance, and Alpha and Despill Bias controls just below Screen Colour. Screen Strength helps define the saturation of the background pixels, and Screen Balance delineates its hue. The Bias controls color correct the image. All of these controls differ from the controls below them in Keylight in that they work on the color comparison process itself, rather than the resulting matte.

The major enemy of a successful blue-screen shot is muddy, desaturated colors. One clear symptom that saturation in your background isn't sufficiently high for an easy key is that areas of the background are of a consistent hue yet fail to key out. Similarly, a clear symptom that your foreground has become contaminated with reflected color from the background is that it becomes semi-opaque after setting the Screen Colour. In either case, the Screen Strength control becomes useful.

The Screen Strength control boosts or reduces the saturation of each pixel before comparing it to the screen color. This effectively brings more desaturated background pixels into the keying range if raised or, if lowered, knocks back pixels in the foreground containing the background color.

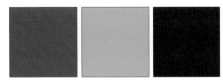

Figure 6.22 The Rosco colors: Ultimatte Blue, Ultimatte Green, and Ultimatte Super Blue. The blue colors are not pure blue, but contain twice as much blue as green, and twice as much green as red. The green is nearly pure, with only a quarter the amount of red and no blue whatsoever. Lighting will change their hue, which has also changed by being taken to print. They're called Ultimatte because that's the hardware system for which they were initially optimized.

NOTES

Not only is it good form to derive the best matte you can with these core tools, there are extra, hidden reasons to do it. For one thing, none of the core controls described in this section slows the keying process down, while the other controls within Keylight, and outside of it, will to an extent dependent on the size of your source footage. Also, tools discussed in the next section, such as Clip Rollback, depend on the core matte as a reference.

TIP

Saving a stage of your shot that you might want to revert to is conveniently done with the Increment and Save feature in the File menu.

That takes care of saturation, but what about hue? Keylight is designed to expect one of the three color values to be much more prevalent than the other two. But it can do an even better job if it knows which of the two remaining colors is more prevalent.

By default, the primary color is weighted evenly against the two other components of a pixel. In the real world, however, there might be far more of one than the other, and Screen Balance allows you to alert Keylight to this fact. A Rosco Ultimatte Blue screen will have quite a bit of green in it—much more than red, unless someone has lit it wrong. Ultimatte Green screens are almost pure green (**Figure 6.22**).

On this theory, you would use a balance of 95% with blue screens and leave it at 50% for green screens. The true recommendation from The Foundry, however, is to put it near 0, put it near 100, and compare these to the default setting of 50 to evaluate which one works best. In other words, you should think of there being three settings to try (instead of 100): 5%, 50%, and 95%.

The Bias settings, Alpha Bias and Despill Bias, effectively color correct the image before the key is pulled, by scaling the primary color component up or down (enhancing or reducing its difference from the other two components). Use the Bias settings if the screen color has been infected with a secondary color, causing it to turn muddy, moving it toward gray.

Focusing In: Clean-Up Tools

Once you are satisfied that you have as good an edge matte as possible, you are ready to zoom in on a detail area and work on solving specific problems.

If you see an area that looks like a candidate for refinement, save (so that you can Revert to this as your ultimate undo point), zoom in, and create a region of interest around the area in question.

Now take a look at some common problems you might encounter and the tools built into Keylight to solve them.

Holes and Edges

The double-matte method shortcuts a lot of the tug of war that would otherwise exist between filling holes in the foreground and increasing the chunkiness to the edge, which inevitably results. Even with this advantage, your edge matte probably will require adjustments to the Clip Black and Clip White controls that you used on the core matte to reduce noise in the background and make foreground edge detail more prominent.

The game is to keep as large a difference between the two settings as possible. The closer those two numbers approach one another, the closer you are to having a bitmap alpha channel in which each pixel is either black or white—a bad thing (**Figure 6.23**). The delta, or difference between the clipping numbers, represents the area in which all your gray, semitransparent alpha pixels are allowed to exist, so the goal is to give them as much real estate as possible.

If you take the Clip controls too far and are looking for a way out of the corner without starting over, raise the Clip Rollback setting. This control is designed specifically to restore detail only to the edge, and used in moderation and with a close eye on the result it can be quite effective (**Figure 6.24**).

Screen Strength versus Clip Black

These two controls seem to have a similar effect on the result, causing the background to become more transparent. How do you know which one to use? You can get the same result from both, but there are differences.

Screen Strength
- Is part of the basic screen matte calculation and doesn't slow the process down
- Is not affected by edge rollback
- Does not trigger color replacement if the matte is made more or less transparent

Clip Black
- Is a post process requiring extra time and memory
- Is affected by edge rollback
- Triggers color replacement if the matte is made more or less transparent

So although it is not crucial to choose one of these over the other at any given time, understanding the differences can certainly help you along.

Figure 6.23 This is why you divide difficult shots into pieces. Eliminating all the problems with this key has resulted in a chunky, chewy, quantized matte.

Figure 6.24 In this case, raising the Clip Black setting and rolling it back, instead of raising Screen Strength (as was advocated for this shot in the step-by-step) gets the nod. The hair detail can be given a thicker matte without introducing noise into the background.

Here's how Clip Rollback works: The number assigned to this control is the number of pixels from the edge that are rolled back. The edge pixels reference the original, un-hardened screen matte. So if your edges were looking nice and soft on the first pass but pulling noise out of the matte hardened them, this tool could help you out by restoring them.

Noise Suppression

Are your mattes chattering? Keylight includes a Screen Pre-blur option that you should use only in the zoomed-in view and only with footage that has a clearly evident noise problem, such as source shot on miniDV. Essentially, this option is the same as blurring your source footage before keying it, so it adds error and is something of a desperation move. The result of the blurring does not appear in the footage itself; it is visible only internally to Keylight.

A better alternative if your matte is fundamentally sound is Screen Softness, found under the Screen Matte controls. The difference is that Screen Softness blurs the matte itself after the key has already been pulled, so it has a much better chance of retaining detail. As was touched upon in Chapter 3, edges in nature are slightly soft for various reasons; so used to a modest degree (considering that it is introducing error into your key), this control can enhance the realism of your matte (**Figures 6.25a**, **b**, and **c**).

Figures 6.25a, b, and c Okay, you might have to squint your eyes, but look closely enough and you'll see how much more hair detail is retained using Screen Softness (6.25b) than Screen Pre-blur (6.25a). Both have a nicer look up so close than the unsoftened matte (6.25c).

A more drastic approach, when softening and blurring cannot reach larger chunks in the footage, is to use the Despot controls to simplify the matte. If you use these at all, use them at low levels. Crank them up, and you'll see that they cause an undesirable blobbiness in your matte. For this reason, I've never quite trusted these controls and usually leave them alone.

A better approach, particularly with miniDV and HDV footage (which by the way are both guaranteed to add undesirable noise and are typically not recommended for blue-screen and green-screen shoots), is one that was refined to perfection by a member of the After Effects community at large, Mats Olsson (and drawn to my attention by Alex of Disciple Films in Paris). The steps are

1. Convert your footage from default RGB to YUV using Channel Combiner (the From pull-down). This will make your clip look very strange. Do not be alarmed (**Figure 6.26**).

2. Apply Channel Blur to the green and blue channels only, at modest amounts (to gauge this, go to each channel–press **Alt+2**/**Option+2** or **Alt+3**/**Option+3**— and zoom in on a noisy area of the frame). Make sure Repeat Edge Pixels is checked.

3. Round-trip back from YUV to RGB, again with Channel Combiner.

4. Apply Keylight, and breathe a sigh of relief.

YUV is a color space associated with broadcast video and used in component PAL television. It is functionally similar to YIQ, the NTSC variant. In After Effects YUV, the red channel actually displays the luminance value of the shot, while the green and blue channels display blue and red weighed against green. It's a complicated analog color method, which is why you may never have encountered it, but DV formats work in a similar manner, giving more weight and clarity to luminance than to color (and giving the least weight and clarity of all to the blue channel, an obvious drawback).

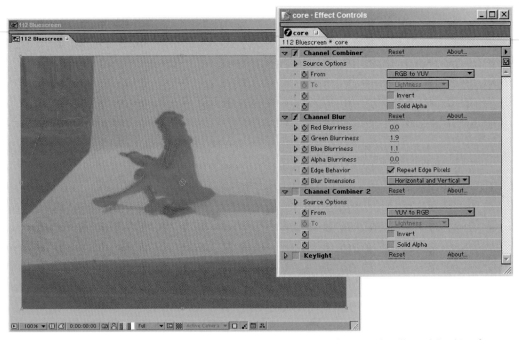

Figure 6.26 Do not attempt to adjust the controls. Someone, somewhere, must have mistaken Channel Combiner for a trippy color effect, but the truth is that After Effects is set up to display only RGB, not YUV (which conveniently also uses three channels, just not those three). The round-trip around a Channel Blur appears in the Effect controls (but the second Channel Combiner effect is temporarily disabled, hence the strange look).

Fringing and Choking

Sometimes, despite all best efforts, you will work on a matte and find that you are left either with extra unwanted edge pixels (fringing) or that your keyed subject has lost all subtle edge detail because the matte is overchoked.

On the one hand, Keylight does include the Screen Grow/ Shrink control for such situations. On the other hand, if you find yourself having to shrink or expand your matte, it may be a symptom of other problems. Faced with the need to choke or spread my matte (another way of saying shrink or grow), I typically go back and try my initial key again, possibly breaking it down into more component parts using holdout masks. (More on choking and spreading coming up.)

Spill Suppression

The thing to understand about Keylight's suppression of *color spill* (foreground pixels contaminated by reflected color from the background) is that spill suppression in Keylight all happens when the matte is initially pulled. Whatever matte you get from Keylight's core controls has spill suppression. So spill-kill is practically automatic if you pull a good initial key (**Figures 6.27a** and **b**).

When does this lovely elegant freebie disappear? First of all, when it's an unwanted by-product. There are situations when parts of the foreground that you want to keep are close enough in color range to the background that their color is suppressed. On *The Day After Tomorrow* our problem was that the helicopter pilots on their way to Balmoral were wearing blue uniforms, which would turn gray with spill suppression. For example, I had to rotoscope an epaulet to bring it back to blue.

Furthermore, adjustments to the matte can expose areas of the clip that didn't get the spill suppression. Those are the green pixels in the Status view (back in **Figure 6.20**); these show the areas of the matte whose spill suppression may now be off. In such cases, you specify a Replace Method; Soft Colour set to medium gray is a good choice if the only

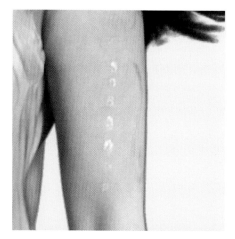

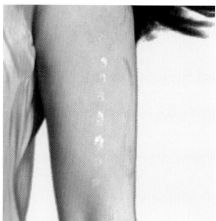

Figures 6.27a and b Setting the correct Screen Balance is critical not only to pulling a good key but to getting automatic spill suppression. If you see spill with Screen Balance at the default 50% (6.27a), just try 5% and 95% (6.27b) before you move on to more drastic measures.

affected pixels are at the edge. It is a cheat, but it will make your key look better by gently desaturating pixels that might otherwise pop.

If too much of your edge will be affected for replacing in gray to work, you still have an option in Keylight: Uncheck the Lock Biases Together toggle and raise the Despill Bias, leaving the Alpha Bias at 0. This tells Keylight that there is more of the foreground color than expected to suppress, but that the areas that are contaminated with blue should not be made more transparent.

Finally, in cases in which Keylight's spill suppression becomes unwieldy or not useful (as with the soldier in dress blues), there is an easy out. Create a good key without worrying about blue spill, pre-compose the result, and apply it as an alpha matte to the foreground source. You can then use one of the methods described in the next section to try and remove color spill without adversely affecting your footage.

Fixing Typical Problems

As you now well know, because I've taken every opportunity to drill it into your head, the number one solution to most matte problems is to break the image being matted into multiple sections rather than trying to get one matte in one pass. You can divide the matte as follows:

▶ Core and edge matte (hard and soft matte)

▶ Holdout masks for particular areas of the frame (useful if lighting varies greatly within the frame, or if one area contains a particularly challenging element, such as hair or motion blur)

▶ Temporal split (if light conditions change as the shot progresses)

All other tricks fall short if you're not willing to take the trouble to do this. And now for some more bad news.

On Set

No matter how advanced and well paid you are, in most cases, your time is going to be far cheaper than that of a film crew on set. That means—shocking, I know—you're going to have the opportunity to fix some things in post that should have been handled correctly on set, but weren't. I would call it job security but that's just too cynical.

If you're fortunate enough to be supervising the effects shoot itself (it's worth it for the craft services alone), you can do all sorts of things to ensure that the footage will key successfully later on.

A hard *cyclorama*, or *cyc* (pronounced like psych), painted a uniform key color is far preferable to a temp cloth background. If you can't rent a stage that has one, the next best thing might be to invest in a roll of floor covering and paint that, so that you get the smooth transition from floor to wall, as in **Figure 6.28** (assuming you're including the floor in your shot). Regarding the floor, it's also important for people not to walk across the cyc in street shoes, which will quickly contaminate it.

Assuming you're starting with a background that is not only the correct color but is footprint free and has as few seams and other variations as possible, the most important concerns are lighting it correctly and balancing the foreground and background lighting.

The Right Color Background

The digital age has made some directors pretty fast and loose with what they consider a keyable background. You may be asked (or try on your own) to pull mattes from a blue sky, from a blue swimming pool, or from other monochrome backgrounds.

If you are looking to create a colored backdrop that you will key, however, there is one brand to look for when purchasing your paint, fabric backdrop, or adhesive tape: Rosco. Rosco's Digicomp products are of a color designed specifically to allow for the most effective keying, with a purity and intensity of saturation unavailable at your local paint store. They are available in three colors—you guessed it—blue, green, and red.

In terms of how different the background color has to be from your foreground, the answer is "not very." Red is generally avoided not least because human skin tones contain a lot of it, but a girl in a light blue dress or a soldier in a dress blue uniform would probably key just fine from a blue screen (although spill suppression might require special attention).

Figure 6.28 On a stage with no hard cyclorama, you can create the effect of one—the curve where the wall meets the floor—using blue-screen cloth instead. It doesn't behave as well (note the hotspot on the curve), but it will certainly do in a pinch and is much preferable to removing the seam caused by the corner between the wall and floor.

This job is, of course, best left to a professional, and any kind of recommendations for a physical lighting setup are beyond the scope of this book. But, hey, here are a few things you can keep in mind even if your role is only that of the effects supervisor on set:

▶ Ideally, the light levels on the foreground and background should match. A spot light meter will tell you if they do.

▶ Diffuse lights are great for the background (often a set of large 1 K, 2 K, or 5 K lights with a silk sock covering them), but fluorescent lights will do in a pinch. With fluorescents you just need more instruments to light the same space.

▶ It is helpful to keep a good deal of space between the foreground and background. Ten feet is ideal.

▶ Avoid unwanted shadows like coal in your stocking, but by all means light for shadows if it looks like you can get some clean ones on the floor.

▶ If your scene is set outdoors, consider shooting it outside (almost certainly in that case with solid color cloth backdrops and carpets). You may need fill lights on the background, but daylight is a difficult—almost impossible–light quality to re-create on a stage, especially for a large exterior shot.

▶ Record on the highest quality, least compressed component video format you can afford. Even if the rest of your project will be shot on miniDV, it might be worth shooting the effects on Digital Betacam and converting them later if you can.

If the setup permits, bring a laptop with After Effects on it and with some representation of the scene into which the footage you're taking is going to be keyed. This can be enormously helpful not only to you but to the gaffer and director of photography, to give them an idea of where to focus their efforts. You will have to work with the camera operator to get a live signal, and with a film camera it may require the addition of a video tap, but it is possible and useful.

Finally, particularly if you're on set when a locked shot is being set up, once the lighting has been finalized and before action is called on the shot, ask the camera operator to shoot a few frames of clean plate—the background with no foreground characters or objects to be keyed out later. There are all sorts of ways this can be handy.

Matte Problems

It's an ugly fact of life that there will be times that you have to cheat and alter your matte. If you're going to do it and you're not using the built-in tools for it in Keylight, make sure you're at least using the right tool for the job—and that you're using it with as light a touch as you can manage.

For whatever reason—the placement of the effect in the Effects menu or maybe the name—Minimax is employed by artists who would enjoy far more success with one of the Matte Tools: Matte Choker or Simple Choker. Minimax is old school: It works in whole pixel increments to choke and spread pixel values. It has some interesting uses—but not for subtle matte edits. It is a quick way to spread or choke a matte, particularly when you lack alpha channel information.

In most cases, however, Simple Choker is the tool you're looking for. It allows you to choke or spread a matte (by entering a positive or negative number, respectively) at the subpixel level (by inputting decimal values). That's all it does. It's really no different from the corresponding control in Keylight, but you can use it on any alpha channel, not just one created by Keylight (or any keyer).

Matte Choker adds tools to introduce softness to the choke. The good thing is that its default is set at an effective starting point for many mattes. The bad thing is that softness controls tend to add more error to the process and are often the sign of a bad key. Don't be afraid to "settle" for Simple Choker: It is often up to the job without monkey-wrenching anything.

Isolating and Working with Edges

It's a pity that some of the best tools for dealing with mattes are found in a third-party collection of 8-bit plug-ins that haven't been updated in years. But there it is. The collection is, at least, still available from Red Giant Software—it is called Composite Wizard.

For the most part these plug-ins do not do anything you can't do on your own in After Effects. They just save you some steps. The "Edge Selection" section outlines some of the more useful tools in Composite Wizard and the workaround if you don't have the plug-ins. Only one effect in Composite Wizard, the Miracle Alpha Cleaner, has no equivalent that you can create on your own, but it's a slightly dangerous tool anyhow.

Edge Selection

If you have a copy of the Composite Wizard plug-ins, Deluxe Edge Finder is one of the most useful tools in there: It allows you to make a grayscale map outlining only the edges of your alpha channel, which you can apply as a luma matte to an adjustment layer. Then you have an adjustment layer whose effects—a blur, a levels adjustment, or a holdout—apply only to the edge.

If you don't have Composite Wizard, no worries; you just have to take a few extra steps to make your own. The simplest way to do this is to apply Shift Channels with Take Alpha From set to Full On and the three color channels set to Alpha. Next, apply Find Edges (often mistaken for a use-less, trippy, psychedelic effect because, as with Photoshop, it appears in the Stylize menu), and check the Invert box (**Figure 6.29**).

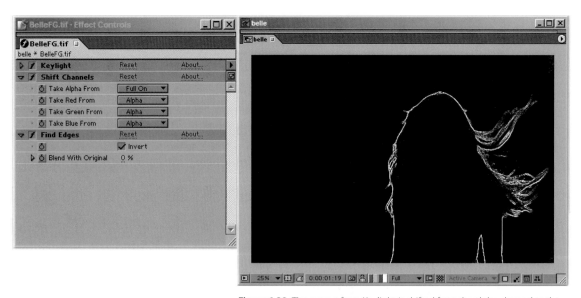

Figure 6.29 The output from Keylight is shifted from the alpha channel to the color channels. Find Edges then takes all the contrast (gray) areas and makes a lovely edge selection from them, which can be used as a luma matte applied directly to the footage or to an Adjustment layer with the effects you want to apply. A typical use is to blur the edge slightly using this selection, in which case you want to blur the background and foreground together.

If you want to choke or spread this edge matte, this is a good time to bust out Minimax. The default setting under Operation in this effect is Maximum, which spreads the white edge pixels by whatever amount you specify in the Radius setting. Minimum chokes the edge in the same manner. If the result appears a little crude, an additional Fast Blur will soften the edge (**Figure 6.30**).

Once you're done, apply the result as a luma matte. You should not need to pre-compose before doing so.

So what can you do with an adjustment layer with an edge matte applied to it? One great use is to apply a blur on the adjustment layer in the master comp, so that any blur you apply affects the blend area between the foreground and background. This is another way around a matte that is too hard and crunchy. Sometimes a subtle Levels adjustment helps your composited edge, and a desaturation operation using Hue/Saturation has the same effect as choosing gray as an edge replacement color in Keylight.

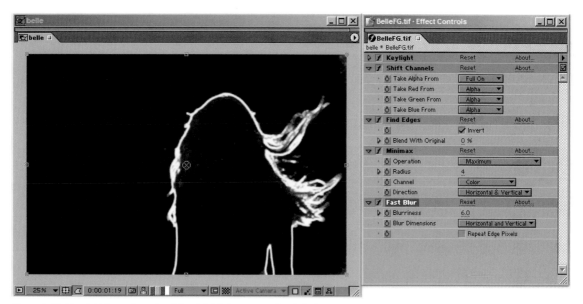

Figure 6.30 Need thicker, softer edges? A quick Minimax set to the default Maximum allows you to specify a Radius by which the white area will grow. If the result looks a little chunky, a quick Fast Blur will soften it back. This is very useful, for example, when there is motion blur on the object that needs to be controlled in the edges.

Matte Holes

If you followed my instructions for keying closely, you should not have a problem with noise or holes in your foreground, because you are using a heavily choked core matte to close them.

However, in cases where your background on set had fundamental problems—uneven lighting, seams, dirt on the floor—you may find noise and holes in your background. You need a way to close these without affecting your edges. The perfect software solution for such cases exists, but unfortunately it is a third-party tool: Miracle Alpha Cleaner, which is also a part of the Composite Wizard set. But before you run out to buy Composite Wizard, a further caveat: Most artists ultimately give up using Miracle Alpha Cleaner because they stop believing in miracles. That is to say, it's an automated tool that frequently fills holes that should have remained unfilled, such as the little triangular gap that sometimes opens up under outstretched arms (**Figure 6.31**).

I hate to be the one to break it to you, but holes in your matte present a situation in which you're probably going to have to break out your rotoscoping skills (or refine them

Figure 6.31 Using an automated solution, such as Pinnacle's Miracle Alpha Cleaner (part of the Composite Wizard pack), to fill holes in the foreground matte will also close holes that you want to keep, such as this tiny gap under the pitcher's arm. For that reason, veteran effects compositors tend to avoid these solutions, although they are tempting.

using tips from the next chapter). It's usually not as bad as you think to work this way; the painstaking part of keying is defining the edge. Things like holes can be fixed with crude masks or by tracking in paint strokes (more on this in the next two chapters).

Matte Fringing

Fringing around the edge of a feather matte is usually the result of an alpha having been applied separately. For example, it could occur if, in attempting to process color spill outside of Keylight, you applied the Keylight matte as a track matte.

Don't panic and choke all that detail out of your edge! There is a better solution, but it is hidden away in the Channel menu. Remove Color Matting is designed specifically to suck color out of edges that are behaving as premultiplied rather than straight (if that distinction eludes you, review Chapter 3).

Typically, premultiplied images have been matted against black, leaving a dark fringe around the edges. Remove Color Matting uses black as the default Background Color, and this is the only user-adjustable parameter in this effect. Therefore you may apply this plug-in and find that, boom, your problem is solved.

If not, you can use the eyedropper to sample the background. If the fringing is bright colored, premultiplication may have occurred against white or gray.

Color Spill

Color Spill doesn't have to be a big deal. If you're not happy with the spill suppression you get from Keylight or whatever keyer you are using, you have other options once you apply the matte as an alpha track matte to the source footage.

Sometimes the Spill Suppressor tool that is included with After Effects will do the trick for you. It uses a simple channel multiplication formula to pull the background color out of the foreground pixels. All you have to do is use the eyedropper tool to select a sample from the background

TIP

If the fringing seems to be black but applying the default black Background Color in Remove Color Matting causes the edge pixels to pop to bright white, try creeping up the values slightly: Click on Background Color, and raise the RGB values from 0, 0, 0 to 1, 1, 1. The black in this case has been "contaminated" and the image pedestal somehow raised.

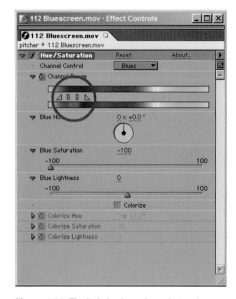

Figure 6.32 The little hash marks and triangles under the upper gradient of the Channel Range control let you specify a region to desaturate. It's crude but in some cases effective for knocking a particular color out of your scene.

color (you can even copy your original choice of screen color from Keylight) and leave the setting at 100%.

If even Spill Suppressor pulls out foreground color that you want to keep, then it is probably advisable to open up Hue/Saturation and try to target and desaturate the specific hue that is causing you problems.

This sounds positively Neanderthal in its lack of subtlety, but it works a surprising amount of the time, provided you can identify the spill color that needs to be removed. Open Hue/Saturation, and select a channel under Channel Control that you think might be the one that needs attention—say, blues.

Look closely at Channel Range. You might not have noticed the little controls underneath the upper color spectrum (**Figure 6.32**). These allow you to set the color range as precisely as you like. The inner hash marks control the range affected by the controls below; the region between those and the outer, triangular markers is the feather area.

In most cases what you'll be doing to remove spill is selecting a channel, refining it, and lowering Saturation to reduce spill. Here's how to gauge which pixels are affected: Before lowering saturation, crank it up to 100. The pixels in the affected range will be easy to spot.

Conclusion

Keylight is a great tool, and tips in this chapter should help you get the results you're after. It's not the only option, of course. Primatte Keyer is just as powerful, with a completely different methodology, but you must purchase it separately. (The book's CD-ROM includes a demo if you want to check it out.)

The other potential candidate for pulling a professional blue-screen or green-screen key is Color Difference Key, which like Keylight is available as part of After Effects Professional. It uses an old and straightforward method of comparing the primary color being keyed (blue or green) against the other two color channels and using whichever channel offers the greatest difference to create the matte. This is similar to how optical keyers operate, although they do it photochemically, and how mattes were created in the earliest days of digital compositing—say, on *Terminator 2*. If you want to try it, follow the directions under "Applying the Color Difference Key" in the online Effects Help.

The next chapter offers assistance for situations where keying can't do the job, or can't do everything, and rotoscoping is necessary.

Rotoscoping and Paint

It's a small world, but I wouldn't want to paint it.

—Steven Wright

Rotoscoping and Paint

So, you've gritted your teeth, girded your loins, and opened up the rotoscoping chapter. There's no way to paint an utterly pretty picture, so to speak, of the task you face: Rotoscoping and paint tools are generally a last resort, employed when there is no other way to fix your matte. Rotoscoping is the art of fixing a shot frame by frame, generally using masks. Cloning and filling using paint tools are variations on this task.

To compound matters, After Effects did not gain its fame as a rotoscoping tool. You *can* get good results with the program, but its interface and tools aren't set up expecting rotoscoping to be your main task, as they are in such dedicated programs as Curious gFx Pro or the no-longer-updated Pinnacle Commotion.

Although sometimes you just can't get around having to clean up footage by hand in After Effects, it's often not as bad as you think if you follow a few basic guidelines:

▶ **Ascertain that rotoscoping is definitely necessary.** Novices and even pros sometimes will bite the bullet too quickly and assume it's time for frame-by-frame work without looking at other ways to break down the problem at hand. Specifically, make sure that these other tools won't help at least part of your problem:

  ▶ Keying. See Chapter 6, "Color Keying," for more on using luma mattes (including matting footage with itself), color keys, and difference mattes.

  ▶ Tracking. See Chapter 8, "Effective Motion Tracking," for more on the many ways to track in selections. Paint, by the way, is fully trackable.

▶ **Keep it simple.** This is the number one piece of advice for any rotoscoping the world over. If you're articulating a mask, do it with as few points as possible. When keyframing that mask, use as few keyframes as possible.

▶ **Paint is a last resort.** It is very hard to re-create realism with paint tools, and they will always be slower than masks. Assume that paint is an option only when you can't achieve a similar result with a mask. There are, of course, exceptions, such as cases in which you can easily track a paint stroke, and cases in which you're rapidly painting holes in an alpha channel.

▶ **Review constantly at full speed.** Don't waste time heading down the wrong road. Carefully assess your footage via a RAM preview every few frames, and determine if your approach is working. If it's not, be prepared to switch tactics.

▶ **Combine strategies.** Effective rotoscoping may employ a mixture of keying (whether color keying or a *hi-con matte*), tracking, animated masks, and paint. Start with the one that protects the most crucial edges, and work your way down to the cruder stuff.

With these guidelines in mind and a solid grasp of the fundamentals of creating selections (remember Chapter 3, "Selections: The Key to Compositing"), you're ready to consider some rotoscoping specifics.

Articulated Mattes

I've said it before, and I'm saying it again here: When animating, or *articulating*, mattes, keep it simple. All of the strategies offered here are for setting up and animating your mattes with as few steps as possible. Not only will this save you time in setup, you'll have fewer elements to fix if something goes wrong. Each new edit you keyframe introduces the possibility for more error. Focus on staying simple.

The first question to decide when starting a roto job is whether you want to mask in the Composition window or in the Layer window. The advantages of the Composition

NOTES

A *hi-con*, or *high-contrast matte*, is created by taking luminance data from an image—typically one or all of its color channels—and raising the contrast to create a luminance matte, typically to hold out areas of the same image. Chapter 6 explores this process in greater depth.

window are that you can see the layer in the composition and that it updates live as you work. This approach, however, does have several potential pitfalls:

▶ On a large scene you may have to wait for the screen to redraw for each point you draw.

▶ If the layer you are masking has been transformed, particularly rotated in 3D, you may find it difficult to edit a mask cleanly.

▶ You may need to select and lock all of the other layers to be sure that you're editing the correct layer, particularly if you're creating more than one mask.

▶ As you create the mask, the masked areas disappear, which can make it impossible to draw complex shapes.

▶ You lose some of the useful selection tools that exist only in the Layer window.

I could go on, but by now, you have probably guessed that opening the Layer window is generally preferable for creating masks. Tweaking mask points in the Composition window is often useful, but I recommended this only as a secondary approach. If you start to create a mask in the Composition window and realize you're in trouble, you can go to the timeline and double-click the layer; your mask will remain live in the Layer window, ready for you to continue drawing and editing wherever you left off.

The Layer window includes a couple of important pull-down menus you should be aware of: View and Target. You select your display mode from the View menu (**Figure 7.1**), choosing Masks, Anchor Point Path, or any effect you might have applied to this layer. Keep it set to Masks (the default) to be able to edit masks in this window. If Anchor Point Path is selected, you may be unable to edit your masks. If you choose None or any effect, your masks will disappear altogether.

Beside the View menu is a Render check box; with a mask selected, disable it if you want to see the full frame source of your footage without disabling a mask (**Figure 7.2**).

Figure 7.1 The View menu specifies what is active in the Layer window.

Figure 7.2 The Render check box, if unchecked, disables whatever is selected in the View menu.

The Target menu resides along the bottom bar of the Layer window (**Figure 7.3**) and does one thing. It enables you to select a target mask to replace if you draw (or paste) in a new mask. This would seem to be a boon for rotoscoping, allowing you to draw in a new mask at any time, but there's a gotcha: The first vertex of the mask shape (which you can control) and the direction in which its points are numbered (which you can't) must match the target's.

RotoBeziers

An invention unique to After Effects among Adobe applications, RotoBezier shapes are great for creating a mask that has to change over time because they are much simpler than Bezier shapes (discussed in Chapter 3). Fewer controls, theoretically at least, mean less ability to inadvertently create the pops and bubbles (also known as *boiling* mattes) that can send your rotoscoping job in the wrong direction (**Figure 7.4**).

There's only one problem: RotoBeziers can look really, really wrong while you're in the midst of setting them up. If this is a problem, you can even try initially setting up your masks as Beziers and then switch them to RotoBeziers for animating. To use RotoBeziers from the start, choose

Figure 7.3 Choose a mask from the Target menu and start drawing a new mask (or paste in a mask shape). The target mask shape will be replaced.

The first vertex of the mask is slightly larger than all of the rest. If you're having trouble matching an animation between shapes and need to specify it, context-click on the mask in the Layer window and select Set First Vertex from the resulting menu. More on First Vertex in the Morphing section of this chapter.

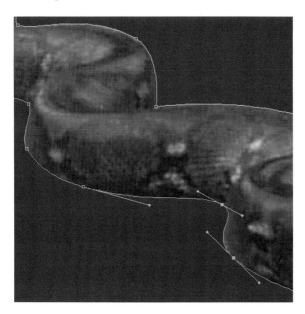

Figure 7.4 With moving footage, Bezier shapes are prone to crimping; managing the length of the handles can lead to error.

the Pen tool (**G** key selects it, pressing **G** repeatedly toggles through the associated variations) and check the Roto-Bezier box that appears in the Tools menu. To switch a mask shape from Bezier to RotoBezier after, or even while, creating it, context-click on the shape and look for the RotoBezier toggle halfway down the list (**Figure 7.5**).

In RotoBezier mode, try drawing a mask around an object. If possible, choose something that has a combination of curved edges and corners. For now, don't worry about how well the mask conforms to the edge, just try following this one instruction: Place a point at the center of any curve and on any corner you can perceive (**Figure 7.6**). As using Beziers did, this takes practice, so don't worry. The mask isn't initially going to look right until you adjust tension on the points.

Okay, now how do you edit this RotoBezier? The literal key to your success is the Alt/Option key. After you've drawn your final point, keep the Pen tool and all of the mask points selected and hold down **Alt/Option**. You will see a double-ended arrow appear. This is the Adjust Tension pointer. Dragging it to the left increases tension (counter-intuitive, but you get used to it quickly). Try this, and all of your points become corners (**Figure 7.7**). Now slide it in

Figure 7.5 There are lots of useful options tucked away in the Mask context menu, including the ability to lock and hide other masks, to close the shape, and to set the first vertex for use with such features as Smart Mask Interpolation and the Reshape tool.

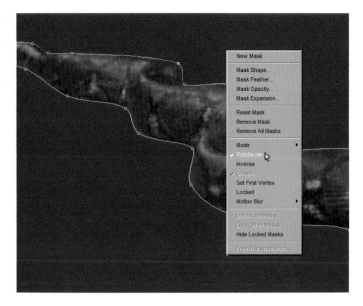

the opposite direction, and all of the points seem to have had their Bezier handles extended to the limits.

Although it does help dispel the myth that Beziers are easier for shapes that consist mostly of corners, dragging the Adjust Tension pointer is not how you will edit Roto-Beziers in most cases. Instead, after laying down the initial points of a RotoBezier mask, deselect it (**Control+Shift+A/Cmd+Shift+A**) and then Alt-drag the Pen tool on each point that needs its tension adjusted.

TIP

If the Selection tool (**V**) is active, use **Ctrl+Alt** (**Cmd+Option**) to activate the Adjust Tension pointer.

Figure 7.6 Your first pass with Roto-Beziers should be fast and will have inaccuracies. Just place a point at the apex of each curve you find, as well as at each corner. The next step is to tighten or loosen individual points.

Figure 7.7 Contrast all RotoBezier points at full tension and no tension (inset) to see how easy it is to adjust. Generally you will adjust points one or two at a time, however, not all at once.

Figure 7.8 You can use the Add Vertex tool (one of the Pen tool's modes) simply to select an existing point, without creating a new one. This means that you can always work with the Pen tool active, using the G key to cycle through its variations.

You can freely add or subtract points where needed by toggling the Pen tool (**G** key; look for the pen cursor to add a plus or minus sign beside it). With the Pen tool in Add mode you can also simply select a point by clicking on it, and deselect a point by Shift-clicking on it. This means that you never have to switch to another tool—a big advantage over Beziers (**Figure 7.8**).

But the thing you probably still don't like about Roto-Beziers is that the shape is so dissatisfying when you first lay in your points. So now that you're used to the basics of how RotoBeziers work, try drawing another mask this way: When you place a point on a corner, before moving on to draw the next point, Alt/Option-drag to the left on the corner point. Voila: It's already a corner, and your shape is much closer to final on the first pass (**Figure 7.9**). As you become more skilled with RotoBeziers you may even become adept at preselecting other tensions, although it's not necessary.

Or you can just draw the initial shape as a Bezier, if you prefer that, and consider context-clicking to change it to RotoBezier once you're done if you think you're going to want to animate that way. The real advantages of RotoBeziers show up when you animate them; you take advantage of their ability to resolve transitions with fewer variables than Beziers.

Strategies for Complex Shapes

Whether you've been won over to RotoBeziers for creating animated masks or not, the strategies for masking a complex moving shape are largely the same. Here are the main points:

1. Start with whatever matte you can pull to keep as much of the edges as you can. If no color key is possible, carefully examine all three channels of the footage for the one with the greatest contrast and pull a hi-con matte.

2. Narrow down the work area to just the section you need for your shot. Do not rotoscope even one frame more than you need.

TIP

Although each new mask keeps the same color as its predecessor by default, your life will be made easier with overlapping mattes if you give each one its own color, and if you choose colors that are easy to see against your source. In the Timeline window, select the masked layer and press **M** to reveal its masks, then click on the colored square beside each mask to edit its color in the user interface.

Figure 7.9 While drawing a Roto-Bezier shape, you can add a corner on the fly. Before moving on to the next point, Alt-drag (Option-drag) to the left to tighten the corner point. Draw the next point or two, and you see clearly that you have a corner and that your shape is already more accurate.

Figure 7.10 One key to working quickly is to intentionally create overlapping, separate mask shapes for different parts of your masked area that you know will move independently of one another. As a guideline, if any one shape has more than 20 or so points, you'll have difficulty retaining accuracy over time.

3. Use multiple overlapping masks instead of a single mask on a complex, moving, organic shape (**Figure 7.10**).

4. Go through the clip, and block in the major keyframes for a given shape. This will be the point at which a change of direction, speed, or shape begins or ends.

5. Start a mask on the frame on which you can draw it with the fewest points, and add points as needed to progressively more complex frames. Be prepared to break down the shot as much as necessary so that each of your masks describes only one part of the shape, and *each shape stays simple.* Stay under a dozen points if you can.

Block in and refine the first shape, then refine as necessary. Check the result at full speed against a contrasting background, just as you do with color keys. Then move on to the next shape.

In some cases, you can finish the matte this way. In other cases, you'll be left with a few stray holes in your matte here and there that you can go back and clean up with paint strokes. The process for working with paint is detailed in the next section; first, take a look at some of the other strategies at your disposal for masking and evaluate their effectiveness.

CLOSE-UP

Working Quickly

Here are some tips for working more efficiently with masks:

▶ The **G** key activates the Pen tool and cycles through its modes to add and subtract mask points.

▶ **Alt/Option** activates the Adjust Tension slider, if the Pen tool is active.

▶ **Ctrl+Shift+A** deselects the active mask; **Ctrl+A** activates all masks.

▶ The **V** key activates the Selection tool. To switch a mask to Translate mode, double-click it with this tool; your mask will transition to Free Transfer mode and be outlined by a gray box with a center that you can offset for rotation and scaling.

▶ With the Selection tool active, context-click on a mask for quick access to most of its editable properties.

▶ If you have a scroll wheel on your mouse, scrolling with the Layer window active zooms in and out of frame. Holding down the spacebar activates the Hand tool for fast panning around the frame.

▶ To replace a Mask shape, select the shape from the Layer window's Target menu and start drawing a new one; whatever you draw replaces the previous shape, creating a Mask Shape keyframe if the stopwatch is enabled. Beware: The first vertex point of the two shapes may not match, creating strange in-between frames. To set the first vertex point, context-click on the mask.

Working Around Limitations

At the opening of the chapter I came right out and admitted that After Effects is not most artists' first choice as a dedicated rotoscoping tool. This is not a generalized complaint or simply a matter of taste: Other programs' masking tools perform useful things that are impossible to do with After Effects 6.5. This section will identify some of those holes and focus on the strategies that can help you make the best of the situation. For example

▶ There is no way to apply a tracker directly to an After Effects mask, let alone track individual mask points. That doesn't mean there's no way to track in a mask selection, however.

▶ You can't translate a mask the way you would a layer, by selecting all of the keyframes you want to translate and performing the move; After Effects applies the move to the current keyframe only. The workarounds are similar to those for tracking.

▶ After Effects lacks the ability to specify whether a feather is applied to the inside or outside of a mask, nor can you vary feather settings on a per vertex basis (**Figure 7.11**).

Figure 7.11 All of the motion blur in this shot is left to right, so the ideal mask for the front of this truck would have heavy feathering on the right edge and none on top. Because After Effects lacks per-vertex mask feather settings, however, you have to handle this with two masks—not so bad in this case because the motion is highly predictable.

▶ Adding points to an animated mask has no adverse effect on other keyframes applying to that mask; the mask retains its shape. Deleting points, however, deforms the other keyframed versions of the mask. Avoid deleting points on a mask animation at all costs. Always start by keyframing the simplest shape, with the fewest points, and work your way up to the most complex.

▶ There is no dedicated morphing tool in After Effects. The elements to do a morph, however, exist in the program.

In the following sections, you'll explore the above points in depth.

Tracking and Translating

If you cannot apply a tracker directly to a mask, even using expressions, what are your alternatives? The next chapter will concentrate on successful tracking, so here I'll focus on simply getting set up.

One workaround that is effective in limited cases is to stabilize the layer, pre-compose it into a composition large enough not to crop the result, and mask the stabilized element; you would then reapply the stabilization by linking Position keyframes to the stabilized Anchor Point either via expressions or a simple copy and paste. This might simplify matters when the element being rotoscoped is itself relatively static but the camera is moving; however, it would not work so well if the element is moving around enough to generate substantial motion blur. Really, it's just an idea to keep in the back of your mind that might be useful once in a great while.

More likely, you will have luck tracking in a mask when articulating its points with the track isn't so important. One example is tracking an element with a solid surface that doesn't change shape. The workaround in this case is to use the masked layer as a track matte and track the transforms of that. The tracked layer would carry the mask with it and then be applied to the alpha of the same layer (**Figure 7.12**).

TIP

In General Preferences, there is a preference, on by default, to preserve a constant vertex count when editing masks. Leave this on to prevent inadvertent popping of extra vertices and awkward tweening around missing vertices. But in cases where in-betweening is not an issue (presumably because you're creating a mask on every frame), you can consider unchecking this preference.

Figure 7.12 if you're creating quick holdout masks of items that don't change shape, such as the windows of this car, you can set the masked frame to be a separate layer and apply your track to that, then use the result as an alpha track matte. It's somewhat of a kludge, but it can be helpful (especially when creating garbage mattes, as seen in the next chapter).

NOTES

It is possible to apply a tracker to a mask point using scripting, but I've never heard of anyone trying to design a script to do it in any useful way. One problem is that the user interface is beyond what is readily possible with a script, because you would want to be able to apply an arbitrary number of tracks to an arbitrary number of points.

This same not-very-pretty workaround can also get you out of a tight spot in which you have dozens of mask keyframes that simply need to be offset, scaled, or rotated. Duplicate the masked layer and set it as an alpha track matte, offsetting the track matte layer instead of each individual mask keyframe. Here's where you're truly out of luck, however: If only one or some subset of the points of your mask needs to be offset, there is simply no way to get that edit to ripple through all instances of that mask point. Features for future versions, perhaps.

Auto-trace

Wouldn't it be great if there were a tool in After Effects that would track masks for you? The good news is there is. The bad news is the cases in which it would be useful are cases in which you should be pulling high-contrast luminance mattes instead. The further bad news is that the process is much slower and more cumbersome than using the techniques from Chapter 6 to create a hi-con matte.

Here's the problem: Auto-trace is a threshold tool that looks either at overall luminance or a specific color channel. You set the threshold (which you can guess reasonably intelligently by sampling pixels using your cursor and the Info palette in Percent 0-100 mode. Next, add a pixel tolerance setting (whole values only), and then let Auto-trace work its magic (**Figure 7.13**). The result is an arbitrary number of masks, each describing a single area that meets the criteria. Over the course of the shot, some of these masks will reshape, some will disappear, and some new ones will appear.

It ends up being a pretty unwieldy result, albeit cool for the motion graphics designers who want to play with those masks. For effects work, however, it's largely pointless compared to trackable mask points, which After Effects lacks.

Masking Motion Blur

Motion blur happens. That's a good thing; it's a natural artifact of seeing on object in motion captured over a short period of time, and on moving footage it reinforces the persistence of vision required to make a series of still frames look like a moving image (when in fact, a moving image is always just a series of stills). But masking motion

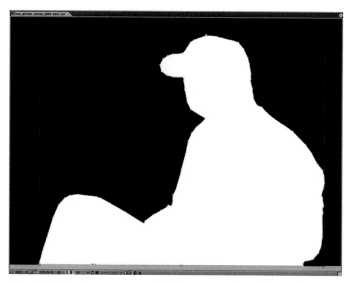

Figure 7.13 For the most success with Auto-trace, apply it to footage that is already high-contrast, such as this keyed matte, which was created with a 50% threshold and a two-pixel blur. Even this clean a result will chatter over time, however, but if you ever find yourself needing a vector shape based on a high-contrast image or alpha channel, this is a way to get it.

blur would seem to be something of a nightmare, as its edges defy careful observation.

Well, true, it's not easy by any means, particularly if the masked object is also articulated—a bird flying through frame, for example. Remember to carefully evaluate whether you can pull any kind key or hi-con matte on a blurred element to get all of those lovely edges before you get out the masking tools.

You can even evaluate whether the blurred element is really enhancing your scene. (Hopefully, we're not talking about the starring element of your shot.) Because you didn't shoot it on a proper color matte, maybe you'd be better off eliminating the element from your scene.

Otherwise, there is one thing to think about. Masks respect the motion blur settings of the composition; a masked element in motion will have motion blurred edges. That means you have a chance of matching the motion blur with a mask whose contours would fit the shape of the object if it were stationary (**Figure 7.14**). To make the mask work with the moving element is a matter of getting the composition's Shutter Angle and Shutter Phase settings right. For details on doing that, see Chapter 2, "The Timeline."

Figure 7.14 Don't forget that putting a rotoscope mask in motion allows motion blur to come along for the ride, simplifying a seemingly difficult masking situation, as was shown in **Figure 7.11**.

This will probably leave you with edge problems that you will have to cleverly conceal, whether by choking, further blurring the edges, forcing them to the background color, and so on.

Morphing

Let's talk about morphing—that's right, that craze of the early '90s. Trivia question: What now major studio raised its profile by pulling off the morphing effects in Michael Jackson's "Black or White" video? Hint: It raised its profile quite a bit further a decade later with *Shrek*.

Thing is, morphing could conceivably come in handy, without being so blatant and obvious. Think of it as a concealing tool, useful when you don't want anyone to notice a transition between two objects or even a transition between one object and itself at a different point in time. Or heck, go crazy morphing together members of your extended family to see if you look anything like the result.

What exactly is a morph? It is, quite simply, a combination of two warps and a dissolve. Given two images, each with a corresponding shape (say, the features of the face), you warp the source image's face shape to the face shape of the target, warp the target from something that matches the source to its face shape, fading the target in over the source.

After Effects has no tool called Morph, and for a long time, the program offered no good way to pull off this effect. In After Effects Professional, you now can use Reshape, a tool that lays the groundwork for simple morphs. You can then build these up into more complex morphs, with separate individual transitions occurring within the overall transition.

Using Reshape to Morph

Unfortunately, creating a morph with Reshape is nowhere near a one-button process, and the simple formula I just mentioned will not provide enough detail for you to be successful. This book generally steers away from step-by-step recipes in favor of helping you solve larger problems

Figure 7.15 This is me and my doppelgänger, and that awkward phase in which Jekyll turns into Hyde.

creatively, but in this case, it's easy to get confused. Let me walk you through the creation process, using a demonstration of my own resemblance transitioning to that of my evil twin (**Figure 7.15**):

1. Start with two elements that have some basic similarities in their relative position of features. The subtler the distortion required, the more you can get away with.

2. Isolate the two elements you will be morphing from their backgrounds to prevent contamination. If you're working with elements shot against a blue screen, key them out first. Otherwise, mask them. In my example, I have created masks for each layer.

3. Ascertain that the two layers are the same size in the X and Y dimensions and as closely aligned as possible. If they are not, pre-compose one layer to match the other. *This step is important because it will make matching the source and target masks much, much simpler.* Name the two layers Source and Target (as they are in the example) if it helps you follow along.

4. Choose matching sections from your two clips for the duration of your transition (say, 24 frames). If you have still elements, no worries. The closer your moving elements are to still, the more likely you'll get a clean result.

5. Draw a mask around the boundary that is going to morph in both layers. Be as precise as possible, erring to the inside if at all (**Figure 7.16**). This could be the masks created in step 2, if you created masks there. It does not have to be active; if you don't need it to mask out the background, you can set it to None. Rename each mask something descriptive like outer (the name used in my example).

6. Create a mask around the area of the Source layer that is the focus of the morph. In my example, it is the facial features: the eyes, nose, and mouth (**Figure 7.17**). Make this mask as simple as you can; use RotoBeziers and as few points as will work to outline the features in question.

Figure 7.16 The outline of each head has been carefully masked. These two masks do not have to correspond to one another; they are defining the boundary for the Reshape effect. You don't want to pull bits of background into your morph.

7. Set the mask mode to None; this mask is your first shape, you don't need it to influence the layer at all; you will use it for the Reshape effect only. Give it a name (mine is called "me").

8. Copy this mask shape and paste it in the Target layer. If the two layers are the same dimensions, it should be an identical size and position as it was in the Source layer. The name does not copy with the mask, so you can restore the name (me).

9. Duplicate the mask. Give it a different color and re-name it. In my case, I called the mask "it."

10. First scale and rotate, then if necessary move individual points (as little as possible!) so that the it mask surrounds the equivalent area of the Target layer that me does of the source: in my example, the eyes, nose, and mouth.

11. Copy the resulting it mask shape, and paste it to the Source layer to create a new, third mask. Restore the name "it" for this mask. (Don't ask me why names don't copy with masks—perhaps someone should report it as a bug.)

12. You now have three masks for each of the Source and Target layers. Now apply the Reshape effect to each layer.

13. Starting with the Source layer, set the Source Mask (me), the Destination Mask (it), and the Boundary Mask (outer). Set Elasticity to Liquid (you can experiment with other settings later if need be). Set Interpolation to Smooth.

14. At the first frame of the morph transition, still in Source, set a keyframe for Percent (at the default, 0.0%, meaning no reshaping is occurring). At the last frame, set Percent to, you guessed it, 100.0%. Now sit back and wait for the gruesome transformation. Don't worry about how it looks yet.

15. Repeat steps 12 and 13 for the Target layer, with the following changes: Set Source Mask to it and Destination Mask to me. The Percent keyframes should be set to 0.0 at the *last* frame of the transition (where it is keyframed to 100.0 on the Source layer) and, you guessed it, 100.0 at the first frame.

16. You've created the warps, now you just need the cross dissolve. Set an Opacity keyframe for Target at the last frame of the transition (leaving it at the default 100.0%), and then add a 0.0% Opacity keyframe at the first frame.

TIP

If at any point during setup it becomes difficult to interact with the UI because After Effects is taking so long updating a frame, enable Caps Lock on your keyboard to prevent any further frame rendering until you're done.

You should now be ready to preview. The preview may take a long time to build the first frame; subsequent frames write much more quickly, so be patient. The main question you must now resolve is whether the features lined up properly; if not, you must adjust the source and destination mask shapes accordingly. I'm sorry I can't be more specific, but for example, if the eyes are too low to match the target halfway through the animation, then dragging the destination mask (it in my example) upward a few pixels in the Composition window, for both layers, should help.

At this point my example is looking good in terms of the face transition (**Figure 7.17**), but, of course, I've made life hard on myself by transitioning from a head of one size to a larger one, and the edges just kind of fade in. Therefore—and this is where it can get really complicated– I add a second morph, using the same steps as before, but all new masks.

Why complicated? Why new masks? These two questions are interrelated. If you set a second Reshape effect, the key is that you don't want it to influence the result of the first Reshape effect whatsoever. Therefore, this time your Boundary mask is going to be the boundary of the object *minus the area covered by the original source and destination masks* (it and me). Likewise, my new shapes cover the ears and top of the head, but avoid the area of the previous masks completely (**Figure 7.18**).

TIP

The Correspondence Points property in Reshape can be raised from its default of 1 to make the distortion more precise (and in some cases less twisted). That's cool, but the downside is that it makes this slow effect even slower. Better to try to simplify what you're attempting to do with your masks and fix things there, and try raising this value only as a last resort.

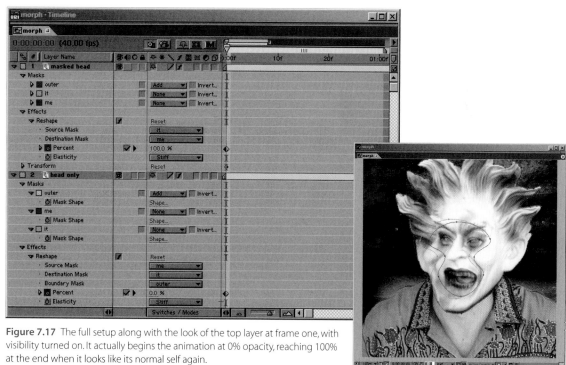

Figure 7.17 The full setup along with the look of the top layer at frame one, with visibility turned on. It actually begins the animation at 0% opacity, reaching 100% at the end when it looks like its normal self again.

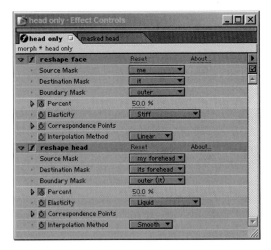

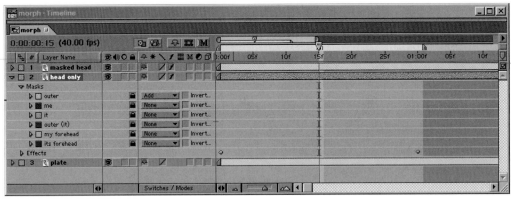

Figure 7.18 The full setup to do more than one morph on a single image is pretty gnarly. Renaming masks and effects to specify which is which, with individual colors and judicious use of mask locks and the Caps Lock key, can help a lot.

Because I know this is complicated, I've included the source project and the final result as projects on the book's CD-ROM. Please do me a favor and don't show the results to my mom. Now a quick look at something I left out (by having you duplicate the Source and Destination masks rather than draw them from scratch).

First Vertex

The Reshape tool relies on a concept that was touched upon already, but is now very significant: that of the First Vertex that exists on every mask. Look closely at any mask you draw, and you will see that one vertex on the mask is larger than all the others. This is the First Vertex.

Reshape relies on the First Vertex to determine which point on the source mask corresponds to which on the destination mask. I had you duplicate the source mask to create the destination mask, because this is the easiest way to satisfy two criteria that are essential for a smooth Reshape effect:

▶ Placement of the First Vertex corresponds on both masks

▶ Each mask has the same number of points

If either of these criteria is not fulfilled, Reshape will do some not very pretty things to try and compensate. I mention this just in case you try to customize your own mask transitions and don't like what you see. The easiest approach will always be to duplicate the source mask and edit it, keeping the same number of points. The next easiest method would be to draw a new mask with the same number of points, drawn in the same direction (clockwise or counterclockwise), and set to the First Vertex where you need it (by context-clicking on the mask and choosing Select First Vertex from the menu).

Worrying about this stuff is not fun, which is why I avoided the need to do so in the previous section.

Paint and Cloning

Paint is generally your last resort, and for a simple reason. Paint work is typically more painstaking and more likely to show flaws than approaches involving masks. Of course, there are exceptions. The ability to track clone brushes gives paint work a huge advantage over masks, which are not so easy to track.

Other tasks are just plain tedious no matter how you look at them, but they are sometimes necessary or inevitable. Plate restoration and *dust busting* are entry-level jobs at many effects facilities; there's no way to get around them on shows whose shooting conditions and standards demand them.

For effects work, you will use the paint controls in After Effects in two predominant ways:

▶ Cleaning up an alpha channel mask by painting directly to it in black and white. This approach is best suited for touching up animated masks.

▶ Using the Clone Stamp tool. This is for cases in which overwriting part of your frame with other source is most effective.

Assuming you're using the Professional version, you're lucky. Prior to version 6.0, paint was a convoluted, tacked-on afterthought in After Effects. It was available only via a licensed effect that was so counterintuitive that most users had to re-read the manual each (infrequent) time they used it. Now the brush tools are more robust and fully integrated with the application.

Paint Fundamentals

Activate any of the three brush-based tools in the Tools palette—Brush, Clone Stamp, or Eraser—and the palette that contains the Paint and Brush Tips tabs automatically appears (**Figures 7.19a, b,** and **c**).

The After Effects tools are designed with a user interface and functionality patterned after the brushes in Photoshop, but there are a couple of important differences between

Figures 7.19a, b, and c Use the keyboard shortcut **Ctrl+B** (**Cmd+B**) to cycle through the three basic brush tools (7.19a) and open the Paint and Brush Tips tabs (7.19b and c).

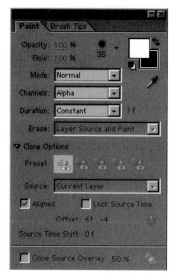

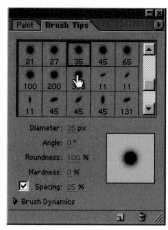

After Effects brushes and those in Photoshop. After Effects offers fewer customizable options for its brushes (you can't, for example, create your own brush tips) and fewer UI shortcuts for editing brushes on the fly, so don't expect all those nifty tricks you've learned with keyboard shortcuts in Photoshop to work here. Also, After Effects brushes are vector based, while those in Photoshop are raster based. This is generally a good thing, as it makes all paint edits in After Effects editable after you've already drawn with them.

Say that you have an alpha channel that needs some touching up (**Figure 7.20**). With the Brush tool active, go to the Paint palette and switch Channels to Alpha if it is not there already (this palette remembers the last mode you used); the foreground and background color swatches in the palette will switch to grayscale, and you can switch them to black and white by clicking the tiny black-over-white squares just below the swatches (**Figure 7.21**). To see what you are painting, switch the view to the Alpha Channel as well (**Alt+4/Option+4**).

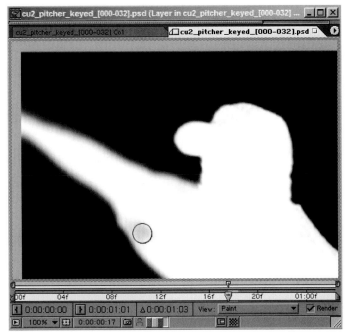

Figure 7.20 To touch up an alpha channel matte, select Alpha in the Channels drop-down menu (in the Paint palette) and then make the alpha channel visible (**Alt/Option+4**).

Figure 7.21 Ever wonder what those little squares are for? They reset the foreground and background colors. To swap white and black, just as in Photoshop, press the X key; this only works when the Paint palette is visible.

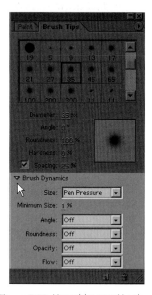

Figure 7.22 Hey tablet users! Look at all the useful brush settings tucked away under the Brush Dynamics twirly arrow at the bottom of the Brush Tips palette!

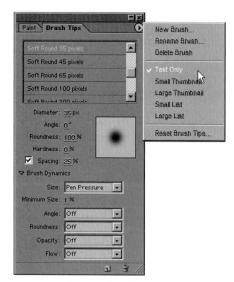

Figure 7.23 If you use brushes a lot, you may find it helpful to make your own and list them by name.

Here are the other things you need to know to make use of the paint tools:

▶ Brush-based tools operate only in the Layer window.

▶ Brushes include a Mode setting (analogous to Transfer Modes). For alpha channels, you'll almost certainly leave this at the default of Normal.

▶ If you use a tablet, you can use the Brush Dynamics settings, at the bottom of the Brush Tips palette, to set how the pressure, angle, and stylus wheel of your pen affect strokes (**Figure 7.22**).

▶ Brushes are adjusted in the Brush Tips palette, where you can either select a preset brush or customize your own by inputting numerical settings for diameter, hardness (which affects the amount of feather on the edge), and so on.

▶ The Duration setting and the frame where you begin painting are crucial.

By default, the Duration setting in the Paint menu is set to Constant, which means that any paint stroke you create on this frame continues to the end of the layer. For cleaning up an alpha channel, this is typically not the setting you want, because you're presumably using paint only to catch stray holes in your matte here and there. The Single Frame setting confines your stroke to just the current frame on which you're painting, and the Custom setting allows you to enter the number of frames that the stroke will persist.

The other option, Write On, records your stroke in real time, re-creating the motion when you replay the layer; this stylized option is for such motion graphics tricks as hand-written script, and it does not seem to have much of an application for effects work, unless, of course, your effect is re-creating a signature.

You can access various display options available for brushes from the Brush Tips wing menu (**Figure 7.23**). Here you can add, rename, or delete brushes, as well. You can also do this using the small icons at the bottom of the palette and by double-clicking the brush in question.

For an alpha channel, you typically work with the Brush tool in Single Frame mode, looking only at the alpha channel (**Alt+4**/**Option+4**) and progressing frame by frame through the shot (press **Page Down**). You can switch as needed between painting white into the foreground and black into the background; just use the **X** key to swap foreground/background colors with the Brush tool active.

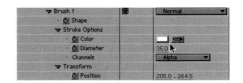

Figure 7.24 The real benefit of nondestructive vector paint strokes is how many properties each one contains that can be edited after the fact.

You may end up with dozens of paint strokes in your timeline, each of which contains numerous options that you can edit after the fact (**Figure 7.24**). If you simply want to select a stroke to edit, delete, or redo it, use your Selection tool (**V**) to directly select it in the Layer or Composition window rather than hunting it down in the Timeline window. You can drag it into place or delete it and start over.

Cloning Fundamentals

The benefit of cloning is that you get all of the grain and other organic peculiarities that go along with using moving footage as a source. There are many cases in which it will be the quickest and most effective solution, particularly if you are cloning out a trackable area of the frame (more on this in the next section).

Cloning in After Effects opens you to several possibilities beyond what would be possible with, say, the same tool in Photoshop. Not only can you clone pixels from a different region of the same frame, you can clone from a different frame of a different clip at a different point in time (**Figure 7.25**). In Commotion, the tool that could do this was christened the Superclone tool; the After Effects implementation is actually more straightforward in many cases:

▶ **To clone from an offset area of the same frame:** This works just the same as in Photoshop. Choose a brush, Alt/Option-click on the area of the frame you wish to sample, then paint over the area to be replaced. Remember that by default, Duration is set to Constant. If you want to clone for only one frame, choose Single Frame; for a subset of frames, choose Custom.

TIP

The biggest downside to the paint tools is that you can do your painting in the Layer window only. To paint in the context of a comp, the Vector Paint effect remains useful, as it operates only in the Composition window. However, it does not include cloning. And beware: It's not always clear in the After Effects online help which is which if you search on paint, so if you're looking for particular information, you can be misled.

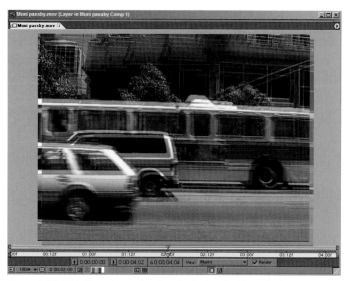

Figure 7.25 With Clone Source Overlay checked under Clone Options, you can see a preview of your clone source overlaid on the current frame. Click on the small spheres to the right of the check box, and the overlay is displayed in Difference mode, which makes for easy alignment of matching images. If initially this option doesn't seem to be taking effect, move your cursor into the frame of the Layer window to activate it.

▶ **To clone from an area of the same clip, offset in time:** The offset is specified in the Clone Options, and you enter the offset value in frames. Note that there is also an option for setting spatial offset, so if you want to clone from the exact same position at a different point in time, set the Offset to 0, 0 and change the Source Time.

▶ **To clone from a different clip:** The source from which you're cloning must be present in the same composition; if you don't want it to display in final output, make it a guide layer and, optionally, turn off its visibility in the timeline. Select the source from the pull-down menu under Clone Options. By default, cloning takes place from the same frame at the current comp time; use Source Time to specify an offset.

For the most part, cloning is just that straightforward, but of course, nothing about visual effects work is *always* straightforward.

Tricks and Gotchas

So, where can cloning trip you up? For example, say that offsetting the time or selecting a different layer causes the clone tool to attempt to sample beyond the last frame of the source clip. What happens? By default, After Effects automatically loops back to the first frame of the clip and keeps going. This is dangerous because you may not even have any idea it has occurred; it is an automatic, default setting.

This is one of several situations where you can get into trouble because of a temporal mismatch. Not only might you not have enough source frames for the target layer, your layers might have different frame rates, or you might want to sample from just one or just a few frames from the source clip.

You can take control of this process by editing the source clip. Time remapping is one potential way to solve these problems, allowing you to stretch a source clip or loop it the way you want to. If you want to sample only one or a few frames from the source, you can time remap it or you can do the even simpler thing: Shorten the layer to just the frame or frames you want to use as source, and take advantage of the automatic looping I referred to as "dangerous" a couple of paragraphs back.

What if your source is a different scale from what it should be for the target? Shockingly, even though temporal edits, including time remapping, in the source show up directly in the target, other types of edits—even simple translations or effects—do not. As always, the solution is to pre-compose with any scaling, rotation, motion tracking, or effects that you want to clone embedded in the subcomposition.

Finally, and perhaps even more shocking: Paint is an effect. Don't believe me? Apply a stroke or two and then take a peek in your Effects Control window. You'll see an effect called Paint with a single check box labeled Paint on Transparent, which causes only the strokes you've painted to show up for that layer.

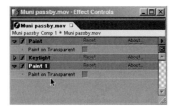

Figure 7.26 Paint strokes and effects are interleaved.

But there's an extra benefit to doing it this way: You can change the render order of your paint strokes relative to other effects. So, for example, you could do some cloning on your raw footage, then apply an image adjustment, and then add some other cloned strokes that are applied to the adjusted image, all on one layer, no need to precompose (**Figure 7.26**). To get the new paint strokes to appear in a new Paint effect instead of the previous one, however, you must actually apply the Paint effect before you start painting again.

But this means that you could conceivably touch up a bluescreen background, then apply a keyer, and then apply a second instance of Paint to touch up the resulting alpha channel.

Finally, to help you take control of this process of interleaving paint strokes and effects, note the View pull-down menu in the Layer window (**Figure 7.27**). It lists, in order, the paint and effects edits you've added to the layer. To see the layer with none of these applied, you can clear the Render box next to the pull-down, and to see a particular stage of the edit—after the first paint strokes, but before the effects, say—you can select a prior stage of the layer edits in the View menu, disabling the steps below it. These settings are for previewing only; they will not enable or disable the rendering of these items.

Tracking Strokes

One really cool thing about paint strokes is that they have their own editable properties. Not only can you change your mind about how they draw later on, which isn't useful as often as you might think, you can apply the motion tracker directly to a paint stroke.

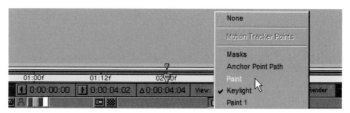

Figure 7.27 The Layer window's View pull-down menu is a useful method for working with interleaved paint strokes and effects.

Cases come up all the time where artists can save themselves a ton of work by attaching paint strokes to motion-tracked objects. However, to do so requires use not only of the tracker, which is covered in the next chapter, but also of basic expressions. Thus this topic is fully covered in Chapter 10, "Expressions," as an excellent example of a simple use of expressions and offsets; look at that chapter if you are dealing with a case where tracking in a cloned paint stroke would help you.

Wire Removal

Wire removal and rig removal are two terms often bandied about in the visual effects industry. Generally speaking, *wire removal* means painting out a wire on a blue-screen shot, a wire usually used to suspend an actor in mid-air. *Rig removal*, meanwhile, is even less glamorous: It's just garbage masking any equipment that showed up in frame.

Some rotoscoping applications have dedicated wire-removal tools, but in After Effects, you're on your own. However, wire removal need not be a painstaking process in After Effects simply because there's no dedicated tool for it. There are several approaches that could conceivably work; if the ends of the wire are trackable, you could track position and rotation and apply these to a null, which would be the parent of a masked element to replace the wire. More about tracking and applying tracks is found in the following chapter.

Rig removal is often trackable, because rigs don't move. The key is to make a shape that mattes out the rig, then apply that as a track matte to the foreground footage and track the whole matte.

Plate Restoration via Cloning

This is as nitty-gritty as rotoscoping gets. For various reasons, even on the highest budget visual effects film, footage digitizes with flaws visible on a frame-by-frame basis: Dust and scratches made their way onto the pristine master sometime between when it was shot and when it was digitized.

Most of these flaws, alas, will be corrected via frame-by-frame cloning, sometimes known as "dust busting." Large visual effects houses have teams dedicated to this work, a motley crew of mostly entry-level folks who strap on an iPod and lose themselves in the zen of cloning (or a good audio book). I mention this here not because it requires a different approach than what has been previously discussed, but only because neophytes do not always believe that such a job exists, let alone that it could be their entry level job at a major facility.

One final note about this work: Despite its apparent tedium, it's not all done with a single approach. In some cases, cloning with an offset will work. In other cases, you're better off masking out a part of the source to reveal the footage you want to replace by placing that clean version behind it. Never treat any task as utterly mind-numbing, because you might be cheating your brain out of an opportunity to help you think of a better way.

Conclusion

And so, like rain, into every effects artist's life a little rotoscoping must fall. The tools outlined here are mostly sufficient for the type of rotoscoping work that compositors will have to do. Dedicated rotoscope artists would likely choose software other than After Effects to ply their trade, but as long as rotoscoping is in your stock and trade, the After Effects tools will usually let you complete your shot without having to go find other software.

The next chapter completes the picture by adding motion tracking to your areas of expertise. As I mentioned earlier, you can combine motion tracking with rotoscoping as a shortcut around tedious tasks.

8

Effective Motion Tracking

Image courtesy of Tim Fink Productions.

Even if you're on the right track, you'll get run over if you just sit there.

—Will Rogers

Effective Motion Tracking

The After Effects tracker is a semi-automated solution for two-dimensional match moving and stabilization. Set up correctly, it allows you to click a button and get a result more refined than anything you could ever animate by hand. It can save you piles of time, too, such as the several months I spent hand match moving shots for Rebel Assault II using After Effects 2.0, which had no motion tracker whatsoever. It wasn't added until version 4.0, allowing me to learn everything I know about keyframes. But, having the tracker doesn't mean you get to click a button and put your feet up on the desk, George Jetson style.

First, you need to make sure you're using the tracker to best effect. Some of the most common ways people go wrong are

▶ Failing to choose good track points

▶ Misunderstanding how the tracker does its job, and not knowing when to change the default settings

▶ Giving up on tracks that seem to have gone wrong (although abandoning them is a good idea once you understand what may have gone wrong)

▶ Forgetting about motion blur

▶ Failing to realize all the different ways tracking data can be applied

This chapter will help you with all of the above and much more.

Once you've nailed down these essential techniques, you can move on to some elegant uses of the tracker, including

▶ Using the After Effects 3D camera as if it were a physical camera, matching objects you insert in the scene to the scene motion automatically

- Procedurally smoothing a camera move (as opposed to simply stabilizing a static shot)

- Using a simple expression to continue tracking an object that has moved offscreen

- Giving your effects three-dimensional depth even though After Effects does not support 3D objects

Don't forget, the tracker's uses go beyond those clearly spelled out in the Tracker Controls palette (which can always be revealed by choosing it in the Window menu, although it appears automatically upon applying a track).

The tracker is available only in After Effects Professional. If you are using After Effects Standard, skip ahead to the final section of this chapter, which focuses on importing 3D match moves from third-party software.

The Essentials

There's no point in learning about all the cool tricks you can perform with the tracker if you're still fighting it for a good basic track. If you still find your tracks going astray after doing everything according to the After Effects documentation, read on and don't despair. Just because it is automated doesn't mean that you don't have to come to a certain "understanding" with this feature set.

Tracking is a two step process: First, you set up and run the tracker, then you apply the tracking data thus created. Each step contains unique pitfalls. Once you learn to recognize them and take action, however, you can avoid them easily enough.

Choosing a Good Reference Point

There are trackers out there that don't require you to decide what to track (predominantly dedicated third-party 3D trackers, discussed later in this chapter). After Effects, however, relies on you to choose a reference point that will track effectively, and it is the most important choice you will make (**Figure 8.1**).

Make sure the feature you plan to track

- Contrasts in color, luminance, or saturation from the surrounding area

- Has defined edges that fit within the feature region

- Is identifiable throughout the shot

 If your target feature changes or even disappears as the shot progresses, just hang on. Later in the chapter, I'll give you strategies for dealing with this.

Figure 8.1 After Effects tracking is done by setting manual track points in the Layer window.

▶ Does not have to contend with similar distinct features within the search region at any point during the track

▶ Is close to the area where the tracked object or objects will be added

To find a good candidate for tracking, look for "corners" in your image—places where two edges meet. If you can get more than one corner into your feature region, so much the better. **Figures 8.2a**, **b**, and **c** show examples of this set of criteria.

Here's something to keep in mind as you set the search and feature regions: They don't have to be square! If the feature you want to track is wide and short, make the feature region wide and short. And if the motion of the shot is only in one direction—say, a left-to-right pan—then make the search region not only wider and barely taller than the feature region, but offset it to the right. The search region needs to include only the area where you think the feature region is likely to appear on the very next frame—no more, and certainly no less. Be generous when setting this region, but don't give the tracker any reason to search where it has no business looking (**Figure 8.4**).

Figures 8.2a, b, and c Here are shown excellent (8.2a), fair (8.2b), and poor (8.2c) candidates for track points. A high-contrast, clearly defined corner, such as that of the painted flag (a) is perfect as long as it stays in shot. The sun glint off the back of the spare tire (b) is also high-contrast with clearly defined edges, but if light conditions in the shot change, the track will no longer work. Although the region in the trees has enough contrast (c), there is way too little distinction between the patterns inside the feature region (the small center box) and the search region (the larger outer box).

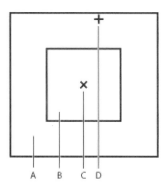 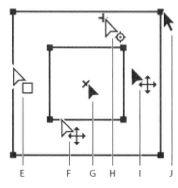

Figure 8.3 As this diagram from the After Effects documentation illustrates, knowing where to click when working with trackers can be elusive. Identified here are: **A.** Search region, **B.** Feature region, **C.** Keyframe marker, **D.** Attach point, **E.** Moves search region, **F.** Moves both regions, **G.** Moves entire track point, **H.** Moves attach point, **I.** Moves entire track point, **J.** Resizes region. Most useful (and most elusive if zoomed out) is F.

Figure 8.4 I happen to know that this shot tracks right to left, so I offset my search region (the outer box) to the left of the feature region (inner box). Customizing the track regions in this manner speeds up the track and reduces the margin of error considerably.

Figure 8.5 You typically have to zoom way in to see your controls. Here the tiny icon to the left shows where the attach point is being moved. This is handy when a better trackable feature is nearby, but not exactly where you want the track point to be.

Figure 8.6 The various available track types are accessed via the Tracker Controls palette.

No Good Reference Point in Sight

Sometimes you get lucky, and you find trackable features that are right in the area where the target layer is supposed to appear. It's almost like being able to return to the time and place where the scene was shot and place an object exactly where it was supposed to be.

Other times, however, you may not find very many trackable features of a shot, or your feature may exit the frame at an inconvenient moment (a solution to this is coming in the section called "Continuing a Track with Expressions"). For such cases, you could use an attach point, which is that little x in **Figure 8.5**. Although the attach point defaults to the center of the feature region, you can offset it anywhere in the frame.

Later on, however, I'm going to show you how to pretty much ignore the attach point by using nulls and parenting instead, which let you offset this point. This isn't how the documentation would have you do it, but it's much more flexible.

Optimizing Tracker Options

Prior to version 6, the After Effects tracker was tricky to use because the default settings were practically guaranteed not to produce a good track. Life is much better now. Thanks to new defaults, you can just click Play after you set your tracking regions and be assured of a good track.

Nevertheless, defaults will take you only so far. The tracker is packed with plenty of powerful options designed for specific scenarios that, sooner or later, you will encounter. Be prepared by getting to know the tracker's options now.

Typology

It's easy enough to get an idea of the types of tracks available in After Effects: Just have a look at the Track Type menu (**Figure 8.6**). But what exactly are the differences?

Stabilize and *Transform tracking* are very similar, until you are ready to apply them. At that point, click Edit Target, and the singular difference between them emerges. Stabilize tracks are always applied to the *anchor point of the tracked layer.* Transform tracks are applied to the *position of a layer other than the tracked layer.*

With Stabilize, the animated anchor point, which is the center of the image by default, works in opposition to Position. Increasing the anchor point's X value (assuming Position remains the same, which it does if you adjust the Anchor Point value in the timeline) moves the layer to the left, just as decreasing the Position value does.

Animating only the anchor point gives a certain advantage to Stabilize: For example, if you scale or rotate the layer at a later time, these transforms occur from the corrected (and now consistent) center of the footage. Also, you are free thereafter to edit or even animate the position of the layer without disrupting the tracking data.

As you will see, you can, and quite likely should, use Stabilize, exclusively, even when tracking footage. I'll get to how and why in a moment.

Corner Pin tracking is something else altogether—essentially a cheat to skew a rectangular source so that its four corners appear to be tracked in 3D space. This is not, however, 3D tracking in any sense. Rather than moving the target layer around in 3D, Corner Pin tracking applies data to a 2D layer via the Corner Pin plug-in. Think of replacing a billboard on the side of a moving bus (something you'll look at later in the chapter), and you get the idea.

There are two types of Corner Pin tracking. Both generate four points of data, one for each corner of the target layer, but Parallel Corner Pin does so with only three track points. This works as long your target is perfectly rectangular and remains so throughout the shot—a shot of a door, head-on, with the camera at a perpendicular angle, for example. In most cases, you will use Perspective Corner Pin (**Figure 8.7**).

One tricky thing about both types of Corner Pin tracking is that offsetting the track points tends not to work, particularly if there is any variation at all in scale. You pretty much have to track the actual corners of your target, therefore, and leave the keyframe markers right at the center, on those corners (**Figure 8.8**).

Figure 8.7 The basic Corner Pin setup. Corner Pin tracking is normally applied to a target layer with the same rough dimensions as the source. The results show up in the Corner Pin effect on that layer, which translates its corners to those in the tracked source.

Figure 8.8 Sometimes the corners you want to match don't make good track targets. You can offset them, as shown, but this can lead to trouble, particularly if the camera pushes or zooms in at all, in which case the offset will probably be wrong.

Finally, *Raw tracks* generate track data only, graying out the Edit Target button. What good is track data that isn't applied anywhere? It can be useful to drive expressions, or you can save it to apply it later. You can derive the same result by simply never clicking Edit Target; you still get the raw track data stored within the source layer (**Figure 8.9**).

Rotation and Scale

Stabilize and Transform tracks can also include rotation and scale data. This is straightforward enough: You use two track points instead of one. Because of the phenomenon of parallax, you must be sure these two points reside at the same depth in the scene as the item being tracked. In other words, you have to imagine where, in Z space, the object is going and track points that are at that relative depth, or your track will be way off. In such a case no bag of tricks—not offsets, not 3D extrapolation—is likely to help.

The big catch about Rotation and Scale is that they essentially never look right when first applied directly to a target layer, because the relationship to the actual layer you are tracking in is arbitrary. After Effects has no way of knowing

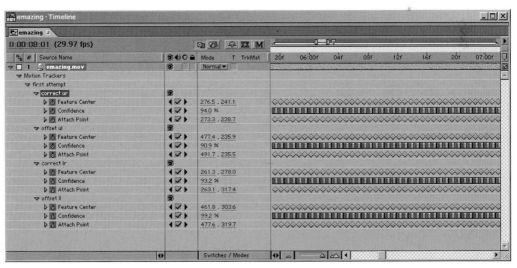

Figure 8.9 Every track generates raw data, whether you specify it as a Raw track or not. The data is stored under Motion Trackers for the tracked layer. As shown, you can rename the full track and individual points for future reference, which is handy on a difficult track for which you attempt multiple passes.

what the target layer's scale and rotation at any given frame should be, it can only get all the frames consistent with one another once one of them is correct.

So what do you do to correct for this? See the later section called "Using Nulls to Solve Transform Problems."

Another big tip about tracking rotation and scale: The fact that these are changing over time gives you nearly 100% certainty that you will want to go into the Motion Tracker Options palette and check Adapt Feature on Every Frame, which is like restarting the track on each and every frame. This might be a bad idea on a more static track because, theoretically at least, it adds a greater margin of error per frame, but I have often found turning it on delivers much better results.

Finally, perhaps the biggest tip of all: If things aren't going well tracking footage forward, try going to the end of the clip and tracking in reverse. Particularly when tracking an object moving away from the camera, working backward will prove far more effective, especially with Adapt Feature on Every Frame checked (**Figure 8.10**).

Confidence

Below the Adapt Feature check box you'll find a pull-down menu that allows you to work with After Effects' mysterious Confidence settings. Take a closer look at what shows up in the Timeline window after a track has been performed.

Lo and behold, in addition to data about the feature center (the center of the feature region) and the attach point, there is keyframe data labeled Confidence, a new feature as of 6.5. Twirl its arrow to reveal a graph of the confidence values and you may see some surprises (**Figure 8.11**).

What does this figure mean? It's an algorithm used to extrapolate the relative accuracy of a given track point according to pre-established criteria—which still doesn't explain much, without some frame as a reference. My experience is that good tracks tend to stay in the 80% to 90% region, and as soon as there is a major problem, confidence drops way off to 30% or less.

Figure 8.10 For tracking items that become more prominent later in the shot, try reverse tracking. The tracker does a much better job of tracking a large pattern as it gets smaller than the reverse.

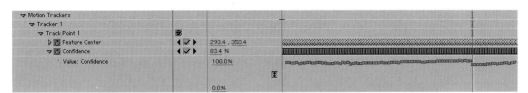

Figure 8.11 Twirl down this graph and you can easily see where the tracker's confidence has been shaken, so to speak. Just because a frame has low confidence doesn't mean there's a problem. This track had confidence values in the "healthy" 80% and 90% region. If you want to more easily see whether any of your values went below 80%, set the lower boundary of the Value graph to 80%.

You don't have to take a manual approach to checking confidence, however. The feature is designed to be used with a setting in the Motion Tracker Options dialog for what to do according to the Confidence amount (**Figure 8.12**).

This menu and the Confidence rating that accompanies it open a world of options for those of you wrestling with a wandering track. Adapt Feature below the default of 80% is a pretty good as a default. Look at a healthy motion track, and you'll see most of the confidence numbers are somewhere in the 90s and 80s, with the occasional inexplicable dip.

Other Options

The rest of the options in Motion Tracker Options (**Figure 8.13**) have to do with examining the footage in a different way. Instead of tracking a clip's luminance (the default), for example, you can track its RGB color values (for unique cases where you have contrasting colors of a similar luminance) or saturation (should you ever track a feature with extraordinarily high and low color saturation

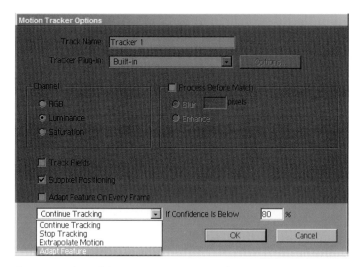

Figure 8.12 This pull-down menu at the bottom of Motion Tracker Options (accessible from the Tracker palette) enables you tell the tracker what to do if the Confidence rating suddenly drops below a certain threshold during the track. A good default setting is 80%. Which setting you choose depends somewhat on your specific situation.

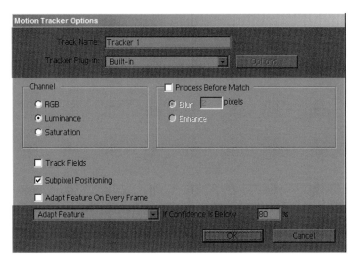

Figure 8.13 These tracker options pertain to looking at your footage in different ways.

Figure 8.14 What do you mean, options? The tantalizing Tracker Plug-in pull-down yields but one choice, and the Options button is in a permanent state of gray. Evidently no third party has, as yet, seen a market for a custom After Effects tracking plug-in.

but similar color and contrast, something I don't think I've encountered in tracking). Generally, luminance does the trick, provided you can locate trackable areas of strong bright/dark contrast.

You probably won't need to check Track Fields unless you are working with video footage in which you've decided to leave the fields unseparated. The thing is, as soon as you start seeing your tracks go astray, as a precaution you'll probably go back and separate fields anyhow. Likewise, you can elect to use the Process Before Match options to pre-blur or pre-sharpen (Enhance) your clip, but honestly, it may indicate that your footage needs de-graining or, conversely, is too blurry to track.

Tracker Plug-In

So, what's with the mystery pull-down menu with only one choice and an Options button that seems to be permanently grayed out (**Figure 8.14**)?

Adobe considers itself to be in the application business, and where possible it leaves specialized features to third-party developers. Hence, the most powerful color keyers are not the ones made by Adobe. (Although Adobe does bundle the excellent Keylight, the company didn't create it).

Thus, although the development team put quite a lot of effort into refining the built-in tracker, the idea was to open the API for tracking so that one of the many specialists who make software that just does tracking would have the opportunity to embed their own.

Thus far, however, no one seems to have stepped up.

In such cases, you might also want to try a third-party automated tracker if you have access to one (see the section "Making Use of 3D Tracking Data").

Fixing Tracks That Go Wrong

The feature you're tracking changes as the shot progresses, and the tracker suddenly jumps to a different, similar feature within the search region. You pounce on the Stop button in the tracker controls (**Figure 8.15**). But now what? The tracker has probably created a few frames' worth of bad data.

It's no big deal! Just drag the time needle (in the Layer window) back to the last well-tracked frame and click Play again. In so doing, you have reset the process, so there is a higher likelihood that the tracker will succeed. If not, and the tracker drifts away from the feature multiple times in succession, the next line of defense is Adapt Feature on Every Frame, followed by altering the Confidence options:

▶ If the problem was caused by some other object briefly passing in front of the object you're tracking, try the Extrapolate Motion option when confidence is below

Figure 8.15 Everything was fine until the tail lights suddenly went off, causing the tracks to jump as they tried to find an equivalent shape. You can restart a track at the frame where it went off the rails without having to do anything with the bad frames, other than overwrite their tracks. In this case, I need to find new points with good contrast (perhaps the corners of the trunk) and offset the Attach Point back to the tail light positions.

80% (or whatever threshold at which your track went wrong, which you can check in the timeline).

▶ If the problem was caused by a feature that has changed its shape, color, or luminance, try Adapt Feature in the pull-down menu (as shown back in **Figure 8.12**) to see if the tracker can pick up the change automatically. Keep in mind, however, that the Adapt Feature option can instead widen the margin of error for features that change too much over time. In such a case, there's no hard and fast rule for what to do other than look for a different feature to track.

▶ If there is truly a problem for which neither of these helps, then Stop Tracking is probably your best option. Sometimes manually resetting the track point at certain key moments of failure is worth the trouble.

Stay flexible, be creative about your choice of points, and be ready to bail and start over if things aren't working too well, and you can get a good track with the minimum of hassle.

Using the Timeline

It seems as though the Tracker Controls palette is where all the heavy lifting of tracking is done, but in fact the decisions you make in that palette actually end up residing in the timeline. This has been alluded to several times already, but I want to take a moment to spell it out for you so that you don't get frustrated. Any track that you begin for a layer remains a property of that layer unless you twirl down the layer's properties and then delete it. Otherwise, the track sticks around.

For example, you are simply exploring the various Track Type options and discover that the Corner Pin options give you four track points. You don't want four points, so you

Subpixel Motion

The key feature the After Effects tracker offers is subpixel positioning. You could never achieve this effect manually, and it can rescue a scene that requires stabilization despite being a locked-off shot in which no object in the scene ever moves even a full pixel. Yes, your eye's ability to detect motion is that good. Look closely at subtle motion in a scene that is almost locked off, and you can actually see motion occurring below the single-pixel level.

Although it is on by default, you can turn off subpixel positioning from the Motion Tracker Options palette if for some reason you need motion in whole-pixel values. In most cases, disabling subpixel positioning will make your track look strange and crude.

Do not be fooled as you watch a track in progress, however; the tracker icons themselves move in whole pixel values only. You will see them bounce around as if they're deriving a very crude track! Only after you've seen the result or checked the resulting values to see that they go down to 1/10,000 of a pixel (four places below the decimal point) do you discover that the tracker is, in fact, properly doing its job (**Figure 8.16**)—despite having bounced along like granny in the rumble seat on her first date in the horseless carriage.

Figure 8.16 Click on a keyframe holding a motion track result, and you'll see that its accuracy extends down four decimal places below the whole-pixel level. This is essential to a realistic-looking track.

Figure 8.17 Easily overlooked, the Motion Source pull-down menu is your one-stop location for finding all layers in the timeline containing motion tracks.

NOTES

If you have several layers that need to be tracked and motion blurred to match a background plate, the next section, "Optimize Tracking with the 3D Camera," offers a method for automating this process, saving you the trouble of applying your motion track to each added layer.

switch back to a simple transform but four track points remain, and you can't seem to click in the Layer window to delete them. The Timeline window is the place to search and destroy those unneeded points.

Should you find later on that you need to reapply track data, there's an even easier way to find it than hunting around in the Timeline window. With the comp in question open, go to the Tracker Controls palette (under the Window menu if it's not already revealed) and look in the Motion Source pull-down menu. Layers with no tracks will be grayed out, but the black layers have track data that you can then select using the following menu, Current Track (**Figure 8.17**).

Matching Motion Blur

Don't forget about the possibility of motion blur! It's your friend until it's unwanted, and then it's like a malingering houseguest—impossible to ignore. There are two situations in which you would think about motion blur relative to tracking:

▶ When you want to add motion blur to foreground layers to match motion in the background plate; you don't have motion blur and you want it.

▶ When motion blur already exists in a shot you're trying to stabilize; you have motion blur and you don't want it.

The solution to the former problem is relatively simple, and the methodology is along the lines of what you did for color matching a few chapters back. Zoom into an area of the image that would be well defined if there were no motion blur on the image—a high-contrast object with well-defined edges, if possible. Now turn on motion blur for your foreground layers, and see if the length of the blur matches. Adjust accordingly, in the Composition Settings window (**Ctrl+K/Cmd+K**), Advanced Tab (**Figure 8.18**). To get the setting right, you may have to revisit this window several times in a row, as there is no interactive portion of the timeline that allows you to control motion blur.

The latter problem, however, implies a nearly impossible situation, that of removing blur from footage that contains it. The truth is, however, that footage that is heavily enough blurred to give away that it has been stabilized is probably going to exhibit other problems when stabilized, such as a large gutter area around the tracked image (**Figure 8.19**). The best solution is probably to forgo the locked stabilization in favor of smoothing the camera motion but leaving in the move. I'll explain how this works more thoroughly in the section "Smoothing a Moving Camera."

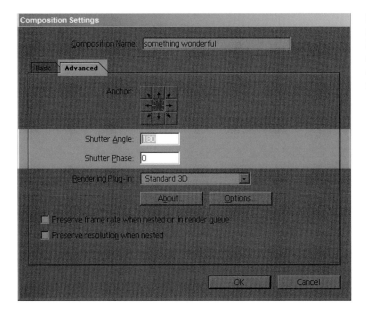

Figure 8.18 In case you missed discussion of motion blur earlier in the book, I'll reiterate: This is the one and only place you can adjust motion blur settings for layers that have keyframed motion.

Figure 8.19 The double whammy of stabilization: Not only has the frame leapt sufficiently away from center that it leaves a large gutter in the lower left, but this particular frame of footage contains motion blur. The former problem can be fixed only by scaling and repositioning the shot; for the latter problem, there is, alas, no good solution.

Using Nulls to Solve Transform Problems

Having a problem matching your track to its target? Nulls are the solution. It can be disconcerting to apply a track to a layer and see it repositioned, rotated, or scaled. Luckily, there's a relatively easy fix: Apply the track to a null, then parent the layer to be tracked to the null at a point where it is correctly positioned. Actually, doing this is a good habit with track data in general.

Why? For one thing, you can lock the null once you've applied the tracking data. Locking prevents you from making one of the easiest mistakes you can make with tracked layers: transforming it without having all keyframes selected.

As you'll see in the next section, and again in the next chapter, nulls can be useful for animating the 3D camera. Because the 3D camera does not use anchor points, you cannot apply a motion track, which depends on anchor point controls, directly to a 3D camera. Therefore, parenting a camera to a null is the most sensible and straightforward method for passing data to it from the Tracker.

If you prefer not to add a null layer, perhaps because it's just one more layer to manage, there is, of course, another solution. You can, instead, use expressions to offset the track the way you want it. If that sounds tempting, check out Chapter 10, "Expressions." For most users, however, nulls are the simplest solution.

Optimizing Tracking via 3D

So you get the idea how to set and apply a tracker. Is that all there is to know about tracking in After Effects? Not by a long shot—you've only laid the groundwork for the good stuff. Say you want to track an arbitrary number of overlaid elements into a scene, matching the movement of a camera. You may think that you would have to track each layer individually.

Wrong. There is a way to set up tracking so that adding in tracked elements, including motion blur, rotation, and even scaling of elements, requires no extra steps. You drop

TIP

When Corner Pins miss: The trick of using a null to offset tracks that aren't perfectly placed will not work with Corner Pins because it is an effect, not a transform operation. In such a case, expressions will help you out; see Chapter 10 for details.

them into the scene as easily as you might have added them when the shot was taken, and they look just as natural. That's right, you can come very close to the look of 3D tracking on many shots without a 3D tracker.

The key is to stabilize the background layer (it will not appear stabilized in the final shot, although it could, or you can smooth out a rough camera motion) and then parent a camera to that stabilization. You now have the motion captured in the movement of a camera, just as it was when shot, so that any elements you add to the scene just pick up on that motion. It's really cool.

The 3D Camera: The One-Stop Solution

Suppose you need to add an arbitrary number (more than one, maybe more as you go along) of foreground layers to a motion-tracked background plate: CG objects, color corrections, effects with hold-out masks, you name it. Applying track data to each of those layers individually would be a time-consuming headache.

Skip it. Don't apply your tracker at all. Instead, create whatever type of track your shot needs: Position only or with the addition of Rotation or even Scale. Now try this:

1. In the Tracker Controls, change the Track Type from the Transform (the default) to Stabilize. (This method is not meant for corner pinning.)

2. Apply Stabilize to the track that generated it. You actually have no other choice; try choosing a different layer than the source track layer by clicking Edit Target, and you'll find the other layers grayed out.

3. Your layer has now been stabilized and will probably slip and slide around in the frame to maintain stability (**Figure 8.20**). No, this is not what you're after, but don't worry. It's only one step from looking normal again.

4. Return to the first frame of the track (quite possibly frame 0 of your comp). Turn on its 3D switch. Add a 3D camera (context-click in an empty area of the Timeline window) and parent it to the tracked background layer (**Figure 8.21**).

Figure 8.20 By the end of the shot, the motion stabilizer has managed to keep the world's most obnoxious stretch Humvee perfectly in place, but there's that gutter problem, and anyhow, you wanted that bit of camera shake and wobble associated with a handheld shot here. What to do?

Figure 8.21 All is now looking normal again at the end of the shot with the addition of a 3D camera, parented to the stabilized background layer, which had already been switched to 3D so that the camera would pick up its motion. If you watch this shot, you cannot see that anything has changed with it.

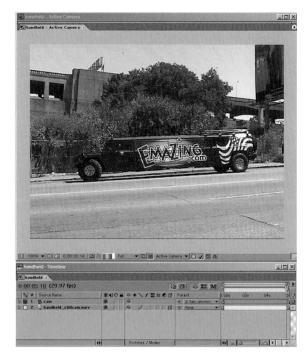

Everything now seems back to normal, but any new item that you add to the scene joins the motion track as soon as you switch it to be a 3D layer. Any layer that you don't want to join the track, such as an adjustment layer, can remain 2D (**Figure 8.22**).

Figure 8.22 It's very hard to show how impressive the result is in a still figure, but believe me, those orange markers now hold their position on that roadway throughout the shot. A look at the perspective view (inset) shows that all layers are essentially 2D, but only the camera and background actually animate.

The Z-depth value of any layers you add will typically remain at 0, so the pylons in Figure 8.22a were scaled and repositioned rather than moved in 3D space. This is not because it wouldn't work to reposition them in 3D space, but simply because it's more work to get the amount of Z depth correct so that the object actually sits where it is supposed to; you have no frame of reference for where it should be in Z space (**Figure 8.23**).

Relocating added layers in Z space might be worth the trouble in extreme cases, such as when you're adding in something that is nowhere near co-planar with the shot. On *The Day After Tomorrow*, The Orphanage had several

Figure 8.23 Instead of faking perspective in 2D, you have the option of actually repositioning layers in 3D space, which yields a shot that looks a lot like 8.22a. The only problem is that now you have to get the View Angle and relative distance of the camera and objects just right or they will start to slip and slide in the shot. It's typically not worth the trouble.

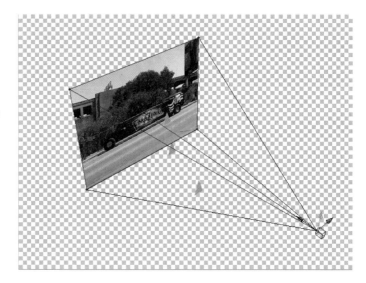

NOTES

When considering the camera lens setting, keep in mind that a 50 mm camera lens introduces no lens distortion to your scene; a set of 3D layers with a Z Position of 0 will look the same as they would as 2D layers. Generally, that's a good thing. It is conceivable, of course, that your scene was shot with a wider (or longer) lens, and that there is some lens distortion in your scene. If this distortion is substantial, and you're relocating items in Z depth, you may want to try to match it. See Chapter 9, "Virtual Cinematography" for details.

shots of a helicopter pilot inside a moving cockpit, with a blue screen outside the window that was replaced with a distant horizon. By moving it back several thousand pixels on the Z axis to approximate the relative depth, we were able to get parallax for free. Of course, we didn't have to worry about anything looking like it was sitting right on the ground plane, as in the Humvee example.

Fake 3D Tracking

As I was writing, I decided to see what would happen if I tried to use the methods I described in the previous section to approximate an actual 3D camera on a shot with a zoom-in—tracking Position, Rotation, *and* Scale. What would happen, I wondered? Would it work, or would the fabric of space and time itself be rent asunder and the universe as we know it come to a screeching halt?

Happily, the result was largely the former. **Figure 8.24** shows my tracked shot in which the camera zooms in on the infamous Hummer. If I switch the Track Type from Transform to Stabilize (I seem to always forget to do that before I start, and luckily the After Effects tracker has improved to the point where you can change your mind), I can apply this to the source plate layer and get a resulting end frame like the one in **Figure 8.25**. Not good. But again, it's just an interim step on the way to tracking glory.

Figure 8.24 It's not hard to get a good track of the zoom in this handheld shot. Most of the movement is straight in (Scale), but there is also some wobble (Position and Rotation).

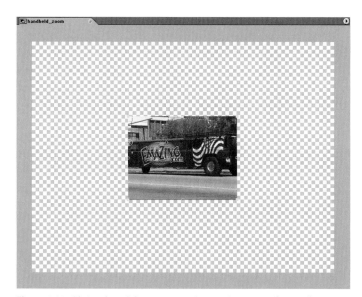

Figure 8.25 Obviously, stabilizing a zoom shot results in a tiny frame, albeit one that is absolutely identical to the first frame of the shot, if it were cropped like this.

Figure 8.26 The result at the beginning, middle, and end of the shot. The pylons are fairly well locked to the pavement, but the quality of the result mostly comes down to how good the track was in the first place, because any slight bump ripples out to all of the objects.

The drill from here is just as before: Add a 3D camera, parent it to this plate layer, then enable the plate layer's 3D toggle. The scaled-down shot pops back to 100% size (make sure the camera covers the whole shot if you set it on the end frame). As before, the magic begins when you drop objects into the scene, but in this case, you definitely want to enable their 3D toggles as well (if there's more than one of them) to get the effect of parallax as you zoom in (**Figure 8.26**).

Now before you get too excited, let me remind you that this works only in certain cases and that true 3D trackers generate true 3D data (including understanding the difference between a camera zoom and a push, which this one decidedly does not). Still, if you pull off a track that looks this three-dimensional using only the tools supplied with After Effects, you will amaze your friends, indeed (at least the ones nerdy enough to know the difference).

Smoothing a Moving Camera

But wait, there's more.

What about stabilizing a shot in which the camera is meant to be moving? There's no track type for this in the tracker controls and simply choosing Stabilize (the closest option) locks the shot in place. This will not do with a pan, tilt, or other camera move (including a handheld shot), and there's that problem with it introducing gutters around the image. Is there any way to reduce some of the jitter or rotation in a shot without removing the camera motion altogether?

Of course! Now that you've re-created the physical camera as an After Effects camera, you apply your smooth to the data that animates that camera, and barring extreme jolts that cause enough motion blur to blow the gag, it just works.

Figure 8.27 features a tilt-down shot taken with an old Arriflex camera that seems to have had a rather serious pin registration problem, causing lots of unwanted gate chatter. The process would be the same if the shakiness was the result of a handheld camera move or a stiff tripod head. As

Figure 8.27 It's difficult to show what a pin registration problem on a film camera looks like in a printed figure, but look at the motion on this simple tilt-down from the sky. In particular, notice the jumps in attach point animation. You can tell something is up. The motion is stuttery and jerky, although the pan was smooth.

you see from the timeline in the figure, the now familiar steps are in place. There is only one problem: The camera has no data to smooth; its motion is derived only from being parented to the stabilized layer, and you don't want to apply a smooth to the source layer. The smoothing effect will come from the difference between that layer's motion and that of the camera.

Therefore, duplicate the tracked layer and turn off its visibility. Rename it "stabilizer," or something like that (I called mine, "Ken Stabler," recalling my early childhood as a Raiders fan), and just to be on the safe side, make it a guide or adjustment layer as well, so that there's no possibility of it rendering should its visibility get checked back on. **Figure 8.27** shows this preparation on a sample shot.

There are a couple of ways to apply smoothing to the motion data of the camera:

▶ Use of The Smoother (**Figure 8.28**)

▶ Use a `smooth` expression (**Figure 8.29**)

Either way, once you've smoothed the duplicated camera motion, don't forget to enable the 3D toggle for the source plate layer.

Figure 8.28 I don't really like The Smoother, a relic from the pre-expressions days of After Effects. You get only one shot using a single Tolerance adjustment, and thereafter your original keyframes are destroyed, replaced by a hodgepodge of new ones. The good news is that the result *is* smoother than the original.

My advice is to take the second of the two smoothing options, and to help get you on board with that decision, I'm going to show exactly how it's done, a few chapters ahead of actually detailing how to create expressions. The main problem with The Smoother is that it's a one shot deal: Once you've applied it, you can undo it, but if later on you decide you need to refine it—good luck. The Smoother

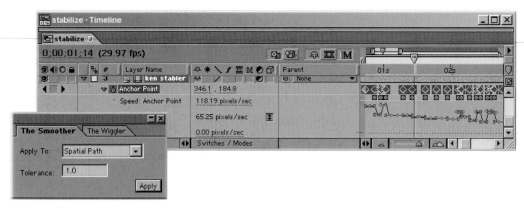

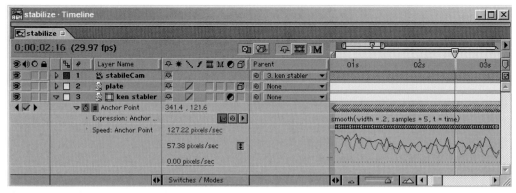

Figure 8.29 Ah, that's better. The source and result motion can be easily compared and adjusted after the fact; you just have to be comfortable changing those little numbers in between the parentheses (known as arguments). If you're not, read on, and check out Chapter 10 for good measure.

actually changes your keyframe data. Furthermore, it offers only one adjustable setting, for Tolerance; it's up to you to guess how that setting will influence your track.

Expressions are completely nondestructive and thus much more in the true spirit of After Effects.

To apply a `smooth` expression

1. Alt/Option-click on the stopwatch for the null to which the camera is parented.

2. With the default expression (`anchorPoint`) still highlighted, go to the Expressions menu (**Figure 8.30**) and under Property choose `smooth(width = .2, samples = 5, t = time)`.

In many cases, this default setting will do the trick. If it doesn't, try changing the width value from the default of 0.2, which is the width of time sampled (raising it will use a larger sampled area but take longer), or increase samples from 5 (increase the number of samples within the specified time) for more smoothing. The final argument, `t = time`, is not applicable unless you need to offset the

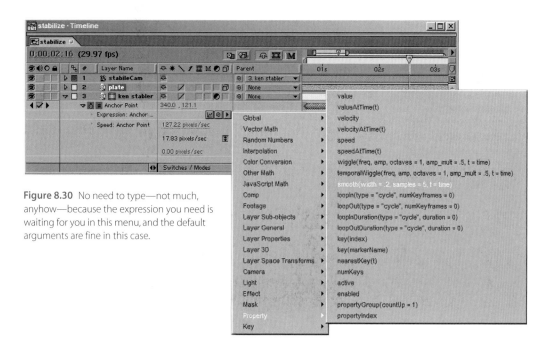

Figure 8.30 No need to type—not much, anyhow—because the expression you need is waiting for you in this menu, and the default arguments are fine in this case.

TIP

The same basic trick will work to destabilize, rather than smooth, a camera motion. Because this expression doesn't simply work with the default parameters, I've left discussion of it to Chapter 10.

smoothing function in time for some reason. If the idea of expressions and arguments seems like gobbledygook to you, take a look at Chapter 10.

What about rotation? If your shot has unwanted rotation, and you've managed to track it, you may wish to eliminate it altogether by setting a static rotation value to the camera null or to use a high smoothing value on it.

And what about compositing other elements into this now smoother scene? You can do it, but you have to pre-compose all of this and retrack the result, as if the smoothed shot was the one you started with. Next, follow the instructions on compositing objects into a tracked shot. Use the same track point that worked for you before with the same settings, and it should be a piece of cake— honest!

Continuing a Track with Expressions

Ever have your track point disappear before you're done with it? Perhaps you were tracking a point moving across the screen with the target offset such that the tracked point exited frame before the target. Maybe your track point was obscured at some point in the scene, obscured too badly for the tracker to extrapolate motion.

Other effects software might have an option for continuing the track, but in After Effects, you use a simple expression to do it. This will work only in cases where your tracked item is traveling more or less steadily in more or less a singular direction. A classic example is the sign on the side of a bus moving across frame because whether or not you do it with a corner pin, the point you're tracking is likely to exit frame before your added sign (**Figure 8.31**).

Here I'll offer the simple trick for continuing positional data; for a more thorough explanation of what's going on, and variations on the theme (looping incoming frames, repeating a movement pattern, or looping in *and* looping out) take a look at Chapter 10.

For now, make sure there are no unwanted keyframes at the end of your animation, where the tracked area of the

Figure 8.31 The wheel of the bus provides a good track target, and offsetting the track point to the fender panel behind the wheel means that our track comes into frame right from offscreen. Unfortunately, the wheel disappears behind the van that it's passing before even exiting the frame. Note the evenness of the track points. This is a perfect candidate for continuing the track.

clip moved offscreen; the expression you will create pays close attention to the final two keyframes to make its estimate of what will happen next.

Find the property that contains the keyframe motion you want to continue (Position in this case), and Alt/Option-click on its stopwatch. In the text field that appears, replace the current text (position) by typing in `loopOut("continue")`. Yes, that's right, typing; don't worry, I won't tell anyone you were typing code in After Effects (**Figure 8.32**). With a corner pin, you might apply this expression to two or even all four of the corner properties.

Would this trick work with other parameters that don't deal with position? Of course. **Figure 8.33** shows it being applied to the tail end of the track for **Figure 8.26**, in which Position, Rotation, and Scale were tracked to simulate 3D tracking on a zoom. In fact, this expression will work in any

Figure 8.32 Ladies and gentlemen, a miracle: A broken motion track has been healed with a mere line of code, and the orange target now exits frame with the bus.

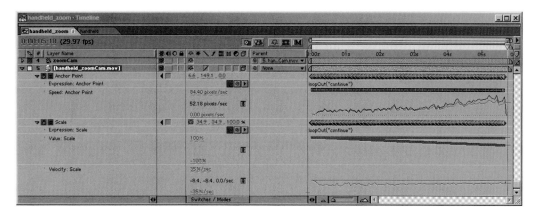

Figure 8.33 It's easy to get away with a continue loop over a short number of frames like this. What you lose over time is all of that lumpy, bumpy organic motion that you see in the graphs.

case where the last two frames of animation reflect a delta (change) in values that you wish to continue, ad infinitum. In Chapter 10 you'll see how it's not even restricted to the last two frames, nor is continuing the only option.

Tracking for Rotoscoping

Other compositing programs, such as Apple's Shake, allow you to track masks, something that is not directly possible in After Effects. So you should give up on the idea of trying to make rotoscoping work easier using the tracker, right?

Wrong, of course. I feel a little sheepish writing something so obvious amongst more advanced After Effects tips, but the number of times I've seen fellow artists overlook situations where the tracker would help compels me to bring this up.

What you cannot do with the After Effects tracker is track individual mask points, which means you can't use the tracker to articulate an animated mask. That's too bad, but it's not the end of the story. I've run into numerous cases where I needed precise tracking but did not need to articulate the matte—for example, tracking the edge of the stage in a green-screen shot in which the camera pushes in. I was interested in masking out a linear edge as it moved across frame.

NOTES

As this book was going to press, Silhouette FX (www.silhouettefx. com) announced a new plug-in that has an integrated motion tracker for applying motion data to mask points. It might be worth checking out if you do want to track articulated masks.

Yes, it's true that there's no way to apply track data (or position data for that matter) to masks, but you can work around the problem, as long as you're not actually trying to articulate your masks using the tracker. Here's how:

1. Line up a solid (with or without a mask) to mask out your layer (**Figures 8.34a** and **b**).

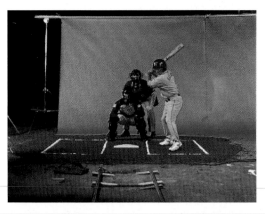

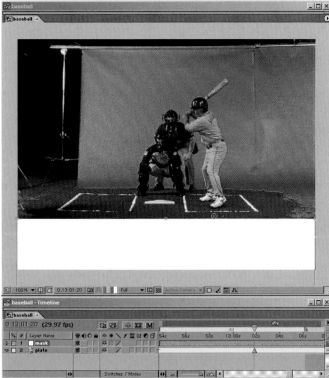

Figures 8.34a and b This plate needs garbage mattes on all sides, but in this case focus on the tracks in front of the set that have to go. The shot tracks in down those rails. The first step is just to add a solid where the front edge of the action area should be (8.34b). (All baseball images courtesy of Tim Fink Productions.)

2. Track the background plate and apply the track to the
solid. Reposition it (either selecting all Position keys
or using the anchor point values) as needed (**Figures
8.35a**, **b**, and **c**).

Figures 8.35a, b, and c This track is one of the few times
you actually might want to use the feature of being able to
restrain the track to one axis only. In this case, keeping it to Y
only keeps the mask solid-centered in frame at the middle
(8.35b) and beginning (8.35c) of the track as well as the end.
I tracked it in reverse to take advantage of how much more
prominent the trackable features are at the end of the shot.

Scripting actually offers access to individual mask points, so it is theoretically possible to apply data to them automatically. The reality, however, is that to work properly the script would need a user interface that is complicated enough to make this a very difficult task indeed, unless you happened to be working with the same mask over and over.

3. Apply this masked solid as an alpha track matte to the layer you're masking (**Figure 8.36**).

Of course, you will have to account for such variables as making the solid big enough to cover the full area being masked over the length of the shot, but you knew that. The main thing about this is that once you get it working, you might actually enjoy creating garbage mattes, thanks to this extra boost of automation.

Paint, of course, is a different story and a much simpler situation if you're comfortable with the basics of expressions. Each paint stroke has its own transform data, including a Position property that is separate from the layer's property. Using the pickwhip, you can link this property to tracking data from the same layer. (For more details, see the "Tracking Brushes and Effects" section in Chapter 10.)

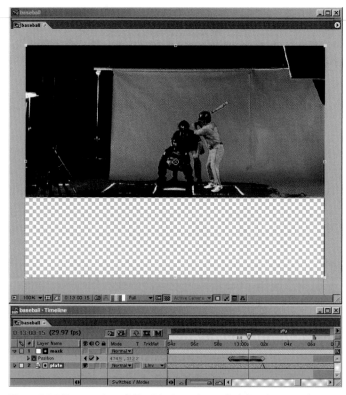

Figure 8.36 Because the solid is white, it can be applied directly as a track matte in Luma Inverted mode (Alpha Inverted will also work), and the first holdout area has been created. The process can easily be repeated for the sides and top of this shot. Ambitious trackers might want to try to nail the whole thing with a single tracked and scaled mask.

Using 3D Tracking Data

2D tracking is, of course, only the beginning of the story. After Effects added tracking prior to adding 3D layers, but as of yet it has not included dedicated 3D tracking, in which the entire scene is tracked to match a virtual 3D camera, rather than individual 2D layers. Fortunately, you can easily work with data from 3D tracking programs, such as 2D3's Boujou and RealViz MatchMover Pro.

Early in this chapter, I told you about a cheat for 3D tracking in certain situations, but that wouldn't help you at all if you were trying to integrate a rendered 3D object in your scene. After Effects does not work with 3D mesh objects, of course, so the workflow with true 3D tracking usually goes like this:

1. Track the scene in a dedicated 3D tracking software program. This generates 3D camera data, typically in a format to match whichever 3D system you're using. It may also generate helpful elements, such as nulls corresponding to where solid objects were in the original scene or a "floor" that matches the ground plane of the shot.

2. Import the camera data into a 3D animation program. This step assumes you're going to be integrating match-moved computer-generated elements into your scene; you might, instead, be doing everything 2D in After Effects.

3. Import the camera data into After Effects, and finish the scene, integrating the plate, computer-generated elements, and any 2D elements or final touches (adjustment layers tracked in 3D, separate passes of lights and shadows, whatever you need), all from the point of view of the camera in After Effects.

Figure 8.37 shows the final shot that resulted from the baseball plate; the camera follows the pitch all the way to the plate, where the batter hits it out of the park (of course). This shot is a complete mishmash of 2D and 3D elements. The ball, field, and front of the stands are computer generated, but the crowd was lifted from a videotape of an actual game.

Figure 8.38 shows a completely different type of shot that also began with a 3D track in Boujou. The fires that you see in the after shot are actually dozens of individual 2D fire and smoke layers, staggered and angled in 3D space as the camera flies over to give the sense of perspective. You'll find more on this shot and how it was set up in Chapter 14, "Fire and Explosions."

Figure 8.37 True 3D tracking (done in 2D3's Boujou for this shot) was essential here because the feet of the characters had to be completely locked to the computer-generated ground, and even a camera on dolly tracks wobbles and bounces quite a bit. The full shot follows the ball to the plate.

Figure 8.38 Just because you're placing elements in a supposedly "2D" program like After Effects doesn't mean you can't stagger them all over 3D space to give the illusion of depth, as was done on this fly-by shot. Tracking nulls from Boujou helped get the relative scale of the scene, important because the depth of the elements had to be to exact scale for the parallax illusion to work. (Final fire image courtesy of ABC-TV.)

Working with 3D Tracking Data

Many people don't realize that After Effects is able to import Maya scenes (.ma files). The only elements that are imported are the rendering cameras, including all translation and lens data (even animated zooms) and nulls that are in the scene. The camera data should be "baked," which is Maya parlance meaning that it should have a keyframe at every frame (search on "baking Maya camera data" in the online help for specifics on this).

3D trackers tend not to require (or even easily allow) you to set track points manually; they create a swarm of hundreds of points that come and go throughout the shot, and they choose the ones that seem most consistent. These points can be saved with the resulting scene as nulls. If you're working with Boujou (among others), the camera solve can contain literally hundreds of nulls. This may be overkill, but some of these nulls will be very useful because they give you the exact 3D coordinates of something in the scene that Boujou decided to track—often a clear detail on an object or the object's boundary. After Effects has the huge disadvantage of not displaying 3D grids, and these nulls can be invaluable for getting your bearings as to the proper scale and positioning of layers that you will insert into the scene.

Besides Position and Rotation data, the Camera may also have keyframes for Zoom. Keep in mind that, unless Sergio Leone has started making spaghetti westerns again, zoom shots will be the exception rather than the norm and any zoom data that you get from the 3D tracker should be checked against your camera report (or any other data you have indicating whether there was, in fact, a zoom in the shot, including your own observations). Most 3D trackers will be helped out a lot if you can tell them whether the shot was taken with a prime lens, in which case zoom is out of the question.

TIP

Once you find all of the nulls that are useful to you in the scene, which will usually number two dozen or less, you can select them in the timeline along with the camera and its parent null (if any). Now context-click on the selected layers and from the context menu choose Invert Selection to select the potentially hundreds of other unused nulls. Delete them.

NOTES

Maxon's Cinema 4D has added its own support for 3D integration with After Effects via a plug-in available from Maxon (www.maxon.net).

Importing a Maya Scene

So, how do you import a .ma scene containing 3D camera data? Just look for the file with the .ma extension. After Effects will import it and set it up either as one or two compositions: one if the Maya project has a square pixel aspect ratio and two for nonsquare (so that a square pixel version is still available as a child composition of the nonsquare one).

Your camera may be *single-node* (in which case the camera holds all of the animation data) or *targeted*, in which case the transformation data resides in a parent node to which the camera is attached.

Depending on your tracker and your scene, you may get too many nulls with the scene. A composition with 500 layers, even if they are only nulls, becomes quickly unwieldy, so assuming you have software (such as Alias Maya or the tracker itself) in which you can weed out the useless nulls and keep only the ones that correspond to points where you want to place objects in the scene, you can pare it down to a couple dozen (and maybe even give them descriptive names). You can usually easily make out what the nulls correspond to in the scene if you watch them over the background plate; they tend to cluster around certain objects.

Keeping some of the nulls is essential because not only does After Effects not even have such basic viewport orientation tools as a visible grid, but the scale of the scene relative to the real world is quite arbitrary, as is the placement of the ground plane unless you have been careful to set it up in the tracker.

Try It Out for Yourself

If you'd like to try out a 3D tracker, look no further than the book's CD-ROM. It includes a demo of SynthEyes, a reasonably priced 3D tracker from Andersson Technologies that has been used on feature films (**Figure 8.39**). For about the cost of a typical After Effects plug-in set, you can have your own 3D tracking software for either Mac or Windows. The demo is the full version but with a time limit, and you will not be able to save your SynthEyes projects, so you must perform and export your track start to finish before quitting. But the output data will be fully usable.

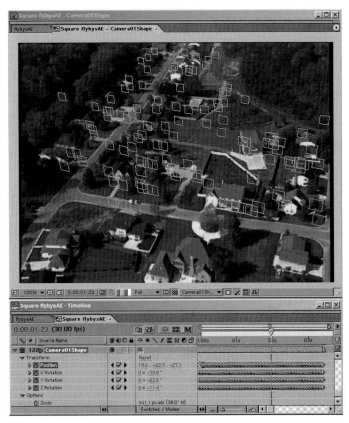

Figure 8.39 This composition began as a Maya (.ma) scene file created by SynthEyes 3D tracker. The squares are nulls that were track points and that now serve as handy references for layer placement. The camera includes a keyframe on every frame (the Maya camera was baked) but only a static value for Zoom (because this flyover shot was taken with a prime lens). This scene is available for download from www.ssontech.com if you want to try it yourself.

There are also sample files to try out before you create a scene of your own. You may have luck simply importing your shot into Syntheyes, clicking Full Automatic, and exporting the result as AfterEffects via .ma. If there's more involved in getting a good track, however, you will need to learn a bit more about how the software works, and it's beyond the scope of this chapter to document it. Instead, I highly recommend you take a good look at the Syntheyes online documentation, which is available from the Help menu.

NOTES

If you'd like to learn more about the complex subject of match moving, check out *Matchmoving: The Invisible Art of Camera Tracking* (Sybex Inc.) by Tim Dobbert, one of my former colleagues from The Orphanage.

Conclusion

Despite all attempts to make it standardized and automatic, tracking remains as much art as it is science, which is probably why most large effects facilities retain match-move artists on staff. Even if you've understood everything in this chapter and followed along closely, therefore, working on your own shots will no doubt prove to be a process of trial and error.

The next chapter will delve further into the ways in which After Effects can replicate what a physical camera can do, expanding on some of the concepts touched on earlier in the "Optimizing Tracking via 3D" section.

9

Virtual Cinematography

A film is never really good unless the camera is an eye in the head of a poet.

—Orson Welles

Virtual Cinematography

As visual effects artists, we strive not only to re-create the natural world realistically, but also the camera's view of the world. These goals are by no means the same. The camera sees only a limited part of the world, and from a specific perspective.

Capturing a scene from this perspective requires a host of decisions that constitute a full-blown storytelling art known as cinematography. After Effects offers compositors the opportunity to re-create and even change some of these decisions, long after the crew has struck the set and called it a wrap. The title of the chapter may seem grandiose, given how many cinematographic choices are out of reach to compositors, but thinking like a director of photography and understanding the workings of the camera are the goals if you're going to fool the viewer into believing your effects shot.

This far-reaching chapter deals with several aspects of replicating a physical camera in After Effects and matching, influencing, or changing the camera's perspective, including

▶ Taking control of the After Effects 3D Camera to replicate the settings of a physical real-world camera

▶ Interpreting, managing, and re-creating other effects of using a film or video camera, including grain and lens distortion

▶ Camera mapping a scene, making a 2D source three dimensional

▶ Recreating both the look of camera blur and the effects of depth of field in the camera

> ▶ Exploring different camera looks, including the fundamental distinctions between film and video, and how to recreate each

These seemingly disparate points all involve understanding how the camera sees the world and how film and video record what the camera sees. All of them transcend mere aesthetics, influencing how the viewer perceives the story itself.

2.5D: Using the Camera

What if you could pick up a camera and move it around a world of objects that were flat and two dimensional, yet were related to one another and to a virtual camera in 3D space? As was explored toward the end of the previous chapter, that's pretty much the dimensional model After Effects offers you. It's sort of a 2.5D world, comprised of objects that can exist anywhere but have no depth themselves.

There are a lot of fun, stylized ways to play around with 3D in After Effects, but there are also ways in which you can get the After Effects 3D camera to match the behavior of a real camera, if you understand how they are similar, and how they differ. Therefore it's worth taking a closer look at how 3D works in After Effects, and how its various features—the camera, lights, and shading options—correspond to their real world counterparts.

Understanding the After Effects Camera

You can use 3D in After Effects without setting a camera—just toggle a layer to 3D and *voila*—but it's little bit like driving a race track using a car with an automatic transmission: You can't maneuver properly, and before long you'll probably crash.

Furthermore, when you set a camera, you encounter one of the more helpful and visually descriptive portions of the After Effects user interface: the Camera Settings dialog (**Figure 9.1**). If you know how to interpret what it is showing you, the dialog's diagram tells you virtually everything you need to know about how the After Effects camera sees the 3D world.

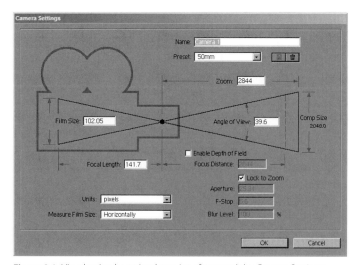

Figure 9.1 Visual artists love visual user interfaces, and the Camera Settings dialog is one of the few to include a diagram. That's a good thing because it also contains a lot of settings that most users find a bit abstract. Here are the default settings for a 50 mm preset, which happens to be the setting that introduces no change of lens angle from a flat 2D view.

Virtually everything is an apt description, moreover, because one thing that is confusing about After Effects' camera is its use of lens settings from still SLR (single lens reflex) cameras to describe how long or wide a lens is. The diagram in Camera Settings, however, is helpful not only in making some sense of the numbers involved, but also in learning how cameras—be they real or virtual—operate.

Lens Settings

The default camera in After Effects uses the 50 mm preset (listed in the Preset pull-down menu in the Camera Settings dialog). Switching all of your layers to 3D and setting this camera does not change the appearance of your scene whatsoever, which is significant. Like many added features in After Effects, it is specifically designed not to fundamentally change (or corrupt) the appearance of your work when you switch it on.

But hold on—there's no such thing as a 50 mm virtual camera lens because virtual space doesn't contain millimeters anymore than it contains kilograms, parsecs, or bunny rabbits. The virtual world is generally measured relative to pixels. Everything else is just kind of made up until you find its analogue in the real world. So where did the name come from?

On any physical camera, there is a lens length that would be considered neither long nor wide. This lens captures a scene without the shifts in perspective and distortion of features—not all of them displeasing, mind you— associated with lenses that tend more toward the fisheye or telephoto perspective (**Figures 9.2** through **9.4**).

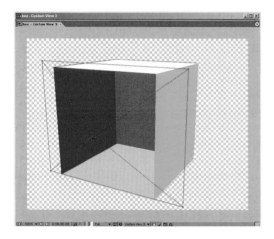

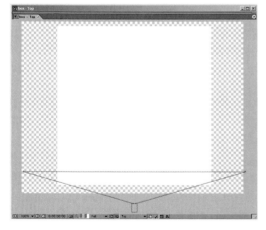

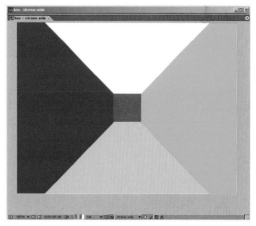

Figure 9.2 The extreme wide or *fisheye* lens pointed inside an evenly proportioned 3D box. Note that the "long" look of the box is created by this "wide" lens, which tends to create very strange proportions at this extreme. A physical lens with anything like this angle would include extremely distorted lens curvature.

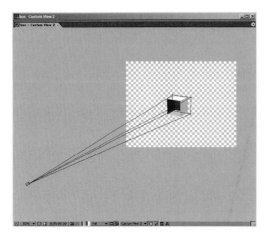

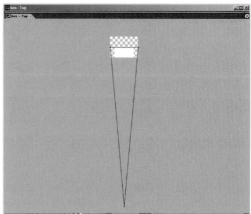

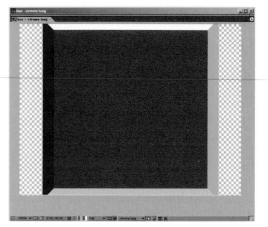

Figure 9.3 A telephoto lens (using the 200 mm setting) pushes items together in depth space, shortening the distance between the front and back of the box dramatically.

On a 35 mm SLR still camera such as has been used for professional photography for decades, 50 mm is the median lens length and the namesake for the After Effects preset. SLR cameras are familiar to many more people (including After Effects developers) than professional film or video cameras. But how many movies have been shot predominantly using an SLR camera? Not many; in fact, only one candidate comes immediately to mind, *La Jetée*, the 1962 Chris Marker film that was the inspiration for Terry Gilliam's movie *12 Monkeys*.

Your source more likely would be from a 35 mm motion picture camera shooting Academy ratio, on which, it just so happens, a 35 mm lens is considered flat or normal. But if

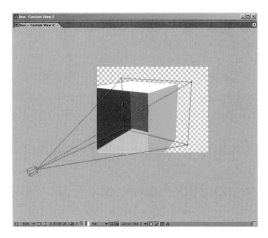

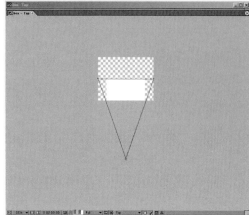

Figure 9.4 The default lens (50 mm setting). If the Z Position value is the exact inverse of the Zoom value, and all other settings are at the default, this is the view you get, and it matches the appearance of setting no After Effects camera whatsoever.

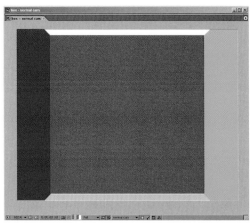

your footage would come from a miniDV camera, the tiny CCD requires an equally tiny default lens length of around 4 millimeters. The appearance of different lens lengths is directly related to the size of the backplate or video pickup, the area where the image is projected inside the camera. The smaller the film size (or CCD size), the shorter the default lens.

The point is that millimeters don't mean much without a physical lens and a physical camera. The only setting in the Camera Settings that truly, universally applies, whether images were shot in IMAX or HDV or created in a 3D animation package, is the Angle of View.

NOTES

Yes, there is an optional, indirectly related, fifth numerical field in the Camera Settings diagram: Focus Distance, which you enable by checking the Enable Depth of Field toggle. This is more like a camera's aperture setting; I'll touch on it separately later.

Real-World Camera Settings

So how exactly do the After Effects camera's settings line up with those of a camera in the physical world? If you know a camera's settings, how do you use them?

First, look again at the diagram provided in the Camera Settings dialog. Four interrelated numerical fields—Film Size, Focal Length, Zoom, and Angle of View—are oriented around two triangles sharing a common hypotenuse (**Figure 9.1**). On a physical camera with a prime lens, these values would all be fixed. With a zoom lens, the Film Size would be fixed (as it always is in a physical camera), but the Zoom and Focal Length could be changed, resulting in a change in the Angle of View. These four settings, then, are interrelated, as the diagram implies.

And so it is with the After Effects camera: Change Angle of View, Zoom, or Focal Length and the other two values among those will change correspondingly, but Film Size will remain fixed. Film Size is useful only if you're trying to emulate a specific camera, which I'll get to in a moment.

Lengthen the lens, and Focal Length increases as Angle of View decreases. A physical telephoto lens really is longer from lens to back plate, and adjusting its zoom does make the lens longer or shorter. The only feature that would make this diagram any clearer is if it actually articulated to visually display the difference in Angle of View as clearly as it can be seen (particularly in the top views) in **Figures 9.2** through **9.4**.

Making Your Adjustments

The only two settings to focus on (no pun intended) are Zoom (for animation) and Angle of View (to match source where that measurement is available). Film Size and Focal Length, measured in pixels, make sense only relative to those two. Angle of View is the actual radius, in degrees, that the camera sees. The setting corresponds directly to real world cameras, and Angle of View is a setting you will see in other computer graphics programs, so you can match it precisely if you need to.

The Zoom value is the distance of the camera lens, in pixels, from the plane of focus of its subject. By default when you set a new camera, After Effects always sets that camera's Z Position value equivalent to the negative of its Zoom value, so that everything that is at the default Z position of 0.0 remains framed the same as it was before the camera was activated. The plane of focus represents an area the size of the composition (**Figure 9.5**), so wherever it is relative to the camera is the point where all items will be framed by that area exactly.

There are several cases in which having the Zoom value in pixels is ideal. It helps for reference when creating depth of field effects, and it makes it easy to tie the position of the camera and the zoom together via expressions for depth of field and related effects (discussed later).

Emulating a Real Camera

And how do you put all of this knowledge to work? You probably have one of two goals: Either you're matching settings that came from a real camera in order to match

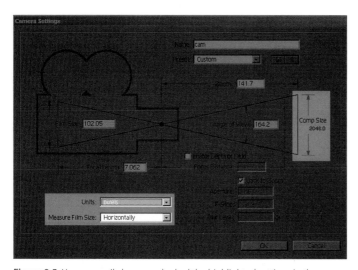

Figure 9.5 You can easily have overlooked the highlighted settings in the Camera Settings dialog. Comp Size (on the right) shows the horizontal size of the composition, in pixels, if the Units and Measure Film Size settings are as shown. This makes the relationship between Zoom and Plane of Focus clearer, although Comp Size is showing a horizontal measurement while the diagram makes it appear vertical.

your elements to images taken with that camera, or you're creating a shot from scratch but want it to look like it was shot with a particular camera and lens. Here are some of the things you have to consider:

▶ **Depth of Field:** Is everything in the shot in focus, or does the shot require a narrow depth of field with elements in the foreground and background drifting out of focus?

▶ **Zoom or push:** If you are moving in or out on the shot, which type of camera move is it (discussed further in the section called "Moving the Camera")?

▶ **Motion blur and shutter angle:** These settings aren't part of the 3D camera, they're composition settings. If you're unclear about these, review Chapter 2, "The Timeline." Note that camera movement can generate motion blur, just as layer movement does (**Figures 9.6a** and **b**). The key is that the objects to be blurred by the motion of the camera must have Motion Blur toggled on.

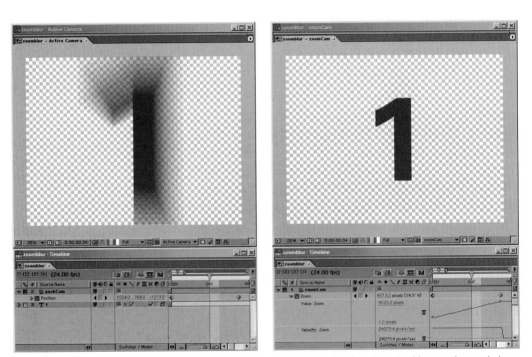

Figure 9.6a and b The blurred object (9.6a) is not moving, the camera is, but the object's motion blur must be toggled on to track the camera's motion. Just in case you were wondering, there is no motion blur associated with zooming (9.6b).

▶ **Lens angle and distortion:** The perspective and parallax among objects in 3D space changes according to the angle of the lens through which they are seen. Real cameras also introduce lens distortion, a curving toward the edges of the image, especially apparent with wide angle lenses, which require a good deal of lens curvature (hence the fisheye lens) in order to take in such a wide angle of view. The After Effects 3D camera does not need a physical lens and does not cause lens distortion on images, but you may need to add it to match existing footage (see the "Optics Compensation" section).

▶ **Exposure:** The After Effects camera has no direct corresponding adjustment for this feature (and limitation) of physical cameras. Therefore you needn't worry about it. But if, on the other hand, you want to create effects that emulate changes in exposure, you may be best off working with eLin (from Red Giant Software and on the book's CD-ROM) in a 16-bit linear image pipeline. For more on that, see Chapter 11, "Issues Specific to Film and HDR Images," and for an example of working this way, look at the last section in Chapter 12, "Working with Light."

One specific piece of information that can help you match existing footage is a camera report, a record of the settings used when the footage was taken. If the crew was large enough to include an assistant cameraman, this information was taken down and can be made available.

Making Use of a Camera Report

If you know the type of camera and the focal length used for your shots, you have enough information to match the lens of that camera with your After Effects camera.

Researched by Stu Maschwitz, author of Chapter 15, "Learning to See," **Table 9.1** details the sizes of some typical film formats. If your camera is on the list, and you know the focal length, use these to set your camera in the Camera Settings dialog. The steps are

1. Set Measure Film Size to Horizontally.

2. Set Units to Inches.

TIP

A potentially easier alternative to the listed steps, for those who like using expressions, is to use the following expression on the camera's Zoom property:

```
FocalLength = 35
//change to your
➡value, in mm
hFilmPlane = 24.892
//change to your
➡film size, in mm
this_comp.width*(Focal
➡Length/hFilmPlane)
```

3. Enter the number from the Horizontal column of the chart that corresponds to your source film format.

4. Set Units to Millimeters.

5. Enter the desired Focal Length.

TABLE **9.1** Typical Film Format Sizes

FORMAT	HORIZONTAL	VERTICAL
Full Aperture Camera Aperture	0.980	0.735
Scope Camera Aperture	0.864	0.732
Scope Scan	0.825	0.735
2:1 Scope Projector Aperture	0.838	0.700
Academy Camera Aperture	0.864	0.630
Academy Projector Aperture	0.825	0.602
1.66 Projector Aperture	0.825	0.497
1.85 Projector Aperture	0.825	0.446
VistaVision Aperture	0.991	1.485
VistaVision Scan	0.980	1.470
16 mm Camera Aperture	0.404	0.295
Super-16 Camera Aperture	0.493	0.292
HD Full 1.78	0.378	0.212 (Full Aperture in HD 1.78)
HD 90% 1.78	0.340	0.191 (90% Safe Area used in HD 1.78)
HD Full 1.85	0.378	0.204 (Full Aperture in HD 1.85)
HD 90% 1.85	0.340	0.184 (90% Safe Area used in HD 1.85)
HD Full 2.39	0.3775	0.158 (Full Aperture in HD 2.39)
HD 90% 2.39	0.340	0.142 (90% Safe Area used in HD 2.39)

Your shot now has the correct Angle of View to match the footage, and so any objects that you track in (perhaps using the techniques described in Chapter 8, "Effective Motion Tracking") will maintain the correct position in the scene as the shot progresses. It's vital to get this right if your camera is going to move during the shot, and especially if the lens used was at one extreme or the other, wide or long.

Lens Distortion

If a virtual camera is set with a wide lens angle, the software simply samples a wider (and taller) area of the scene, as you saw in **Figure 9.2**. This dramatically changes the perspective of 3D space, but it does not actually distort objects the way a real camera lens does because it relies on no lens whatsoever. All the software is doing is widening the view area and scanning, in a linear fashion, each pixel that falls in that area.

A real camera cannot simply widen its view area, which is essentially fixed. It can only "see" what is perpendicular to the surface of the lens glass, so it uses a more convex lens combined with a short lens length to pull a more disparate (wider) range of view.

At the extremes, this causes lens distortion that is easily visible; items in the scene known to contain straight lines don't appear straight at all, but bent in a curve (**Figure 9.7**). In a shot taken with a fisheye lens, it's as if the screen has been inflated like a balloon. It's rare, but not unprecedented, for a shot in a movie to look like this (but there are always exceptions, for example the point of view of a droid in a certain big-budget science fiction film).

As you work with more and more footage, particularly at film resolution (where the phenomenon is often more apparent), you start to notice that many shots that don't seem so extreme as a fisheye perspective have some degree of lens distortion. Even if you can't spot any curved edges that should appear straight at the edge of frame, you might notice that motion tracks from one side of the frame don't seem to apply equally well at the other side of the frame, proportions go out of whack, and things don't quite line up as they should (**Figure 9.8**).

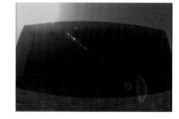

Figure 9.7 The somewhat psychedelic look of lens distortion at its most extreme. The lens aberration in this case is so extreme that even the flare caused by the front lens element is extremely aberrated. You could easily set an equivalently wide lens with the After Effects 3D camera, but none of the curving of what should be straight lines (the ground plane, the building outline) would occur.

Figure 9.8 The curvature of items that you expect to be straight is one clear clue that there is lens distortion in this scene, but the surest sign is that an attempt to corner pin a yellow solid to the side of the building fails; it is not possible to make all four corners and edges line up properly.

There's no way to introduce lens distortion directly to a 3D camera, but the Optics Compensation effect (Professional version only) is designed to add or remove it in 2D. **Figure 9.9** shows this effect in action. Increasing the Field of View makes the affected layer more fisheyed in appearance; to correct a shot coming in with lens distortion, check Reverse Lens Distortion and raise the Field of View (FOV) value.

This process is not exactly scientific, because the Field of View settings don't correspond to measurable phenomena, such as difference in Lens Angle. You have to look for what should be a straight line in the scene and adjust the setting until you're happy with the match. The specific workflow is

1. Having identified that there is lens distortion on a background plate to which you must add foreground elements (as in **Figure 9.8**), drop the background into

Figure 9.9 The process of removing distortion must take place in a composition larger than the source, padded to allow what happens to the corners of the image. The Beam effect is used on an adjustment layer, below the Optics Compensation effect, to act as a virtual "plumb line" to check the precision of a line near the edge of frame (where lens distortion is strongest).

a new composition that is at least 20% larger than the plate to accommodate stretching the corners.

2. Add an adjustment layer above the plate layer, and apply Optics Compensation to that layer. Check Reverse Lens Distortion and raise the Field of View (FOV) setting until lines that should appear straight in your image look straight.

3. Add a Beam effect below the Optics Compensation effect. Make its Inside Color and Outside Color settings match (using any color you'll be able to see easily), and align the Starting Point and Ending Point along an apparently straight line near the edge of frame. Fine-tune the Field of View setting a little more until the line is plumb (as in **Figure 9.9**).

4. Pre-compose all of these layers and set this new composition as a guide layer. In **Figure 9.10**, you can see that the corner pin is now successful, but you actually want to match the distortion of the source shot.

Figure 9.10 Over the undistorted background plate, you are able to freely position, animate, and composite elements as if everything were normal. Note that the perspective is still that of a very wide angle lens, but without the curvature. Any elements you positioned in 3D space would need to have a similarly wide Angle of View to match this perspective.

5. Create a new master composition containing the background plate and the laid-out foreground element. Copy Optics Compensation from the adjustment layer where you undistorted the background and paste it to the foreground element but turn off Reverse Lens Distortion. You have applied the exact distortion of your background to your foreground elements, and they now match up (**Figure 9.11**).

You have tricked After Effects into compositing elements into a distorted environment. Stu Maschwitz, who supplied me with the example used for the step-by-step figures, notes that it is important not to undistort and redistort the plate image itself, which will soften it dramatically. He summarizes the process with the following haiku:

undistort, derive
reunite distorted things
with an untouched plate

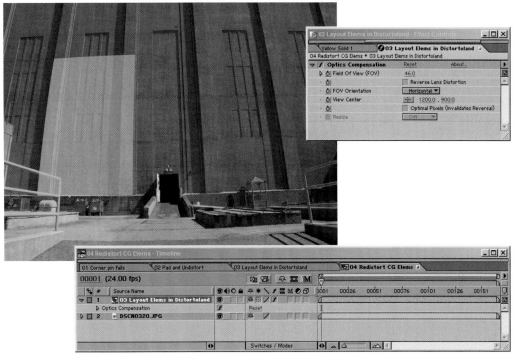

Figure 9.11 Back where you started, by applying the same Optics Compensation effect that was used to undistort the background to the foreground layers, but with the Reverse Lens Distortion box now unchecked, the foreground distorts to match the background, and features now line up properly.

Mixing 2D and 3D

Using a 3D camera in an effects situation typically entails compositing 3D elements over a 2D plate background. This is no big deal. After Effects does not force you to decide up front whether your composition consists of a 2D or a 3D world, and it can contain both, layered together. This is a huge advantage as long as you're clear about managing the composition properly.

And why is it an advantage to mix layers in this manner? Once you understand it, you have a lot less to worry about:

▶ A background stays in place no matter how you move the camera (as in the motion tracking examples using the 3D camera in the previous chapter).

▶ 2D adjustment layers set to comp size and default position affect the whole composition, including 3D layers, without budging.

▶ Foreground from 3D programs that come in with 3D camera tracking data can be augmented in 3D while remaining rendered 2D elements.

Everybody wins.

Where are the gotchas of this approach? They are all special cases:

▶ A 2D layer can use a 3D layer as a track matte and vice versa. Beware of using a 3D track matte on a 3D layer: It's rarely (if ever) what you want. One or the other layers typically needs to be locked in 2D space.

▶ Some effects that emulate 3D perspective make use of the After Effects camera. Typically, and paradoxically, these work correctly on 2D layers only. Examples of this are Trapcode's Particular and 3D Stroke (**Figure 9.12**).

▶ Pre-composing a set of 3D layers effectively makes them behave like a single 2D layer. They no longer interact with other 3D layers or with the camera unless you

Figure 9.12 It seems incredible, but the particles generated by Particular, a Trapcode plug-in, are true 3D, as is evident in perspective view. Paradoxically, this 3D effect occurs when Particular is applied to a 2D layer. It calculates the 3D positions internally using the After Effects camera as a reference, an elegant workaround for the fact that 3D layers in After Effects are always flat planes.

enable Collapse Transformations for the pre-comp. Doing so bypasses the camera in the embedded composition, but respects the 3D position of the object. (For details, see Chapter 4, "Optimizing the Pipeline.")

So go ahead, freely mix 2D and 3D layers. Just make sure, if it gets confusing, to double-check the gotchas list and ascertain that you know what you're doing.

Storytelling and the Camera

A decision as simple as creeping the camera slowly forward can change the whole dramatic feel of your shot. The main limitation you face is the two-dimensionality of After Effects layers, but that's a huge step forward from the bad old days of optical compositing, when it was hardly possible to move the camera whatsoever.

Nowadays, most directors aren't satisfied with a locked-off camera for effects shots, yet it's often simpler to shoot an effects plate that way and leave the camera movement to the compositor. That's no big deal, as long as you don't completely break the rules for what you can get away with.

Keep in mind, moreover, where the audience is likely to be focusing their attention—every once in a while you get away with something you shouldn't. Robert Rodríguez made his entire directing career possible with this realization when he made *El Mariachi*, in which the many continuity errors failed to disrupt an action-packed story.

Specifically, I'm talking about not worrying about the effect of planes of motion and parallax for elements that are in the background, near the edges of the frame, appear for a few frames only, or otherwise won't be noticed by the viewer. The "Sky Replacement" section in Chapter 13, "Air, Water, Smoke, and Clouds," contains just such an example, in which a flat card stands in for a fully dimensional skyline; people aren't watching the skyline for shifts in perspective, they're watching the lead character walk through the lobby and wondering what he's got in his briefcase (**Figure 9.13**).

Figure 9.13 Prominent though it may appear in this still image, the audience is only subliminally aware of what is going on with that skyline outside the window. As the camera pans and tracks to the right, the pyramid building should creep out from behind the foreground skyscraper. It doesn't, because the background skyline is a tracked still, and no one notices because they're wondering what that silhouetted character in the foreground is going to do. (Image courtesy of The Orphanage.)

Figure 9.15 Many 3D camera tragedies could have been avoided if more After Effects users knew about this dialog box, (accessible via **Ctrl+Alt+O** or **Cmd+Option+O**). By turning off auto-orientation, you are free to move the camera anywhere without changing its direction. People who don't know about this end up trying to animate the camera's Position and Point of Interest values together—a nightmare.

Moving the Camera

You may feel you know all about working with a 3D camera already, but the After Effects version is slightly different from the 3D camera in other applications. For example, the After Effects camera has Transform options that are unique from all other types of layers (**Figure 9.14**), and a couple of things about them are a little strange to people used to other types of layers in After Effects, or other 3D programs. Take a closer look.

▽ ▨ 3 🎥 Camera 1	👁 ▢▢ 🔲
▽ Transform	Reset
▸ 🔘 Point of Interest	360.0 , 270.0 , 0.0
▸ 🔘 Position	360.0 , 270.0 , -480.0
▸ 🔘 Orientation	0.0 ° , 0.0 ° , 0.0 °
▸ 🔘 X Rotation	0 x +0.0 °
▸ 🔘 Y Rotation	0 x +0.0 °
▸ 🔘 Z Rotation	0 x +0.0 °

Figure 9.14 The Transform values for the camera include no anchor point and two sets of rotation data: the Orientation of the camera (its basic position), as well as separate X, Y, and Z rotation values. Separating these obviates the need for separate nulls to solve complex 3D rotations. The Point of Interest appears only with the default Orient Towards Point of Interest option (see **Figure 9.15**).

Camera Orientation

Certainly the biggest confusion about the After Effects camera stems from the fact that by default, it includes a *point of interest*, a point in 3D space at which the camera always points, for auto-orientation. To clarify

▸ Auto-orientation via a point of interest is *fully optional*. You can turn it off (making the camera a *free* camera) or change it to orient automatically along the path of camera motion. To do so, context-click on the camera, then choose Transform > Auto-Orient or use **Ctrl+Alt+O** (**Cmd+Option+O**) to access the menu of settings (**Figure 9.15**).

▸ If you need to move the camera and its point of interest, don't try to match keyframes for the two properties—this is sheer madness! You can parent the camera to a null and translate that instead.

▸ Orientation works differently depending on whether auto-orientation is on (in which case it revolves around the point of interest) or not (in which case it rotates around its center).

▶ The auto-oriented camera flips itself so that its view remains oriented, top and bottom, when crossing the X/Y plane while orbiting the center, but the free camera does not. This is great for positioning but not for animating—don't let it surprise you.

So although the default camera in After Effects includes a point of interest, it's often useful to do without it if you want to maintain or control the direction of the camera as you translate it through space. This may not come up in normal visual effects use very often, however, because the camera is often put to more modest uses, such as a simple-camera push.

Push versus Zoom

Knowledgeable effects artists understand that there is a huge difference between a camera push, in which the camera moves closer to the subject, and a zoom, in which the camera stays in place and the lens lengthens. You must make a conscious decision which type of move you're doing and adhere to the rules.

Figures 9.16a and **b** demonstrate the difference between pushing and zooming a real camera. Remember that zooming changes the actual lens angle, and has more of an effect on the immediate foreground and faraway background framing than a push.

Most of the time, you will animate a push; zooms, generally speaking, had their heyday in the era of Sergio Leone. That's a good thing because it is evidently easier to get away with a 2D push than a 2D zoom due to the static lens angle. The relationship and perspective of objects close up does not change with a push the way it does with a zoom.

Push it Good

Why use a 3D camera for a simple push when you could instead scale up the contents of a comp in 2D? If you're traveling any significant distance at all, a scale is too linear to achieve the illusion of moving in Z space. Instead, pick up a 3D camera and move that. You can add eases, stops and starts, a little bit of destabilization—whatever works for your shot.

Figures 9.16a and b The difference between a push in (9.16a) with a wide angle lens and a zoom (9.16b) from a distance is evident especially by what happens to the perspective of the orange ball in the background. With the zoom, its apparent scale is much greater, and it is much more prominent in shot. It seems to be closer to the foreground figures than in the image that was shot wider, but close-up.

TIP

The Keyframe Assistant called Exponential Scale (in the Animation menu) is the old-school, pre-3D way to fake the illusion of a push on a 2D layer. As far as I'm concerned, there is no reason to use it, given how limited it is compared with creating your push in true 3D space.

When you perform your 3D push, however, do it on a single pre-composed layer rather than individual coplanar 3D layers, unless you're separating your source layers into planes of varying depth. Why? Because coplanar 3D layers easily lose proper layer order as After Effects calculates their movement in floating point space. There's no reason it should work, and you should avoid even attempting it.

Your camera move will look more natural if you add keyframe eases, giving the impression that there was a real camera operator behind the lens; if you're unclear about how to create an ease, check Chapter 2. You may even want to add a little extra hesitation or irregularity to the default ease curve to give it that feeling of a camera operator's personality (**Figure 9.17**).

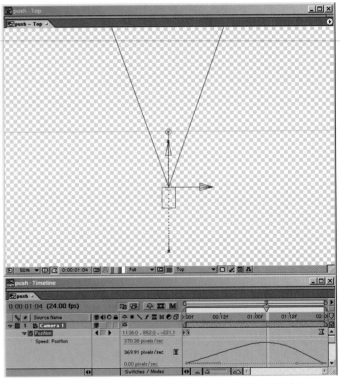

Figure 9.17 You can finesse a simple animation just by highlighting the keyframes and adding Easy Ease (**F9** on your keyboard), but why stop there? Lengthening the Bezier handle for the first keyframe gives the camera that added realistic inertia moving from a static position.

But wait—a move in or out of a 2D shot—isn't that going to look wrong because it lacks any kind of parallax? It might, unless it's subtle. If you're dealing with enough of a move that planes of depth should change their relative perspective, 2D objects are probably not going to hold up. This goes doubly for tracking and panning shots, crane-ups, and other more elaborate and dimensional types of camera moves. Unless these moves are very small, you're going to blow the 2.5D gag. If in doubt, try it and ask neutral observers (or your effects supervisor) to tell you if they buy it.

The exceptions to the 2D object limitation are soft, organic shapes, such as clouds, fog, smoke, and the like. With these, you can fool the eye into seeing 3D depth where there is none, and you can get away with staggering them; the parallax even helps sell the shot. (For more on this, see Chapter 13.)

Camera Projection

Camera projection (or *camera mapping*) is the process of taking a still photo, projecting it onto 3D objects that match the dimensions and placement of objects in the photo, and then moving the camera—typically only along the Z axis—providing the illusion that the photo is fully dimensional (right up until the camera move reveals some area of the image that wasn't part of the photograph). It has been used for some very elaborate visual effects sequences over the years and is often employed by matte painters as a way to keep 3D modeling simple and to focus efforts instead on painting.

Figures 9.18a, **b**, and **c** show a camera projection that Stu Maschwitz set up, ambitiously featuring the shapes of two parked military vehicles. Typical camera projection examples consist of such cube-shaped items as crates and boxes. In this case, a dozen separate planes were created to form a crude 3D model, all white and ready to receive a projected image (**Figures 9.19a**, **b**, and **c**). This example shows both the magic of this technique—deriving perspective shifts from a flat, still image—and the associated problems of image tearing when an area of the frame is revealed that had previously been obscured in the source photo.

NOTES

Remember that toggling on Collapse Transformations causes any 3D layers in a subcomposition to look at the camera in the current comp, rather than in the subcomp. If you don't know to expect this, it may baffle you.

Figures 9.18a, b, and c The progression from the source image (9.18a) through the camera move. By the final frame, image warping and tearing are evident, but the perspective of the image is essentially correct for the new camera position. The tearing occurs simply because as the camera moves it reveals areas of the image that don't exist in the source.

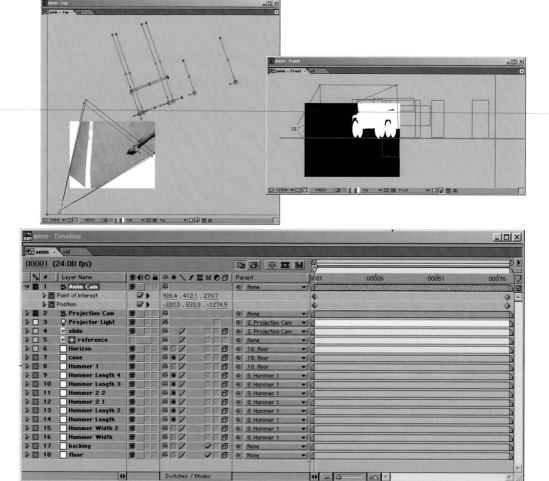

Figures 9.19a, b, and c The rather complicated setup for this effect: from the top (9.19a) and side (9.19b) views you can see the planes that stand in for the vehicles and orange cone. Once setup is complete, animating the camera is a relatively simple matter (9.19c).

The key to pulling off an effect like this is obviously the setup: How is it that the one "texture" of the image (the photo) sticks to the 3D objects? The fundamental concept is actually relatively simple; getting it right is a question of managing details, and that part is fairly advanced and not for the faint of heart. The steps to projecting any still image into 3D space are as follows:

1. Start with an image whose most prominent objects can be modeled as a series of planes. This typically includes rectilinear objects, although in this example it also includes masking off such details as wheels.

2. Create a white solid for each plane in the image. Set each one to be a 3D layer, and under Material Options, change the Accepts Lights option to Off. This means that the planes will retain a pure white surface, ready to receive the projection of the image.

3. Add a camera called Projection Cam; if you know the Angle of View of your source image, set this camera to have that value. If not, you can experiment with zooming this camera in a moment, once setup is complete.

4. Add a light. Normally you would use a Spot light for projection maps, but After Effects lights have no fall-off so you're just as well creating a Point light. Give it the same position as Projection Cam, then parent it to Projection Cam. Change its Casts Shadows setting to On.

5. Rename the source image to reference, and duplicate it, naming the duplicate Slide. Turn on 3D for the duplicate, then under its Material Options, change Casts Shadows to Only and Light Transmission to 100%. This image now is cast by the light onto the white planes, as if it were a slide in a projector.

6. Parent Slide and Projector Light to Projection Cam. Now, no matter how you reposition the camera as you set up, those layers follow.

7. Next comes the potentially painful part: masking, scaling, and repositioning those white solids to build the model, ground plane, and horizon onto which you will project your slide. If it helps, toggle on the reference

layer and build your model to match that, checking it with the slide every so often. Parent each set of planes to a null object so that you can easily change the position and scale of the whole object.

8. If planes that you know are at perpendicular 90 degree angles don't line up properly, you need to adjust the Zoom value of the Projection Cam, scaling the model and slide as needed to match the new Zoom value. The example file on the book's CD-ROM includes an expression applied to the Scale value of the slide layer so that the slide scales up or down to match however you adjust the Zoom of the camera. This isn't necessary but it's helpful in this example.

9. Once everything is lined up, duplicate Projection Cam, and rename the duplicate (the one on the higher layer) Anim Cam. This is the one you can now try animating, using the Point of Interest, Position, and Zoom from the Projection Cam as the default view at which everything looks just like the source photo.

The number of variables that may come up as you employ this technique with your own images are many, and the result is likely to exhibit the problems shown in the figures, so if this sounds like more trouble than it's worth, it probably is. If, on the other hand, you're feeling daring and ready to try something tricky, take a look at the example file, and feel free to give it a whirl.

Camera Blur

Real cameras blur images in a particular way when areas of the image are out of focus. Plenty of camera operators in the history of filmmaking have regarded defocused areas of the frame as mistakes; Gregg Toland, visionary cinematographer of *Citizen Kane*, went to extraordinary lengths to keep items in the extreme foreground and background of that film in sharp focus, even devising (with Orson Welles) a customized camera for this purpose.

Nowadays, however, good-looking camera blur is not typically seen as a flaw. It has a practical purpose, putting the audience's attention where the director wants it, which is why a *rack focus* shot, in which the focus changes from a figure in the background to one in the foreground, or vice versa, is part of the cinematographer's palette of storytelling tools. It also is often considered beautiful to behold, so much so that the Japanese coined a term for the quality of the out-of-focus image, *boke* (also spelled *bokeh*, which is closer to a phonetic spelling).

So what's the big deal? Just blur the areas that should be out of focus, and you're done, right? Typically not, for a couple of reasons. First of all, as with lens flares, the design of the lens influences the look of the blurred image. Second, as is explored further in Chapter 11, if there are actual points of luminance in a blurred image. Be they lights or even specular highlights or glints reflected off of objects, they will retain their full brightness when blurred in a manner that images that simply have a blur applied to them do not.

Before I get to these special case scenarios and a discussion of what, exactly, boke means to your shots, take a look at a setup where the 3D camera in After Effects can help you re-create the type of blur caused by focal limitations in a physical camera.

Image Planes and Rack Focus

If your source footage can easily be divided into planes of depth, you can achieve a rack focus effect that matches the way this effect is achieved in a physical camera. The focal point passes from an object in the foreground to one in the background or vice versa, and the depth of field is narrow enough that only the immediate plane of focus is seen in sharp detail.

With a physical camera, this type of shot requires a narrow depth of field, which is created by lowering the f-stop value. Doing so influences shutter angle and the amount of light passing through the aperture, so the color response and likelihood of motion blur in the shot are affected.

Not so with the After Effects 3D camera, which has Aperture and F-Stop settings as well (**Figure 9.20**), but they affect only focal depth. The two settings are tied together; changing one in the Camera Settings dialog has an inverse

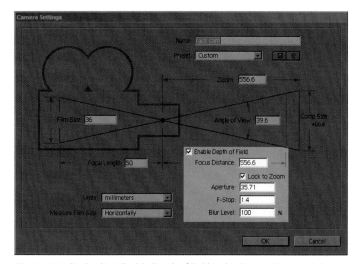

Figure 9.20 By checking Enable Depth of Field in the Camera Settings dialog, you enable the settings associated with it, including Focus Distance (the distance in pixels that is in focus, which can be locked to the Zoom value using the check box just below it), as well as Aperture and F-Stop, which are different methods of controlling the same thing: the relative depth of field. A low F-Stop (or high Aperture) as shown here with a Blur Level of 100% will create a shallow depth of field.

effect on the other and the mathematical relationships are not linear. F-Stop is the setting more commonly referenced by camera operators, and yet only Aperture is available to be adjusted and keyframed in the timeline.

After Effects depth of field settings can be matched to a camera report, provided that you have the camera f-stop setting that was used when the footage was shot. If so, open up the Camera Settings dialog (**Ctrl+Shift+Y/ Cmd+Shift+Y**, or click on the Camera in the Timeline window), check the box labeled Enable Depth of Field, and enter your value for F-Stop.

The key to this effect is to offset at least one layer in Z space so that it is out of focal range. Now you can animate Focus Distance in the timeline; in the Top view, set the Focus Distance (under Options) to match the layer that will be in focus at the beginning of the shot, and keyframe it, then change the Focus Distance to match a second layer later in the shot (**Figures 9.21a** and **b**).

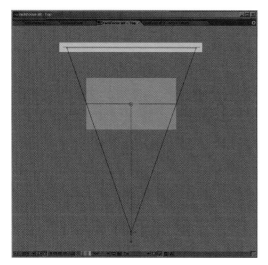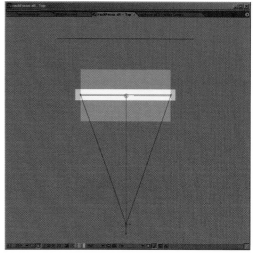

Figures 9.21a and b In the Top view it is easy to animate the Focus Distance, denoted by a red boundary line, to animate from the far plane (9.21a) to the near plane (9.21b).

A static focus pull doesn't look quite right; changing focus on a real camera always alters the zoom slightly. To sell this shot, which starts on a view of the city and racks focus to reveal a sign in the foreground, I add a slight camera pull-back, which takes advantage of the nice shift in planes of motion that I get from my repositioned layers (**Figure 9.22**).

Boke Blur

The rack focus method generates camera blur that is realistic as far as moving and changing focus on a camera go, but the After Effects camera is not capable of generating the look of a truly defocused lens because of what happens to out-of-focus points of light that pass through a camera lens and aperture.

Boke is meant to connote the look and feel of how points of light become discs of light (also called circles of confusion) that take on the character of the lens itself, as with lens flares (another effect that is the result of the lens interacting with light, covered in Chapter 12). This would seem to be rather obscure and arcane, except it produces beauty and suspense in a movie.

Figure 9.22 The final shot is a rack focus combined with a gentle pull-back, with eases at the start and end of the Position and Focus Distance animations.

How so? Shots create suspense by keeping elements out of focus. We may have a notion of what we are seeing, or we may not (**Figure 9.23**). We remain intrigued as viewers as the shot focuses in from a strange wash of color and light (**Figure 9.24**).

So what, exactly, causes this phenomenon, and how should you think about it? A perfect lens, photographing a point of light that is out of focus, creates a soft, spherical blur to represent that point. What was a bright point is now an equally bright, larger, softer area. If you tried to re-create this effect by simply blurring an image, the blur would

Figure 9.23 Offered a dollar by Stu if I could guess what this image is, I guessed a beanbag chair. I was wrong. The correct answer is at the end of this section.

Figure 9.24 Even in the very first, most blurred frame of this shot pulling back from the lawn, you have a good idea what you're looking at, yet the appearance is strange and compelling. Note that a few blades of grass in the extreme foreground retain the quality of boke although most of the shot is in focus.

have the effect of graying out toward the edges rather than retaining the brightness of the source. This is true not only of blurs that result from defocusing, but of motion blur as well (**Figures 9.25a**, **b**, and **c**).

Moreover, most camera lenses are not perfect, so you will not see perfect blurred spheres. The digital images in **Figure 9.24** show spheres that are brighter toward the edges than in the middle; an anamorphic lens will show squashed spheres, and as with lens flares, the blades of the aperture diaphragm will sometimes be visible in the circles of confusion, making them hexagonal (or pentagonal, and so on, depending on the number of blades in the opening).

Go for Boke

Okay, let's say you're sold on the look of boke blur and want to incorporate its effect into your shots. What can you do in After Effects to recreate it?

In Chapters 11 and 12, guest author Brendan Bolles and I look at ways in which working in true linear color space can help recreate at least one aspect of realistic camera blur—that the hotspots do not dim down as they are blurred, but retain their brightness. True linear color includes overhead for overbright pixels, and so you can build up a boke-like effect by building up (via Add mode) and blurring elements in the scene that should appear brighter than the surrounding scene. The re-lighting tutorial at the end of Chapter 12 includes creation of a sun sphere in just this manner.

There are also third-party solutions out there to help you fake this effect. I don't mean the verb "fake" to connote that you should instead go for the "real" method. This phenomenon occurs only when a blurred or defocused element passes through a physical lens, so if you're recreating this in After Effects, faking it is your only option. The best tool on the market for creating good-looking lens blurs is probably Frischluft's Lenscare (for After Effects and Photoshop). The default settings are not reliable, but if you're willing to make some adjustments and use such optional additions as depth maps (for 3D footage), you can derive some lovely results with this plug-in (www.frischluft.com).

Figures 9.25a, b, and c Motion blur generated the standard way (9.25a and b) literally pales in comparison to true motion blur on illuminated elements (9.25c).

If you're interested in learning more about the phenomenon of boke, good information is available on the Web. At www.bokeh.com you will find links to essays and tests exploring camera blur, including an excellent essay from luminous-landscape.com written by Michael Reichmann.

The day may come when digital cameras are capable of delivering moving footage that has no grain whatsoever. Already, high-definition video cameras used to shoot movies pick up clearer detail than film cameras, all other things being equal. For example, miniatures for *Star Wars, Episode One: The Phantom Menace,* the first big-budget film to be shot on digital video, had to be created with greater detail than typical film miniatures because of what the digital camera exposed.

You might not be able to recreate the look of that twenty-dollar bill in **Figure 9.23** so easily, but if you pay attention to what happens in these surprising reference images, your camera blur will be that much closer to what you would get out of a real, defocused camera.

The Role of Grain

Beyond lens effects, you will need to consider another attribute of images shot with a real camera: grain. Grain is essentially high-frequency noise that occupies every channel of your shot to some degree. And grain is your friend, as long as you give it the proper amount of attention.

Grain can give texture and life to images and help to conceal a multitude of small details, enabling compositors to get away with illusions. Just like depth of field and motion blur, grain can be a problem or the key to a whole cinematic look.

For compositors, perhaps the most important role of grain is its role integrating a flat, static layer with moving footage, adding life to an element that otherwise looks oddly suspended out of the time and place of the rest of the scene **(Figure 9.26)**.

Figure 9.26 Solid areas of color are always the best for examining grain, and it always appears, even on perfectly shot 2 K film plates (here zoomed in to 400%). Drop in a solid the same color as the plate, and you see that it fails to blend with its surroundings. The effect is even more pronounced with moving footage, especially at film resolution.

Proper grain is not simply switched on or off, however; it needs to be carefully adjusted. You can become quite theoretical about all this, but really you need to concern yourself with only two basic factors:

▶ Size of the grain

▶ Amount of grain, or amount of contrast in the grain

The trick is that these factors typically vary from channel to channel. Blue is almost universally the channel likeliest to have the most noise; happily the human eye is less sensitive to blue than red or green, but this can be bad news for blue-screen shoots.

How much grain is enough? As with color in Chapter 5, "Color and Light: Adjusting and Matching," your goal is typically to match what's there already. If your shot has a background plate with the proper amount of grain in it, you match your foreground elements to that. In the case of a fully computer-generated scene, you might have to match surrounding shots that have plate reference, which you would match in the same manner.

Grain Management Strategies

After Effects 6.5 Professional includes a suite of three tools for automated grain sampling, grain reduction, and grain generation: Add Grain, Match Grain, and Remove Grain. Add Grain you adjust entirely manually, but Match Grain and Remove Grain sample a noise source layer to give you an initial result that you can then adjust.

If you've been reading closely up to this point, you know I'm not a fan of using the automated solutions. Not so in this case. The Match Grain effect does not seem to be appreciably slower due to grain sampling than Add Grain, which does not perform any sampling and includes all of the same controls. Therefore, I recommend you see what Match Grain can come up with as a starting point, and then work from there. In either case, the steps are the same:

1. Look for a section of your source footage that contains a solid color area and little or no motion for 10 to 20 frames. Most clips have this, and those that don't tend to let you be a bit more fast and loose with grain anyhow.

NOTES

Grain is often the result of a low amount of light coming through the lens combined with a low-quality image-gathering medium, such as 8 mm film or miniDV, that has poor light-gathering abilities or large silver particles (typical of faster, cheaper film stocks).

2. Zoom to 200% to 400% on the solid color area, and create a Region of Interest around it. Set the Work Area to the 10 or 20 frames with little or no motion.

3. Add a solid that is small enough to occupy part of the Region of Interest. Apply a Ramp effect to the solid, and use the eyedropper tools to select the darkest and lightest pixels in the solid color area of the clip. The lack of grain detail in the foreground gradient should be clearly apparent (**Figure 9.27**).

4. Apply the Match Grain effect to the foreground solid. Choose the source footage layer in the Noise Source Layer pull-down. As soon as the effect finishes rendering a sample frame, you have a basis from which to begin fine-tuning. You can RAM preview at this point to see how close a match you have. In most cases, you won't be done yet.

5. Twirl down the Tweaking controls for Match Grain, and then twirl down Channel Intensities and Channel Size. You can save yourself a lot of time by doing most of your work here, channel by channel.

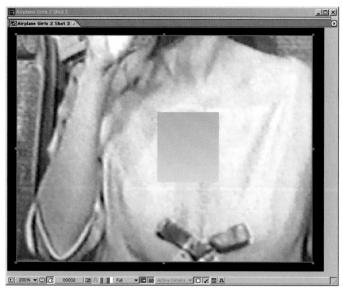

Figure 9.27 Inserting a small solid with a Ramp effect, and then using the eyedropper tools in Ramp to sample the brightest and darkest areas of the background will give you a much clearer idea of how good a grain match you're getting once you apply the Match Grain or Add Grain effect.

6. Activate the red channel only in the Composition window (**Alt+1/Option+1**) and adjust the Red Intensity and Red Size values to match the foreground and background (**Figure 9.28**). Repeat this process for the green and blue channels (**Alt+2/Option+2** and **Alt+3/Option+3**). RAM preview the result.

7. Feel free to adjust the overall Intensity, Size, or Softness controls under Tweaking according to what you see in the RAM preview. You may also find it necessary to reduce Saturation under Color, particularly if your source is film rather than video.

In most cases, this is all you need to do for a result that will work. You can copy the effect and paste it to any foreground layers that need grain. If the foreground layer already contains noise or grain, you may need to adjust the Compensate for Existing Noise percentage for that layer.

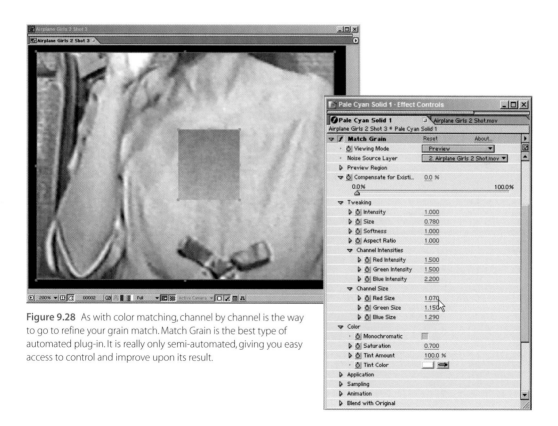

Figure 9.28 As with color matching, channel by channel is the way to go to refine your grain match. Match Grain is the best type of automated plug-in. It is really only semi-automated, giving you easy access to control and improve upon its result.

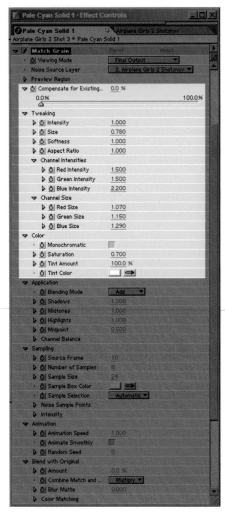

Obviously, I left a lot of other controls alone (**Figure 9.29**); the Application category, for example, contains controls for how the grain is blended and how it affects shadows, midtones, and highlights individually. Typically these are overkill, as are the Sampling and Animation controls, but how far you go in matching grain before your eye is satisfied is, of course, up to you. This is one more case in which slamming the result can help ascertain its effectiveness (**Figure 9.30**).

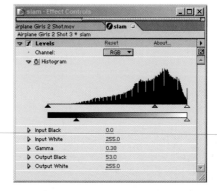

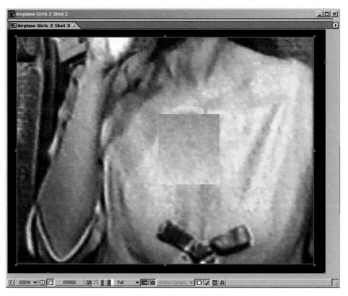

Figure 9.29 Match Grain clearly has a lot of controls, and yet the ones you will use most often are in the highlighted region, mostly under the Tweaking and Color categories. It is best to go top to bottom, first adjusting overall Intensity, Size, and Softness, then refining the individual Channel Intensities and Channel Size (as in **Figure 9.28**).

Figure 9.30 How good a match? As always, slam the result—with an adjustment layer containing a Levels effect with its Gamma and Output Black raised—and behold. Adjust Match Grain as needed. Not bad in this case.

Grain Removal

Removing grain, or sharpening an image in general, is a completely different process from adding grain. Typically on a production that has been well shot, however, you'll rarely have a reason to reach for the Remove Grain tool.

If you do, your reason will probably be unique to your particular footage. In such cases, you may very well find that Remove Grain at the default settings gives you a satisfactory result. If not, check into the Fine Tuning and Unsharp Mask settings to adjust it.

Remove Grain is often most useful sort of "behind the scenes," in other words not across the whole final shot (**Figure 9.31**), or in combination with other effects. If you're using Remove Grain to improve the likelihood of a clean blue-screen or green-screen key, apply the resulting matte back to your source footage as an alpha track matte. That way you get the best of both worlds: a clean matte channel and realistic grain on the source color layer.

Using Noise for Grain

Prior to the addition of Add Grain and Match Grain to version 6.5 Professional, the typical way to generate grain was to use the Noise effect. The main advantage of Noise effect over Match Grain is that it renders 20 times faster. The downsides are that After Effects doesn't make it easy for you to separate noise channel by channel, nor can you hold out noise to foreground elements only while viewing the background. Scaling it requires a separate effect. But adding grain is one of those areas where you can often get away with less than 100% accuracy.

. . . .

You can use three solid layers, with three effects applied to each layer: Shift Channels, Noise, and Transform. You use Shift Channels to set each solid to red, green, or blue, respectively, set their Blending Modes to Add, and set their Opacity very low. Next, set the amount of noise and scale it in the Transform effect.

. . . .

If the grain is meant to affect a set of foreground layers only, hold them out from the background plate either using pre-composing or track mattes. If this sounds complicated, it is, which is why Match Grain is the better choice if it's available.

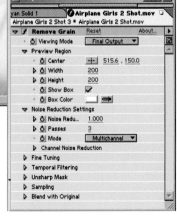

Figure 9.31 Although it may look nice for a still figure in a book, the results of Remove Grain applied to the whole shot at the default settings are rarely what you want. The solid with the Ramp effect now matches quite well with no grain applied to it whatsoever, but in full motion the grain-reduced shot looks a bit strange and retains a certain soft lumpiness. Still, it's a powerful tool if you need it, and you can certainly dial it back.

Chapter 10, "Expressions," offers a unique and highly effective strategy for removing extreme amounts of grain from a locked-off shot using expressions.

When to Employ Grain Strategies

The most obvious time to add grain to a layer is in cases where the layer is computer-generated or a still image. In either case, it will lack any of the moving grain that you would find in film or video footage. Pixar does not add grain to its final shots because they are internally consistent; none of the shots originated on film or video, so they all lack appreciable grain. As soon as your shot has to match anything that came from a camera, and particularly if it's going to be projected, you need to manage grain.

You also may have to add grain to an element if it has blur applied to it. Blurry source shots can still contain quite a bit of grain over the blur because the grain is an artifact of the medium recording the image, not the subject itself. Elements that are scaled down in After Effects also have the grain scaled down, another case in which it may be necessary to restore it.

Blue-screen footage that has been keyed may also need grain added. Remember, the blue channel contains more grain, typically, than red or green. Suppressing the blue channel in a color key operation, therefore, can also suppress grain too much for it to match other footage.

Other compositing operations can enhance the grain of an element. Sharpening, if it is not done via the Remove Grain tool, can strongly emphasize grain contrast in an element, typically in a not-so-desirable manner. Sharpening also brings out any nasty compression artifacts that come with footage that uses JPEG-type compression, such as miniDV video.

Lack of grain, however, is one of the big dead giveaways of a poorly composited shot. It is worth the effort to match the correct amount of grain into your shot even if the result isn't apparent as you preview it on your monitor. Especially when outputting to film, but even with video, elements with the wrong amount of grain stand out unpleasantly and fail to look natural.

Film and Video Looks

Grain is only one of the many properties associated with a film look. People tend to mean different things when they speak about a film or video look. That's because they have different purposes in mind for creating these looks.

I can think of two very different reasons to shoot video and try to make it look like film:

▶ The story calls for a sequence to appear as if it was shot on old home movie stock, such as Super 8 (a popular format from the '60s and '70s).

▶ The filmmaker wants to shoot as cheaply as possible, yet achieve the look of an expensive feature film.

The first situation is relatively simple and straightforward. In the same way that you match the color and grain of foreground elements to the background, you can match a whole shot to the look of an old film stock using those same grain and color tools, plus maybe extra tricks, such as a vignette effect, which offers the look of projected film, brighter in the center and fading to black at the edges (**Figure 9.32**). As always, I encourage you to get reference if you're not sure what to do.

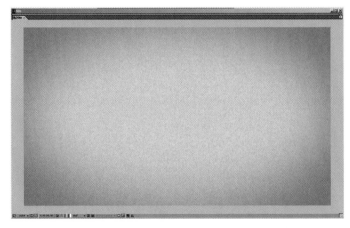

Figure 9.32 The easy clichés of film: heavy grain, a light vignette effect, a slight leaning away from saturated reds and yellows. These are stylized ways of telling the audience it is looking at a filmic image.

NOTES

This discussion, by the way, is nothing against the look of video. There could, hypothetically, be a situation in which you wanted something shot on film to look as though it were video. That's unlikely given basic economics, however; film is far more expensive than video, and although we may see its virtual demise in our lifetimes, it retains a cachet that video lacks. On the other hand, if you submitted a reel to any of the top of visual effects facilities in the world and you had convincingly made it look like your visual effects shot was taken with a Handycam, there is no doubt you would get the job.

The second situation, however, is nearly broad enough to constitute a whole other book. I almost hesitate to bring it up in the context of a visual effects book, but I've seen enough situations in which a student or low-budget filmmaker clearly went for a filmic look and missed in elementary ways that it seems helpful to offer a few pointers. If, for example, you are just starting out and creating a shot to go on a reel to apply for jobs in the film industry, your work will be judged more harshly if it seems to have gone for a film look and failed.

Here are three important distinctions that come into play differentiating film from video that I have seen novices overlook:

▶ **Garbage in, garbage out.** It sounds obvious, but if you're shooting your own footage (say, on miniDV tape), simple decisions that you make when you shoot can have profound consequences when it comes time to make the shot look its best. Too often, artists learn too late what they end up trying (and failing) to fight against in postproduction.

▶ **Frame rate and format matter.** Frame rate and format might seem to be inconsequential or a matter of personal preference, but I would argue that when low-budget video producers are trying to make shots look filmic, frame rate, at least, might be the most important ingredient.

▶ **Color affects story.** Changes to color and contrast can change the overall mood of a shot.

The following sections offer a few simple pointers for anyone with an effects shoot on a tight budget and the goal of producing a shot that will stand up against feature film footage.

Garbage In, Garbage Out

Garbage in, garbage out isn't a new principle. But what does it mean in this context? Here are some specifics (with details following):

▶ Don't try to do things on set that you can easily add in post, but equally, don't neglect things on set that will be difficult if not impossible to fix in post.

▶ Don't underlight a scene, but for God's sake don't over-light it. Keep the contrast low.

▶ Plan carefully: Storyboard, scout, and eliminate variables.

The most radical thing you can do on set to ensure a good result when shooting miniDV or HDV video is to aim for a low-contrast master that looks horrible to the director of photography. As Stu Maschwitz said about shooting this way, "The on-set monitor [is] not the answer print but the negative." Whites in particular, once blown out, are impossible to recover (**Figure 9.33**).

Most camera operators would be inclined to deliver an image on set that looked as close as possible to how the final should look. This is often an appropriate strategy with film. With digital video, however, shooting a low-contrast source leaves ample room to bring out a high dynamic range using tools such as Levels and Curves in After Effects.

Figure 9.33 Sunsets are notoriously difficult for digital cameras to capture. Once those hot areas of the image are blown out, they're not coming back, nor is detail returning to the foreground. Even in lower-contrast images, as the color levels approach full white or black, you lose all room to maneuver in After Effects. This problem is a centerpiece of Chapter 11.

Frame Rate Matters

Many artists would argue this point, but I'm going to go out on a limb and say it straight out: If you want your footage to look filmic, the frame rate had better be 24 fps.

One of my favorite demonstrations of the difference between 24 fps film and 60 field per second NTSC video dates back to the Golden Age of television and is available on DVD. In 1960, when the original *Twilight Zone* was in production, the crew decided to shoot on video rather than film during the second season as a cost-cutting measure.

The experiment lasted six episodes ("Static," "Night of the Meek," "The Lateness of the Hour," "The Whole Truth," "Twenty-Two," and "Long Distance Call"), then was abandoned. The difference in how the drama "reads" on video versus film is simply incredible. The video versions are almost like watching a soap opera; the film versions retain all of the spare, noir ironic distance and mystique that made the series famous. In short, the videotaped versions have immediacy, but the film versions seem timeless.

If you're with me on this, but you're still faced with shooting NTSC video, consider carefully if there's any way to capture your footage using the slower frame rate. It is certainly possible to convert 29.97 fps video to 23.976 fps (otherwise known as 24 fps), but the resulting motion will stutter as every fifth frame is skipped. Many contemporary video cameras include a 24 fps mode; prior to that, digital filmmakers would use 25 fps PAL format cameras and slow the footage down to 24 fps. These options are worth considering.

Again, if the immediacy of the reality television look is what you're after, by all means, go for it: Shoot your source with a consumer video camera and match elements to that. It's not a question of better or worse, it's a question of immediate versus timeless.

Format Matters

As the world transitions from standard definition to high-definition broadcast television, formats are making the same transition that they made in film half a century ago. The nearly square 4:3 aspect ratio is giving way to wider formats: 16:9, 1.85 Academy aperture, even 2.35 Cinema-scope, and who knows what next.

Big-budget films are often made for more than one format, and you can do the same with some preplanning. When the film is intended both for theatrical release and the home video market, all of the effects might be created at a 4:3 aspect ratio and then masked off for the wider theatrical version. This is fine as long as you're aware at every stage of production what the safe areas of your frame are. For example, on *The Day After Tomorrow* the theatrical mask sat near the top of the frame, so that all of the less-essential action had to be planned for the bottom of the frame. This one had the nickname Ueli-mask, after the film's cinematographer, Ueli Steiger.

Color Affects Story

The influence of color decisions on the final shot, and by extension on the story being told in the shot, is a big topic, discussed by cinematographers and colorists the world

NOTES

The numbers "1.85" and "2.35" referred to the ratio of the width to a height of 1, so it's the same as saying 1.85:1 or 2.35:1, respectively. The 16:9 format, which has become popular with digital video, is equivalent to a 1.77:1 ratio, slightly narrower than Academy, but wide compared to the standard television format of 4:3 (which translates to 1.33:1). See Chapter 11 for more on this.

over. Trying to distill it into a few pithy paragraphs here would do it a disservice.

So here's a suggestion: If you're new to the idea of developing a color look for a film or sequence, get reference. Study other people's work for the effect of color on the mood and story in a shot, sequence, or entire film. **Figure 9.34** is taken from an independent short film series shot on DV but intended to parody the look and attitude of big budget action movies; the transformation of before and after is fairly radical.

You can find third-party plug-ins dedicated specifically to lending a film look to video. Many are dedicated to the first motivation for creating a film look: They can make your shot look grainier, scratched, vignetted, jittery, and generally like it was shot with the oldest, most poorly maintained film camera in the world, with the negative being dragged across the floor of the lab and stepped on for good measure.

Reliable methods for fabricating the expensive film looks of twenty-first century Hollywood, however, are harder to come by. Stu Maschwitz developed the Magic Bullet Suite (a set of plug-ins for After Effects and Apple's Final Cut

Figure 9.34 Radical color transformation is undertaken to give this no-budget action movie parody the feel of one of the films it satirizes. Techniques such as using a color solid to transform the lighting and color of footage are explored throughout Chapter 12. (Images courtesy of markandmatty.com.)

Pro) so that The Orphanage could help filmmakers who want to shoot on cheap and easy miniDV cameras, but who demand the look of film; thereafter, the software was made publicly available. Amongst the suite's many tools are Magic Bullet, which converts video footage to 24 fps with special emphasis on de-artifacting, and Look Suite, which contains preset looks designed to match existing film styles and processes. There is no direct replacement for these tools (which you can check out for yourself on the book's CD-ROM), but Chapter 12 looks at simpler ways to match certain looks.

Conclusion

And really, you've just scratched the surface of what's possible. The inventive compositor can and should always look for new methods to replicate the way that the camera sees the world, going beyond realism to present the realism we've become so accustomed to seeing—realism through the lens.

CHAPTER

10

Expressions

Music is math.

—Michael Sandison and Marcus Eoin
(Boards of Canada)

Expressions

Expressions open up a whole new realm of functionality in After Effects by enabling you to link elements of your project together and apply logic and bits of math to the connections.

Here is where the standard disclaimer is usually added about how artists don't like logic and bits of math and where I promise to shield you from it as much as possible. But I don't buy the underlying assumption that because you are a visual artist, you don't want to be bothered with pesky numerical data, technical details, logic, or math.

Admit it: You deal with that stuff all the time. Of course you do, you're an After Effects user. The job of expressions is, generally speaking, to make logical connections easier and to automate the tedious parts of animating. So it's not like you get out of having to deal with this just because you don't fully understand expressions—you still have the problem, just with a less-elegant solution.

There is one thing about expressions, however, that strikes the majority of After Effects users as inelegant: They require the use of code. To harness the power of expressions, you have to examine, think about, and occasionally type little bits of code.

In this chapter, I will try to make the case that it's worth dealing with a little bit of code—often just one line in these examples, all or part of which can be entered automatically—to get the flexibility and power of expressions. If you're still not convinced to at least give it a try, realize that you have condemned yourself to spending more time piecing together solutions in the UI to perform operations that expressions are designed to do.

With that out of the way, let's look at an overview of what is possible with expressions. Some of the most typical things you might do are

▶ Create a one-to-one relationship between data from two different animation channels (whether from the same layer, separate layers, or even separate compositions)

▶ Scale and offset keyframe values

▶ Link values to a slider control for easy access

▶ "Mute" keyframe values by replacing them with a constant value

▶ Loop

▶ Destabilize or smooth camera moves or any animation data (while the source data remains in place)

▶ Use time and index values to progress animation data and specifically, to remove noise from a locked shot when it is too prominent for the Remove Grain effect

▶ Create a conditional statement that causes something to happen when specified criteria are met and specifically, to trigger a film dissolve using comp markers

▶ Emulate 3-D tracking (in case you don't have access to a third-party 3D tracker)

In looking at that list, you may see things that you've always wanted to do in After Effects and things you'd never thought of doing. If you can get the hang of how these examples work, you'll be able to apply the same principles to similar but unique situations on your own.

Rather than taking you step by step through learning expressions from scratch, this chapter outlines and deconstructs useful applications of expressions to demonstrate how they work, moving from the simplest to the most complicated examples. I'll do my best to fill in the gaps for you, and at the end of the chapter, I'll touch on what to do to go beyond what's here.

Logic and Grammar, in that Order

There are only two components to learning how to use expressions:

▶ You must be able to reason out the solution you are pursuing in a methodical, step-by-step fashion.

▶ You must translate this ordinary language methodology to the logic and syntax of expressions into lines of code.

Expressions really do only one thing: translate data values. Granted, that's a little bit like saying your computer's hard drive only has ones and zeros on it, but it's useful to think of this.

Fundamentally, there are three types of data with which expressions work:

▶ Numbers

▶ Booleans (True/False or Yes/No)

▶ Text strings

Expressions can either link to these values where they are found among data in After Effects or fabricate the data using criteria that you, the user, specify. And generally, text is used as only a label for a layer or effect, not as an input/output value—so text almost doesn't count.

So where do these numbers come from? Almost anywhere. They can derive from the basic transform data (position, rotation, scale, opacity, anchor point) of a layer, the current position on the timeline, the number in which the layer appears in the composition, the pixel dimensions of the source footage, whether or not a layer has a parent, and on and on. Pretty much every piece of numerical or Boolean data that exists in your After Effects project is accessible to expressions and can be used to create animations.

Okay, What *Can't* Expressions Do?

Expressions cannot evaluate certain types of data:

▶ Pixel values

▶ Audio waveforms

▶ Mask data

Nor can they handle certain complex effects data, such as effects channels that can be keyframed but whose keyframe values are not made up of four or fewer numerical values. For example, expressions work with RGBA data—red, green, blue, and alpha channel values normalized between 0 and 1—but they can't handle the Channel Range color control in Hue/Saturation.

So, although you can change the pixel values and audio levels of a layer using expressions, you can't sample a given pixel's RGB values, the decibel level of a soundtrack, or the position of a mask point.

One other major limitation is that expressions are incapable of compounding data over time. In other words, calculations that involve a progression from frame to frame cause expressions to recalculate all frames prior to the current one as each new frame is loaded; in such cases, the further you get down the timeline, the longer frames require to render. For example, in *After Effects 5.5 Magic* (New Riders Publishing), I demonstrated drawing a spirograph shape over time using the Write On effect to add a series of dots to make a line. Each successive dot took longer to calculate its position than the one previous, because it had to know the positions of all of the dots up to that point to know what came next. If that still sounds confusing, don't worry about it; until you find yourself writing an expression that increments with time, you won't likely run up against it.

Muting Keyframes

How many times have I heard someone wish for the ability to temporarily disable keyframes in After Effects? You can do this with just about the simplest expression it is possible to write. Not only is disabling keyframes useful when working with an element that is meant to be barely or only occasionally visible (say, one with a keyframed Opacity level below 10%), but you can also use this trick for any property that will let you set an expression. This method of applying expressions is so elementary, there is no excuse for anyone not to use it.

Creative Accounting

There are, of course, workarounds to the limitations of expressions. The commonly used Levels effect, for example, has an Individual Controls version that was created expressly (pun intended) for use with expressions.

For sampling sound, Trapcode (www.trapcode.com) offers Sound Keys, which can translate waveforms into numerical data suitable for expressions.

As for such unreachable data as mask vertices, it is theoretically possible to sample and adjust them using scripting. I've just never known anyone geeky enough to try it.

NOTES

The After Effects expressions language is based on JavaScript, a scripting language that was originally devised for Web browsers. Many functions that are fundamental to JavaScript, such as the ability to perform mathematical operations, work identically with expressions. Of course, many other functions from JavaScript are specific to the Web and interactivity, and have no application in After Effects. Likewise, After Effects adds its own keywords, functions, and attributes; these use the same basic syntax and rules of JavaScript but would not be recognized by it.

Consider the opacity example: You have an element that is flickering at low opacity, that is blinking, or that for some other reason has Opacity keyframes assigned. You don't want to lose these keyframes, but they prevent you from properly seeing the layer for setup.

The expressions solution for this is trivially easy, and it doesn't require an understanding of JavaScript. It might even help you understand something basic about expressions, especially if you've ever tried to decipher one and wondered where the value is held.

With keyframes already set to the Opacity of a layer, set an expression for Opacity. There are several ways to do this once you've selected the property to receive the expression. For example, you can use the Animation menu or a keyboard shortcut (**Alt+Shift+=/Option+Shift+=**), but it's usually done by Alt-clicking (Option-clicking) on the stopwatch of the property (in this case, Opacity).

Before solving the example's problem, take a quick look at what occurs when you set an expression (**Figure 10.1**). Note the equals sign toggle that appears next to the stopwatch; you can use this to turn the expression on and off. Also, note that After Effects adds a new line below the property. This line contains text that is automatically highlighted directly after you apply the expression. In this case, the text reads `opacity`, and the cursor blinks to indicate that the text is live. This is useful, because the first thing you want to do is usually to replace or augment this text.

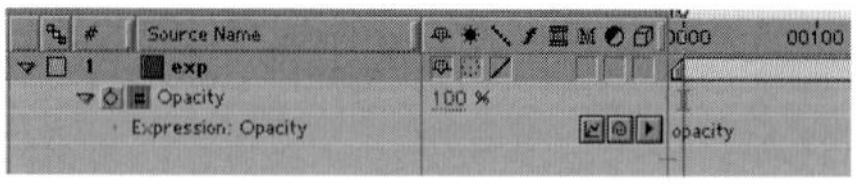

That one word, "opacity," is an expression. It tells After Effects to look at the layer's Opacity channel for its value, which is, of course, what happens under normal circumstances. Nothing about the functionality has changed. If you moved opacity over to an expression on the Rotation property, however, then Rotation would get its value from the layer's Opacity value, including any keyframes and expressions, as well. But I'm getting ahead of myself.

Replace `opacity` with `100` and either press Enter (not Return) or just click outside the text area. Now, instead of looking back at its own keyframe data, Opacity looks at this

Figure 10.1 With the default expression activated for the Opacity channel, the opacity value of 100% turns red and a new cursor with an equals sign appears next to the stopwatch; this toggles the expression on and off. The following line, revealed by the twirly arrow, contains the expression itself along with icons for the graph, pickwhip, and keywords.

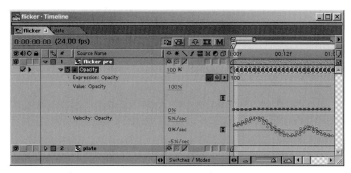

Figure 10.2 If Opacity (or any property) has keyframes set, a number in the expressions field overrides them and sets it to that value. The flat red line in the graph shows you what's going on.

one value, 100, on every frame of the composition (**Figure 10.2**). The keyframes have effectively been "muted," replaced with a constant value.

Toggle the Expressions button (the equals sign next to the stopwatch) to enable/disable the keyframes. The only danger here is that you'll forget to turn this expression off when you're done with it, but that's not really the fault of expressions, now is it? You can optionally delete the expression instead, the same way that you set it—by Alt/Option-clicking on the stopwatch.

Things work a little differently with properties that contain more than one value, such as Position. These are called *arrays* and are detailed in the next section.

Linking Animation Data

It's good to start simple, but the bread and butter job of expressions is to link animation data when, for whatever reason, the other means of linking data will not do. Other linking methods all have their place, but have their limitations as well:

▶ **Parenting** is a great way to link translation data between layers, but not if you want to exclude part of the data—for example, to include position but not rotation—or if you want to link translation data to properties, such as brushes and effects positions, that are tied to effects rather than the layer itself.

▶ **Pre-composing** allows you to group layers, but not to link their actual data in more sophisticated ways.

▶ **Copying and pasting** keyframes is possible and will even allow you to copy data from one property over to a completely different property, but the link is not "live." If anything changes with the source, you have to recopy to the target, and you cannot easily scale or offset the result, nor go from a one-channel to a multiple-channel property or vice versa. Furthermore, this method has a high possibility of user error and is largely outmoded by the expressions pickwhip (**Figure 10.3**).

None of these methods lets you do more complex relationships, such as setting up a nonlinear relationship between two sets of values (for example, doubling or squaring the keyframe values).

Following are some practical examples of linking data via expressions, with explanations of what is really going on so that you can devise your own practical applications. These examples save you from having to type code by leveraging use of the pickwhip, a nifty tool for grabbing bits of data and turning them effortlessly into useful bits of code (which you've already seen used with Parenting and Post Render Actions).

Tracking Brushes and Effects

Chapters 7, "Rotoscoping and Paint," and 8, "Effective Motion Tracking," alluded to a method for combining paint tools and the tracker. The problem is a simple one: How to apply tracker data to a brush to automatically paint out an element in motion?

The only one of the above alternatives to expressions that could work in this case would be copying the attach point

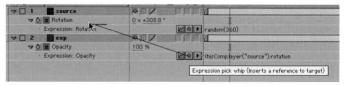

Figure 10.3 The pickwhip in action: Set it by dragging from the pickwhip item to the target property.

of the tracker, highlighting the Position value of the brush in question, and pasting, but what if the result doesn't look quite right and you need to retrack it?

The simpler, more flexible solution is to use the pickwhip, and in cases where you are setting up a one-to-one relationship between two properties, that is all you need. I'll show you some less straightforward cases in a minute.

Figure 10.4 shows a clip of a plane landing in the distance; let's say that this plane needs to be painted out to be replaced with a 3D model of a flying saucer. The Track Type could be set to Raw because I'm applying the tracking data via expressions only. The attach point can be offset so that it sits at the center of the airplane, although offsetting it is also simple, as you'll see.

Having tracked the plane, I return to the first frame and use the Clone Stamp tool to eliminate the plane on that frame by painting over it with surrounding cloud cover (any adjacent area of the same frame works). I can use a nice big brush (100 or more pixels) to eliminate the plane by clicking once in roughly the same place as I placed the attach point (the center of the airplane). Best in this case is

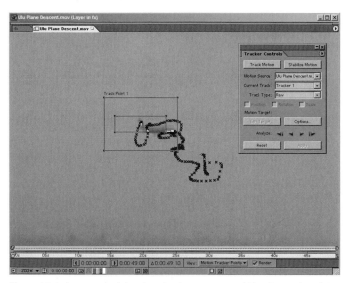

Figure 10.4 A raw track of the plane has been generated. The dips and swirls in the motion are due to the shot having been taken with a hand-held camera. The camera Track Type is set to Raw.

Geek Alert: Unpacking Syntax

Okay, so you're not satisfied until you understand that little piece of code you just grabbed, although you're wary of delving into code. Take a closer look at the syntax of that brush stroke:

```
motionTracker("Tracker
➥1")("Track Point 1").
➥attachPoint
```

This works similarly to how pathnames work in Unix or Windows: Starting at the left, `motion-Tracker` contains Tracker 1, which has a Track Point 1, which in turn contains the property you're after, the attach point.

What's up with the parentheses, the quotations, and the dot? Parentheses in JavaScript contain *arguments*, which are specifics needed to clarify settings, in this case, telling After Effects which point, in which tracker, you're after. The `motion-Tracker` property is unusual in that it needs two sets of arguments, each in its own set of parentheses. The dot works the same way a forward slash would in Unix (or a back slash in Windows): It identifies the next level down in the hierarchy, like looking inside a folder.

Keywords in expressions use inter-caps, so that a keyword is made of two words with no spaces. For example, motion tracker and attach point, end up as `motionTracker` and `attachPoint`, respectively.

to clone out the unwanted object in one stroke, so that you only have to join the tracker to that one, but it's possible to repeat this step.

With the layer highlighted in the timeline, I press **UU** to expose the tracker and brush data. I set an expression on the Position of the brush, then drag the pickwhip—the swirly icon in the center of the three—up to where I see the words, "attach point."

Done. The resulting expression looks something like

```
motionTracker("Tracker 1")("Track Point 1").
➥attachPoint
```

But why sweat the syntax? I've just set up an automatic link between these two properties, and with the pickwhip, I can always grab available data in this manner.

Offsetting an Element

Now let's say that instead of painting out the plane, I want to add a flying saucer tracking it from a higher altitude and left of frame. I could apply the tracker to a null and parent the repositioned element to that, but it would be simpler to offset the same expression I just used, now applied to the Position value of the saucer. To start, I again pickwhip from the saucer's Position to the track's attach point.

Offsets are quite intuitive even to people who don't understand JavaScript very well. Perhaps you want to offset a value by –100. What would you add at the end of the default expression text? That's right, –100. Try it on a Position value and it works—kind of. The object moves 100 pixels, but on the X axis only.

Position is an array, a property with multiple values. A 2D Position property has two values, X and Y, and a 3D layer's Position would add a third (as would Anchor Point and Rotation, which otherwise has one value). So while offsetting and scaling values is simple—you use the basic math operators (+, -, *, /)—things get slightly less straightforward with arrays—but only slightly.

An array value is written in expressions as [x, y] for a 2D value or [x, y, z] for 3D. So if you want to mute a Position keyframe at the center of a 720, 540 frame, you enter [360, 270] (half each value), and if you want to offset each value by negative one hundred (-100), you add -[100, 100] after the pickwhip data to add the offset (**Figure 10.5**). If you needed to mix a positive and negative offset of 100, that would be simple too: instead, add + [-100, 100] or +[100, -100] and so on.

Yes, this is quick and dirty; the goal here is to offer you the low-hanging fruit, the things you do all the time with expressions that are easy to pick up. A more elegant way of setting a constant position at the center of the frame would be

```
[thisComp.width/2, thisComp.height/2]
```

because this expression would adjust itself to any composition size. There are typically many ways to write any expression; the simplest (with the fewest lines or operations) that applies to the greatest number of variables (such as changes in the comp size) is typically the preferable one, as with all coding.

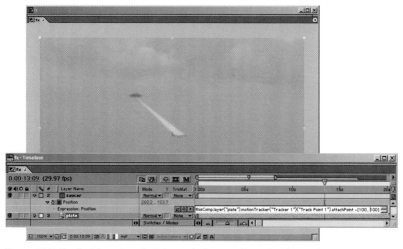

Figure 10.5 The Position value of a Paint stroke is a two-dimensional array; the highlighted text shows how to perform a simple offset of such an array.

One Channel Only

Okay, now suppose you need to link something on one axis only: say, heads-up display pointers that move up and down along the left and bottom edges of the frame, tracking the enemy craft (not a typical effects scenario, but one that easily demonstrates what I'm after). This time what you want to do is keep the value of one axis in a static position, and to apply your track to the other axis.

This gives you the opportunity to learn a useful new bit of syntax. You know how to write an array, but how do you identify one portion of the array? Like this

```
[position[0], position[1]]
```

Whoa, more brackets. Once again, you're expressing position as two values separated by a comma in brackets, but the values themselves are identified by trailing numbers in brackets. The numerical order starts at 0, not 1, because this is how programming languages generally work.

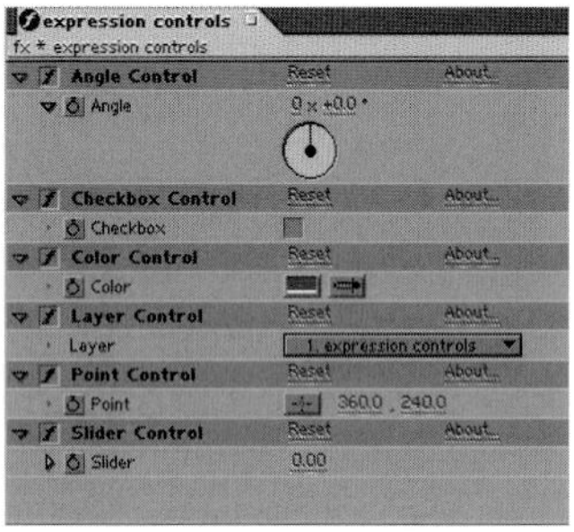

So, to keep the existing value on the X axis and the track on the Y axis, you would enter position[0] (or a static value, like 400) before the comma and pickwhip the Y value to the Y value of the attach point. That's right, not only can you pickwhip to the attach point, but if you drag the pickwhip instead to just one of its values—the second one, in this case—you get the code linking you only to that value (**Figure 10.6**). Once again, the pickwhip has saved you from typing in some gnarly code, but you need to know the simple stuff.

To do the same on the other axis, just reverse the steps, pickwhipping before the comma and entering position[1] following it.

This rather trivial example has hopefully elucidated a powerful concept, of using expressions to apply data to one channel only. This is the first example we've examined that would truly be impossible without expressions—none of the alternative methods offer a method to apply animation data to only one channel of a property.

Figure 10.6 You can pickwhip from a single channel of an array (a property with multiple values) to the corresponding single channel of a separate array.

Building Your Own Controls

Here's another really cool, really basic thing you can do with expressions: link effects controls to properties to allow you to control them in the Effects Control window. It's incredibly simple, too.

The effects found within the Expression Controls sub-category don't do anything until you attach an expression to them. That's all they're for, to offer you a user interface for adjusting your expressions values on the fly. The one you'll most often use is likely Slider Control, but look carefully at the other five, as each produces a different result (**Figure 10.7**).

Anyhow, for now, say you want to make yourself a zoom control slider for a 3D camera. You may never have needed to do this, but it hardly matters—it won't be long before you think of another property you want to attach to a slider, and once you see how easy it is, you'll be actively looking for opportunities to use this.

You can't apply effects to a camera, so you need to apply the slider to a different layer, and it hardly matters which one. The slider will affect only a layer containing an expression pointing to it. The normal method would be to put it on a null or adjustment layer named Controls or something similar so that it's easy to find later.

To the Controls layer you apply Slider Control. Now to be really organized you might as well rename this control something intuitive and unique, such as Zoomer, by highlighting the effect name and pressing the Return key, then typing in the new name. It's important to do all of your renaming before applying an expression, because, lamentably, expressions do not auto-update their contents to reflect changed target names, so they will break, generate an error, and disable themselves.

Now the easy part: Apply an expression to the Zoom property of the camera, and pickwhip to the Zoomer property. You can even pickwhip up to the Effects Control window instead of revealing it in the timeline. The zoom will snap to the value shown on the slider, which by default is 0, so your camera position now needs to be adjusted.

Figure 10.7 Here's the full array of available expression controls, all applied to a single layer. These look familiar because they are standard to other effects as well. Each generates a unique type of data: Angle generates radians and degrees, Checkbox is a Boolean, Color three values between 0 and 255, Layer a layer in the current comp, and Point an array of two values. Only Slider generates a single floating-point number.

Figure 10.8 Slider range values can be set anywhere between the specified maximum and minimum values, not only for the Expression Slider but any effect.

You can raise the slider to zoom in, but the 0 to 100 range is probably not going to be sufficient. This can be changed by context-clicking on the Zoomer value, choosing Edit Value, and then setting new Slider Range values (**Figure 10.8**).

In this case, however, there's an alternative. Say that you want the zoom to increment logarithmically, by powers of 2. That means the slider value is multiplied by itself, and you probably now know how to set the expression to do this. You take the existing pickwhip path, copy it, add a * symbol directly after the original version, and then paste in the copy. Voila, it's multiplied by itself, and the zoom control feels more like a real zoom.

NOTES

What's up with spaces? Typing "x * x" or "x*x" in an expression has the same result. In fact, you can put as many spaces as you want between the operator (*) and its operands (x). It's purely a matter of what you prefer to look at. Where you get into trouble is in adding spaces where they don't belong, such as in the middle of a name; valueX is not the same as value X. If there are spaces in a name you pickwhip, the name appears in parentheses, for example:

`motionTracker`
➡ `("Tracker 1")`
➡ `("Track Point 1")`.

Looping Animations

Maybe the coolest feature unique to expressions (one that users often wish was built into the After Effects user interface) is the ability to loop a set of keyframes. It's so easy to learn and powerful, however, that once you understand it, you might even like it.

Much of the time, you just can replace your source expression text with one of the default loop expressions and be done. These are found in the Property submenu of the Expressions menu (**Figure 10.9**).

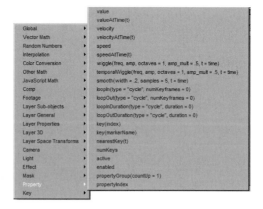

Figure 10.9 Try not to be overwhelmed. The expressions menu is a well-organized cheat sheet of After Effects keywords. Once you understand a little bit about how it's organized and where the most useful items are located, you can open this with confidence. The Property submenu, shown here, might be the one you visit most often because it contains several essential functions.

The loop effects have two arguments, the settings found in parentheses after the command. The first one is mandatory; you have to specify the type of loop you're requesting by choosing one of the three loop types. The second is optional and, in some cases, unavailable.

I'll start with a basic example and then detail out the various permutations, and then show you a specific problem that looping solves.

I'll use the example of a blinking light that is animated via keyframes to its Opacity control. To blink, these keyframes, which turn it on and off, must repeat. Begin by creating one cycle of this animation, start to finish. For example, it could be a burst of light (100% Opacity) followed by a hold and a decay at or near the beginning of the composition or wherever you want it to begin (**Figure 10.10**).

Now set an expression for Opacity, and with the default expression still highlighted, choose

```
loopOut(type = "cycle", numKeyframes = 0)
```

Press the Enter key or click outside the text area. Your keyframes now loop.

Specifically, the loop acts as if the first keyframe followed one frame after the last keyframe; this is always how it works. So, if for timing purposes you want a pause at the end, you build that into your keyframe pattern. **Figure 10.11** shows the animation with a hold at 0 Opacity added at the end.

Expressions Menu and Hierarchy

The Expressions menu is a bit overwhelming to the uninitiated—nearly two dozen submenus with several entries each. How do you know where to find anything?

Two significant observations can make this menu less daunting:

▶ Most of the entries don't do anything, technically speaking, other than point to a value that you can sample.

▶ The menus are organized hierarchically, from most global to most local. So at the top is the Global submenu, which has shortcuts to areas of After Effects that are available on the broadest or most global level. At the other end of the menu are Property and Key, which work on an individual property of an individual effect applied to an individual layer in an individual comp. In other words, these are the most nested expressions.

So don't worry, it's not as gnarly as you might think.

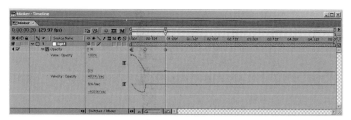

Figure 10.10 Opacity of this light decays over ten frames, with an ease added out of the first frame, followed by a hold between frame 10 and 20, at which point you are in need of a loop.

Extraneous Verbiage

How can two expressions

```
loopOut(type = "cycle",
➥numKeyframes = 0)
loopOut("cycle")
```

achieve the exact same result? Here's a quick explanation: Expressions don't do a lot of hand-holding in terms of telling you what to enter and where, but the default settings sometimes come with extra keywords that are totally optional; their only purpose is to remind you what the values are for. In the case of this example, not only are the keywords "type =" and "numKeyframes =" optional, but the whole second argument will default to 0 if it's missing.

Now how the heck would you know this? After a while, you start to anticipate it because it's somewhat standard. As you begin, however, the only way to know it is to read it in a book like this one. Sad but true.

Figure 10.11 A loop has been added to the animation in Figure 10.10. The default expression (chosen from the menu in the instructions) would work, but unnecessary arguments have been removed here to shorten it (see the sidebar, "Extraneous Verbiage").

Before looking at the other loops available, check out the other arguments you can set for this expression. For example, numKeyframes specifies how many keyframes before the final one are used in the loop; set to the default of 0, it uses all keyframes. You can get rid of this argument altogether in such a case (see the sidebar, "Extraneous Verbiage"); in fact, the expression would work the same if it read loopOut("cycle"). Set numKeyframes to a value of 2 and it uses the last three keyframes for the loop, ignoring the first hold keyframe (**Figure 10.12**).

The more useful argument is probably the first one, because it changes the fundamental type of loop, and there are three possible arguments:

```
loopOut("cycle")
loopOut("pingpong")
loopOut("continue")
```

You've seen the results of cycle, and I will cover continue in the next section. The pingpong option is like cycle except that it alternates looping the keyframes forward, then backward, then forward to ping-pong them back and forth (**Figure 10.13**).

Figure 10.12 The hold keyframe, added at the beginning, is ignored because of the numKeyframes = 2 argument, which limits the loop to the two keyframes preceding the final one (which, as you may have noticed, the loop ignores, using it only as a placeholder for the first keyframe of a new loop).

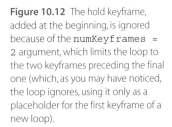

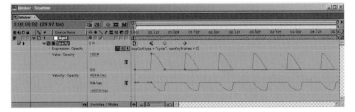

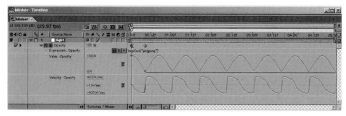

Figure 10.13 The eminently useful `pingpong` loop is applied here.

As for the other loop types available, `loopIn("cycle")` works identically to `loopOut` with one exception; the loop is created prior to the existing keyframes, rather than following. Both `loopOutDuration()` and `loopInDuration()` enable you to specify an interval, in seconds, between loops. For example, `loopOutDuration("cycle", 2)` cycles a loop every two seconds.

Smoothing and Destabilizing

Chapter 8 alluded to methods for smoothing and destabilizing a camera that are preferable to the Smoother and the Wiggler, After Effects' built-in solutions that pre-date expressions. As with looping, these are pretty easy to learn and will expand your capabilities quite a bit.

Steadicam and Camera Shake

There are effects applications out there with specific effects for smoothing or destabilizing the camera, and I've seen at least one other author claim that After Effects has no tools for camera stabilization and destabilization. I'd like to disprove that assertion right now.

If you followed the steps in Chapter 8 for using a 3D camera to motion track a scene in such a way that the track is applied only to the layer and camera, you're ready to proceed. If not, please review that section briefly if you want an idea of how the setup can be applied to a motion-tracked camera. Using `wiggle` to destabilize a camera will work without tracking data (see **Figure 10.14**).

Once again, application of the expression is easy. Given a set of keyframes, you can smooth them—averaging them

CLOSE-UP

Extending a Motion Track

Chapter 8 contains tips for continuing a motion track using a simple loop expression. What if your footage needs both a `loopIn("continue")` and a `loopOut("continue")` to extrapolate the track not only beyond the end but before the beginning of the keyframe data?

You could do this with conditionals, telling expressions to execute `loopIn` before a certain frame and `loopOut` after a certain frame, but a simpler way if you're just getting comfortable with expressions would be to split the layer at the beginning or end of the keyframe data and apply `loopIn` to the first portion and `loopOut` to the second portion.

Remember that this trick only works if the first (`loopIn`) or final (`loopOut`) two frames accurately represent a steady state at which the layer should continue animating. It only typically holds up for a few frames.

against the closest adjacent keyframes (you control how many)—or give them more noise and jitter, by applying one of the following expressions:

```
smooth()
wiggle(freq, amp)
```

There are, actually, more default parameters than I've included here, but I'm hoping that presenting them this way will make them appear easier to use than they do with the menu defaults, which are nonetheless explained below.

You can apply `smooth` as is, and you can clearly view the result without ever previewing any animation, just by looking at the velocity graph showing the source animation curve (in black) and the result of the `smooth` operation (in red). This graph is an additional advantage to applying smoothing with an expression (**Figure 10.15**).

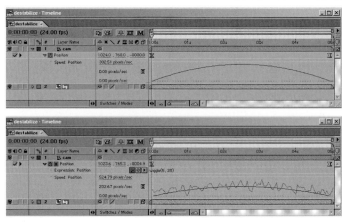

Figure 10.14 Contrast a simple camera push with an ease (top) with the result of applying a modest Wiggle operation to it (bottom: overlaid in red on the curve).

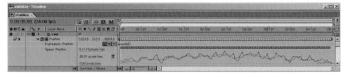

Figure 10.15 Camera jitter, smoothed. The delta (change over time) of the smoothed motion (in red) is much less than that of the source (in black).

You can of course tweak the amount of smoothing using the parameters shown in the default expression:

```
smooth(width = .2, samples = 5, t = time)
```

These are the same settings as in the example above, with no arguments used. The `width` setting specifies the amount of time, in seconds, to either side of the current frame that is averaged into the smoothing calculation. The `samples` setting specifies how many increments to examine within that keyframe range (typically, you should choose an odd number to include the current frame in the calculation). The `time` setting allows you to offset the effect of the smooth, something you'll rarely, if ever, need to do.

The `wiggle` expression needs a couple of arguments by default, and has the option for more. At the very least, you need to enter `freq`, or frequency (the number of wiggles per second), and `amplitude` (the maximum amount the wiggle can change a value—in other words, the number of pixels). The full default expression reads

```
wiggle(freq, amp, octaves = 1, ampMult = 5,
➥t = time)
```

For the most part, `freq` and `amplitude` are all you need, but if you must know, `octaves` has to do with how much noise is added together, and won't usually need to be more than 1. A higher value for `octaves` doesn't mean more noise, it just means more samples, and `ampMult` multiplies the result—again, it's about variety. For just plain more, add to the frequency and amplitude. Time, once again, is an offset.

To apply `smooth()` and `wiggle()` expressions to a 3D camera that has been tracked to match the background (as demonstrated in Chapter 8), make sure that you apply them both to the null layer to which the camera is parented and to the background plate.

Alternatively, if you're just looking to apply random numbers within a certain range rather than wiggling keyframe values, you can use the various random, Gaussian random,

NOTES

Although it wasn't possible in earlier versions of After Effects, in 6.5 you can apply `wiggle()` to a property that has no keyframe data whatsoever, useful for adding the jitter of a handheld camera to a static setup.

CLOSE-UP

Geek Alert: Wiggle versus Random

The `wiggle()` function adds random data to an animation channel. How does it differ from the functions in the Random Numbers submenu?

Random numbers are truly random; any number generated has no relationship to the number preceding it. They can be constrained to a particular range, and Gaussian random numbers will tend toward the center of that range (following a Gaussian distribution pattern that weights random numbers toward the median), but the effect is one of values that pop around completely randomly.

With `wiggle()`, the seeming randomness is generated by adding an organic noise function to existing data. The randomness is not quite so random: It takes existing data and deviates from it, within a set range (`amplitude`) and at a set number of times per second (`freq`). The `wiggle()` function, then, not only has the advantage of using animation data to determine its range, but of generating an effect that does not feel so chaotic as random data.

and noise functions found in the Random Numbers submenu (see the In Depth box). Or, if you want to wiggle the temporal position of the keyframes themselves (to wiggle them in time), try

```
temporalWiggle(freq, amp)
```

It's not the most commonly used, but it is useful if you need the animation values to stay in exactly the same range (to follow a path, for example) but to move back and forth semi-randomly on that path.

Offsetting Layers and Time

Some of the coolest things you can do with expressions involve incrementing either layer index numbers (the number of the layer that you always see to the left of the source name) or time itself. Time in expressions is measured in whole seconds. Frames and fields are calculated as decimal fractions of seconds. Of course, if you're ever worried about calculating this, you can use fractions instead: in 24 fps footage, frame 65 would be `time = 65/24` (or 2.7083 seconds). See how easy?

A frame's index and time become especially useful when using conditionals. In the example expression, you will use index and time to average grain between several frames of a sequence. Although I'm still trying to keep this simple, this means moving beyond the one-liner expressions that can be applied and tweaked easily.

Grain Averaging

In some cases, the normal methods of dealing with grain just don't do the trick—even methods as powerful as the Remove Grain effect (detailed in Chapter 9, "Virtual Cinematography"). The noise simply obscures too much of the frame. If the shot is locked off, there is an interesting alternative, one that came in handy for me on one shot in *The Day After Tomorrow*.

This effects shot started with a plate that was taken on a huge blue-screen stage of actors trudging across a snowy plain. It was meant to be snowing fairly hard in the shot, and for whatever reason it was decided to use practical snow on set. Usually, as in **Figure 10.16**, this means little bits of plastic confetti or corn flakes painted white. With 20/20 hindsight, this was clearly the wrong decision, because we were adding computer-generated snow to all kinds of exterior shots, and furthermore, the way it was shot, the lighting grid was too far in shot so I had to mask out a big hole where the falling snow should have been. So, what was needed was to get rid of the plate snow altogether and start over. Happily it was a locked-off shot, so the following trick worked, and then I added a gentle camera push-in to the final composition.

First I'll describe the solution so you understand it logically, then we'll look at the pair of expressions that accomplished this. First, I determined that the frames I wanted to average were the ones at the end of the shot, where I could easily eliminate the one moving element in the shot, some figures walking across the horizon. I did not know how many frames I would need to average, but I knew that if I took a series of different frames and set their Opacity so that collectively, it added up to 100%, I would get an average of all of them. On a given frame, a given snowflake would appear on a given pixel, but it would be missing

Figure 10.16 Artificial snow falls on a blue-screen stage.

from the other frames, and therefore would be averaged out. If I needed to average ten frames, then each would have Opacity at 10%, adding up to 100%.

Without expressions, this process would be a real pain. Each added layer would have to be adjusted to the proper frame and would have necessitated adjusting the opacity of the other layers so that they all still added up to 100%. Instead, I was able to apply two expressions to one layer and simply duplicate that layer until I had enough iterations to accomplish the effect of averaging.

First, I took care of the Opacity settings by applying

```
100/thisComp.numLayers
```

to Opacity. This expression simply says, "Take 100, my target Opacity total, and divide it by the number of layers in this composition." The `thisComp` and `numLayers` keywords are found in the expressions menus, in case you're wondering where they came from. Truth be told, I had a couple of extra layers in my actual comp (for adjustment and rotoscoping), so I wrote the real expression with an offset to compensate:

```
100/(thisComp.numLayers-2)
```

The parentheses are necessary to force the offset to occur before dividing the result into 100.

Next, I wanted to average together the last few frames of the composition, but I wasn't certain how many. As the solution, I applied Time Remapping to which I added the expression

```
thisComp.duration—(index / 24)
```

The duration of a composition is measured in seconds, and this was a 24 fps comp. By dividing the index number by the frame rate and subtracting that from the total number of seconds, I caused each successive frame in the timeline to increment backward one frame.

With these two expressions applied, I was able to do the artistic work of choosing the optimal amount of frame averaging in real time, by duplicating (**Ctrl+D**/**Cmd+D**) and deleting the layer until I'd nailed it. In the end, it required fewer frames than expected—just four, but in deciding to use that number I tried as many as ten, and handling these changes with expressions made it a breeze (**Figure 10.17**).

Conditionals

Also known as *If/Then statements*, conditionals open up a host of possibilities. They allow you to use any circumstance that expressions can recognize—pretty much any numerical or Boolean condition in the timeline—as a condition for an event or a series of events to occur.

If you're really going to harness the power of automation in expressions, it's extremely helpful to understand how to set up conditionals. All kinds of effects shots feature a cause-and-effect relationship that you can set up logically with expressions so that, even if the timing or other parameters change, the amount of busywork involved in rippling those changes through is minimized.

Triggering a Filmic Dissolve

Here's a simple example of conditionals: using layer markers to trigger a one-second filmic dissolve. This expression could just as easily be set up to trigger a different operation, such as a simple opacity fade to black or white, but once you understand the basics, you'll be able to adapt it however you like.

A composition marker can be set by pressing **Shift+1** (or Shift plus any number, 0 through 9, on the top of the keyboard—not the numeric keypad). For the following example to work as-is, if you want to try it yourself, place marker number 1 (**Shift+1**) at the frame at which you want the fade to begin.

Add the Levels (Individual Controls) effect. Reveal controls for Input Black and Output White; you'll be applying the same expression to each, with the variation that they will be animated in opposition (**Figure 10.18**). The expression for Input Black is

```
mark = thisComp.marker(1);
linear(time, mark, mark+1, 0, 1)
```

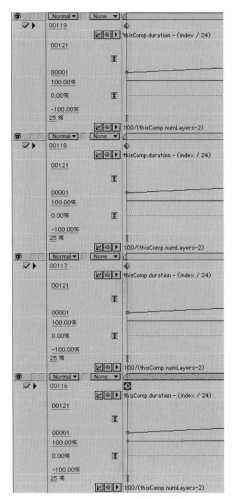

Figure 10.17 With deepest apologies that I was not able to secure permission to break down this shot for you visually, here are the expressions that propagate and offset themselves automatically simply by duplicating any of the layers.

345

Figure 10.18 The expressions have been set for Input Black and Output White; values appear in red in the Timeline and Effect Controls windows.

TIP

You can apply an expression directly from the Effect Controls window by Alt-clicking (Option-clicking) on the stopwatch, the same way you would in the Timeline window. This can be convenient because the property with the expression is revealed in the timeline as well, where you can edit the expression.

The inversion for Output White is

```
mark = thisComp.marker(1);
linear(time, mark, mark+1, 1, 0)
```

What the heck? Here's what's happening. This is the first example in this chapter in which you're setting a *variable*. This one is called `mark`, named for the fact that it identifies a marker (and also for the author's vanity). How do you know it's a marker and which one it is? The variable's argument tells you; the `thisComp.marker` portion signifies a marker and `(1)` specifies which one. Any time you use a unique name followed by an equals sign, you are telling After Effects to save you the trouble of having to repeatedly type whatever comes after that equals sign. That's all. No big deal about variables.

The linear(t, tMin, tMax, value1, value2) command is so compact and efficient that it's easy to forget it even exists. It has five (count 'em) required arguments that identify, in order, the

▶ Time that the effect evaluates

▶ Time to start a linear transition

▶ Time to end a linear transition

▶ Value at the start

▶ Value at the end

With this in mind, you can see that the expression first evaluates the current time (time). When that time reaches mark (marker 1), After Effects should perform a linear transition from 0 (0%) to 1 (100%), and the transition should last one second (until mark + 1, or one second past marker 1). You can see what's going on in the expressions graphs, and the result is reflected in the Composition window (**Figure 10.19**).

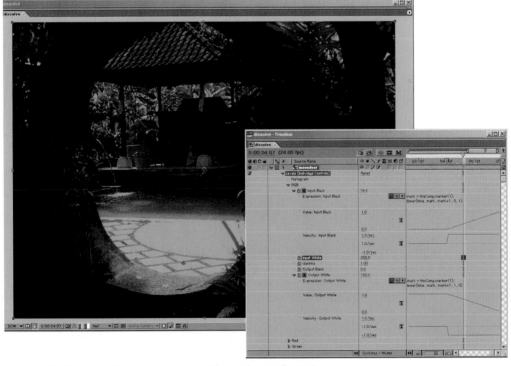

Figure 10.19 The result of the dissolve appears in the graphs as well as in the composition itself. A filmic dissolve re-creates what happens to film densities when film is faded to black.

Now, why go to all that trouble to do an effect that would take a few keyframes? Because you can save the effect into your favorites and apply it whenever you want to trigger a filmic dissolve using a layer marker, without having to do any keyframing or setup at all, and you can change this animation, which would require four keyframes, using only the marker. Not life-changing, perhaps, but satisfying and one more indication of the many applications of expressions.

How will you ever remember how to do this again? Most of the components of this expression are organized into the Expressions menu. A variable is always set by naming it and then adding = after the name; whatever follows the equals sign is the variable setting. (There's no need to type variables in JavaScript, in case you were wondering about that.) The shorthand `thisComp` is in the Global category of the menu, which also tells you that it sits at the top level of any hierarchy, such as `thisComp.marker(1)`. Look in the Comp category for `marker(name)`; you need to add the dot separation between them and the semi-colon at the end yourself. As you've seen already, these are basics of JavaScript. With all of its defaults, `linear()` is an interpolation function and found in the Interpolation category. (You'll see two versions there, one showing the option of fewer arguments).

Emulating 3D Tracking

Finally, there has to be something to make everyone's head hurt, not the least mine. Although most major studios have access to 3D tracking these days, you may run into a situation where you don't. This workaround will do the trick for you, using the plain old After Effects 2D tracker. Just keep in mind that it will work only on shots in which the ground plane is clearly visible as you travel forward (or backward) in imaginary Z space.

I first used this setup on an aerial shot of a forest for the television movie *Superfire*; images from the movie appear in Section III of this book. For this shot, the forest needed to be covered with smoke, but the point of view was from a moving helicopter, banking slightly to the right. The idea was to track in a series of smoke planes to give the illusion of a bank of smoke, but each one had to be positioned separately because of the movement in 3D space.

You could track each smoke layer separately, but for five layers, this would take, oh, about five times as long to set up. Instead, for a shot that travels along the imaginary Z axis, it's possible to triangulate the relative position of the smoke layers as they offset into the distance and foreground and average them to create an offset.

Here's basically how it works for a shot in which the camera tracks forward over the ground plane:

1. Create a rotation/scale track on two points that represent the background of your plate—they are the most distant trackable points (visible at the start and end of the shot) from the camera's point of view. Apply this track to a new null called layerMotion1 (**Figure 10.20**).

2. Create a separate one-point track that represents the foreground of your plate, closer to the camera position. Apply this track to a new null called FG. Along with the two previous points, this completes the triangle you need to re-create distance effects (**Figure 10.21**).

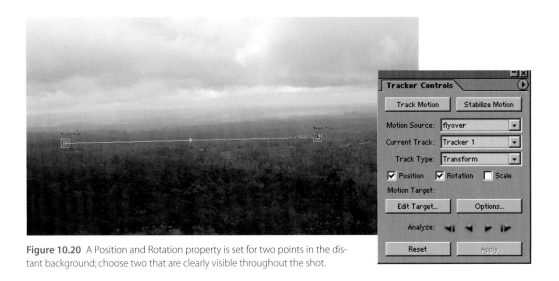

Figure 10.20 A Position and Rotation property is set for two points in the distant background; choose two that are clearly visible throughout the shot.

Figure 10.21 To be sure that the foreground point remains in frame to the end of the shot, it can be helpful to track it in reverse.

3. Apply a Slider Control to layerMotion1. Change the Slider Control's name to Distance. (The names are for clarity; you can create whatever names you like.)

4. Create two more nulls, name them BG1 and BG2, expose their position values (P), and then apply an expression to each. Pickwhip the value of each of the two attach points from the two-point track you made in step 1. Yes, the resulting code path is gnarling-looking. This step is mostly just to bury these paths so they don't show up in the main expression!

5. Now comes the expression. To the Position property of layerMotion1, apply the following expression:

```
fg = thisComp.layer("FG").position;
(this_comp.layer("BG1").position + this_comp.
➥layer("BG2").position) * 0.5;
placement = effect("Distance").
➥param("Slider")/-100;
bg + ((bg - fg) * placement)
```

And you're done—almost. What you now have is a null, layerMotion1, that can be offset using the Distance slider value. You then parent any layers that belong to that plane of motion to layerMotion1. You next duplicate layerMotion1 to create layerMotion2 with a different offset value, to create a separate plane of motion, then layerMotion3, and so on until you have enough layers to create the illusion of depth.

Tell Me More

So there you have some useful practical applications for expressions in visual effects work. Maybe you still want more—a more thorough understanding of the basics, if you're a beginner, or more advice on developing your own expressions, if you're an expert.

Unfortunately, expressions is one area where the official After Effects documentation falls short. Plenty of information is there, but it's organized in such a way that you already need to know quite a bit about expressions before you can understand it.

Happily, a couple of Web sites take up the slack. They are excellent, and at this writing they are still very much up to date:

▶ **www.motionscript.com:** This site is the work of Dan Ebberts, a prolific contributor of expressions information in various online forums. One section of the site, Mastering Expressions, thoroughly explains how JavaScript works as is implemented in After Effects. The Expressions Lab contains more hands-on examples for you to dissect.

▶ **www.aenhancers.com:** This is a forum-based site filled with sample expressions and scripts created for specific purposes, as well as areas for discussion about how they work.

Both sites also include information on scripting, an automation feature set in After Effects that, alas, makes creating expressions look like child's play (and I should know, having documented this feature for version 6.0 and 6.5). Someday, perhaps the development team will be able to add recordable Actions as are found in Photoshop, and scripting will be unlocked for the masses. For now, however, the scripting controls are double black–diamond expert features, for the most part requiring full-fledged programming capabilities to accomplish anything truly significant.

And hold onto your hats, because the complicated stuff isn't over with yet. The next chapter deals with issues specific to film, most of which have never been handled in any book on After Effects.

11

Issues Specific to Film and HDR Images

True realism consists in revealing the surprising things which habit keeps covered and prevents us from seeing.

—Jean Cocteau (French director, painter, playwright, and poet)

Issues Specific to Film and HDR Images

The difference between jaw-dropping movie effects and the motion graphics made by a budding artist comes down to one thing: details. The real world is full of detail we take for granted and rarely articulate, but it is the job of visual effects artists and supervisors to recognize where real-world detail is missing in a shot and then know how to add it.

The basic principle behind visual effects is that we are trying to replicate how each shot would look if it had simply been a real-world event captured on film. For example, when shooting a cruise ship seen from the air, a camera will shake as the helicopter it is mounted to hits turbulence and wind blows against the lens. Nature can sometimes be a nuisance, but it is unavoidable. So in creating a computer-generated boat, these motions also need to be added to the virtual camera to achieve movie-like realism. Such "imperfections" won't hurt your beautiful computer graphics, they will sell them.

Another unavoidable fact about movies is that they are always made with cameras—cameras that capture light, light that exposes film. So we need an understanding of light and film to perform our job of creating images that could have come from the real world. Because this is a matter of physics, the details can get pretty technical and the points they make may seem trivial, but grasping them will help turn a shot that looks great into one mistaken for real.

This is a chapter about details.

Film 101

The first step to understanding film is simply knowing the basic format it comes in. Thomas Edison created 35 mm film in 1889, and it remained the standard for decades. In response to the growing popularity of television in the 1950s, Hollywood conjured up a number of different widescreen formats through experiments with anamorphic lenses and film stocks as wide as 70 mm. These systems—CinemaScope, VistaVision, Panavision, and so on—haven't completely faded away, but their presence in the modern era is mostly felt in the way that films are displayed, not how they are shot. 35 mm is once again the most popular shooting format, specifically the full-aperture version known as Super 35 mm.

Standard 35 mm film has an aspect ratio of 4:3, which is not coincidentally the same as a television. Almost all current movies are filmed in this format as if originally intended for the small screen. When shown in a theater using a widescreen aspect of 1.85:1 (also known as 16:9, the HDTV standard) or 2.35:1 (CinemaScope/Panavision), the full 4:3 negative is cropped (**Figure 11.1**). Theater patrons actually pay $10 to see *less* than if they waited for the movie to get broadcast full screen on cable! You may be surprised that movies are shot with TV in mind, until you consider that home video sales have surpassed theater revenues recently. But rest assured, directors still compose their films with the theatrical aspect ratio in mind.

After a movie has been filmed, the negative is developed, and then shots destined for digital effects work are scanned frame by frame, usually at a rate of about 1 frame per second. During scanning, the Telecine process (pronounced Tell-eh-sin-ee), some initial color decisions are made before the frames are output as a numbered sequence of *Cineon* files, named after Kodak's now-defunct film compositing system. Both Cineon files and the related format, DPX, store pixels uncompressed at 10 bits per channel. Scanners are usually capable of scanning 4 K plates, although most elect to scan at half resolution, creating 2 K frames around 2048 by 1536 pixels and weighing in at

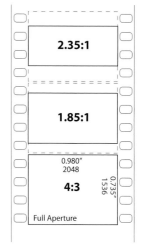

Figure 11.1 Super 35 mm film format is always 4:3 at full aperture; the typical ratios at which Super 35 is projected are crops of the full aperture, still occupying four perforations of the negative.

Figure 11.2 To find out what working with film is like, you can download this Cineon file from Kodak's Web site.

almost 13 MB. Cineon files used to be transported to visual effects companies using computer tape formats, but now portable FireWire hard drives are the method of choice.

Working with Cineon Files

Because the process of shooting and scanning film is pretty expensive, almost all Cineon files ever created are the property of some Hollywood studio and unavailable to the general public. The only free Cineon file I know of is Kodak's original test image, affectionately referred to as Marcie (**Figure 11.2**) and available from Kodak's Web site. To get a feel for working with film, download Marcie from Kodak's Web site (www.kodak.com/ US/en/motion/ support/dlad/) and drop the file into After Effects, which imports Cineon files just fine.

The first thing you'll notice about Marcie is that she looks funny, and not just because this photo dates back to the '80s. Cineon files are encoded in something called *log color space*, which I will explain shortly. To make Marcie look more natural, apply After Effects' Cineon Converter, found under Channels in the Effects menu. The Cineon Converter follows equations described by Kodak for converting log space images to the video space of your monitor.

In working with film, the goal is to add whatever magic on top of the original image and then return it to the studio. Because the Cineon Converter can also convert video images back to log space, it would seem natural to convert everything to your monitor's color space, work as you always have, and then convert the end result back to log. But upon further examination of what happens in After Effects when you convert from log to linear (as After Effects calls it) and then back to log, you see a problem: The bright details in Marcie's hair don't survive the trip (**Figures 11.3a**, **b**, and **c**).

The obvious alternative is to not convert Marcie, leave her in log space, and use the Cineon Converter for preview only. Although this is a workable plan, there are many pitfalls with this method because none of the tools in After Effects were designed with log images in mind.

Figures 11.3a, b, and c When you convert an image from log space (11.3a) to linear (11.3b) and then back to log (11.3c), the bright details are lost.

What's going on with this mystical Cineon file and its log color space that makes it so hard to deal with? And more importantly, why? Well, it turns out that the engineers at Kodak know a thing or two about film and have made no decisions lightly. But to properly answer the question, I first have to step back and explain some basic principles of photography and light.

Dynamic Range

I took the pictures shown in **Figure 11.4** within a minute of each other from my roof on a winter morning. Anyone who has ever tried to photograph a sunrise or sunset with a digital camera should immediately recognize the problem at hand. With a standard exposure, the sky comes in beautifully, but foreground houses are nearly black. Using longer exposures you can bring the houses up, but by the time they are looking good the sky is completely blown out.

The limiting factor here is the digital camera's small *dynamic range*, which is the difference between the brightest and darkest things that can be captured in the same image. An outdoor scene has a wide array of brightnesses, but any device will be able to read only a slice of them. You can change exposure to capture different ranges, but the size of the slice is fixed.

Figure 11.4 Different exposures of the same camera view produce widely varying results.

Our eyes have a much larger dynamic range and our brains have a wide array of perceptual tricks, so in real

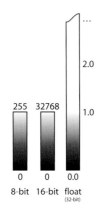

Figure 11.5 8-bit and 16-bit pixels stop at white, while floating point can go beyond.

life the houses and sky are both seen easily. But even eyes have limits, such as when you try to see someone behind a bright spotlight or use a laptop computer in the sun. The spotlight has not made the person behind any darker, but when eyes adjust to bright lights (as they must to avoid injury) dark things fall out of range and simply appear black.

White on a monitor just isn't very bright, which is why we use them in dim rooms with the blinds pulled down. When you try to represent the bright sky on a dim monitor, everything else in the image has to scale down in proportion. Even if a digital camera could capture extra dynamic range, you still couldn't display it on a monitor. And how would that extra range be stored in an image?

A standard 8-bit computer image uses values 0 to 255 to represent RGB pixels. If you could record a value above 255—say 285 or 310—that would represent a pixel beyond the monitor's dynamic range, brighter than white or *overbright*. Because 8-bit pixels can't actually go above 255, overbright information is stored as floating point decimals where 0.0 is black and 1.0 is white. Because floating point numbers are virtually unbounded, 0.75, 7.5, or 750.0 are all acceptable values, even though everything above 1.0 will clip to white on the monitor (**Figure 11.5**).

In recent years, techniques have emerged for taking a series of exposures (such as my sunrise shots) and creating *high dynamic range* (*HDR*) images—floating point files that contain all light information from a scene (**Figure 11.6**). The best-known paper on the subject was published by Malik and Debevec at SIGGRAPH '97 (go to www.debevec. org for more details). In successive exposures, values that remain within range can be compared to describe how the camera is responding to different levels of light. That information allows a computer to connect bright areas in the scene to the darker ones and calculate accurate floating point pixel values that combine detail from each exposure.

But with all the excitement surrounding HDR imaging, many forget that for decades there has been another

Darker Sky: 1.9

Bright Sky: 7.5

Dark Tree: 0.03

Houses: 0.8

Figure 11.6 Consider the floating point pixel values for this HDR image.

medium available for capturing dynamic range far beyond what a computer monitor can display.

That medium is film.

Cineon Log Space

A film negative gets its name because areas exposed to light ultimately become dark and opaque, and areas un-exposed are made transparent during developing. Light makes dark. Hence, negative.

Dark is a relative term here. A white piece of paper makes a nice dark splotch on the negative, but a lightbulb darkens the film even more, and a photograph of the sun causes the negative to turn out darker still. By not completely exposing to even bright lights, the negative is able to capture the differences between bright highlights and *really* bright highlights. Film, the original image capture medium, has always been high dynamic range.

If you were to graph the increase in film "density" as increasing amounts of light expose it, you'd get something like **Figure 11.7**. In math, this is referred to as a logarithmic curve. I'll get back to this in a moment.

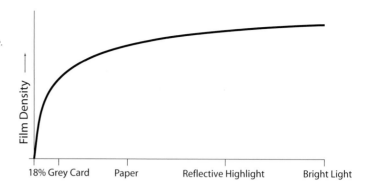

Figure 11.7 Graphing the darkening of film as increasing amounts of light expose it results in a logarithmic curve.

18% Grey Card   Paper   Reflective Highlight   Bright Light

Digital Film

Because all the computer film work is essentially the processing of Cineon files and then sending a new set back to the client to be printed on film, some further examination of the Cineon log color space and its properties will serve you well.

I'll tell you now that if a monitor's maximum brightness is considered to be 1.0, the brightest value film can represent is considered to be 13.53. Note this only applies to a film negative which is exposed by light in the world as opposed to a film *positive*, which is limited by the brightness of a projector bulb and is therefore not really considered high dynamic range. A Telecine captures the entire range of each frame and stores the frames as a sequence of 10-bit Cineon files. Those extra two bits mean that Cineon pixel values can range from 0 to 1023 instead of the 0 to 255 in 8-bit files.

Having four times as many values to work with in a Cineon file helps, but considering you have 13.53 times the range to record, care must be taken in encoding those values. The most obvious way to store all that light would simply be to evenly squeeze 0.0 to 13.53 into the 0 to 1023 range. The problem with this solution is that it would only leave 75 code values for the all-important 0.0 to 1.0 range, the same as allocated to the range 10.0 to 11.0, which you are far less interested in representing with much accuracy. Your eye can barely tell the difference between two highlights that bright—it certainly doesn't need 75 brightness variations between them.

A proper way to encode light on film would quickly fill up the useable values with the most important 0.0 to 1.0 light and then leave space left over for the rest of the negative's range. Well, fortunately, the film negative itself with its logarithmic response behaves just this way.

Cineon files are often said to be stored in log color space. Actually it is the negative that uses a log response curve and the file is simply storing the negative's density at each pixel. In any case, the graph in **Figure 11.8** describes how light exposes a negative and gets encoded into Cineon color values according to Kodak, creators of the format.

One strange feature in this graph is that black is mapped to code value 95 instead of 0. Not only does the Cineon file store whiter-than-white (overbright) values, it also has some blacker-than-black information. This is mirrored in the film lab when a negative is printed brighter than usual and the blacker-than-black information can reveal itself. Likewise, negatives can be printed darker and take advantage of overbright detail. The standard value mapped to monitor white is 685, and everything above is considered overbright.

Although the Kodak formulas are commonly used to transform log images for compositing, other methods are

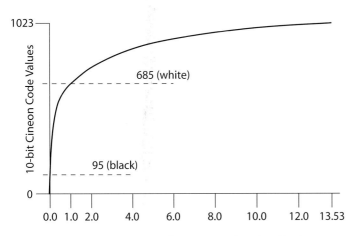

Figure 11.8 Kodak's log Cineon encoding is expressed as a logarithmic curve, with labels for the visible black and white points that correspond to 0 and 255 in normal 8-bit pixel values.

All About Log

You may first have heard of logarithmic curves in high school physics class when talking about the decay of radioactive isotopes.

If a radioactive material has a half-life of one year, half of it will have decayed after that time. The next year, half of what remains will decay, leaving a quarter, and so on. To calculate how much time has elapsed based on how much material remains, a logarithmic function is used.

Light, another type of radiation, has a similar effect on film. At the molecular level, light causes silver halide crystals to react. If film exposed for some short period of time causes half the crystals to react, repeating the exposure will cause half of the remaining to react, and so on. This is how film gets its response curve and the ability to capture even very bright light sources. No amount of exposure can be expected to affect every single crystal.

emerging. The idea of having light values below 0.0 is dubious at best, and many take issue with the idea that a single curve can describe all film stocks, cameras, and shooting environments. As a different approach, some visual effects facilities take care to photograph well-defined photographic charts and use the resultant film to build custom curves that differ subtly from the standard Kodak one.

As much as Cineon log is a great way to encode light captured by film, it should not be used for compositing or other image transformations. This point is so important that I just have to emphasize it again:

Encoding color spaces are not compositing color spaces.

Thank you, I feel much better. To illustrate this point, imagine you had a black pixel with Cineon value 95 next to an extremely bright pixel with Cineon's highest code value, 1023. If these two pixels were blended together (say, if the image was being blurred), the result would be 559, which is somewhere around middle gray (0.37 to be precise). But when you consider that the extremely bright pixel has a relative brightness of 13.5, that black pixel should only have been able to bring it down to 6.75, which is still overbright white! Log space's extra emphasis on darker values causes standard image processing operations to give them extra weight, leading to an overall unpleasant and inaccurate darkening of the image. So I'll say it again: If you're working with a log source, don't do image processing in log space!

Video Gamma Space

Because log space certainly doesn't look natural, it probably comes as no surprise that it is a bad color space to work in. But there is another encoding color space that you have been intimately familiar with for your entire computer-using life and no doubt have worked in directly at some point: the video space of your monitor.

You may have always assumed that 8-bit monitor code value 128, halfway between black and white, makes a gray that is half as bright as white. If so, you may be shocked to hear that this is not the case. In fact, 128 is much darker—not even a *quarter* of white's brightness on most monitors.

A system where half the input gives you half the output is described as linear, but monitors (like many things in the real world) are nonlinear. When a system is nonlinear, you can usually describe its behavior using the gamma function, shown in **Figure 11.9** and the equation

$$\text{Output} = \text{input}^{\text{gamma}} \qquad 0 <= \text{input} <= 1$$

In this function, the darkest and brightest values (0.0 and 1.0) are always fixed and the gamma value determines how the transition between them behaves. Successive applications of gamma can be concatenated by multiplying them together. Applying gamma and then 1/gamma has the net result of doing nothing. Gamma 1.0 is linear.

Mac monitors usually have a gamma of 1.8, and the gamma value for PCs is 2.2. What this really says is that the electronics in your screen are slow to react from lower levels of input voltage and everything is darkened as a result. The reason digital images do not appear dark, however, is that they have all been created with the inverse gamma function baked in to pre-brighten pixels before they are displayed (**Figure 11.10**). Yes, *all* of them.

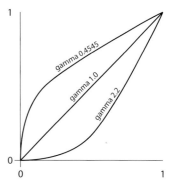

Figure 11.9 Graph of monitor gamma (2.2) with file gamma (0.4545) and linear (1.0). These are the color curves in question, with 0.4545 and 2.2 each acting as the direct inverse of the other.

I am somewhat oversimplifying my description of gamma in video because the subject is complex enough to get a book of its own. An excellent one is Charles Poynton's *Digital Video and HDTV Algorithms and Interfaces* (Morgan Kaufmann Publishers).

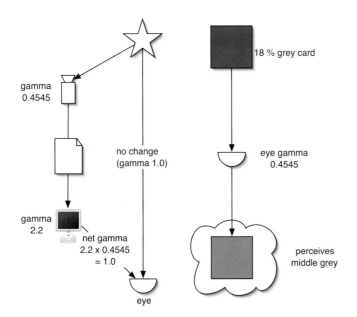

Figure 11.10 Offsetting gammas in the file and monitor result in faithful image reproduction.

Gamma-rama

In case I haven't already blown your mind with all this gamma talk, allow me to mention two other related points.

First, you may be familiar with the standard photographic gray card: the 18% gray card. But why not the 50% gray card?

Second, although I've mentioned that a monitor darkens everything on it using a 2.2 gamma, you may wonder why a grayscale ramp doesn't look skewed toward darkness. 50% gray on a monitor looks like 50% gray.

The answer is that *your eyes are nonlinear too!* They have a gamma that is just about the inverse of a monitor's, in fact. Eyes are very sensitive to small amounts of light and get less sensitive as brightness increases. The lightening in our eyeballs offsets the darkening of 50% gray by the monitor. If you were to paint a true gradient on a wall, it would look bright. Objects in the world are darker than they appear.

Getting back to the 18% card, try applying that formula to our gamma 0.4 eyes:

$$0.18^{0.4} = 0.504$$

Yep, middle gray.

Because encoding spaces are not compositing spaces, working directly with images that appear on your monitor can pose problems. Similar to log encoding, video gamma encoding allocates more values to dark pixels, so they have extra weight. Video images need converting just as log Cineon files do.

Battle of the Color Spaces

Right about now, many of you are looking around to see which window to throw this book out of. You have been working with digital images since before I could spell RGB and have done perfectly fine working with unconverted video, thank you very much.

Truly, much great work has already been created by artists working in nonlinear color spaces, some even in log space. But the color space you work in is going to affect the final image, so you must pick the one that helps you accomplish what you've set out to do, which is to simulate how the world is photographed by a camera. When you brighten a scene, you want to mimic the addition of another on-set floodlight or an expanding camera aperture. An image is blurred to imitate light from out-of-focus objects spreading out across the film gate. To do this properly, you need the compositing math to mimic light in the real world.

In the real world, light behaves linearly. The nonlinear encoding in video and film is introduced *after* all the light has been added linearly. Turn on two lightbulbs of equivalent wattage where you previously had one and your entire scene will become exactly twice as bright. By working in a linear color space, you can perfectly simulate this effect simply by doubling your pixel values. You are getting back to the color space of the original scene. For this reason, linear pixels are often referred to as *scene-referred values*.

The examples in **Table 11.1** show the difference between making adjustments to digital camera photos in their native video space and performing those same operations in linear space. In all cases, an unaltered photograph featuring the real in-camera effect is shown for comparison.

TABLE 11.1 Comparison of Adjustments in Native Video Space and in Linear Space

	BRIGHTEN ONE STOP	LENS DEFOCUS	MOTION BLUR
Original Image			
Filtered in Video Space			
Filtered in Linear Space			
Real-World Photo			

The table's first example brightens the image by one stop. A stop refers to clicks on a camera's aperture—the iris that controls how much light coming through the lens will expose the film within. Widening the aperture by one stop allows twice as much light to enter, and each additional stop redoubles the exposure again. An increase of three stops brightens the image by a factor of eight (2*2*2, or 2^3).

Doubling the pixels in video space causes bright areas in the image to blow out very quickly. Video pixels are already encoded with extra brightness and can't take much more. Notice how the curtain and computer screen have lost detail in video space, while the same operation performed in linear space has retained detail. Also notice how the linear image is nearly indistinguishable from the actual photo for which camera exposure time was doubled (another practical way to brighten by one stop).

The second example simulates an out-of-focus scene using Fast Blur, one of the most common operations performed in After Effects. You may be surprised to see that it actually causes an overall darkening with bright highlights fading into the background—at least when applied in video space. In linear, the highlights pop much better. See how the little man in the Walk sign stays bright in linear but almost fades away in video because of the extra emphasis given to dark pixels in video space.

Try squinting your eyes as you look at these images to see how only the video image has darkened overall. Because a defocused lens doesn't cause any less light to enter it, the video blur is not behaving like a true defocus. Comparison with the real-world defocus drives the point home even more, although this simple linear example doesn't mimic the camera's aperture shape or the scene's overbright information, so it isn't completely identical to the real photograph either, but it's close.

The table's third example uses After Effect's built-in motion blur to simulate the streaking caused by my quickly panning as I take a photo. Pay particular attention to the highlight on the lamp; notice how it leaves a long, bright streak in the linear and in-camera examples. Artificial dulling of highlights is the most obvious giveaway of nonlinear image processing.

Artists have dealt with the problems of working directly in video space for years without even knowing. A perfect example is the Screen transfer mode, which is additive in nature but actually much more convoluted than the pure Add transfer mode. Screen uses a multiply-toward-white

Figures 11.11a, b, and c Adding in video space blows out (11.11a), but Screen in video looks better (11.11b). Adding in linear is best (11.11c).

function with the advantage of avoiding the clipping associated with Add. But Add's reputation comes from it being applied to bright video-space images. Screen was invented only to help people be productive when working in video space and without overbrights; Screen *darkens* overbrights (**Figures 11.11a**, **b**, and **c**). Real light doesn't Screen, it Adds. As Stu Maschwitz says, "Add is the new Screen."

Floating Point

A common misconception is that if you work solely in the domain of video you have no need for floating point. But just because your output will ultimately be restricted to the 0.0 to 1.0 range doesn't mean that overbright values above 1.0 won't figure into the images you create.

In the Figures **11.12a**, **b**, and **c**, each one of the bright Christmas tree lights is getting severely clipped when shown in video space, which is not a problem so long as I'm only displaying the image. In the center image, I followed the rules and converted the image to linear before applying a synthetic motion blur. Indeed, the lights are creating pleasant streaks, but they are not reflecting their true overbright nature. In the third image, I processed the HDR image in floating point, and the lights have a realistic impact on the image as they streak across. Even stretched out across the image, the streaks are still brighter than 1.0. Considering this printed page is not high dynamic range, I think this

Figures 11.12a, b, and c An HDR image is blurred without floating point (11.12a) and with floating point (11.12b), before shown as low dynamic range in 11.12c. (HDR image courtesy Stu Maschwitz.)

example shows that HDR floating point pixels are a crucial part of making images that simulate the real world through a camera, no matter what the output medium.

Floating point's benefits aren't restricted to blurs, however. Every operation in a compositing pipeline will gain extra realism from the presence of floating point pixels. The simple act of floating one layer over another with a transfer mode also potentially sees big benefits.

In **Figures 11.13a**, **b**, and **c**, I took an HDR image and performed a simple composite once in video space and once using linear floating point. In the floating point version, the dark translucent layer acts like sunglasses on the bright window, revealing extra detail exactly as a filter on a camera lens would. The soft edges of a motion-blurred object also behave realistically as bright highlights push through. Without floating point there is no extra information to reveal, so the window looks clipped and dull and motion blur doesn't interact with the scene properly.

And now you might have noticed another red flag: *After Effects 6.5 does not support floating point.*

So how can you hope to work in linear color space or retain Cineon values over 1.0 in After Effects if it has no floating point? The answer is you have to cheat.

eLin

Developed by The Orphanage, eLin is a plug-in set for getting After Effects to behave like it has floating point. At The Orphanage, eLin has already been used in such films as *Jeepers Creepers 2*, *Hellboy*, *The Day After Tomorrow*, *Sin City*, and *Harry Potter: The Goblet of Fire*.

Working in eLin involves converting between three color spaces:

▶ **log:** The logarithmic encoding found in Cineon film scans

▶ **vid:** The video color space used by an image destined for a computer monitor or television

▶ **eLin:** A linear color space where all compositing operations are performed

The eLin space is what was first described as the "obvious" way to encode Cineon files: the scheme where all the dynamic range of a film negative was compressed linearly into 10-bit values. But whereas the 10-bit Cineon left only 75 code values for the all-important 0.0 to 1.0 range, the 16-bit mode of After Effects allocates 2400, much more than an 8-bit file and (as experience has shown) enough to perform linear compositing without noticeable banding. In addition, eLin allows its white point to be lowered by the user in order to give 0.0 to 1.0 even more values if necessary (**Figure 11.14**).

As footage is brought into an eLin project, each RGB image is converted to eLin space using the plug-in vid2eLin or log2eLin, depending on the original color space. Those pixels remain in eLin space through the entire flow of the

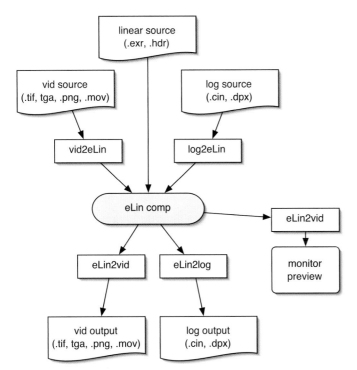

Figures 11.13a, b, and c A source image (11.13a) is composited without floating point (11.13b) and with floating point (11.13c). (HDR image courtesy of Stu Maschwitz.)

Figure 11.14 The eLin workflow is depicted with all of the optional inputs and outputs. There is an eLin effect to transition your image to and from true linear space, regardless of whether the desired input or output is in video or Cineon log color space.

project until the very end when they are converted back to the appropriate output space using eLin2log or eLin2vid.

Of course, eLin space itself is very dark and does not look anything like the final output, but you must preview everything in your monitor's space, while working using a *View LUT* (look up table). In eLin this is accomplished by floating an adjustment layer over every comp and applying the eLin2vid effect. Be sure to make this layer a guide layer as well, so that downstream comps continue to receive pixels in eLin space.

Considering how strange the eLin workflow may seem, it's not surprising that some things in After Effects do not function properly with it. For example, transfer modes, such as Hard Light, pivot around middle gray, but what eLin sees as middle gray After Effects sees as nearly black. You'll need 16-bit support for all plug-ins operating in eLin space, and even then, many filters, such as Levels, are built with firm ideas of what black and white are—ideas that eLin instantly destroys.

But plenty of After Effects operations work just fine in eLin. The most important transfer modes, such as Normal, Add, and Multiply, all perform even better in eLin thanks to the truly linear space. Hue/Saturation, Fast Blur, and After Effects' built-in motion blur also function naturally. The plug-in also includes eLevels, which functions the same as Levels with awareness of eLin's adjusted white point and overbright headroom.

Not Just a Hack

Although eLin is a tricky way to cheat floating point in After Effects, the concepts in the eLin workflow are universal to any compositing package, *especially* one that supports floating point such as Apple's Shake, Eyeon's Digital Fusion, or Digital Domain's Nuke. Video and film images always need to be converted to linear space where all the processing will take place, and you will always need a View LUT to preview linear compositing space on a monitor. The lessons learned by working in eLin will apply to any

View LUTs

The term "look up table," or LUT, is often confusing because it has been used in many different contexts over the years. In the early days of color computer games, look up tables were required to convert all imagery to a 256-color palette. Ah, the good old days.

In this case, a clearer term for LUT might be "conversion layer" because the lookup process here is to covert imagery back from true linear, or *scene-referred*, pixel values to values that you can actually see properly on your monitor. It's not a table so much as an adjustment layer with a gamma adjustment.

However, LUT is common parlance for "the thing that makes it look like it's supposed to," so it's a term you may as well become used to using in this context.

digital compositing program you can buy today and all coming in the years ahead.

If you want to check out eLin and its associated tools (such as the OpenEXR importer), they are included on the book's CD-ROM, ready for installation and use with After Effects 6.5. The eLin software is essentially shareware; you are free to use it with no restrictions (other than an occasional reminder to buy it), but if you use it commercially, you are obligated to purchase a license.

A specific example of implementing eLin into a color adjustment workflow, including its benefits and challenges, is included at the end of the next chapter.

Conclusion

This chapter concludes Section II, in which you've delved into the most fundamental techniques of effects compositing. In the next and final section, you'll apply those techniques. You'll also learn about the importance of observation, as well as some specialized tips and tricks for specific effects compositing situations that re-create particular environments, settings, conditions, and natural phenomena.

CLOSE-UP

Floating Point Files

There is one class of files that does not need to be converted to linear space: floating point files. These files are already storing scene-referred values, complete with overbright information. Common formats are Radiance (.hdr) and floating point TIFF, but the newest and best is Industrial Light + Magic's OpenEXR format. OpenEXR uses efficient 16-bit floating point pixels, can store any number of image channels, supports lossless compression, and is already supported by most 3D programs thanks to being an open source format. eLin includes a plug-in for reading OpenEXR in After Effects, presenting files in log space to preserve overbrights on import.

If the knowledge that Industrial Light + Magic created a format to base its entire workflow around linear doesn't give it credence, I don't know what will.

SECTION III

Creative Explorations

12

Working with Light

There are two kinds of light: the glow that illuminates and the glare that obscures.

—James Thurber

Working with Light

Light is the most complex phenomenon a compositor must understand. In other areas of digital production, elaborate models are derived to simulate the way light works in the physical world. Accurate modeling of the physics of light is crucial to a good 3D rendering program. The science of light phenomena, such as radiosity, caustics, the inverse square law, environment mapping, and many more, have transitioned from theoretical papers delivered at SIGGRAPH to features readily available in high-end 3D software.

The world of the compositor is less pure and scientific, which if anything makes it that much more important to understand the workings of light phenomena in your scene. Like a painter, you must observe the workings of light in the three-dimensional world so that you can re-create them in a two-dimensional frame, using your software toolbox.

Several chapters in this book have already dealt with some of the principles of the behavior of light. Chapter 5, "Color and Light: Adjusting and Matching," focused on the most fundamental work of the compositor: matching the brightness and color of a foreground layer to a background source. In Chapter 11, "Issues Specific to Film and HDR Images," guest author Brendan Bolles explained alternate models for dealing with light at the bottom and beyond the top of the visible range.

This chapter is dedicated to situations in which you as a compositor must create or emulate specific light conditions in your scene. You'll explore the actual behavior of light, its direction, intensity, color, position, reflection, diffusion, occlusion, and volume, as well as look at

NOTES

Chapter 11 introduced the radical idea that there are alternative color models to the ones with which you're already familiar and that one of these in particular, linear color, represents the direction in which digital imaging is headed. Although linear color is not officially supported in After Effects, it is available via shareware called eLin. Buckle your seatbelt because the last section of this chapter is dedicated to exploring this, hands-on and in depth.

methods of mimicking these in realistic and dramatic ways, including such special situations as backlighting, flares, glints, blurs, and defocused lenses. I'll distinguish between lighting conditions you can easily emulate and those that are essentially out of bounds—although, for a compositor with a good eye and patience, the seemingly "impossible" becomes a welcome challenge.

Light Source and Direction

Often, when you need to match elements to a source, the steps outlined in Chapter 5, "Color and Light: Adjusting and Matching," for matching brightness and color are sufficient. In many scenes, however, there is clearly more involved with light than brightness and color. In some cases, the direction of the light plays a role, especially where the quality of the light is *hard* (direct) rather than *soft* (diffuse).

There is such a huge variety of light situations possible in a shot, and in an infinite array of combinations, that it becomes difficult to make any broad statements stand up about lighting. This section, however, tries to pin down some general guidelines for manipulating the light situation of your scene.

Location and Quality

You may have specific information about the lighting conditions that existed when your plate footage was shot. On a set, you can easily enough identify the placement and type of each light; this information is contained to some extent in a camera report also. If the source shot was taken only with natural lighting, you're seeking the position of the sun relative to the camera (**Figure 12.1**). This information can help you puzzle out highlights and shadows when it's not clear how to match the lighting of the plate.

Sometimes the location and direction of light is readily apparent, but surprisingly often, it's not. As I write this, I'm looking out the window on an overcast day. The sunlight is coming from the south (on my left), but as I look at objects in my backyard, it seems to have no direction at all, because it's not direct, it's diffuse. Furthermore it keeps changing.

Figure 12.1 Three shots lit only by the sun; in each case shadows tell you the light is coming from behind and to the right of camera, but as the sky becomes more overcast, the light becomes more diffuse and its direction more difficult to discern.

The quality of light in this scene is the most subjective and elusive of criteria. Hard, direct light casts clear shadows and raises contrast, and soft, diffuse light lowers contrast and casts soft shadows (if visible at all). That much seems clear enough. But these are broad stereotypes, which do not always hold as expected. For example, hard light aimed directly at a subject from the camera's point of view flattens out features, effectively decreasing contrast. And when multiple lights combine to light a subject, hard shadows can be diffused, a typical situation with artificial light (**Figure 12.2**).

Figure 12.2 To simulate the artificial lighting of a baseball stadium at night, this scene was lit from both sides with nearly equivalent key lights, causing light and shadow areas to overlap and cancel one another out to some degree. (Image courtesy of Tim Fink Productions.)

Heightening Drama with Light

Although the color and contrast of the scene can be nailed down precisely, light direction and quality can be slippery, surprising, changeable, and difficult to re-create. All true, but there's still plenty you can re-create—or get away with—if you follow a few basic guidelines:

▶ **Use elements with a similar quality of light.** Matching hard- and soft-lit elements is generally going to be difficult, if not impossible. Sometimes you can raise contrast on soft shadows, or even lower it to soften existing shadows, but there's always a limit. If you can, start with elements that were shot, rendered, or painted with a similar quality of light to the plate.

▶ **Changing apparent light direction is just about impossible, particularly in a hard-lit scene (Figure 12.3).** Incorrect light direction, in cases where it's evident, is one of the big giveaways of bad compositing, although for whatever reason it isn't always noticed by the audience the way matte lines and other such basic compositing mistakes are noticed. If you minimize its effects, this is one category where you can get away with something.

▶ **Shadows are often broken up by indirect or reflected (bounced) light in artificially lit scenes.** This is the phenomenon that gave rise to radiosity rendering in 3D rendering programs. Study the world around you, and you start to notice that some of the most interesting things that light does are the result of reflected light mixing with direct light. A clear, black cast shadow is often not nearly so interesting as one contaminated by secondary light, and this can free you from the need to faithfully play it straight with cast shadows.

Figure 12.3 Trying to convince the viewer that this figure was not key-lit from the upper-right of frame? Good luck. (All Newton images courtesy of Tim Fink Productions.)

▶ **Natural light can change rapidly over time.** Clouds overhead, trees rustling, an open flame, the sunlight reflected off of a shimmering pool—all of these create dramatic, interesting interactive lighting in your scene, helping bring it to life (or distracting the viewer if there's too much of it). If they're part of the story, you want these elements, but there are only limited ways you can add them in 2D (**Figure 12.4**). Some of these are explored in this chapter.

▶ **Foreground elements that you add can change the lighting situation.** Be aware that if the element you're adding to your scene is highly reflective (and obviously, if it is self-illuminating), you must account for its interacting with the other elements.

Mastering the use of light in a scene is no simple matter. For centuries, painters defined themselves as much by their observation and use of light as anything; a new school of thought would develop, typically driven by a "master" who had observed something novel and revolutionary about how light works, and the course of art history would be changed. So instead of looking for the lazy quick fix, you are encouraged as always to keep shooting reference and scouring it for details you can steal.

Figure 12.4 Trying to re-create the effect of dappled natural light caused by an overhanging canopy of trees blowing in the breeze? Good luck. Although with planning, you can fake this lighting on set using the old trick of a bicycle wheel with pieces of paper woven through its spokes. Spinning the wheel slowly back and forth in front of the key light re-creates the effect of the moving canopy.

Neutralizing Light Direction

If your source was shot with a light direction that is incorrect for the composited shot, that's a pretty big problem, depending on how hard and directional the light actually is. The solution is generally to neutralize, rather than to try to fix the discrepancy.

For the purposes of discussion, consider a situation in which shadows and highlights give a clear indication from where the light is coming. Also assume that a simple quick fix, such as flopping the shot, is not possible, which it usually isn't.

In such a case, you would first look for light direction clues that you could remove from the element; for example, look for cast shadows falling on an area of the shot that can either be removed or replaced (probably via matting and rotoscoping, as in **Figure 12.5**). In areas of the footage that can't be removed or replaced, use the Levels control to reduce contrast, raising Output Black to neutralize shadows and Output White to knock down highlights. There will likely be unwanted side effects, so you must do your best to strike a happy medium (**Figure 12.6**).

Figure 12.5 The most immediate indication that Sir Isaac has been lit from the left is his long cast shadow, but you have the option of including it or not when pulling the key.

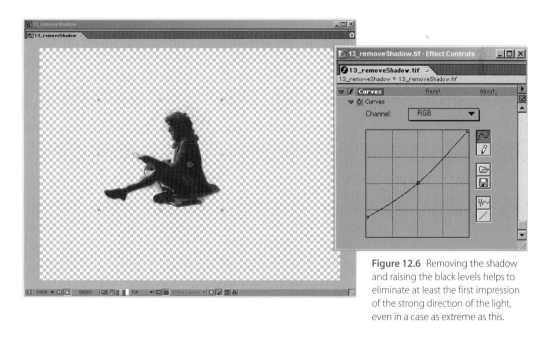

Figure 12.6 Removing the shadow and raising the black levels helps to eliminate at least the first impression of the strong direction of the light, even in a case as extreme as this.

Figure 12.7 The effect of a soft lens filter is created with two extra duplicates of the source, each blurred and then set to Add (or Screen) and Multiply, respectively, each with an Opacity of approximately 30%.

If adjusting the image directly to soften highlights and shadows isn't looking so good, you can get creative in adding the equivalent of a soft filter on the image. To do this

1. Duplicate the image.

2. Set a modest Fast Blur (say, 10 pixels for a film-resolution source) and an Add (or Screen) blending mode to the duplicate.

3. Knock down Opacity to 30%.

4. Make a second duplicate with the new settings, and change the blending mode of the top layer to Multiply (or Overlay).

These blurred layers soften the highlights and shadows, respectively. With Screen mode, the overall levels will not change; with Add, they will brighten slightly (**Figure 12.7**).

Far from being the only such adjustment you can make, this is one pretty much devised on the fly to give a specific example; different shots might well require different settings. More generally, the principle of combining an image with blurred and matted versions of itself can be a highly effective way to change not only its lighting qualities but also its overall look.

Leveling Uneven Light and Hotspots

There is a simple trick that you can use to even out the lighting in cases where it should appear uniform. The basic idea is simple: Create a counter gradient and use it to weight to your image adjustment by bringing up the shadows, bringing down the highlights, or both. What's surprising is how powerful the technique is—and to how many situations it applies.

You can create the gradient to do this by eye. In some cases, such as scenes with low contrast, you can use the inverted, blurred source itself to create the matte. But as a compositor used to looking at light, you should be able to discern where the hotspot is, and how far it reaches (**Figure 12.8**). You might even find this kind of fun.

The next step is to create a white-to-black gradient using the Ramp effect that matches your perception of the hot-spot in the scene (**Figure 12.9**). You could apply the result directly to the scene with a blending mode, but you'll have more control if you apply it as a luma track matte to an adjustment layer containing a Levels or Curves effect. This allows you to select whether you're adjusting highlights and shadows or gamma.

The result won't necessarily obliterate all evidence that there was hot lighting in some area of your scene (**Figure 12.10**), but as always, the goal is not only aesthetic beauty

Figure 12.8 This scene is lit by a single key light aimed at the center of the scene, causing a distracting hotspot on the torso of the second bunny from the left.

Figure 12.9 A simple gradient created to match the offensive area of the hotspot. The center and edge of the radial gradient, created with the Ramp effect, have been positioned by eye to match **Figure 12.8**.

Figure 12.10 It's not as though all traces of the single hard key light have been eliminated, but that was not the aim of this adjustment. Instead, the effect of the light has been reduced so that it no longer puts the viewer's focus in the wrong place.

but also the viewer's focus. If there seems to be a distracting spotlight on the middle of some part of the scene, there's a problem. The same technique can even help when you're attempting to pull a key from an unevenly lit set, although tools such as Keylight already compensate for these types of image defects. Should the camera move during the shot, you can even consider marrying the gradient start and end points to a tracker with an offset, either via expressions or parenting. (See Chapter 8, "Effective Motion Tracking," for more on this.)

Conversely, you can also create a lighting effect this way; a radial gradient at the center of the frame, with the corners slipping away to darkness, creates a *vignette* or *eye light* effect, often associated with projected or heavily treated film and with handheld low-light shooting. The easiest way to do this is not with Ramp but with a heavily feathered and inverted elliptical mask applied to a black solid (**Figure 12.11**).

Figure 12.11 Reference of film footage that was shot and processed with a vignette, and addition of the equivalent vignette effect in After Effects, by double-clicking the Elliptical Mask tool to fill the frame, then opening the mask controls (**MM**), checking Invert, and setting a very high Mask Feather (500 for this 2 K resolution source) and Mask Expansion (50 pixels).

Figure 12.12 The same gradient as in **Figure 12.9**, but duplicated with the duplicate layer set to Multiply mode, creating the inverse-square fall-off that is a phenomenon of light. Because the example in **Figure 12.8** has only a single light that would fall off in this manner, this gradient was used to create **Figure 12.10**. Ordinary incandescent lights exhibit this phenomenon.

Creating a Look with Color

Go back and study a movie that you consider to be visually compelling. Chances are that the use of color in that film was bold and deliberate. If you ever saw behind-the-scenes footage of one of your favorite films, you might be startled at how flat and boring all the action seems, taken directly on set with standard video ENG (electronic news gathering) equipment.

Some of that movie magic process is the direct result of photochemical processes applied to the film. For example, much of the strange, detached, futuristic appearance of the film *Minority Report* was derived from the use of the bleach bypass method in processing the film. To some degree, it is possible to re-create these kinds of looks purely in After Effects, particularly if you have good reference.

Geek Alert: Inverse Square Law

3D artists and lighting directors out there will be aware that a linear gradient is not the perfect model for light falloff and that light's intensity diminishes proportionally to its distance from the source squared. So if I'm twice as far from a single light source as you are, I will be illuminated by one-quarter the amount of light.

So I suppose you want a gradient that behaves this way? Simple. Duplicate your layer with the radial gradient, and set the upper of the two layers to a Multiply blending mode. There you have it: inverse square dissipation of intensity (**Figure 12.12**). Instead of using a gradient layer directly as a luma matte, put the two combined gradients into a single pre-composition, and you're good to go.

Who knows, maybe you'll even find a situation where you notice the difference; the number of shots taken with a single light source is not high, but the same adjustment would work with any single light that is too hot. If nothing else, you've just avoided paying money for one more third-party plug-in that offers one more capability you can easily create for yourself.

TIP

To see what I mean, compare the behind-the-scenes footage on *The Matrix* DVD with the look of the film itself.

Using a Solid

Suppose your client or supervisor asks you to make your overall shot look warmer or cooler. What tool do you reach for first? Levels, Hue/Saturation, Tint, Color Balance—all of these effects and more are capable of satisfactorily altering the color look of your shot.

You don't have to use an effect at all, however, because there is a more direct and interactive way of doing this. The results look like you added a colored filter over the imaginary lens of your virtual camera. Add a colored solid with its blending mode set to Color. Choose a color that is pleasing to your eye, has brightness and saturation well above 50%, and fits your criteria: blue or green for a cooler look, red or yellow for a warmer one (**Figure 12.13**).

At 100%, this is the equivalent of a full-color tint of the image, which is not really what you're after, so don't be horrified by how your shot looks when you first turn this

Figure 12.13 The source shot and four different colored looks blended over it, each using deep-colored, saturated solids: blue, yellow, green, and blue and green combined. Each is set to Color mode at 33% Opacity. Note how this method permits the source colors to be perceived, while changing the feel of the shot.

on. Instead, reveal the Opacity control for the solid (keyboard shortcut: **T**), and dial it back to somewhere between 10% and 50%. You are looking for the threshold where the source colors still come through but are filtered by the color you're adding. What I find powerful about this approach is that, assuming you've gotten the color right, you need only adjust it with that Opacity slider. With this approach, you are only ever two adjustments away from transforming the look of your shot. Furthermore, the effect is more natural and subtle, allowing more of the source color through than the alternatives of adding a Tint or an HSB effect (**Figures 12.14a**, **b**, and **c**).

The last section of this chapter discusses using overlaid colors to create a more deliberate film look.

Figures 12.14a, b, and c Three methods for tinting the plate green; the timeline exposes the effects used for each. The effects of a solid (12.14a) and an HSB adjustment (12.14b) probably appear similar in print, but note that colors such as the yellow blanket on the wall at the left of frame change disproportionately (to orange in that case). The Tint approach has the shot looking like it was taken in a fog of pea soup (12.14c).

Day for Night

It's such a classic old Hollywood effect that it became the title of French "new wave" filmmaker Francois Truffaut's ode to filmmaking: the day-for-night effect, or as he would have called it in French, *la nuit américaine.* The trick is a simple one: Shoot a normally lit scene with a dark blue filter on the lens, giving the appearance of night. This was done, especially prior to the introduction of much faster film stocks in the 1970s, because of the low light-gathering capabilities of film stock, particularly in sweeping exterior shots as were favored by westerns. Ideally, the scene would be shot with diffuse, cloudy light, but circumstances didn't always cooperate, so the shadows cast by the sun were supposed to become moonlit shadows. Sometimes it was amazing how bright a specular highlight the moon could cause, kicking off the barrel of the hero's drawn gun.

Lighting techniques and film itself have improved at the high end, but the context in which you would want (or need) to completely change the lighting conditions of a shot have by no means vanished. Digital cameras are notoriously poor at getting anything but grain out of low-lit scenes; witness the popularity of the cheesy Sony Handi-cam Nightshot feature, which is destined to go down as a hallmark look of our era the way Super 8 film says 1960s and '70s.

Figure 12.15 shows a demonstration of a day-for-night effect achieved primarily with a very dark, desaturated blue solid, applied with the Overlay blending mode. In this case, simply overlaying the solid is only part of the job: the underlying image has had its gamma and Output White values knocked down significantly, as well as lowering the Blue Output White. (I use Levels terms to describe these, having actually made the changes using Curves, as shown in **Figure 12.16.**)

The other key here is to desaturate the background image; bright colors will punch through, when the reality is that color cannot be seen without light. This is not to say that no color will come through, but in this example Master

Figure 12.15 Day-for-night effect accomplished with a deep-blue solid and lowering of the white point, gamma, and saturation of the plate. You'll have to trust me that the effect is quite spectacular onscreen; in print, most of the color subtleties are lost.

Saturation is reduced by –60. The effect of yellow moonlight on the clouds is achieved not in Hue/Saturation but by the drop in the Blue Output White. Drop one color, and you raise its opposite (yellow in the case of blue). Of course, the yellow does not really show up very well in print—sorry about that.

Using Effects

Solids are great for instantaneously filtering the color of an entire shot, but what about cases where you want to colorize just a single element or take it from color to grayscale? In such a case, color solids become cumbersome, and you will most typically want to employ either Hue/Saturation or Tint.

For cases in which you want to remove color from footage, there is an important distinction between these two effects. Tint maintains the difference in luminance perceived by the eye between red and green and blue. Hue/Saturation does not. **Figures 12.17a** through **d** illustrate this distinction using the Mars flag, a red, green, and blue tricolor selected by the Mars Society and flown into orbit by the Space Shuttle *Discovery*. Seriously.

Each color of the flag is fully saturated in one channel. Mathematically, the correct thing to do is to average the luminance of each channel for each color, turning them all an equivalent gray; this is what Hue/Saturation does. It causes all of the apparent contrast between the colors to vanish, because it ignores the way the eye sees color.

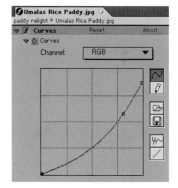

Figure 12.16 Here is the Curves equivalent of reducing Output White and gamma in the RGB channel of the plate image.

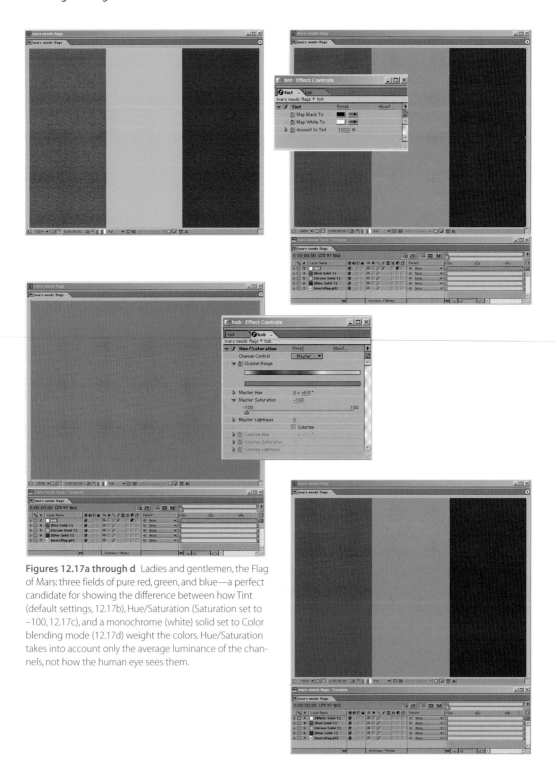

Figures 12.17a through d Ladies and gentlemen, the Flag of Mars: three fields of pure red, green, and blue—a perfect candidate for showing the difference between how Tint (default settings, 12.17b), Hue/Saturation (Saturation set to −100, 12.17c), and a monochrome (white) solid set to Color blending mode (12.17d) weight the colors. Hue/Saturation takes into account only the average luminance of the channels, not how the human eye sees them.

As was mentioned in Chapter 6, "Color Keying," there is a standard weighting used in digital imaging programs to replicate the relative brightness at which the eye sees color. This weighting comes into play when using the Tint effect, and in most situations where After Effects is converting color into luminance. For example, a solid with a 0% Saturation value set with the Color blending mode has a similar result to a black-and-white Tint at 100%.

Therefore, Hue/Saturation is ill advised for desaturating footage. It is, however, very useful and convenient for quickly colorizing an element. On *The Day After Tomorrow* all of us on the compositing team at The Orphanage came to memorize the exact Hue value that the supervisor tended to love (if I recall correctly, it was 237°) and applied it to various snow and fog overlay elements that had been created as grayscale mattes.

The other obvious use for Hue/Saturation is to desaturate footage (or less often, to boost saturation). What is not so obvious to the novice artist is when to desaturate an element or a whole shot. The most succinct advice I can offer is that if you find yourself fighting a color correction and you're focused only on brightness and contrast (say, because you're using Levels), keep in mind that your contrast may be just right, but your overall saturation may be too high.

TIP

One seldom-used effect that is rather nice is Color Balance, not to be confused with Color Balance (HLS), which is useful only for animating Hue/Saturation channels individually. If you find yourself wanting to shift a color channel only in one luminance range and you like thinking in terms of shadows, midtones, and highlights, give it a whirl (**Figure 12.18**).

Figure 12.18 The soil in the image from **Figure 12.11** is given a nice reddish appearance by increasing Shadow Red Balance in the Color Balance effect. According to the After Effects documentation, toggling on Preserve Luminosity "preserves the average brightness of the image while changing the color. This control maintains the tonal balance in the image," which strengthens the overall effect.

NOTES

"Kiss of love" is not a technical term. It is attributed to Stu Maschwitz from when he supervised *Star Wars, Episode One: The Phantom Menace* at Industrial Light + Magic. "I still use that term today," he says. "It's a great way to get an artist to think of a shot as theirs. Examples of kisses of love are reflections in things that might not strictly need it, aperture flares for lights leaving the frame (carefully matched to reference), or animating a starfighter pilot's head to turn as he banks."

Backlighting, Flares, Light Volume

Situations in which light sources appear prominently in a scene are something of a gift to a compositor: They give you a very direct detail to shoot for. Get these right, and you will sell your scene in ways that the viewer can hardly perceive. This is the *kiss of love*, that something extra that isn't necessary to get the shot finaled but that adds to the shot.

The early days of computer graphics were littered with bad examples of light artifacts. Any shot, say, in outer space that had a sun or a star appearing in shot would be accompanied by a big, prominent lens flare, and these seemed to appear with such regularity, it was as if the camera was always being pointed at the sun, which it probably was. These were largely failures on the part of visual artists to recognize what really goes on with light; instead they used stereotyped ideas and tricks that seemed cool at the time. It was years before NewTek's LightWave 3D, which actually can render beautiful images, lost its reputation as "the lens flare software" due to its overuse in science-fiction television of the 1990s.

Ironically, big, bold, daring choices about light can and should become almost invisible if they are appropriate to a scene. Generally, the rule about strong lighting choices is this: If the choice is going to stand out, it should do something to place the viewer's attention where it needs to be to serve the story. If a strong choice doesn't serve the story, it had better not take focus in the shot.

Backlighting and Light Wrap

The conditions of a backlit scene are a classic example of when the compositor typically does not go far enough to match what actually happens in the real world. This is the general subject of Chapter 15, "Learning to See," in which guest author Stu Maschwitz alludes specifically to light wrap. Here, then, is his methodology for creating your own light wrap.

True, light wrap plug-in effects have been developed by third-party developers for After Effects. As is often the case, however, there is an easy way to develop your own equivalent that works as well as, if not better than, what is available out there. Say you began with a background that contains backlighting conditions and a foreground that is lit to match those conditions but does not have any light wrapping around the edges, as is called for (**Figure 12.19**).

You set up the light wrap effect as follows:

1. Create a new composition that contains the background and foreground layers, exactly as they are positioned and animated in the master composition. You can do this simply by duplicating the master comp and renaming it something intuitive, such as Light Wrap. If the foreground or background consists of several layers, it will probably be simpler to pre-compose them into two layers, one each for the foreground and background.

2. Set Silhouette Alpha blending mode for the foreground layer, punching a hole in the background (**Figure 12.20**).

Figure 12.19 I promised myself I wouldn't do any of those classic computer graphics demos with spheres or teapots in them. I lied. That's not an eclipse you see, it's a sphere that has been color-matched to the figures seen on the beach, yet somehow it still appears as a black hole in the scene.

Figure 12.20 Using the alpha of the layer to which it's applied, Silhouette Alpha punches a hole through that layer and all underlying layers.

3. Add an adjustment layer at the top, and apply Fast Blur.

4. In Fast Blur, check the Repeat Edge Pixels toggle on and crank up the blurriness (**Figure 12.21**).

5. Duplicate the foreground layer, move the copy to the top, and set its blending mode to Stencil Alpha, leaving a halo of background color that matches the shape of the foreground (**Figure 12.22**).

6. Place the resulting comp in the master comp and adjust opacity (and optionally switch the blending mode to Add, Screen, or Lighten) until you have what you're after. You may need to go back to the Light Wrap comp to further adjust the blur (**Figure 12.23**).

One final thing to keep in mind as you adjust a scene with backlit conditions: If there is no fill light on the foreground subject whatsoever, most cameras are incapable of

Figure 12.21 Heavy Fast Blur causes the background image color to bleed into the area of the underlying alpha channel.

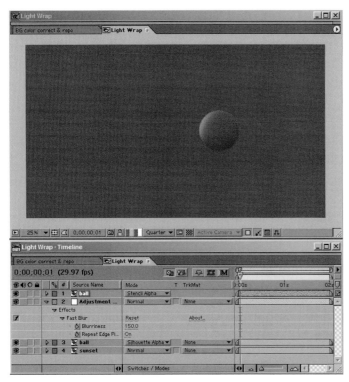

Figure 12.22 Stencil Alpha provides the inverse effect, preserving only the areas of the composition inside the alpha of the top layer to which it is applied. You have your light wrap.

Figure 12.23 It still looks like a black sphere, but it is now light wrapped. This is more light wrap than I would typically add, but the overemphasis shows up more easily in print.

Figure 12.24a, b, and c Three situations in which what the camera yielded in reality might not be what you'd expect in theory. Figure 12.24a has no lens flare, when you might expect one; 12.24b has just the barest suggestion of a flare spiking out of the huge light source pouring in through the window, and 12.24c has a lens flare that is more natural but far less apparent than the flares you would get from the Lens Flare effect.

picking up as much detail in the foreground as your eye might see. In your reference photo, an unlit foreground subject might appear completely silhouetted. Because the foreground subjects are often the actors in the scene, you might have to compensate, allowing enough light and detail in the foreground that the viewer can see facial expressions and other important dramatic detail.

In other words, this might be a case where your reference conflicts with what is needed for the story. Try to strike a balance, but remember, if the story loses, everyone loses.

Glints and Flares

Just because that big lens flare coming from the sun peeking around the side of that sci-fi moon looks cheesy doesn't mean all lens flares are cheesy. Of course, real lens flares are never cheesy: Our eyes accept them as natural, even beautiful artifacts without necessarily understanding anything about what actually causes them (**Figures 12.24a, b**, and **c**).

You won't see lens flares in many films made before the 1970s. Prior to that era, flares were seen as mistakes on the part of the cinematographer, and shots containing them were noted on the camera report and retaken. Then along came such films as *Easy Rider*, whose stories seemed to demand a less casual, more "pick up the camera and shoot" documentary style of filmmaking, as well as pictures coming back from space showing dramatic shots of the sun emerging around the curve of our own planet.

If you are going to get lens flares or even simple glints right, it is vital to get good reference. This will seem strange if you think about it; probably only a tiny percentage of your viewers can tell the difference between lens flares from a 50 mm prime and a 120 mm zoom lens. Yet somehow, if you get the lens flare wrong, it reads as phony to a majority of viewers. Weird.

In Chapter 15, Stu Maschwitz speaks of having created his own lens flare effect using well over a dozen nested compositions, based on reference that John Knoll had taken on set of the kind of flares the camera in use picked up.

Although I'm not going to give an example of doing this, there are two very cool things to be learned:

▶ This is one more case where, with good enough reference, you can roll your own. Lens flares are consistent for a given lens. Their angles vary according to the position of the light, but not the shape or arrangement of the component flares.

▶ Although a 17-element lens flare makes for a good battle story, some of the most natural-looking lens flares barely grab your attention at first and have only one or two simple components—just a bright spot in the frame, sometimes.

Moreover, not every bright light source that appears in frame will cause a lens flare—not even the sun. (Look again at **Figure 12.24a**.)

Most After Effects users will prefer a built-in solution that goes beyond the three settings included with the program's rather useless built-in Lens Flare (useless because everyone knows those three flares; they haven't changed in the better part of a decade). There is more than one option available on the market.

John Knoll himself is responsible for a great lens flare package called Knoll Light Factory, available from Red Giant Software. A demo (Mac only) is included on the book's CD-ROM. Without lapsing into a full-fledged product endorsement, there are two very helpful things about this set: First is that John knows flares, and the presets that are contained in these plug-ins are derived from careful studies of the corresponding lenses. If they're in there, it's probably because Industrial Light + Magic shot a project with that lens, and John took the time to get the preset right. Second, you don't have to rely on presets with this one; it is modular, allowing you to pick and choose various flare effects. In the interest of fairness, I will say that many users like to use the lens flare plug-in offered by The Foundry as part of Tinderbox. You can create a realistic looking flare with that plug-in, but I've seen a lot of pretty goofy-looking flares made with it as well. No matter which software you use, the key, as always, is to do your visual research.

CLOSE-UP

Geek Alert: What Causes Lens Flares?

Lens flares are artifacts that are never seen with your naked eye. They are artifacts created within the camera lens itself, caused by secondary reflections bouncing around between the camera elements. Because they are caused within the lens, they will always appear superimposed over the image, even over objects in the foreground that partially block the background light.

Unlike your eye, which has only one very flexible lens, camera lenses are typically made up of a series of inflexible lens elements. These elements are coated to prevent light reflecting off of them under normal circumstances. Extreme amounts of light, however, are reflected somewhat by each element.

Zoom lenses contain many focusing elements and tend to generate a complex-looking flare with lots of individual reflections. Prime lenses generate fewer.

Several other factors besides the lens elements also contribute to the look of a flare. Aperture blades within the lens cause highly reflective corners that often result in streaks, the number of streaks corresponding to the number of blades. The shape of the flares sometimes corresponds to the shape of the aperture (a pentagon for a five-sided aperture, a hexagon for six). Dust and scratches on the lens also reflect light.

Finally, lens flares look very different depending on whether they were shot on film or video, the excess light bleeding out in different directions and patterns.

Glints

Glints are related to lens flares in that they are also the result of bright light in the scene, but glints are totally different in that they are a natural effect seen with the naked eye rather than being a lens effect. **Figure 12.25** shows an example of a glint in the footage that was used in the Chapter 5 color matching example.

The glints observed on passing cars, then, represent an opportunity to replicate them directly on the computer-generated plane passing through the shot. This is a great example of a detail that is rarely added, which constitutes a kiss of love for the shot.

The great thing about glints is that they're easily observed (especially if they're already in the shot) and easily replicated, although in the taxi example shown, getting them right may involve adding unique glints to several frames in a row. The glint is caused when something in the frame (chrome along the taxi's windows in the example) acts like a mirror, reflecting the overhead sun directly toward the camera.

In the shot from Chapter 5, the plane moves rather quickly through frame, and the glints on the taxi seem to occur

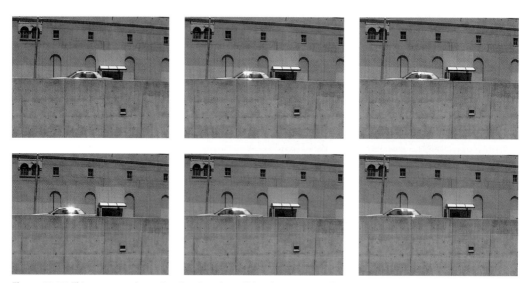

Figure 12.25 This sequence shows the glint that plays off the chrome areas of the taxi as it passes a spot in the frame where the sun is reflected directly into the camera lens.

just to the left of the frame's center, so that's the reference. You're looking for a hotspot on the plane that passes that point in the frame, and you get one on the tail.

By zooming in on your reference, you get the color and shape of a typical isolated glint (**Figure 12.26**). And behold: It's a white blotch with six thin streaks coming off of it (which probably corresponds to a six-sided aperture). Looks like you can paint it in a few minutes, no?

This is a perfect case for not being a perfectionist. Close-up, the result of my quickly painted glint looks most unimpressive indeed. But place it into a fast-moving shot that was never meant to be studied frame by frame, and I've just bought myself a good dose of extra realism for a few minutes' extra work (**Figure 12.27**).

Light Scattering and Volume

The phenomena of light scattering and its most dramatic and visible result, volumetric light, are the result of what happens to rays of light as they encounter particles in the air.

Chapter 5 looked at adjustments for re-creating the phenomenon of atmospheric haze, which causes items in the

Figure 12.26 Yowch, is that all there is to a good-looking glint at video resolution?

Figure 12.27 The plane passes with hand-painted glints added to its tail.

Figure 12.28 The glows of a full moon on a clear night, of a taillight receding into the distance, of stadium lights at dusk—we get so used to seeing the halo around these we hardly notice it after a while.

far distance to appear with lowered detail and contrast. The cause of this phenomenon is that the atmosphere does not permit light to travel directly to the camera, uninterrupted. Instead, the light ricochets off tiny particles in the air, causing it to scatter on even the clearest day.

There are other situations in which this phenomenon occurs, closer up and more dramatically. Lights that appear in the scene, casting their beams at the camera, tend to have a glowing halo around them. If the light traveled directly to the camera, the outline of the source light would be clear. Instead, light rays hit particles on their way to the camera and head off in slightly new directions, causing the halo (**Figure 12.28**).

Place more particles in the air (in the form of smoke, fog, or mist), and you get more of a halo, as well as the conditions under which volume light and such related phenomena as *God rays* can occur. These are the result not only of light scattering, but of the fact that light from an omnidirectional source, such as the sun, travels away from the source at a continuous arc of possible angles (**Figure 12.29**).

Figure 12.29 This cathedral of light is also known as God rays.

What does all this mean to you? You ought to re-create these phenomena when they're called for, not only because they look realistic but because they tend to look cool. As a compositor you don't want to miss an opportunity like that. After Effects has no built-in, one-button function for adding these type of effects, and so your method will vary depending on the shot.

You can do a lot with a soft feathered mask outlining the shape of the light volume, applied to a solid that is roughly the color of the intended effect. For visible particulate matter, you can animate a Fractal Noise effect (as is detailed in the following chapter).

Although After Effects contains no ability to create and render direct visible lights and their effects (for example, if you place a point light in your scene, you see its result but not the light itself), a plug-in from Trapcode called Lux adds that capability, so it is an option as well. A demo of Lux is included on the book's CD-ROM.

Shadows and Reflected Light

Uh-oh, I guess the time has come to talk about creating shadows. If lighting is complex, so are shadows, and maybe more so. At least with lights, if you know where they were placed in your source scene, you can gamely try to directly re-create those conditions. With shadows, however, you could have at your disposal the full dimensional information of the scene and all the lighting, but only a notion of how they should behave (although you have the advantage that your audience wouldn't know, either). Furthermore, because the world of After Effects is not fully three-dimensional, if you have to create realistic shadows from scratch, you're basically faking it.

The addition of 3D features, including lights and shadow casting, to After Effects 5.0 improved the fakery potential, if only somewhat. The problem remains that you're still basically stuck using a flat 2D plane (or planes) to project a shadow and a flat plane (or planes) to receive it, and the greater the angle of difference between the camera and a given light, the less possible it is for that shadow to be accurate.

NOTES

On *The Day After Tomorrow*, one of the shots done at The Orphanage required inverse God rays caused by the Empire State Building blocking the sun in a heavy snowfall. In other words, just as the rays themselves array outward, so do the shadows caused by large objects blocking them. With this phenomenon nailed, the shot was not only more accurate but more interesting to watch.

Figure 12.30 illustrates the problem, using our old friend Sir Isaac lit from the left side with a spot. Keying to keep the shadow proved difficult. But re-creating it using the silhouette of the character is nearly impossible; clearly, his outline from the side bears almost no resemblance to his outline as seen by the camera. As you saw in **Figure 12.6**, there's not much possibility of changing his light direction here; it seems pretty evident that all of his lighting is coming from the left.

Creating Shadows

Figure 12.31 shows the classic 2D solution for cast shadows, corner-pinning the matte to an angle that is something like that at which the camera sees the object, with a figure

Figure 12.30 Positioning a 3D light to the left of the character, where his appearance indicates it belongs, works even worse than you might expect. It yields a fake-looking shadow that includes details that shouldn't be there, such as the extended leg, and misses others that should be there, such as the outline of a head above two shoulders—not to mention how difficult it is to match the ground plane. Horrifying.

Figure 12.31 Sigh. Not much better is the corner pin approach, whereby a duplicate of the layer is made black and semi-opaque, then a Corner Pin effect is added to skew the layer as if it's lying down. This one would need a lot of hand-painting to get it right at all, and the angle in this case is completely wrong. Dismal.

whose outline is complex and lit from an angle more than 10 or 15 degrees off axis from the camera. It doesn't work very well here, but it is certainly possible to pull it off with simpler objects.

Another 2D trick is one borrowed from the games industry; The Orphanage was actually able to use this one extensively for the Level Four sequence of *Spy Kids 3-D* because the story of the movie was characters trapped inside a video game. The cheat is that characters only cast a small pool of shadow beneath their feet or where they're sitting, and so on. The simple way to create this one is to mask off part of the matted character and translate only that into position. By feathering the mask and blurring the matte contained inside it quite a lot, you add some subtle interactivity between the character and the ground plane and basically just hope nobody really thinks about it too much (**Figure 12.32**).

TIP

You can use the shadow matte itself directly, setting its Outpoint White (in Levels) to 0 and then adjusting its Opacity down to soften the shadow. If you instead apply it as a luma track matte to an adjustment layer, then adjust the shadow using a Levels or Curves control, this gives you a bit of extra control over how the shadow interacts with the background, its effect on highlights versus already dark areas, and so on.

Figure 12.32 Not much better, but almost acceptable if you dial it back to where it's almost imperceptible. The pool of shadow is created by masking the parts of the figure nearest the floor, offsetting and blurring them, then using the result as the alpha channel of an adjustment layer (or just sending it to black and semi-opaque and applying it directly). It's basically a hand-done variation on a drop shadow. Yeesh.

Overall, the Sir Isaac example has demonstrated that when there are shadows present on set, it would be preferable to do everything you can to try to bring them back—even rotoscope them and give them a key all their own—rather than submit to the humiliation of the desperate approaches outlined here. Or better yet, composite your character into an environment—say, a grassy clearing—in which the shadows would be mostly obscured.

Reflected and Interactive Light

It's easy to forget the actual physics of what gives an object a certain color, probably because it's strange and even counterintuitive. The color of the surface is made up of the colors of light that it does not absorb. Most of what we see as light and color is the result of reflected light.

Most surfaces in the natural world are diffuse, and the light that they reflect is sent out softly in all directions.

Using 3D Planes

The addition of virtual lights and 3D compositing to After Effects means that you can aim a light at the matted layer and cast a shadow onto a 3D plane that corresponds to an actual surface in the scene (**Figures 12.33a** through **f**). This works especially well if a 3D camera match move has been solved for the scene using third-party 3D tracking software. There are still several strong limiting factors, however. Your shadow is still only as good as the matte that casts it, and the surface receiving the shadow is going to be made up of flat planes only (although you can use several of them if you have the patience). As you saw, this technique has serious limitations if the light angle doesn't match that of the camera that shot the element.

Figures 12.33a through f Here's an opportunity to finally get away with something. The source shot (12.33a) is dominated by a big, brightly lit swath of pavement—not nice. Grab footage of silhouetted trees swaying in the breeze (12.33b), matte them (12.33c), and lay them into the scene as a 3D layer (12.33d). The key to the final result (12.33e) is not to simply layer the shadow directly with opacity (12.33f), but to apply it as an alpha track matte to an adjustment layer and add the shadow effect with color correction. This retains much more of the richness of the image.

Thus in some subtle way, objects in a shot together light one another, and characters or objects that pass through a scene are relit to some degree as they change position. Two objects composited together are completely missing the light interactions that would be present between them had they been photographed together.

Computer software is becoming better at re-creating these types of interactions. Global illumination and radiosity features have been added to 3D rendering programs in recent years to re-create the many effects of reflected light, enhancing the realism of completely synthesized scenes. For the compositor, however, this is still all more art than science, and the subjective evaluation of observed phenomena will in many cases go farther than the application of objective principles. In other words, the 3D artist can be more like a sculptor, letting the light play over the created work, but the compositor is still more like a painter, observing and artistically interpreting the world.

Light that interacts directly with objects in your scene is something of an opportunity for you as a compositor. Nail down appropriate interactive lighting, and you infuse your scene with life and realism, helping to tell the story.

Re-lighting a Scene

Hopefully there will not be too many cases in which your source footage was shot so incorrectly, in terms of fundamentals such as light direction, quality, or intensity that you're asked to do the seemingly impossible: to completely relight a scene. Particularly with exteriors, however, there are bound to be cases in which natural conditions didn't cooperate at the time of the shoot.

Even more likely, there will be cases in which the footage that was shot is adequate but lacks *something*. You could call it visual punch, artistic style, essential drama. With episodic television, your establishing shot can't tell the viewer much more than "downtown, daytime." But feature films and other more ambitious stories demand that the shot do more than that; that it propel the drama and mood of the story forward, and it's not always possible to get what's needed with the camera alone.

The two chapters that follow will look at creating specific effects related to weather and pyrotechnics that would be difficult, expensive, or both to capture on camera. For now, consider taking a source shot with rather ordinary lighting conditions, on a rather ordinary pretty day in Hollywood (**Figure 12.34**) and giving it lighting conditions that could be shot at only one particular time of day and only on certain days of the year (**Figure 12.35**).

This example is directly inspired by a similar video demonstration by Stu Maschwitz, to show the basics of using eLin, the set of tools for linear color compositing that Brendan Bolles described in Chapter 11. Stu and Brendan know a lot about eLin—they worked together to develop it for use at The Orphanage. Most of the rest of the world knows very little about eLin, although the plug-in has been available as shareware for several months at this writing. (It is included on the book's CD-ROM, free for noncommercial use; a pop-up appears on start-up reminding you to register if you're using it commercially, but you are free to work and render with the full features.)

I'm going to show how much less cheating you have to do to make a dramatic metamorphosis of light conditions if you work in true linear color space. I'll also describe where the tried and true method falls short. It's a comparison of old school and new school compositing methods. With eLin, After Effects is among the last of the major compositing packages to have the capacity to work with linear color at a 1.0 gamma (if the concept eludes you, check out

NOTES

The example compares tried and true color models with one that is available in After Effects 6.5 only via particular shareware from The Orphanage. The persons responsible for this shareware were also integral participants in the creation of this book, and have been my colleagues on feature film projects. The following in-depth look at compositing using the eLin toolset is not intended to sell copies of the software, it is intended to open your eyes to how high-end compositing is being done in the twenty-first century.

Figure 12.34 This source shot shows an ordinary day-lit exterior on a pretty, clear day.

Figure 12.35 In the manipulated shot, it's no longer pretty or clear and no longer so ordinary.

Nomenclature

As was already touched upon in Chapter 11, there are terms for color that tend to be used interchangeably, inconsistently, and therefore, confusingly. For example, the Cineon Converter claims to perform "log to linear" conversion, but I would call it log to video and preserve the word "linear" for a color space with a 1.0 gamma, not the 2.2 gamma you are used to working with.

For the purposes of this section, linear, true linear, scene referred, and even high dynamic range color spaces are those in which eLin operates, that look exceptionally dark on your monitor, but that composite together in a nondestructive manner that is faithful to the way light works in the natural world. Video or vid spaces look fine on your monitor and are what you're used to working with, but can easily clip and do not offer the ample benefits of linear.

Chapter 11 for a thorough run-down). For work on feature films, this is fast becoming the standard approach at facilities using such competing packages as Apple's Shake and Digital Fusion's Nuke. If you apply for a job compositing at a company that relies on one of those, you may be downgraded as an After Effects user for not having any familiarity with radiometrically linear images (also called photometrically linear, scene-referred values, gamma 1.0, linear, or lin). Don't let this happen; win them over, if not to After Effects and eLin, then at least to your skills and knowledge.

After using these plug-ins extensively on *The Day After Tomorrow* and subsequent projects, I am convinced that linear color spaces and the ability to calculate brightness values that are higher than your monitor can display are the wave of the future. Most other software used for film compositing includes this feature set, and it is likely to trickle down to other types of users and more software packages because, once you understand the underlying concepts, this method of working makes so much sense. Getting used to it takes time, however; in many ways it marks the biggest change to occur to digital compositing since its inception.

But why take my word for it? Following is my version of the demo that helped convince me. Check out the steps involved in transforming a neutrally lit scene into a dramatically lit one, specifically showing where eLin compositing eliminates compromises that you've probably become accustomed to accepting. Even if you're not ready to switch your workflow, you'll get an idea what's involved with or without linear color

The Basic Linear Set-Up

Figure 12.36 The full set of eLin effects in the Effects palette and the eLin palette. You'll use three effects more than all others: vid2eLin, elin2vid (which convert in and out of lin space, respectively), and eLevels (which gives access to adjusting pixels whose values are above the brightest white your monitor can display).

Before you can compare linear and video workflows, you need to get familiar with eLin. Working with eLin requires a little bit of preparation. If you want to play along, you should first install eLin using the installer from the book's CD-ROM. This adds a set of Effect plug-ins under the category eLin (**Figure 12.36**), as well as a couple of useful scripts that I'll get to in a moment.

As was pointed out in Chapter 11, there are two predominant benefits to working in linear color space. The first is that light adjustments interact as they would in the real world, and the second is that you get access to *overbright* pixels, areas of the image that have become brighter than your monitor can display.

Just in case that doesn't sound life-changing and exciting, there is a major side-benefit to consider: The combination of light adjustments behaving naturally and the overhead for overbright pixels means that you can layer color adjustment upon color adjustment, turning the exposure up and down, dialing color up and then pulling it back, without ever seeing the color turn flat and quantized. This example makes that distinction very clear.

As a source image, the example uses **Figure 12.34**, a normal 8-bit-per-channel file, lightly JPEG compressed, similar to one you would get out of any digital camera (this one came from an Olympus point-and-shoot). The key here is that the source image is not overexposed (save that bright spot on the side of the palm, which can be eliminated). If there were highlights in the sky that were already looking blown out, the image would not be a suitable candidate for this treatment because no matter what you did they would still appear blown out.

Figure 12.37 shows the image looking just the same, but now set to work in linear color space using eLin. If you've installed eLin and want to try this yourself, a few simple steps will offer you this basic setup. You'll use the same basic steps every time you prepare footage for eLin:

1. Create a new composition by importing tower.jpg (found on the book's CD-ROM) and dragging it to the new composition icon at the bottom of the Project window. Rename the comp MASTER, and leave the other settings alone.

2. Choose File > Run Script > 02_eLin_Palette_Rel.jsx. This brings up the eLin palette containing all of eLin's necessary setups as shortcuts.

NOTES

You could get the first benefit simply by changing the gamma setting of all visible layers to 0.4545 (using Levels), compositing them, and viewing the result by setting its gamma to 2.2. Strange, but true (Chapter 11 explains why). To get the tools to properly manage the pipeline in After Effects 6.5, however, you need eLin.

Figure 12.37 The image is the same, but three changes were made automatically using the eLin palette. The layer was set with a vid2eLin adjustment, sending it to lin space and an adjustment guide layer was added with a view LUT, sending it back to vid space so you can see it look as it should.

3. With the image layer selected, click the VID to eLin button on the eLin palette. Clear the warning about commercial usage, and note the red striping across your image (**Figure 12.38**). This is not because you don't own the software, but because you need to use these plug-ins in 16-bit mode.

4. Switch to 16-bit mode by Alt-clicking (Option-clicking) on the 8bpc button at the bottom of your Project window to toggle it to 16bpc.

5. Your image has turned very dark; at best, you can see just the faintest outline of the shapes in it. Your image has had its gamma reduced to 0.4545, changing the standard video gamma to linear gamma. To see the image look normal again, counter-correct this with a view LUT by clicking the eLin LUT button in the palette.

Figure 12.38 If you're trying eLin and you see this striping the first time, don't give up. You just need to switch your project to 16-bit color.

You're now set up for eLin compositing, but your image looks just the same as it did. All of your visible images will include the VID to eLin adjustment, which allows their compositing operations to be performed in linear space, and will have to be converted back out of linear space in order to be seen normally.

And that is the major downside to eLin: You now need that LUT adjustment over the eLin layers for things to look right. A LUT is a *look up table*, a reference adjustment that tells each pixel how it should be displayed differently from its own value.

At this point, nothing is different because you've only lowered gamma and raised it back up again with the LUT. If you were to render this frame right now, you would get the almost black version because the LUT is on a guide layer and does not render.

Experimenting with Exposure

Now you're ready to begin reaping the benefits. Here's the first one: You can change the exposure values of the image in exactly the way a camera would, and freely adjust the image back and forth above and below the top visible white point.

Figure 12.39 shows the completely disastrous result of adding the source layer to itself in regular video space—yuck. As you will recall from way back in Chapter 3, "Selections: The Key to Compositing," Add mode simply adds pixel values together. In this case, many pixels in the image start with a value above the midpoint (0.5 or 128 in RGB colors), so adding that value to itself blows out the value. It looks horrible. You would never brighten an image this way, certainly not without dialing it way back.

Figure 12.39 This is one big reason Add mode is seldom used in normal After Effects work. It is often much too strong an effect when a pixel above middle gray is added to another of that value, in which case the result is pure white.

Figure 12.40 demonstrates the same operation but in linear color space. Only the detail in the clouds and on the palm tree is blown out, and the image looks less like a disaster and more like an image that has been overexposed by one f-stop, which is exactly what it is compared with the source.

That's cool, you think, but I could get the comp in video color space (or *vid space*) to look like that, if I wanted to. All I have to do is reduce the Opacity of the top layer to 45%, and it looks identical (**Figure 12.41**). This brings us to the second cool thing about linear space: You can dial it back without undoing prior corrections. Colors can travel above absolute white and be brought back.

Figure 12.40 Adding an image to itself in eLin space is the equivalent of opening the camera's aperture one stop, and it looks just as natural as a slightly overexposed version of the source image.

Figure 12.41 Add in vid space has been dialed back to roughly match the result of **Figure 12.39**.

Figure 12.42 shows an overlaid solid that is the equivalent of adding a filter over the lens to bring the exposure down one stop; it is masked to cover only part of a cloud so you can see that the masked area looks identical to how the source image looked in that area, yet the previous correction remains behind. This was done by creating the solid at a color of exactly 50% gray (RGB values of R: 128, G: 128, B: 128) and setting its blending mode to Multiply, which is the perfect inverse of Add in linear space.

Figure 12.42 That disc in the image is only a 50% gray solid, but it acts like a filter, knocking the exposure down exactly one stop. Detail that was at values above full white is recovered.

Try the same thing in vid space (**Figure 12.43**), and behold the ugliness of the result. The detail is gone, and the color under the multiplied gray is the exact color of the solid: flat gray. Now you're thinking, "Why would I do that? Ever since I started adjusting digital images I've understood that once my color values are clipped, there's no bringing them back, so I just don't do it."

And what that means is that you've been creating kludges to live with digital color. You may have avoided creating

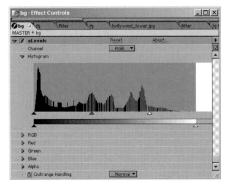

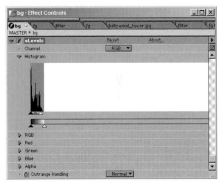

Figure 12.43 Where did the detail go? In video space, once it's gone, it's not coming back, so you've become used to taking great care never to let this happen.

Figures 12.44a and b The normal view of eLevels (12.44a) looks like Levels. But, what happens if you click that white space at the right? You get access to the overbright range (12.44b) where all of the pixels that are beyond white are kept. At this stage, there's not much there.

anything that looks as bad as that darkened area in the adjusted video image, but you haven't been using your digital imaging programs as if they were a real camera, shooting real film.

None of which may bother you—yet. But now, try some practical applications of this information and see what you can learn about the real benefits.

Crafting the Change

An actual Levels adjustment to this image to make it look like it was illuminated by the bright, warm light of dusk will employ the eLin version of Levels, called eLevels. It is similar to Levels with the one major difference that its controls and histogram can account for values greater than 1.0, pure white on your monitor. **Figures 12.44a** and **b** show that there are two modes for eLevels: one for the visible range and one showing the extended range.

TIP

The Curves tool is acceptable for use in linear color as-is. No special eCurves control is needed, but beware: The curves keep going well beyond the visible range in the grid, so adjusting gamma on individual channels is ill advised.

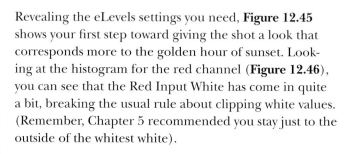

Figure 12.45 You can introduce a more golden hour look with eLevels in much the same way as you would with Levels, channel by channel.

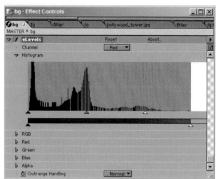

Figure 12.46 In regular Levels this setting, with Red Input White below the visible range, would be considered clipped.

Revealing the eLevels settings you need, **Figure 12.45** shows your first step toward giving the shot a look that corresponds more to the golden hour of sunset. Looking at the histogram for the red channel (**Figure 12.46**), you can see that the Red Input White has come in quite a bit, breaking the usual rule about clipping white values. (Remember, Chapter 5 recommended you stay just to the outside of the whitest white).

That looks pretty good, except for the already clipped values on the palm tree at the left. Those could be painted out, but in this case, you have the option of adding a foreground element instead, heightening the dramatic composition of the shot. Drama in this case means contrast; you've already added a little color contrast and now you're adding contrast between the foreground and background.

Import a close-up of the tree, tree_fg.jpg, which was taken at higher resolution than the same source shot. It needs to have the same settings as the existing tower.jpg layer, so duplicate that one and swap tree_fg.jpg for the duplicated layer (by Alt-dragging/Option-dragging tree_fg.jpg to the selected duplicate layer of tower.jpg). To simplify things, rename these layers bg and fg, meaning background and foreground, respectively.

Next, look at the foreground layer with the same levels settings as the background (**Figure 12.47**). To remove it from its background, give it a quick six-point roto mask; the sky is probably good enough to actually key it, but you only need a quick-and-dirty removal here because the element will also be heavily blurred to match its depth of field in the shot (**Figure 12.48**).

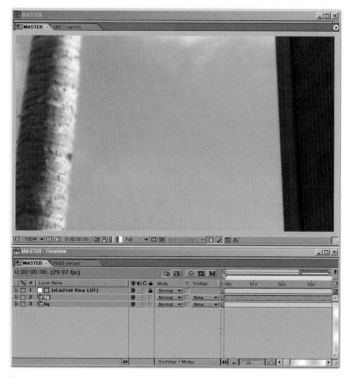

Figure 12.47 The foreground element is added, but not masked. It does not blow out with the levels settings the way the tree at the left of the plate did.

Figure 12.48 The mask is added in the Layer window. The mask doesn't have to be as perfect as a blue-screen key would be because it will be heavily in the foreground and have camera blur.

Figure 12.49 shows the before and after of adding camera blur to the foreground tree. Box Blur is a quick way to create a pretty good-looking representation of a defocused element; Blur Radius is set to 12, and Repeat Edge Pixels is turned on.

The result looks good, but the equivalent settings in video color space aren't holding up so well (**Figure 12.50**). By dialing them back, you're able to visually match the other shot, except that the clouds are becoming more blown out and subtle highlights are lost in the blur of the foreground. These aren't deal-killers yet, although it's not good to see what should be warm highlights turning green (due to the overweighting of the blue sky in vid space).

Now it's time to alter the shot more dramatically. The story calls for it to be a smoggy day, at sunset. You need to add the equivalent of a lens filter over the lens for the smog

Figure 12.49 The masked tree in the scene with camera blur added via a 12-pixel Box Blur.

Figure 12.50 Video color space isn't holding up well.

Figure 12.51 Whoa, what happened to Ramp? It should appear as a smooth black-to-white gradient, but it has been crushed by the LUT. This is exactly what eLin does: pushes the middle gray point down to make room for highlights. I include this image only because these types of surprises will occur along the way as you work with an adjusted gamma.

look (as is often done with a physical camera). To do so, add a solid the size of the comp, call it filter, and place it between the fg and bg layers. The color doesn't matter, because you next apply a Ramp effect. Yes, it looks very strange; that's because it's in video space (**Figure 12.51**).

Anytime something looks completely blown out or dark, there is a missing LUT involved. It's managing little shocks, such as things not looking right because of the view LUT, that constitutes the downside of eLin. In this case, you're not going to add a LUT, however. Solo the layer, disabling the view LUT, and change the Start Color in the Ramp effect to a bright, medium saturation orange smog color. Now apply this with a Multiply blending mode, turn off the Solo setting, and it behaves just like a lens filter (**Figure 12.52**).

The same step applied in video color space lacks subtlety and flattens out detail in the clouds more; the result looks a lot like early computer graphics work, before common cheats were devised. Your best option is to dial back its Opacity to about 70%. That's better, but look at the clouds: They're really starting to look flat and discolored in comparison (**Figures 12.53a** and **b**).

Figure 12.52 The Ramp was adjusted to behave similarly to a real camera's lens filter, creating the smog look. It's multiplied to burnish the image with its orange color.

Figures 12.53a and b The filter doesn't work as subtly in ordinary vid space (12.53a). It has to be dialed back (12.53b), just as with Add earlier, and you're losing detail in the clouds.

To complete the smog look, you can add a couple of layers of haze in the foreground and midground using an orange-hued solid with luminance and saturation values each around 30% (fairly dark and gray). These layers will be visible as-is, no blending mode, so they need the vid2eLin plug-in (click VID to eLin with the solids selected). Dial back midground haze (between the fg and bg layers) to 45% Opacity and the foreground haze (above the fg layer) to 20% Opacity. It's starting to look smoggy enough that I can feel the itch in my scalp (**Figure 12.54**).

In the video version, you'll encounter more trouble with this approach. The overall contrast flattens out even more, and there is a comparatively greenish-gray look to the highlights (although it may not be visible in the printed **Figure 12.55**).

Figure 12.54 I've seen L.A. days like this, achieved by adding dark gray solids with a hint of orange at medium opacity settings.

Figure 12.55 The same trick just doesn't work very well in ordinary vid space. The highlights can't punch through the overlapping layers, so the image just becomes muddy.

At this point the haze has dimmed down the overall image a bit much, so I'd be inclined to add more white contrast by bringing down the Input White value in eLevels for the bg layer and copying the result to fg. And here the video color approach is dealt its final, fatal blow: The equivalent adjustment in vid space makes the image painful to behold (**Figures 12.56a** and **b**). Detail in the clouds is completely gone, and the building, which is real, now looks like a cheap, computer-generated model.

Figures 12.56a and b Here's where the serious benefits start to kick in. The image was looking a bit dim in both versions, so Input White in the background eLevels is moved in to punch up the highlights (12.56a). You can make that simple adjustment in linear color space, but in video color, the image is pretty much wrecked (12.56b). What was a straightforward approach with eLin is untenable with normal methods.

Setting the Sun

Where the benefits of the eLin approach really kick in, though, is with the addition of the bright sun peeking out behind the building. The brightness and glow of the sun can be built up, step by step, without concern for blowing it out and with results in the scene that are very realistic.

Figure 12.57 shows the basic sun glow element: a glowing orange ball, masked by the edge of the building. It looks like a masked solid in the color of a 1970's kitchen countertop, and so it is. How the heck is that going to look like a sun?

You're not going to convert this element to eLin. Instead, you're going to let it blow out the way that Ramp in **Figure 12.51** did. Furthermore, to make it blow out in a really interesting, sun-in-the-sky kind of way, combine it with itself,

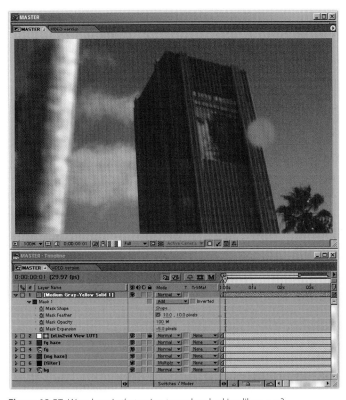

Figure 12.57 Wow, how is *that* going to end up looking like a sun?

Figure 12.58 Still not looking impressive, but now it's ready to be dropped into the master comp.

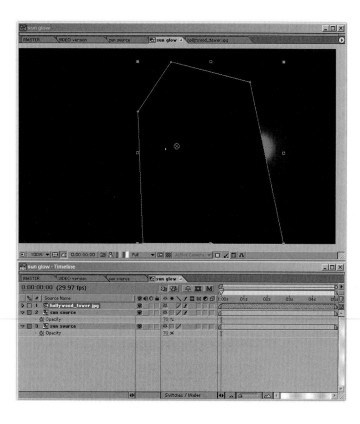

using an Add and a heavy 75-pixel Fast Blur on the upper layer; set both to 70% Opacity to allow them to interact (**Figure 12.58**).

This still looks like a masked orange solid in vid space, but pop the element into the scene, just above the bg layer, and you've already got a pretty nice sun (**Figure 12.59**). The hotspot rolls off well, and the glow interacts with the layers of haze. You can keep building the effect from here, using what you already have.

Duplicate the layer, and the sun gets bigger and hotter. Knock back Opacity to 25%, add a modest Fast Blur, move this duplicate sun above the foreground haze, and you've created a glow that reaches around the edge of the building in a very photographic way. Duplicate this and raise the blur much higher (to 100), and you have your desired result: the dramatic descent of the sun on a smoggy day.

CLOSE-UP

Output

The resulting sun is blown out on three channels. This is how it should look if the camera were pointed straight at the sun. But what if the image needs to be adjusted after you output it?

This is the reason why Cineon log files (described in Chapter 11) are so useful. **Figure 12.60** shows the eLin composite converted to log instead of video, channel by channel. The sun remains hot but is not completely blown out, even on the red channel. So if, at the next stage of production, it is decided that the shot needs to be half a stop darker, this adjustment remains possible without starting over.

Figure 12.59 Suddenly, those dark orange tones are rocketed above whitest white, but the overlaid blur is paying off with a nice glowing decay. The Add trick is performed again, twice, with the Opacity and Fast Blur settings on the upper levels used to fine-tune the look of the glowing ball.

Figure 12.60 The final image has been converted to Cineon format for output to film, where enough white overhead is retained to accommodate even the bright sun; it is not clipping in any of the three color channels.

Conclusion

Even if you only skimmed this eLin discussion, getting the idea from the figures, you have engaged with a complex, bewildering concept: The color model you have used in After Effects and Photoshop is not an accurate model of how light works in the world.

With this model, some of the most pleasing behaviors and phenomena associated with light come along for free. Without this model, I hate to tell you, but you are left to cheat and compensate, boosting and duplicating instances in an attempt to build up the lighting naturally. Often, however, you succeed only in losing the naturalness of the image, or you abandon the idea for an easier work-around.

If you did follow along, you should have an idea of exactly how radiometrically linear color faithfully re-creates the workings of light in the real world and on the medium that is still best designed to capture that reality: film.

I encourage you to keep learning about this subject and to make your own explorations with the eLin demo and its excellent documentation, which further explores topics introduced here. True linear color and the use of a high dynamic range image pipeline undeniably are where the future of digital compositing lies, and that future can be sampled by After Effects users today.

13

Air, Water, Smoke, and Clouds

Conversation about the weather is the last refuge of the unimaginative.

—Oscar Wilde

Yes, yes, let's talk about the weather.
—W. S. Gilbert, *The Pirates of Penzance, or, The Slave of Duty*

Air, Water, Smoke, and Clouds

Even if you're never called upon to re-create the extreme weather events depicted in *The Day After Tomorrow*, climate conditions along with natural elements of water and wind are a constant in dramatic storylines. You may need to re-create these effects from scratch, or you may be called upon to subtly tweak what's already in the shot.

This chapter will give you some pointers on creating such natural elements as particulate matter in the air, replacement skies, mist, fog, smoke, the effects of wind, and water in its three states.

Why would you want to do this? Simply because the crew couldn't get the conditions the story required on the day of the shoot? Well, in extreme cases, yes. But actually, any large exterior shot will exhibit some sort of meteorological influence, and everything in the shot is interrelated. In this chapter, you'll investigate the phenomena that you can influence or even replace wholesale, including

▶ **Particulate matter in the air:** The look of particles in the air can give you important clues to your scene. Is it ever complicated to deal with particulate matter? Where does it not apply?

▶ **Sky replacement:** This is one of those straightforward requests that comes up for effects compositors all the time. What is involved?

▶ **Clouds of fog, smoke, or mist:** You can sense motion, color, and even depth in this element. How can these be created in After Effects?

▶ **Billowing smoke:** What about thick plumes of smoke? Those need to be created with some sort of complex 3D dynamics system, right? Wrong.

▶ **Wind:** How do you re-create something you can't see? Figuring out cheap and easy ways to show its presence via secondary animation can really sell your shot.

▶ **Water and precipitation:** The presence of water can influence your shot either onscreen or off. How do you handle rain and snow?

It's rare indeed that weather conditions cooperate on location. Transforming the appearance of a scene using natural elements is one of the most satisfying things you can do as a compositor. The before and after comparison alone can be stunning, and the result can be worthy of a blockbuster film that is specifically about heavy weather.

Particulate Matter

Particulate matter in the air influences how objects appear at different depths. What is this matter? Fundamentally, it is water, another gas, dust, or some other type of visible particulate usually called pollution. Even an ideal, pristine, pollution-free environment has water in the air—even in the desert. The amount in the air gives you clues to

▶ The distance to the horizon and where objects lie in relation to it

▶ The basic type of climate; the aridness or heaviness of the weather

▶ The time of year and the day's weather

▶ The air's stagnancy

▶ The sun's location

The color of the particulate matter offers clues to how much pollution is present and what it is: dust, smog, dark smoke from a fire, and so on (**Figure 13.1**).

Figure 13.1 The same location looks very different under different weather conditions. But if you start to photograph and study the same location under various circumstances, you begin to get a sense of subtleties, such as how backlighting emphasizes even low levels of haze and reduces color saturation, and how the flat lighting of a foggy day might desaturate and obscure the horizon, but may also bring out colors more.

NOTES

Particulate matter does not occur in outer space, save perhaps when the occasional cloud of interstellar dust drifts through the shot. Look at photos of the moon landscape, and you'll see that the blacks in the distance look just as dark as those in the foreground.

The basic visual result of particulate matter in the air is to lower the apparent contrast of visible objects; the secondary effects are that objects take on the color of the atmosphere around them and become slightly diffuse (**Figure 13.2**). This is a subtle yet omnipresent depth cue: With any particulate matter in the air at all, optics become less contrasty the further they are from the camera, and they may change color and become blurrier. As a compositor, you must use this to your advantage, not only to match the real world, but also to provide clues to the shot's environment.

As an example, consider Figure 13.2, which was shot with a long lens. Zoom or telephoto lenses bring background elements more prominently into the frame; and a common dramatic use of the camera is to employ a long lens when something in the background is meant to loom large. If something that is supposed to be far away looks not only large but crystal clear in the background, however, it will simply look wrong. With the right amount of haze for the weather conditions, even a shot highly compressed with a very long lens will be something the viewer simply believes.

Figure 13.2 This shot was taken with a long lens. The structures one block away retain a good deal in the black of their shadows; buildings a mile or two away, far less; and the foothills ten miles away are so desaturated they begin to fade right into the sky—at first you don't even notice them. The feeling of the shot is one of proximity to a crowded urban environment but with nature always waiting just beyond.

Matching an Existing Shot

The most straightforward scenario in which atmospheric particles come into play is when you place an object in the distance by matching it to a source plate. If the added object is meant to be coplanar with an object already present in the plate, you need only match contrast values using Output Black and Output White in the Levels effect. If you make your adjustments channel by channel (as suggested in Chapter 5, "Color and Light: Adjusting and Matching"), discoloration due to such factors as smog and reflected light simply come along for free.

Similarly, if the added object is meant to be further than one object in the plate but closer than another, you should average the contrast values proportionally.

Where this process can get tricky is if your background does not contain objects with pure black or pure white in the distance. This is less common than you might think because most backgrounds contain shadows that although not pure black are close. In these cases, you're no longer matching exactly, you're eyeballing the shot until the depth looks right (**Figure 13.3**).

Figure 13.3 Not all shots provide a nice, gently shaded white object such as this to match; and yet, if the object you are matching into this scene is hard and metallic, you'd actually want to sample the white of that car in front. But what about placing an item in the background sky, when you can't see any horizon? You start by matching the background and dial down the contrast (using Levels) until it looks right.

If the foreground layer lacks pure black, pure white, or both, that's less of a big deal. You can always start with a small solid set with the default Ramp effect, set Levels to give it the proper depth cueing, and then apply those levels to whatever layer belongs at that depth (**Figures 13.4a, b**, and **c**).

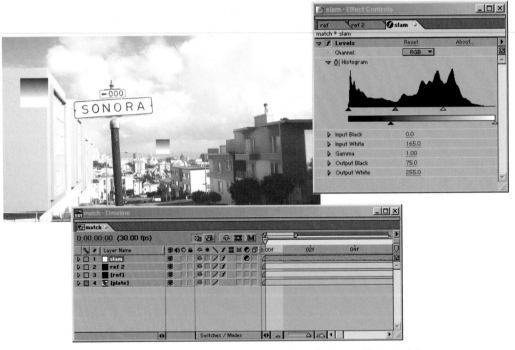

Figure 13.4a, b, and c If a foreground element you are trying to match to a background lacks the full contrast range, you can use stand-ins (13.4a). You apply your Levels adjustments to those (13.4b matches them to foreground and background), matching contrast channel by channel (see Chapter 5 for details). Remember that slamming your comp, temporarily exposing it to higher contrast whites and lower contrast blacks (13.4c), is an effective way of magnifying and checking Levels.

Creating a New Shot

What do you do when you don't have a photographed background plate to match or when your task is to change the conditions in the plate that you do have? Although you no longer have reference built into the shot, you can still use reference. If you can find a photo that contains the conditions you wish to re-create, you can match to that instead.

To start, you must somehow organize the shot into planes of distance. If the source imagery is computer-generated, the 3D program that created it can also generate a depth map for you to use (**Figure 13.5**). If not, you can slice the image into planes of distance, or you can make your own depth map to weight the distance of the objects in frame.

This brings up one of the main reasons that beginning with a basic 3D render of a scene can be useful for matte painters: Not only is perspective and lens distortion included in the render, but a depth map is also easy to generate, and it remains valid as the painting evolves toward completion.

More extreme conditions may demand actual particles, and the phenomena that goes along with them. The rest of the chapter examines these conditions.

Sky Replacement

Sky replacement is one of the cheapest and easiest improvements you can make to a shot. It opens up all kinds of possibilities for shooting faster and more cheaply: You don't have to wait for particular conditions, and you can swap in not only a different sky but also a skyline from a different location.

The sky, after all, is usually part of the story, often a subliminal one but occasionally a starring element. In *Vanilla Sky*, for example, the surreal-looking sky was the first clue we got that maybe Tom Cruise's character was not in the real world. An interior with a window could be anywhere, but show a Manhattan skyline outside the window and New Yorkers will try to place the exact neighborhood and city

Figure 13.5 A basic depth map of a cartoonish 3D city. A map such as this obviates the need for individual layered planes to be rendered separately, to some extent. You can apply this map directly to an adjustment layer as a Luma Inverted Matte (inverted in this example because the most distant objects should be most affected), and then dial in any contrast (via Levels) and softening (via Fast Blur) effects; they are weighted to affect the background more than the foreground, and the contrast of the map itself can be adjusted to change the relative weighting. (Image courtesy of Fred Lewis/Moving Media.)

block of that location, along with the time of day, time of year, weather, outside temperature, and so on, possibly without ever really paying conscious attention to it.

Why spend extra time and money to get the exact distant background conditions you want, if you can get the shot cheaper and more quickly by taking it elsewhere? Why spend tens or hundreds of thousands of dollars for that view apartment on Central Park East and try to get the whole scene done at golden hour (the beautiful time of the sunset, an "hour" that typically lasts about 20 minutes and doesn't show up on an overcast day)? Instead, you could take it in your friend's apartment, shoot all day, and add the sunset view in post. True, sometimes there is no replacement for a real environment. *Days of Heaven*, for example, is as close to being a film about golden hour as you're ever likely to see, and it took a couple of years to shoot. Often, the real story is elsewhere, and the sky is a subliminal (even if beautiful) backdrop that must serve that story (**Figures 13.6a** through **d**).

Figures 13.6a through d For an independent film with no budget set in San Francisco, the director had the clever idea of shooting it in a building lobby across the bay in lower-rent Oakland (13.6a), pulling a matte from the blue sky (13.6b), and match moving a still shot of the San Francisco skyline (from street level, 13.6c) for a result that anyone familiar with that infamous pyramid-shaped building would assume was taken in downtown San Francisco. (Images courtesy of The Orphanage.)

The Sky Is Not (Quite) a Blue Screen

Only on the clearest, bluest days does the sky approach any kind of ideal as a keyable background. The color tends to wash out toward the horizon, cloudless skies are not always so easy to come by, and even clear blue skies are not as saturated with color as they might sometimes seem.

Still, some combination of a color keyer, such as Keylight, and a hi-con luminance matte pass or a garbage matte, as needed, can key out the existing infinite depth in your shot. Chapter 6, "Color Keying," focuses on strategies for employing these, and Chapter 7, "Rotoscoping and Paint," describes the alternative, rotoscoping, when keys and garbage mattes aren't doing the trick.

In any case, the first step of sky replacement is making the existing "sky" (which may include other items at infinite distance, such as buildings and clouds) transparent by developing a matte for it. As you do this, place the replacement sky in the background; a sky matte typically does not have to be as exacting as a blue-screen key because the replacement sky often bears a resemblance to the source (**Figure 13.7**).

Figure 13.7 This rather poor blue-screen matte is acceptable for this type of shot because the color range and contrast of the target background are not so different from the source. The holes in the matte are the result of reflected sky color in the highlights of the foreground; this looks acceptable in the final shot.

Infinite Depth

If your shot is locked off, your job is already complete with the creation of the matte. If, however, there is camera movement in the shot, you might think that you need a 3D track to properly composite in a new sky element.

Typically, that's overkill. Instead, you should consider these options:

▶ If you are matching motion from the original shot and anything in the source sky can be tracked, by all means track the source.

▶ If only your foreground is trackable and you're following the suggestions in Chapter 8, "Effective Motion Tracking," for applying a track to a 3D camera, move the replacement sky to the far background. (This may require a Z Position value in the four or five digits, depending on camera settings.) Scale it up to compensate for the distance. In this case you must essentially eyeball the depth.

▶ If the shot contains a push or zoom (Chapter 9, "Virtual Cinematography," describes the difference), these may be more easily re-created using a 3D camera (although you should look at Chapter 8 for tips on getting away with a 2D track). If you're adding them from scratch, place the sky in the far background as with the last tip and add your camera animation. If the push or zoom is in your source shot, you may need camera data from third-party 3D tracking software (see Chapter 8).

The basic phenomenon you're trying to re-create is that scenery at infinite distance moves less than objects in the foreground, the basic parallax effect. This effect is less pronounced with a long, telephoto lens, and more pronounced in a wide angle. For the match in **Figure 13.6**, a still shot (no perspective) was skewed to match the correct angle and tracked in 2D; the lens angle was long enough and the shot brief enough that they got away with it.

The Fog, Smoke, or Mist Rolls In

Be sure not to confuse the eminently useful Fractal Noise effect, found in the Noise & Grain category, with the far less useful (albeit pretty) Fractal effect in the Render category.

Adding an animated layer of translucent clouds to a shot is easily enough done in After Effects. You can create the basic element by applying the Fractal Noise effect to a solid, and then use a blending mode such as Add or Screen to layer it in with the appropriate Opacity setting.

Fractal Noise, at the default Fractal Type setting of Basic, already looks smoky (**Figure 13.8**); you can refine the look of it somewhat by switching the Noise Type setting from the default, Soft Linear, to Spline. Go ahead and check out the other Fractal Types if you're curious; most of them are more synthetic looking, although some can be appropriate for alternative effects, such as lava. The main thing you must add is motion.

There are two types of motion you typically may want to add: an Evolution animation to cause internal movement, and possibly Transform animations to cause the overall layer to move, as if being blown by wind (**Figure 13.9**). There is no need to create a huge layer and animate its Position value. The Offset Turbulence setting under Transform will do the job for you, and you can reposition it

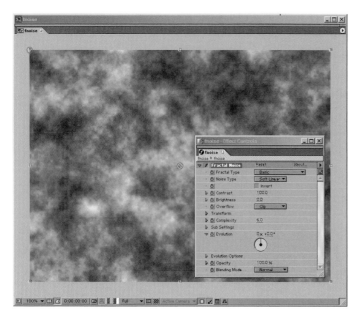

Figure 13.8 Fractal Noise (shown here at the default setting) is a decent stand-in for organic-looking fog. You can try varying the Fractal Type or Noise Type to get different looks, and you must animate the Evolution if you want any billowing of the element.

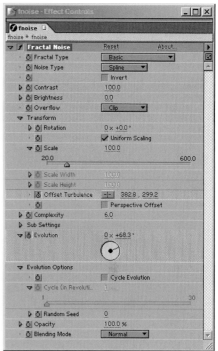

Figure 13.9 The highlighted controls are key-framed; these are the keys to putting your fog element in motion. Note that you can also add Scale and Rotation animations.

infinitely without running out of space to move. The question of how much the settings should change over time is largely one of trial and error according to what your shot demands.

The other main settings to consider are those affecting the apparent scale and density of the noise layer. To influence these, first adjust the Scale (under Transform) and Contrast settings. You will not, generally speaking, want to stray too far from the defaults for Complexity and Sub Settings; these also affect apparent scale and density, but with all kinds of undesirable side effects that make the smoke look artificial.

So now you have an animated smoke, fog, or mist element whose motion you can continue to tweak; the only remaining question is how you layer it in. In virtually no case can you simply blend a single Fractal Noise layer over footage and end up with the look you're after. Instead, you will more effectively sell the effect by combining several layers. Time to examine how that's done.

TIP

If you ever find yourself using Fractal Noise to design a texture map and you need to map the loop seamlessly, go into Evolution Options and check the box marked Cycle Evolution. Now animate Evolution in whole cycles. Try setting the first keyframe to 0° and the final frame to, say, two revolutions and 0° (written as 2 x 0.0°). Set the Cycle (in Revolutions) parameter to the number of total revolutions that complete the loop (2 in this case). The first and last keyframes will now match.

Masking and Adjusting

If you're planning on covering your whole scene evenly with smoke or mist, you will achieve a more realistic look by using two or three separate layers of Fractal Noise. You can even use the same settings, choosing different portions and time offsets and positioning them in 3D space to set the scale as needed (**Figure 13.10**).

The unexpected byproduct of layering 2D particle layers in this manner is that they take on the illusion of depth and volume. The eye perceives changes in parallax between the foreground and background, and automatically assumes these to be a byproduct of full three-dimensionality, yet you save the time and trouble of a 3D volumetric particle render. Of course, you're limited to instances in which particles don't interact with movement from objects in the scene; otherwise, you instantly graduate to some very tricky 3D effects.

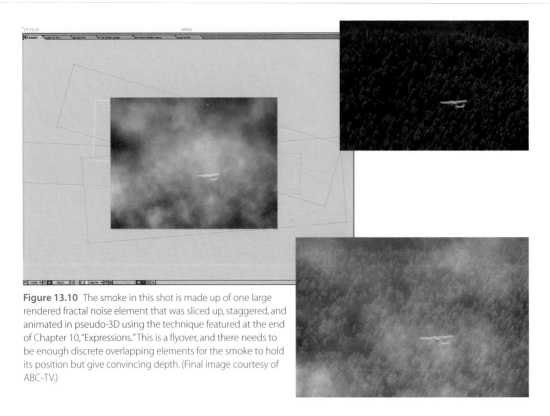

Figure 13.10 The smoke in this shot is made up of one large rendered fractal noise element that was sliced up, staggered, and animated in pseudo-3D using the technique featured at the end of Chapter 10, "Expressions." This is a flyover, and there needs to be enough discrete overlapping elements for the smoke to hold its position but give convincing depth. (Final image courtesy of ABC-TV.)

The best method for blending these particle layers with your background is typically to apply each one as a luminance matte of a solid. That way, you can make the solid whatever color you choose for your particles without having to anticipate what a blending mode choice will do to them.

Often you will want to hold out the particle effect to a particular area of your frame. If you are trying to add smoke to a generalized area of the frame, a big elliptical mask with a high feather setting (in the triple digits even for video resolution) will do the trick; if the borders of the smoke area are apparent, increase the mask feather even further (**Figure 13.11**).

Moving Through the Mist

The same effect you get when you layer several instances of Fractal Noise can aid the illusion of moving forward through a misty cloud. That's done simply enough, but how often does your shot consist of just moving through a misty cloud? Most of the time, you will be adding clouds of smoke or mist to the ground plane of an existing shot.

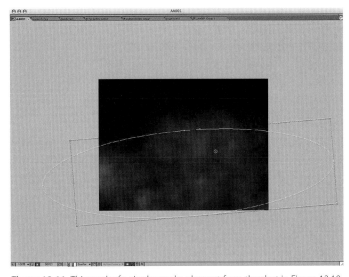

Figure 13.11 This mask of a single smoke element from the shot in Figure 13.10 has a 200-pixel feather, despite that the resolution of the shot is D1 video (720 by 486). The softness of the mask helps to sell the element as smoke and works well overlaid with other, similarly feathered masked elements.

You can use the technique for emulating 3D tracking (see Chapter 10) to make the smoke hold its place in a particular area of the scene as the camera moves through (or above) it. To make this work, keep a few points in mind:

▶ Each instance of Fractal Noise should have a soft elliptical mask around it.

▶ The mask should be large enough to overlap with another masked instance, but small enough that it does not slide its position as the angle of the camera changes.

▶ A small amount of Evolution animation goes a long way, and too much will blow the gag. Let the movement of the camera create the interest of motion.

▶ Depending on the length and distance covered in the shot, be willing to create at least a half-dozen individual masked layers of Fractal Noise.

The shot dissected in **Figures 13.10 and 13.11** features just such an effect of moving forward through clouds. It is difficult to convey with still images how the effect works in motion, but it combines the tracking of each shot carefully into place with the phenomenon of parallax, whereby overlapping layers swirl across one another in a believable manner. Mist and smoke seem to be a volume but they actually often behave more like overlapping, translucent planes—individual clouds of mist and smoke.

Billowing Smoke

Fractal Noise works fine for creating and animating thin wispy smoke and mist. It will not, however, help you re-create thick, billowing clouds. When clouds are opaque enough to have their own shape, shading, and topography, re-creating them with built-in After Effects plug-ins no longer does the job. Luckily, all you need is a good still cloud element and you can animate it in After Effects. And all you need to create the element is a high-resolution reference photo—or a bag of cotton puffs.

That's right, cotton puffs, like you get at the pharmacy. I first heard about this trick on a visit to the digital matte

Selling the Effect with Diffraction

There is more to adding a cloud to a realistic shot than a simple A over B comp; water elements in the air, whether in spray, mist, or clouds, not only occlude light but diffract it. This diffraction effect can be simulated by applying Compound Blur to an adjustment layer between the fog and the background and using a pre-composed (or pre-rendered) version of the fog element as its Blur Layer.

You want details, and you'll get them, but you have to make it to the last chapter of the book, where guest author Stu Maschwitz lays it all out in detail.

department at Industrial Light + Magic about a decade ago (back when the department was made up of four artists), where visionary matte painter Yusei Uesegi was given credit for devising it. He showed me a jaw-dropping shot of a pirate ship in flames, smoke billowing from the masts.

The simplest way to create your basic cloud is to arrange the cotton balls on a large piece of nonreflective black poster board. Take the board outside on a sunny day so you get some nice highlights and shadows. When you photograph it at different angles to the light, the results look like puffy white clouds already (**Figure 13.12**).

To give your clouds some shape and contour, open the image in Photoshop, and use the Clone Stamp tool to create a cloud with the shape you want. You can do it directly in After Effects, but this is the kind of job for which Photoshop was designed. Clone in contour layers of highlights (using Linear Dodge, Screen, or Lighten blending modes) and shadows (with blending set to Multiply or Darken) until the cloud has the look you're after (**Figure 13.13**).

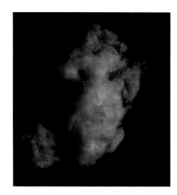

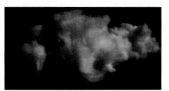

Figure 13.12 You may have noticed how cotton puffs can be arranged to resemble fluffy clouds. But who knew you could get away with sticking them in a movie?

Figure 13.13 The elements from **Figure 13.12** have been incorporated into this Photoshop matte painting, with the shot into which the smoke will be composited in the background for reference (the extended shot moves left to right). The cotton has been painted in via a dozen overlapping layers. The topmost use Screen mode (to highlight) or Overlay mode (to darken), bringing out the contours. Can you tell which smoke is made up of cotton?

So now you have a good-looking cloud, but it's a still. How do you put it in motion? This is where After Effects' excellent distortion tools come into play, in particular Mesh Warp and Liquify.

Mesh Warp

Mesh Warp lays a grid of Bézier handles over the frame; you animate distortion by setting a keyframe for the Distortion Mesh property at frame 0, and then moving the points of the grid, and realigning the Bézier handles associated with each point to bend to the vertices between points. The image to which this effect is applied follows the shape of the grid.

By default, Mesh Warp begins with a seven-by-seven grid. Before you do anything else, make sure that the size of the grid makes sense for your image; you might want to increase its size for a high-resolution project, and you can reduce the number of rows to fit the aspect ratio of your shot, so you begin with a grid of squares (**Figure 13.14**).

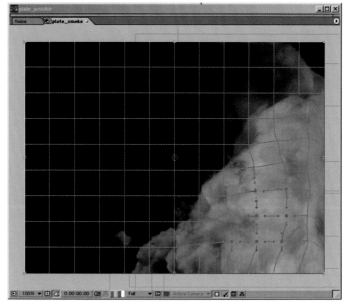

Figure 13.14 The Mesh Warp controls are really quite simple: a grid of points and vectors. You can set the number and quality, and animate the position of the grid overall (one keyframe for all grid points). Points can be multiselected and dragged (as shown) and each point contains Bezier handles for warping the adjacent vectors. It's pretty cool, especially now that machines are fast enough to render the results effectively.

You can't typically get away with dragging a point more than about halfway toward any other point; watch carefully for artifacts of stretching and tearing as you work, and preview often. If you see stretching, realign adjacent points and handles to compensate.

Liquify

The Liquify effect is a brush-based system for distorting footage; as such, it is useful in cases when a Mesh Warp grid is too cumbersome and finer adjustments are needed.

Of the tools included with Liquify, the first two along the top row, Warp and Turbulence, are most likely to be useful (**Figure 13.15**). Warp has a similar effect to moving a point in Mesh Warp; it simply pushes pixels in the direction you drag the brush. Turbulence scrambles pixels in the path of the brush. The Reconstruction brush is like a selective undo, reversing distortions when you use the default setting; other options for this brush are contained in the Reconstruction Mode menu.

TIP

Mesh Warp, like many distortion tools, renders rather slowly. As you rough in the motion, feel free to work at quarter-resolution. When you've finalized your animation, you can save a lot of time by pre-rendering it (see Chapter 4, "Optimizing the Pipeline").

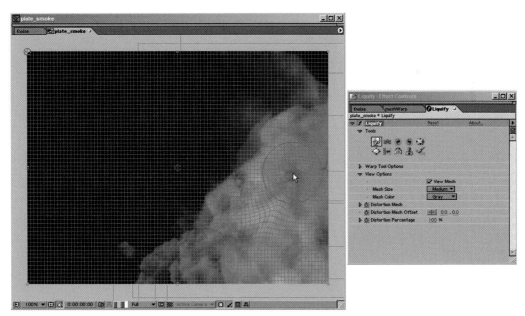

Figure 13.15 Liquify is also a mesh distortion tool, only the mesh is much finer than Mesh Warp's and it is not visible by default. You can choose to display it under View Options in the effect controls. Here the Warp tool is being used to create an effect much like that created by the Mesh Warp in the previous figure, but via a brush rather than a grid.

Liquify also has the advantage of letting you mask out areas that you don't want it to affect. Draw a mask around the area you want to leave untouched by Liquify brushes, but set the mask mode to None, disabling it. Under Warp Tool Options, select the mask name in the Freeze Area Masked menu.

Lest you think the methods described in this section are some crude kludge, inferior to procedural particle dynamic effects created by a technical director in a sophisticated 3D rendering program, here's an anecdote that demonstrates how this generalized approach (refined to a high degree) saved the day on a movie with an eight-figure budget. A few short weeks before the final deadline for all shots to be completed on *The Day After Tomorrow*, the render pipeline at The Orphanage was slammed, but the "super cell" element for the freezing of New York City sequence (that huge cloud bank swirling around on the horizon) had not been approved by the client other than in matte paintings.

It was clear that even if a technical director could re-create the look in 3D—and no one had done so yet—there wasn't going to be time left to render it. By animating the matte paintings using the techniques outlined in this section, the shots were completed and approved within a couple of weeks. As always, the key was breaking the problem down into component parts. The final super cell rig had over a dozen individual component layers and instances of Mesh Warp and Liquify, along with holdouts, overlays, offsets, and blending modes built up among them to give the effect the appropriate organic complexity and dimension.

Combining Techniques

Because each project varies, the techniques offered are meant to form only the basis of your finished effect. The goal is to provide you with a few keys that you can combine or part out on your own, rather than nail you down to specific steps that work only in one context.

So, for example, selling a shot of the smoke plume might involve not only warping effects, but also some thinner, faster-moving smoke nearest the flames or in the fore-ground of the scene, which could be created with Fractal Noise. Or, if the drifting Fractal Noise smoke needed more specific directionality—say, to flow around an object—you could apply a Mesh Warp on top of its animation, or flow it right through the Mesh Warp grid (**Figure 13.16**).

Smoke Trails

Many effects, including smoke trails, don't require particle generation in order to be re-created faithfully. Check out the reference in **Figure 13.17** and you'll notice that smoke trails are just like elongated clouds, revealed over time along a linear path.

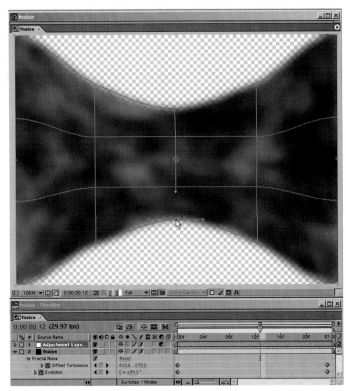

Figure 13.16 You can get pretty creative with your use for Mesh Warp: Here, Fractal Noise is animated to move left to right through a grid that deforms it as it animates. Note how the cursor changes when you are over a Mesh Warp grid point; one of the most difficult things about using this effect is that it's easy to inadvertently move a layer instead of a point.

Figure 13.17 You could easily paint in this effect with no source whatsoever.

Therefore, initial setup of this effect is simply a matter of starting with a clean plate, painting the smoke trails in a separate still layer, and revealing them over time (presumably behind the aircraft that is creating them). The quickest and easiest way to reveal such an element over time is often by animating a mask, but if you want to do it the cool and automatic way, you could use techniques described in Chapter 8 to apply a motion tracker to a clone brush.

The optional second stage of this effect would be the dissipation of the trail; depending on how much wind there was that day, the trail would probably drift, spread, and thin out over time. That means that in a wide shot, the back of the trail would be more dissipated than the front.

A simple method to achieve this (which could work with a distant shot, at least) involves using a black-to-white gradient and Compound Blur. You can use the Ramp effect to create a gradient that is white at the dissipated end of the trail and black at the source (**Figures 13.18a** and **b**). Again, you can apply a motion track to the black gradient point

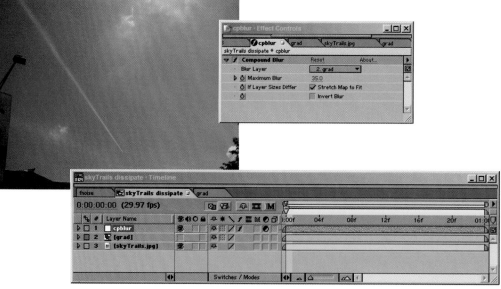

Figures 13.18a and b Getting creative with a quick-and-dirty effect on Figure 13.17: A gradient is created to match the start and end of the plane's trajectory, masked and pre-composed (13.18a). This is then applied via a Compound Blur to the source layer (13.18b)—a simple example of building up your own effect with the tools at hand.

using expressions, or you can just approximate it by hand. To animate the amount of blur applied, animate a Levels adjustment to the gradient, keeping in mind that you may need to pre-compose the result. I offer this not so much because I think your phone will ring tomorrow morning with a client wanting dissipating smoke trails, but as an example of how to combine some of what you've learned into your own effect.

Wind

What is wind doing in this chapter? You can't see it. How do you composite it into your shot? Although it's invisible, re-creating the effects of wind on your shot can help sell its realism. Besides the effect of wind on particles, what other roles does wind play?

As I write this chapter, it is a warm, still, sunny day, but in my backyard leaves and tree branches do sway gently from time to time. If I wanted to re-create the scene from a still or 3D render or if I wanted to add an element to it, the result just wouldn't look right without these subtle bits of motion.

The fact is that most still scenes in the real world contain ambient motion of some kind. Not only objects directly in the scene, but reflected light and shadow might be changing all the time in a scene we perceive to be motionless.

As a compositor, part of your job is to think about these kinds of ambient effects, and to look for opportunities to add to them in ways that contribute to the realism of the scene without stealing focus. Obviously, the kinds of dynamics involved with making the leaves and branches of a tree sway are mostly beyond the realm of 2D compositing, but there are often other elements that are easily articulated and animated ever so slightly. Successful examples of this might not be consciously registered by the viewer, and they often will not have been explicitly requested, but they succeed in bringing the shot to life.

Primary and Secondary

When animating physical objects, it is traditional to speak about primary and secondary animation. *Primary animation* is the gross movement of the object, the movement of the object as a whole. *Secondary animation* is the movement of individual parts of the object as a result of inertia. So, for example, a helicopter crashes to the ground: That's the primary animation. Its rotors and tail bend and shudder at impact: That's the secondary animation. For the most part, in 2D compositing, your work is isolated to primary animation.

Adding and Articulating Elements

To make it easier on yourself, look for elements that can be readily isolated and articulated; you should be able to mask the element out with a simple roto or a hi-con matte if it's not separated to begin with. Look for the point where the object would bend or pivot, place your anchor point there, then animate a gentle rotation.

You also have the option of acquiring and adding elements that indicate or add to the effect of wind motion. **Figure 13.19** shows an element of blowing autumn leaves shot against a black background for easy removal and matting; granted, you could add an element this turbulent only to a scene that either already had signs of gusts in it or that contained only elements that would show no secondary motion from wind whatsoever.

Indirect Effects

Another idea is to add the indirect effects of ambient motion generated by wind; moving shadows and the play of light also enliven a static scene, and capturing or synthesizing these elements to interact with objects in the scene will more readily appear realistic than re-creating them directly.

So, for example, adding the swaying branches of a tree to your scene is complicated, but creating a hi-con matte of existing footage of a tree and turning it into a shadow cast on the ground plane might not be as bad, if the ground plane is flat (**Figure 13.20**). The same goes for fire, which

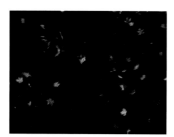
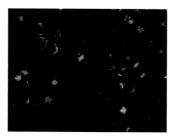

Figure 13.19 An example of an effects element that will enhance something that already is happening in your scene. It would be very difficult to create the impression of a windstorm in a shot from scratch, but if the shot is taken in windy conditions (or using large fans on set) an element like this will enhance the impression of a blustery day.

Figure 13.20 Animating your own trees swaying in the breeze just to make a shadow would be a big pain. Why not steal their silhouettes and get the motion for free? This process is detailed in Chapter 12, "Working with Light."

might flicker and reflect off the faces of characters in the scene, or water, whose rippling reflections can be more easily synthesized than the look of water itself. The simpler the plane receiving the reflection, the more likely you might get away with this.

Water

You've already examined the effect of water in its gaseous form (as fog, mist, or steam); what about water in its liquid and solid states? Although it's not possible to re-create *The Perfect Storm* or *The Day After Tomorrow* without elaborate 3D and practical effects, compositing plays a pivotal role in re-creating rain and snow and in enhancing practical and computer-generated scenes.

Realistically, though, it's rare to do elaborate water effects without relying on some pretty elaborate practical or computer-generated source. I'll assume that you're trying to complete shots only in After Effects, but I'll focus on techniques that are equally valid even if your particle and water animations are coming from elsewhere.

Precipitation

One area where After Effects' built-in features fall short is particle generation. The Particle Playground effect, which ships with the program and hasn't changed much since around version 3.0, is slow, crude, and cumbersome. I have yet to work with anyone who had the patience to coax realistic effects out of this plug-in.

If you're called upon to create rainfall or snowfall from scratch, I highly recommend taking a look at the Particular plug-in from Trapcode (a demo is included on the book's CD-ROM). Not only does it outdo Particle Playground in features and ease of use, but also, if set up correctly, it obviates the need for creating precipitation in a dedicated 3D program.

It's nothing against dedicated 3D programs to note that a faster result, one that is better integrated with source footage, can be achieved in After Effects because of how directly you as a compositor can influence various factors in the scene. When you receive rain or snow elements from another artist working with 3D software (or even if you do them yourself), you may have to go through several rounds just to get the basic speed and density, wind, and turbulence even in the general range where the client wants them because it's so much harder to gain control of the match in 3D.

Creating the Element

Particular has all the controls you need to create a great element of falling rain or snow. You could use a standard particle shape included with the effect, or you can create your own customized particles, such as irregular snowflake shapes. You have several choices of particle emitters; one great option is to use a spotlight as an emitter, so that all of the light layer's Transform controls are available to establish the position and direction of the particles (**Figure 13.21**).

Figure 13.21 If you use a light as an emitter for Trapcode's Particular, you must begin its name with Emitter so the effect knows to use it. You are free to move the light in whatever position or direction you like in 3D space. You are not even limited to some relative size for the light as an emitter; here the emitter size has been raised on the X and Z axes to distribute particles across a wide area (with an optional Gaussian distribution).

The most important settings to adjust are in the Emitter and Physics categories; the former is where you establish the amount, velocity, and direction of your particles (along with the size of the emitter, if you use a light), and the latter contains controls for the environment itself: gravity, air resistance, wind, turbulence, and spin.

The Visibility category contains controls affecting the depth of your particles. In many scenes, the key to pulling off good-looking precipitation will be in creating at least three separate plains: foreground, mid-ground, and background. Separating these gives you far more control when adjusting the look than trying to do it all in one pass; you might find that the client likes the look of the snow except in one area of the shot (say, the foreground).

Particular resides on a 2D layer, but the effect is 3D-aware, so if you add a camera to the composition, the particles will behave as if seen through that camera. Even shots that involve a 3D camera move or a particular lens are possible.

Compositing the Element

When it comes time to integrate falling rain or snow with a background plate, you can do better than a simple A over B comp; in fact, the best way to display these elements might be to show their result in the scene rather than showing the elements themselves.

Raindrops and snowflakes are translucent. Their appearance is heavily influenced by their backdrop. You might presume, therefore, to composite them in either by dialing down Opacity, using a blending mode such as Add or Screen, or a combination of the two. You could conceivably get away with this.

However, these individual bits of precipitation are actually like tiny lenses that diffract light, defocusing and lowering the contrast of whatever is behind them, but also picking up the ambient light themselves. Therefore, on *The Day After Tomorrow* our crew found success with using the rain or snow element as a track matte for an adjustment layer containing a Fast Blur and a Levels effect.

The amount of blur should be set very high (200, for example), so that whatever is behind each individual raindrop or snowflake becomes a wash of color. The Levels effect is then set with a slightly lowered Output White value, and a very much raised Output Black value. The precipitation becomes visible by its effect on the scene, lightening dark areas of the background, darkening light ones, and creating diffusion throughout (**Figure 13.22**).

Waterfalls

Creating the effect of a waterfall remains challenging in software, so here's a cheap and easy practical way to shoot this element as a miniature instead: Use sand.

You can adjust and color correct sand coming out of a funnel or trough to look a lot like a waterfall. Depending on how heavy the sand is, you might even get some of the spray at the base (as a cloud of dust). The tricky part about all this is setting up the shoot properly; everything that is not sand needs to be negative space, so you need to build a miniature stage (it can be all cardboard) in a solid color (Rosco blue, say, or flat black) and light it, then match the camera perspective you're after. Cue the sand and roll the camera.

If your waterfall is more a wall of water than a trickle, you can always consider cloning the result (camera angle permitting).

Figure 13.22 Rain is difficult to see in a still shot because it has no color of its own. For that very reason, it is best applied as a track matte for an adjustment layer that you then set to blur and raise the black values of the plate footage. (It helps if the plate shot was taken under wet conditions as well.)

The best thing about this approach is that it works virtually regardless of what is in the background. There is no need to decide the color of the element for a given shot, and shots match by virtue of retaining their source colors, with precipitation having the same influence on each shot.

Conclusion

To further mess with atmospheric and weather effects may require elaborate 3D simulations, but the principles of compositing them in likely still apply. The chapter's focus has been on how these elements behave in the real world, as well as how best and most simply to emulate that in After Effects. This approach will serve you well even if you have to re-create an element—frost, say, or hail—that is similar but unique from what was covered here.

The next chapter heats things up with fire, explosions, and other combustibles.

CLOSE-UP

Reflected Water Light

Using a variation on Chapter 12, you could demonstrate the presence of water in your scene—off camera—by adding its reflected light in your scene. Light from water has a compelling shape and movement, and if you've set up the scene so that the viewer knows there's a swimming pool or a lake nearby, it will be expected.

The question is how to get the sample of the light playing off of the waves. If you're ready to do some patient adjusting, you could use Wave World, an effect that you get by registering your copy of After Effects. The default settings won't do. For one thing, you have to change the View to Height Map just to preview the effect, and you'll definitely want to raise the Grid Resolution and Pre-roll settings, as well as set Reflect Edges to All. Then the main trick is to get the Position and Amplitude adjusted for a natural look. Use the same technique as with laying in shadows: Position the plane and choose a blending mode, such as Add or Vivid Light.

Fire and Explosions

My nature is to be on set, blowing things up.
> —Ken Ralston (winner of five
> Academy Awards for visual effects)

Fire and Explosions

I have become convinced that a significant number of people first became interested in visual effects work because they qualify as borderline pyromaniacs. Creating fire effects entirely on the computer might not be as much fun as being an on-set pyrotechnician, but hey, keeping these people busy with either job is better than letting them loose on society at large.

This chapter focuses on effects that have traditionally been re-created live on set or via practical elements such as miniatures. The craft of the on-set pyrotechnician is not obsolete by any means, but these days there are many, many cases (particularly the smaller, more common ones) in which compositing can save a lot of time and expense at the shoot, no matter the budget of the production. Blowing stuff up on set is fun, but it involves extensive set up and a not insubstantial amount of danger to the cast and crew, and often you get only one take to get it right.

As a director, I would never subject actors to real gunfire and bullet hits on set unless it was clearly the only way to get the shot. The death of Brandon Lee on the set of *The Crow*, when a gun loaded with blanks shot an empty cartridge (still in the barrel from a previous shot) into his abdomen, was fully preventable—not only by a more attentive arms or prop master, but by never loading the gun in the first place. At the risk of sounding glib, it is indisputable that using compositing in such a scenario could save a life.

And gunfire is only the beginning of what this chapter examines. Equally dangerous on set are explosive bullet hit squibs, small explosives that must be rigged and exploded by an on-set special effects technician, lest anyone damage soft body tissue. You'll learn how to accomplish those in After Effects as well. From there, you'll move on to the science-fiction equivalent of gunplay: weapons of pure energy, such as the *Star Wars* blaster or the *Star Trek* photon torpedo. After that, it's heat distortion, fire, and explosions. Then, perhaps, a nice warm cup of tea.

I hope it won't disappoint you to hear that not everything in this chapter can be accomplished start to finish in After Effects. Some of the effects require extra preparation of elements outside of the application, and all of them will benefit from your familiarity with good reference. There is, alas, no easy way to create realistic fire or explosions from scratch in After Effects, but that does not mean they are off-limits. Often, in fact, the only way to create these on a modest budget, or to enhance what you can shoot on any budget, is to composite them.

And of course, sometimes a storyline calls for the destruction of something that cannot, in real life, be destroyed on any budget. The famous shot of the White House being blown to smithereens in *Independence Day* is one example, but this limitation was also very much in place on a little known ABC-TV movie called *Superfire*, whose concept was often described as "*The Perfect Storm*, but with fire." Infernos consuming acres of forest were central to the plot, and even if the budget had allowed for purchasing and razing hundreds of acres of wilderness, environmental concerns— not to mention horrendous PR—would in all cases mitigate against it. The solution turned out to be varied: in some cases, to composite fire from scratch; in others, to augment what was already there.

To provide examples, this chapter features stills from low-budget independent films that couldn't afford to create the kind of destruction required on screen. *The Last Birthday Card* is a short narrative film that Stu Maschwitz created while still working at Industrial Light + Magic. *Mark and Matty* is a satirical series poking fun at the conventions of action movies with effects (as well as acting) done by Matt Ward, a veteran of Lucasfilm, Industrial Light + Magic, and ESC Entertainment (where he worked on *The Matrix* sequels). In both cases, the effects are quick and dirty, not meant even for the level of scrutiny they are afforded in this book, and intended only to convey the story, which in both cases has hapless victims pursued by unhinged assassins.

Firearms

Re-creating gunplay is relatively straightforward via compositing. There are two basic types of shots to be outlined here: the firing of a gun and the result of bullet hits in the scene. The former can be done entirely with compositing. For the latter, compositing can do the trick in simple cases, but more active scenes of mayhem usually require practical elements on set. I'll discuss both cases, so that the independent filmmakers among you are prepared for either scenario.

There's probably a scene out there, quite possibly from one of your favorite movies, that contains reference very similar to what you're trying to do. As you prepare to stage these effects, I encourage you to carefully study, frame by frame and loop after loop, similar sequences that you like.

Firing the Gun

Sometimes it can be difficult for actors to work on set without practical effects. The firing of a handgun, however, shouldn't be any problem. A prop gun still clicks when you pull the trigger, and the actor need only mime the motion of the recoil, or *kick*. The kick is minor with small handguns, but a much bigger deal for shotguns; again, this is something you can check with reference.

So that's how you start, with a shot of an actor pulling the trigger and miming the kick (**Figure 14.1**). From there, you typically add just a few basic elements via compositing:

> As always, you are encouraged to get reference. Even if you've never been present for the shooting of an actual gun, there's no doubt that you've seen one fired many, many times, running the gamut from cheesy television westerns and cop shows to such gourmet shoot-'em-ups as *The Matrix* and *Terminator 2*.

Figure 14.1 Just by virtue of pulling the trigger on the prop handgun, the actor creates enough motion to set the anticipation of the ensuing muzzle flash to be overlaid. (Image courtesy of The Orphanage.)

▶ The muzzle flash

▶ A smoke puff (optional depending on the lighting and type of gun)

▶ Discharge of the cartridge or shell (on a semi-automatic)

▶ Interactive light on the subject firing the gun (depending on the scene lighting and angle)

The actual travel of the bullet out of the barrel is not something you have to worry about; at roughly one kilometer per second, it is generally moving too fast to see amid all the other effects. The bullet is usually evident more by what it causes to happen when it hits something, which I'll get to in the next section.

Muzzle Flash and Smoke

The clearest indication that a gun has gone off is the flash of light around the muzzle, at the end of the barrel. This small, bright explosion of gunpowder typically lasts only one frame per shot (a repeating firearm is just a series of disconnected single frame flashes), and it can be painted by hand, cloned in from a practical image, or composited from stock reference (**Figure 14.2**).

Figure 14.3 shows the addition of a single-frame muzzle flash for the firing of a handgun. Because it is in close-up, the flash obscures much of the frame. It is a mixture of flash and smoke matted in from a pyrotechnic reference shot. All that is really required for this single shot is a single-frame overlay; there's no need to carefully dissipate the smoke to make the shot believable.

Figure 14.2 The angle of the shot and the type of gun affect the muzzle flash effect. The first image is from an M16 rifle; the other is from a handgun. (Images courtesy of Artbeats.)

Figure 14.3 For this close-up of a muzzle flash and smoke added to the plate from Figure 14.1, only a single frame of smoke was blended in from a photographed source, likely with Add mode. (Image courtesy of The Orphanage.)

Contrast that with **Figure 14.4,** which shows a Gatling gun fired from a helicopter. Clearly, this scene has a lot more going on in it than just muzzle flash and smoke. Because it's a repeating gun, the flashes occur on successive frames and the smoke builds up along with debris caused by bullet impacts. The way the shape of the muzzle flash varies over time as well as its relative size and placement were the keys to the shot, and they required the study of reference.

The shape of the muzzle flash depends on the type of gun being fired, and just as with lens flares and other equipment-specific visual elements, you are heavily encouraged to find a movie that has your gun in it. You can also consult the NRA-ILA Web site (www.nraila.org) to learn how the color and amount of smoke depends on the type of gunpowder. Typically, there is an explosion traveling in two directions from the end of the barrel: arrayed outward from the firing point and in a straight line out from the barrel.

Find smoke, explosion, or fire source, and you can clone in your own on a separate layer, then apply it with a blending mode (typically Add). With automatic weaponry you may have your work cut out for you painting frame by frame, but with good reference to reassure you, this can be quick and dirty work. If you have a budget to purchase stock

Figure 14.4 The fiery muzzle flash of a Gatling gun has a characteristic teardrop profile shape; here it was painted in from fire source. (Image courtesy of The Orphanage.)

footer, you can look for one that contains muzzle flashes (such as the Artbeats Gun Stock collection, www.artbeats.com); these are shot over blue or black, ready to be matted, blended, or painted into your shot.

Shells and Interactive Light

If the gun in your scene calls for it, you can add that extra little bit of realism with a secondary animation of a shell popping off the top of a semi-automatic. **Figure 14.5** shows just such an element in action. All you need is a four-point mask of a white solid, animated and motion blurred (**Figure 14.6**). You don't have to worry about the color; instead adjust the element's Opacity to blend it into the scene.

Depending on the situation, don't forget that the bright flash of the muzzle might also cause just a brief flash on objects near the gun, especially on the subject firing it. From tips in Chapter 12, "Working with Light," you should know what to do: Softly mask in a highlight area, probably using an adjustment layer with a Levels effect or a colored solid with a suitable blending mode. The keys are recognizing that the adjustment is necessary in your particular shot and to what extent.

As a general rule, the lower the ambient light and the larger the weapon, the greater the likelihood of interactive lighting. A literal "shot in the dark" would illuminate the face of whomever (or whatever) fired it, just for a single frame. This is a great dramatic effect, but one that is very difficult to re-create after the fact if you didn't plan for it. If your shot was taken in low light, you will lack any details to illuminate. This is one of those cases where firing blanks on set might actually be called for, assuming the continuity of action in the shot is too visible to be faked by dropping in a single-frame still of the brightly lit assassin.

Figure 14.5 A shell pops off of the fired handgun. Note that the shell appears only as a blurred, elongated white element in frame with no discernable detail. A blue-screen shot of an automatic weapon shows a much more discernable shell. (Images courtesy of The Orphanage and Artbeats.)

Figure 14.6 All that is required to transform a four-point masked white solid to a shell popping off the gun is heavy motion blur and a sufficiently low Opacity setting. (Images courtesy of The Orphanage.)

Figure 14.7 This sequence of frames shows a second bullet hitting the cab of the truck, using two elements: the painted bullet hit and the spark element, whose source was shot on black and added via Screen mode. (Images courtesy of markandmatty.com.)

Figure 14.8 The bullet hit is where you get to become a little bit of a matte painter. The example shows a bullet hole in metal, which has a fairly consistent look. If the bullet were to hit a door frame, you'd need to add irregular splintered wood. One frame is all that's ever required—mayhem happens quickly. Here, the result has been motion tracked to match the source background plate. (Images courtesy of markandmatty.com.)

Bullet Hits

Bullet hits on set are known as *squib hits* because they make use of squibs, small explosives with about the power of a firecracker that go off during the take. Sometimes squibs are actual firecrackers. Under some circumstances, it is possible to add bullet hits without using explosives on set, but with enough gunplay going on, you will probably need a mixture of on-set action (not necessarily actual squibs) and post-production wizardry.

Figure 14.7 shows a before-and-after shot adding a bullet hit purely in After Effects. In this case, the bullet is causing no collateral damage, but it is embedded directly into a solid metal object, namely the truck. In such a case, all you need to do is to paint the results of the damage on a separate layer at the frame where the bullet hits. Then, if necessary, you can motion track that layer to marry it solidly to the background frame (**Figure 14.8**).

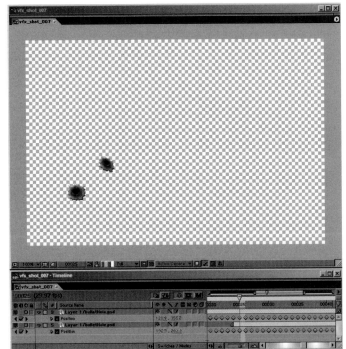

At the frame of impact and for a frame or two thereafter, you usually need to add a shooting spark and possibly a bit of smoke (if the target is combustible—not in the case of a steel vehicle) to convey the full violence of the bullets. As with the muzzle flash, this could be just a single frame, or it can be a more fireworks-like shower of sparks tracked in over a few frames (**Figure 14.9**). For the more elaborate case, you may want to composite in an element shot separately.

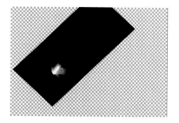

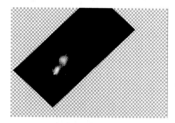

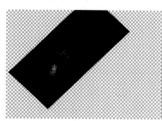

To create an element of a bullet hit, you can set up a little miniature effects shoot using a fire-retardant black background (a flat, black card might do it) and some firecrackers (assuming you can get them). The resulting flash, sparks, and smoke stand out against the black, which you can remove either using a blending mode that removes black (such as Add or Screen) or with the addition of a hi-con matte (Chapter 6, "Color Keying"). Or if dangerous explosives aren't your thing even in a controlled situation, there is stock footage available.

Figure 14.9 You can add the source spark element using Add or Screen blending mode, dropping out all of the black background. (Images courtesy of markandmatty.com.)

Figure 14.10 shows a before-and-after shot of a scene in which a lot of extra debris had to fly around in addition to the bullets to make the shot believable; the character's apartment was being strafed by the helicopter. Compositing in this debris after the shot was taken would be highly inconvenient, causing an impractical amount of extra work compared with firing a BB gun at items on the set and enhancing the effect with sparks and smoke in After Effects.

Figure 14.10 A BB gun was aimed at various breakaway objects on location and assistants hurled other small objects into the scene to add the necessary amount of debris on location. This has to do with compositing only as a reminder that you should try to get action on set when you can, particularly if you're making your own film. Practical debris is very difficult to add after the fact. (Images courtesy of The Orphanage.)

So to recap, a good bullet hit should include

- Smoke or sparks at the frame of impact, typically lasting between one and five frames
- The physical result of the bullet damage (if any) painted and tracked into the scene
- Debris in cases where the target is prone to shattering or scattering

Later in this chapter, you'll learn how much explosions have in common with bullet hits, which are essentially just miniature explosions. In both cases, a bit of practical debris can be the key to believability.

Sci-Fi Weaponry

Science fiction has long foreshadowed reality, so no one should be surprised if we eventually have weapons that resemble the blasters and lightsabers in *Star Wars* or the phasers and photon torpedoes in *Star Trek* (and as an ex-Lucas employee, I'm highly attuned to the distinctions among these). In these weapons of pure energy there are recognizable resemblances to phenomena from our own world: high-powered lasers and high-voltage electrical arcs.

The basic effect is so easy and well known that I almost hesitate to include it, but in the spirit of creating your own effects rather than relying on plug-ins, I'll give it a brief nod. At this point these are virtual clichés of science fiction, but you certainly can customize them with your own additions to the basic formula of a hot white core surrounded by a luminescent glow.

Full Control

A couple of effects in the Render category of the Effects menu automatically create an element with a core and a surrounding glow. For your basic blaster or lightsaber effect, you might be tempted to reach for Beam. And why not? As usual, with a canned effect you are surrendering artistic control for convenience, letting go of an opportunity to stand out a little bit with your attention to detail. In this case, it's things like the shape of the element and the softness of the glow that you can't customize. The result doesn't even look as good as the originals from almost 30-year-old movies, probably because those were done painstakingly by artists by hand. Anything you do in After Effects is going to be a lot easier than hand-rotoscoping lightsabers, I can almost guarantee it.

Figures 14.11a, b, and **c** compare the limits of Beam with a simple method that gives you more control. The steps are

1. Create the shape of a solid white core; this can be done with a four-point mask.

2. Duplicate the core, one layer above.

3. Colorize, expand, and blur it, then give it glow simply using Add mode.

4. Repeat as desired.

It's what you do next that makes it cool, and you have more options than you might think:

▶ Motion blur it.

▶ Add interactive lighting where needed, such as the glow on nearby faces and passing objects.

Figures 14.11a, b, and c Using the Beam effect at anything like its default is a straight-up no-no (14.11a)—it's cheesy. The same settings with Add mode at least give the right feel (14.11b), but you have no control over the look of the core or the glow—it's WYSIWIG. Turn the white core and purple glow into separate elements, combined in Add mode, and you start to get a look you can actually dial in how you like (14.11c).

▶ Add bullet hits, either like those discussed earlier or your own special version of energy coursing through the target.

▶ Layer in your own "special sauce:" Warp the overlay (using Mesh Warp or Liquify), add fractal patterning (with Fractal Noise), cause ripples in the very fabric of time and space (by combining Radio Waves and Displacement Map). Do whatever you can concoct that fits into the world you are re-creating (**Figure 14.12**).

Of course, I'm assuming you have free reign to do whatever you want. Even if you don't, you can still make suggestions. You never know, sometimes you might try something, and it sparks more ideas and gets other people excited.

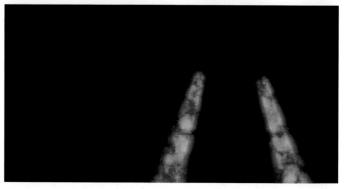

Figure 14.12 A quick and easy further customization to Beam is fractal patterning in the glow. The source layer makes the beams look a bit like they've been tie-dyed, but when added to the core it breaks up the effect in an interesting way that would be simple to animate.

Full Dimensionality

There is one way in which poor Beam does trump the approach of making your own effect in After Effects: It can approximate perspective (as shown back in **Figure 14.11a**). It's a total cheat that doesn't respect After Effects' 3D space at all. It's just a by-product of changing the start and end points to an angle, but it was done to offer a cheap way to send a blaster shot across the room.

So take the good and leave the bad. Use Beam as your core generator—just turn off its outer glow and make your own. Or add your own in addition to Beam's, like a triple-layer glow. There's no reason to abandon ship and head for the nearest 3D package simply because you couldn't see a way to do what you wanted with the default plug-ins, now is there?

Or why knock 3D animation software if you've got it? Create the craziest, most dynamic animated core effect you can devise in Maya (Alias) or 3ds max (Discreet), render it in a couple of passes for the core and glow layers and integrate it with your scene. Or use one of the lightning effects in After Effects as the basis for your energy bolt. Lightning is cruder but animates automatically. Advanced Lightning requires you to keyframe it to animate, but it has many controls and can even wrap around matte areas using the rather tricky Alpha Obstacle feature.

The point is this: No one is asking you to be clichéd. Even if you're doing a straight parody, the world wants to see something new and interesting. The way to get there in After Effects is to keep thinking of fresh ways to combine the tools you've got.

Heat Distortion

Heat distortion, that strange rippling in the air that occurs when hot air is dissipated into cooler air, is another one of those effects compositors love. Like a lens flare, it's a highly visible effect that, if properly motivated and adjusted, lends realism to your scene rather than distracting from its story.

Figure 14.13 shows the fabricated results of heat distortion in a scene. Its rippling effect adds to the dynamism or chaos of the scene. When your eye sees heat distortion, it understands that a strong conflict, accompanied by an abrupt mix of hot air with cold air, is occurring. This adds to the visceral reality of the shot, whether it's a desert exterior, a day at the racetrack, or a jet engine exhaust. When the fire itself is in the shot and you can see through it or anywhere above it, you expect the fire to heavily distort whatever is visible behind its heat.

Figure 14.13 The effect of heat haze has been added to the general mayhem being issued by the helicopter. A comparison with an unaltered shot of the building emphasizes the amount of distortion. (Images courtesy of The Orphanage.)

What Is Actually Happening

Stare into a swimming pool, and you'll see displacement caused by the bending of light as it travels through the water. Rippled waves in the water cause rippled bending of light. There are cases in which our seemingly transparent atmosphere behaves like this as well, when ripples are caused in it by the collision of warmer and cooler air.

As you know from basic physics, hot air rises and hot particles move faster than cool ones. Air is not a perfectly clear medium but a translucent gas that can act as a lens. The lens is usually static and flat, but in the case of heat distortion, the abrupt mixing of fast-moving hot air particles rising into cooler ambient air causes ripples that have the effect of displacing and distorting what is behind the moving air, just like the ripples in the pool.

You might think, therefore, that a physics model devised in 3D animation software would be more accurate than a 2D system. However, 3D software generally does not take into account the role of air in the shot, and in any case, the effect behaves like an overlaid distortion on top of whatever lays beyond the hot air from the point of view of the camera. Therefore it's perfectly appropriate as a compositing effect, useful when there is an object in the scene capable of generating a significant amount of hot air.

NOTES

In some cases it could be useful to generate the particles for heat distortion in a 3D animation package, if the distortion is located somewhere specific in a rendered scene and created by an animated object, such as the exhaust of a jet.

How to Re-create It

The basic steps for re-creating heat distortion from an invisible source in After Effects are

1. Create a basic particle animation that simulates the movement and dissipation of hot air particles in the scene.

2. Make two similar but unique passes of this particle animation—one to displace the background vertically, the other to displace it horizontally—and pre-compose them.

3. Add an adjustment layer containing the Displacement Map effect, which should be set to use the particle animation comp to create the distortion effect, and apply it to the background.

On the book's CD-ROM, you'll find a project file with the effect applied over a checkerboard background. You can easily see the results even in a still image (**Figure 14.14**). Setting up the particles is potentially the trickiest part, and of course the settings are unique for each scene.

I used Particle Playground because it is perfectly adequate for this type of use, and it ships with After Effects Professional. Unfortunately, Particle Playground is slow to render and cumbersome, full of not quite intuitive properties. The help documents are thorough, but there are dozens of pages of documentation. Thankfully, you need to adjust only four properties for this effect:

▶ Under Cannon, move Position to the location in the frame where the heat haze should originate (in this case, the bottom center).

Figure 14.14 A subtle effect, the heat displacement has been laid over a checkerboard where it is clearly visible traveling up the center of the image.

- ▶ Open up Barrel Radius from the default of 0.0 to the width, in pixels, of the source. I chose 50, only because 720, the width of the frame, would require many more particles and slow down the example.

- ▶ Boost Particles Per Second to 200. The larger the Barrel Radius, the more particles needed.

- ▶ Under Gravity, set Force to 0.0 to prevent the default fountain effect.

The default color and scale of the particles is fine for this video resolution example, but you might have to adjust them as well according to your shot. A larger format (in pixels) or a bigger heat source might need bigger, softer particles.

The next step is to duplicate the particles layer and set the color of the duplicated layer to pure green. To vary it slightly so that the particles don't overlap, raise Direction Random Spread and Velocity Random Spread from their defaults of 20 to 25.

The heat animation is almost complete; it only needs some softening, achieved by adding an adjustment layer with a moderate Fast Blur setting of 4.0 (**Figure 14.15**).

Now to put the animation to use: Drag it into the main comp, and turn off its visibility. The actual Displacement Map effect is applied either directly to the background plate or preferably to an adjustment layer sitting above all the layers that should be affected by the heat haze. Displacement Map is set by default to use the red channel for horizontal displacement and the green channel for vertical displacement; all you need to do is select the layer containing the red and green particles under the Displacement Map Layer pull-down.

Variations on the Theme

In many cases, heat displacement dissipates before it reaches the top of the frame. A classic example of this is the heat coming off an airport tarmac or an auto racetrack on a hot summer day. Making your particles behave so that their lifespan ends before they reach the top of the

Figure 14.15 The particles used to create the displacement. By default, Displacement Map uses red for horizontal displacement and green for vertical displacement. A slight amount of blur was added to soften the effect of each individual particle.

frame is an accurate way to model this, but it could become painstaking, whether you use Particle Playground or Particular. A simpler way to deal with the situation is to add a luma matte with a black-to-white gradient (created with the Ramp effect) to the adjustment layer containing the displacement effect.

Fire

Synthesizing fire from scratch is still an advanced topic within the upper reaches of visual effects research and development. I was employed at The Orphanage during its work on *Hellboy,* the film with a leading character whose preternatural gift is that she creates lots and lots of fire when upset. There was no way to use photographed fire for those shots because they required too much interaction with the rest of the scene. I was amazed at what the team responsible for these effects was able pull off.

Within After Effects, synthesizing fire is still way too hot to handle. If the fire is at all prominent in your shot, you will need to work with elements that come from somewhere else—most likely, shot with a camera. Take a look at what's involved.

Creating and Using Fire Elements

Figure 14.16 shows fire elements that were filmed for effects usage. The big challenge for compositing fire realistically is that it doesn't scale very well. You might think that any fire that you shoot with a camera will look better than something you create on a computer, but a fireplace fire always looks like it came from your hearth, no matter how you scale or retime it.

The bigger the fire you need to shoot, however, the more expensive it's likely to be because you really need the fire to be shot in negative space—against a black background—so that you can composite it using blending modes. Fire is obviously capable of illuminating the entire environment around it, so if that environment has specific detail, it can be all but impossible to isolate the fire from the environment.

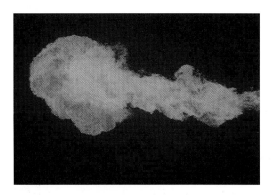

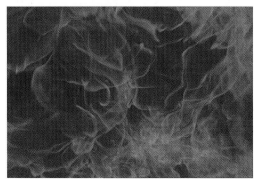

Figure 14.16 Some fire elements are shot in negative (black) space, others in a natural setting requiring a garbage matte in addition to Add or Screen mode to composite them. By adjusting Input Black in Levels, you can control the amount of glow coming off the fire. In many cases, this gives your scene some needed extra interactive lighting for free. (Images courtesy of Artbeats.)

This, then, is a case where it's worth investing in proper elements. In many cases, stock footage companies, such as Artbeats (represented on the book's CD-ROM), have anticipated your needs. Whether you require burning half-height miniature trees or a flamethrower, you're sure to find solutions for a wide variety of shots in these stock collections. Plus, the scale and intensity will be more appropriate than what you can likely shoot on your own.

Comping Fire

If you are starting with a fire element shot against black, the process for integrating it into your scene is highly reminiscent of the techniques for adding fog and mist. These types of elements, however, rely on Screen or Add blending modes rather than mattes to permit the background to be seen behind the fire. As with fog, the secret sauce is to add a Compound Blur effect behind the fire, using its luminance to soften the background behind it (**Figures 14.17a, b,** and **c**).

When you first screen your fire layer over the background, the effect may look rather weak. You need to fine-tune it with a Levels effect, pushing in on the histogram with Input White and Black to strengthen the look (**Figures 14.18a** and **b**).

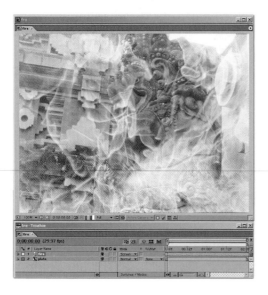

Figures 14.17a, b, and c A simple A over B comp doesn't cut it (14.17a), but add an adjustment layer with Compound Blur referring to the fire luminance as its blur layer and instantly, you begin to have something the viewer could believe (14.17b). A look at just the blurred background shows that a fairly heavy blurring is called for here (14.17c), but the nature of compound blur is that wherever there is a gap in the fire there will be no blur, so at full motion, it's a great effect. (Fire courtesy of Artbeats.)

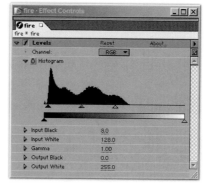

Figures 14.18a and b On first application with Screen mode (14.18a), the fire is barely visible over the background plate. To derive the results shown in **Figure 14.17b**, all you need is a strong Levels adjustment that raises the contrast of the fire element. (14.18b).

Figures 14.19a and b The background plate was stock footage of a raging fire (14.19a), but it wasn't raging quite enough. Compositing in more raging inferno footage required hi-con mattes for the opaque look of such intense fires to break through the overlaid extra layers of smoke (14.19b). (Figure 14.19b courtesy of ABC-TV.)

Only in the case of a raging inferno do you need to go beyond the blending modes approach and create an actual hi-con matte to make the core of the fire opaque (**Figures 14.19a** and **b**).

The Need for Interactive Light

Provided that your camera is not moving too much, a 2D fire layer should read adequately well as being fully three-dimensional. If it's not looking believable in your scene, the problem is probably a lack of interactive light. As was stated above, fire tends to illuminate everything around it with a warm, flickering glow.

Figure 14.20 Depending on the Levels settings you apply to the source fire element that you use, specifically Input White and Black on the RGB and Red channels, you can end up with a lot of extra glow or leave out the glow entirely.

There are a few ways to add this. First of all, as you can see in **Figure 14.20**, your fire element may include a certain amount of glow that you can use. Raising Input Black when adjusting Levels tends to eliminate this glow, so that control is an effective way to dial the glow in and out.

Note, however, that this glow isn't anything particularly unique or special; you can re-create it either via a heavily blurred duplicate of the source fire or using a masked and heavily feathered orange solid, with perhaps a slight amount of wiggle added to the glow opacity to cause a bit of interactive flickering.

If your shot has a close-up of a character or an object that should have fire reflecting off of it, don't immediately assume you have to go crazy projecting fire directly onto the subject. In many cases, it will be enough simply to create some flickering in the character's own luminance values, for example by wiggling the Input White value at a low frequency in Levels (Individual Controls). You can also achieve this by overlaying a colored solid or adjustment layer and wiggling its opacity, affecting the whole frame.

Into the Third Dimension

You can pull off the illusion of fully three-dimensional fire, especially if the camera is moving around in 3D space,

Figures 14.21a and b Before-and-after sequential stills of a flyover shot. Because of the angle of the aerial camera, the shot required 3D motion tracking, originally done using 2D3's Boujou. (Images courtesy of ABC-TV.)

right in After Effects. I was frankly surprised at how well this worked in the shot featured in **Figures 14.21a** and **b**.

As shown, the background plate is an aerial flyby of a forest. Because of the change in altitude and perspective, this shot clearly required 3D tracking (touched upon at the end of Chapter 8, "Effective Motion Tracking"). The keys to making this shot look fully dimensional were to break up the source fire elements into discrete chunks and to stagger those in 3D space so that as the plane rose above them, their relationship and parallax changed (**Figure 14.22**).

It is easy to get away with any individual fire element being 2D in this case. Because fire changes its shape constantly, there is nothing to give away its two-dimensionality. Borders of individual fire elements can freely overlap without being distracting, so it doesn't look cut out. The eye sees evidence of parallax between a couple dozen fire elements, and does not think to question that any individual one of them looks too flat. The smoke elements were handled in a similar way, organized along overlapping planes. As I mentioned in the previous chapter, smoke's translucency aids the illusion that overlapping smoke layers have dimensional depth.

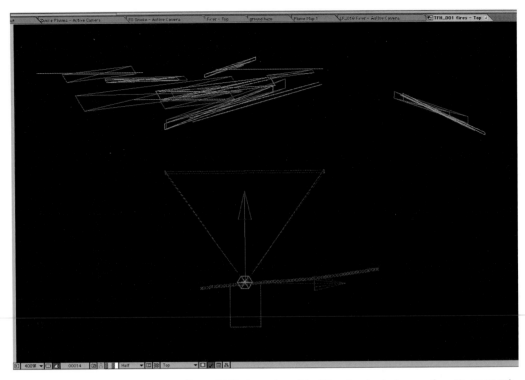

Figure 14.22 A top view of the 3D motion-tracked camera from **Figure 14.21b** panning past one set of fires (of which the final composition had half a dozen). The pink layers contain fire elements, the gray layers smoke.

Explosions

The example forest fire shot also contained a large explosion in a clearing. There is not a huge fundamental difference between how you composite an explosion and how you composite fire, except that an explosion is far more likely to require a mixture of strategies. It is largely a question of what is exploding.

All explosions are caused by rapidly expanding combustible gases; implosions are caused by rapid contraction. Just by looking at an explosion, viewers can gauge its size and get an idea of what blew up, however, so you need to design the right explosion for your situation, or your result will be too cheesy even for 1980s television sci-fi. How do you do it?

Light and Chunky

Each explosion you will see is a little bit unique, but for the purposes of this discussion I'm going to organize all explosions into two basic categories. The easier one to deal with is the *light explosion*, one that is made up only of gas and heat. These behave just like fire; in fact, in the shot in **Figure 14.21b** the explosion is fire, a huge ball of it where something very combustible must have gone up very quickly.

Some shots end up looking fake, however, because they use a light explosion when a more chunky explosion is called for. A *chunky explosion* is an explosion that also contains chunks of various types of debris. The need for debris to be included in the explosion is probably the primary reason that exploding miniatures are still used extensively these days or, when possible, full-scale explosions.

The debris cues viewers to several important pieces of information about the shot. First of all, how big was the explosion? The slower moving and bigger the amount of debris, the bigger it probably was. For this reason, effects pyrotechnics tend to use miniatures shot with a high-speed camera. The resulting slow-motion effect makes the explosion seem much bigger than it was.

If your shot calls for a chunky explosion and you don't have any chunks in your source, you need to add them somehow. Many 3D programs these days include effective dynamics simulations; if you go that route, be sure to generate a depth map as well because each chunk will only be revealed as it emerges from the fireball. There are lots of concerns associated with this that are beyond the scope of this discussion.

The only effect that comes close to doing this for you in After Effects is Shatter, but it's hard to recommend this unless you're specifically breaking a pane of glass in your shot. Shatter isn't bad as a dynamics simulator, but its primary limitation is a huge one: It can use only flat polygons to model the chunks. A pane of glass is one of the few physical objects that would blow up into irregular but flat polygons, and Shatter contains built-in controls for specifying the size of the shards in the point of impact. Shatter was also developed prior to the introduction of 3D in After Effects; you can place your imaginary window in perspective space, but not using a camera or 3D controls.

A wide selection of pyrotechnic explosions is also available as stock footage from such companies as Artbeats. In many cases, there is no substitute for footage of a real, physical object being blown to bits (**Figure 14.23**).

Fiery Conclusion

With good reference and a willingness to take the extra step to marry your shot and effect together, you can create believable footage that would require danger or destruction if taken with a camera. Even in cases when you work on a project that had the budget to actually re-create some of the mayhem described in this chapter, you can use the After Effects techniques to enhance and build upon what the camera captured.

And remember, be careful out there.

 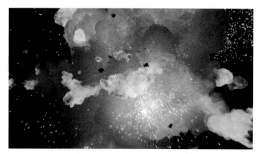

Figure 14.23 Pyrotechnics footage is just the thing when you need a big explosion, filled with debris. (Images courtesy of Artbeats.)

15

Learning to See

Men in the game are blind to what men looking on see clearly.

—Chinese Proverb

Learning to See

In visual effects, we often speak of The Eye, as in, "She has a good eye," or "He's got good technical skills, but needs to develop his eye." Sure, we admire the luminary visual effects supervisors because they can field-strip a Mitchell camera movement blindfolded or code their own HDR exposure-merging Shake plug-in from scratch, but they are most revered because they have The Eye.

What exactly does that mean? It's simple: Having The Eye means knowing the answer to the Ultimate Question:

Why doesn't this shot look real?

It's the question you're implicitly seeking to answer with every tweak of a slider, every opacity adjustment, every key-frame nudge. And it's the hardest question to answer about a shot. Worse still, as the shot progresses from take 1 to 10 to nearly final, the answer becomes more and more elusive.

This chapter focuses on some techniques for honing your eye. These are not compositing techniques—things you'll do sitting in front of your workstation—these are lifestyle techniques. Much to the chagrin of those close to you, being a great compositor means thinking like one all the time. The answer to the Ultimate Question, the hardest question you'll ever face, is all around you in the real world, especially when you're not near your computer.

The only tools you'll need are your eyes, your brain, and a really, really expensive digital camera. C'mon, you were looking for an excuse to buy one, right? No? Fine, a cheap film camera is just as good, if not better. Funny, that.

Why Doesn't This Shot Look Real?

The ability to answer the Ultimate Question comes from developing two distinct skills:

▶ Seeing the shot every time as if for the first time.

▶ Using the left brain to understand what the right brain sees.

If those things sound easy, then this book worked better than I thought it would! Please send your resume to The Orphanage immediately.

Seeing the Shot

The first skill is perhaps the most elusive. It is something I observed sitting in dailies with the great visual effects supervisors of Industrial Light + Magic. Complex shots on their 40th take loop relentlessly on a 30-foot screen. The animator can't see anything but the keyframe tweak he finally nailed five minutes *after* submitting this take. The technical director stares relentlessly at his particle simulation, pondering coefficients of elasticity. The compositor is the last line of defense. She feels like she's done a pretty good job of putting the shot together, but knows that the motion track could use one more pass of fine-tuning.

Everyone in the room has what is known as *Familiarity Disorder*. This is the condition that prevents my health plan administrator from successfully explaining my coverage options: He understands the various plans so well that he cannot possibly put himself in my position, which is that I need it explained to me as if I was four years old and mildly retarded. He can never do that because he's too close to the details. In '80s action movie police-chief-speak, he's "in too deep." Everyone in dailies is in too deep. And that's why the chief needs to take each one's piece and badge and shout a spittle-drenched "You're off the case!"

But not Dennis Muren. His job is to remain objective, and this is a mighty challenge. But I would watch him do this—see the shot every time as if for the first time—and he would skip right past these nuances and details that the various contributors were sweating and say something like, "We should slip the sync of that explosion back a few frames. It will cut better with the next few shots that way."

Not that Dennis would ignore the details. But he would not focus on them when something bigger, something about the storytelling properties of the shot, was still not quite right.

How do you develop this skill? It is a matter of discipline. You need to be intimately familiar with the details of the shot in order to work it to perfection, but to keep it from getting overworked, you have to consciously remind yourself to stand back and at least try to see it objectively. So cure number one for Familiarity Disorder is

1. Try.

As in, remind yourself that it's important. Take a deep breath, count to ten, and hear the chief's voice in your head, "You're in too deep!"

This may seem obvious, but in the heat of battle, with deadlines approaching pointy-end first, it requires a conscious effort to step back and evaluate the shot from as objective a perspective as possible.

Cure number two is

2. Look at it in the cut.

Check your shot in the context of the shots around it, preferably with sound and popcorn. I desperately wanted to add a very expensive, subtle enhancement to a shot I was compositing for *Twister.* An 18-frame shot. With four frame handles. Stefen Fangmeier showed me the cut sequence on the Avid and cured me of my desire in exactly half a second.

Cure number three is an easy one:

3. Flop it.

This is a trick that designers and matte painters use. Flop your shot horizontally and loop it. You'll be amazed how different it feels, and if you're lucky, something new will jump out at you and the problem you've been slaving over will seem far less important.

None of these three cures work as well as the last one. The last one is your ace in the hole—but you have to be selective about how you play it:

4. **Show it to someone who actually _is_ seeing it for the first time.**

   I know, duh. But it's amazing how often we forget to do this. We might even unconsciously not want our peers to point out the thing that we kind of suspect isn't quite working about the shot. Consult cure number one, swallow your pride, and show your buddy your shot.

One of the reasons that working against Familiarity Disorder is so important is, and I really hate to break this to you, there will always be something more you could do to make a shot better. But, chances are, you have a deadline to meet, so you have to pick your battles. I mentioned that Dennis Muren would be selective about how he would nitpick details. What I came to realize was that he was using his ability to emulate the audience's experience to pick which details to sweat. A well-designed shot leads a viewer's eye to specific places. When a defect in some remote corner of the frame was pointed out to Dennis, he'd say, "If they're looking there, we've lost them." He makes shots for the people who are engrossed in the film, and he prioritizes storytelling over immaculateness.

The discipline of maintaining your freshness to the work your doing will be something you struggle with on every shot. But remembering to struggle with it puts you way ahead of the game. Keep at it.

Analyzing What You See

The second skill that is required when struggling with the Ultimate Question is the reason that the chapter is called "Learning to See."

Have you ever taken a life drawing class? You should. The supplies are cheap and you get to look at naked people. Don't make me spell this out for you.

In life drawing you'll learn that you have to fight off the part of your brain that knows what an arm is. You know an arm is a long, skinny thing. But the model has an arm draped over a knee, aiming right at you. You see the arm heavily foreshortened or compressed in perspective. In fact, from your specific point of view, the elbow is directly in front of the shoulder, and the wrist is almost blocking it.

Now, of course your life drawing is perfect, but look what that idiot in front of you did. He drew the arm as a long, skinny thing. He did that because he *knows* that's what an arm looks like. He drew what he knew, not what he saw. And his arm be lookin' fonky.

Knowing What You Know

We do this all the time in visual effects without even realizing it. When asked to add an element, such as a haze effect, a lens flare, or a dust hit, you think "I know what that looks like" and add it to the shot. And it looks stupid. Why? Because in truth, we don't really know what things look like.

Let me use some theatrics here and ask you to read that last sentence again:

We don't really know what things look like.

Our brains are very complicated, sophisticated instruments that connect to our eyes in a slightly fancier way than an S-Video cable. When we visually absorb things, we don't see images, we recognize objects. We don't see colors and shapes, we see people and oncoming trains.

Don't believe me? Pop quiz: What color is the rearmost tomato in **Figure 15.1**?

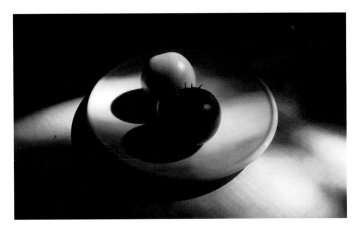

Figure 15.1 What color is the rearmost tomato?

Did you say yellow? If so, you are correct. But check this out: **Figure 15.2** is a crop of that image, showing just the tomato.

That patch of color is clearly green. How did you know it was yellow? Your brain looked past the color on the screen and saw that the whole image has a blue tint to it. Knowing this, and knowing a little about tomatoes, your brain filed that as a yellow object.

Your brain second-guesses your eyes like this all the time. College students quizzed on the height of a guest speaker guessed taller when they were told he was a visiting professor than when told he was a grad student. Eyewitnesses to crimes report widely differing descriptions of the criminal depending on their personal experiences and associations.

As compositors, it's our job to know that our brains are unreliable image banks—they store ideas, not pictures. So we can therefore correlate that if we create images based on what we know, we will be basing them on bad data. This is where that digital camera comes into play.

Figure 15.2 Ok, *now* what color is the tomato?

All Hail Reference

We have a great luxury in our industry, which is that every image we create is meant to look as though it was photographed by a camera. Hey, you have a camera!

You should be taking pictures all the time. Take your camera with you wherever you go. I actually forged a pact with a friend that we would each take a photo every day for the entire year of 2002. Not every one of those was going to be a masterpiece, but it got me thinking about creating an image at least once every day.

The other thing it did was fill my FireWire drive with thousands of photos. Photos of all kinds of crazy things. And these photos are great reference.

The single key to creating believable visual effects is *reference*. If you were to worship a pagan god of visual effects, it would be named Reference.

Now that brings up a catch, which is that the whole reason we do visual effects tends to be to create images of impossible things. You can search your image database all day long for snapshots you may have taken of Nazis opening ancient artifacts and unleashing God's wrath, but chances are the closest thing you'll find is your friend blowing chunks behind a wurst stand in Linz.

But there's always something to look at to help you combat the misconception that you already know what something should look like. What should a star going supernova look like? Better it look like your friend blasting your Digital Elph with a LED keychain light than the default lens flare preset number 47. What does a helicopter look like flying through the Chunnel? Well, the reflections on its metal surfaces won't be terribly dissimilar from those on a Geo Metro stuck in traffic in the midtown tunnel.

Getting in the habit of taking pictures all the time, even of mundane things, and really looking at those photos— examining what's happening with light and surfaces and transparencies—will do more than supply you with reference for future projects. It will get you thinking about these things in ways that will have a direct impact on your work.

Putting Reference to Use

Check out **Figure 15.3**'s picture of the Golden Gate Bridge. Every once in a while this monument is half enshrouded in the "marine layer" like this. (I am told that to call it fog is blasphemous.) But what if it wasn't on the day when your shoot needed it to be, or what if you are compositing a matte painting of a future city with buildings so tall their tops get cut off by clouds?

Zooming way in, you can see how the cloud obscures the bridge in a way that is more complicated than a simple transparent overlay (**Figure 15.4**). The cloud actually acts like mist on your windshield, diffracting the light before completely occluding it.

When I first started seeing this in my photography, it changed the way I composited smoke elements. I got in

Figure 15.3 Here's some big, orange bridge I just found walking around one day.

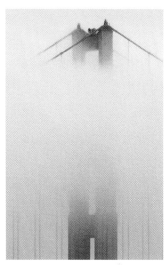

Figure 15.4 An enlargement of **Figure 15.3** shows light diffraction through clouds.

Figure 15.5 The same bridge is bereft of brume.

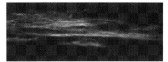

Figure 15.6 If the weather doesn't cooperate, extract a cloud element from another photo.

the habit of using the alpha channel of the fog or cloud or water spray element to drive a compound blur of the background.

Here's an example. **Figure 15.5** shows a clean photo of the bridge, and **Figure 15.6** is the cloud element to be composited over it.

If you do a simple A over B comp, you'll end up with something like **Figure 15.7**.

Now check out that same comp with a subtle compound blur in **Figure 15.8**.

Figure 15.7 The cloud element is simply layered over the bridge photo.

Figure 15.8 The same composite with Compound Blur. See the difference?

The blur simulates the diffraction of the light and ties the cloud element into the shot. This is a great example of how even the most basic layering requires pre-composing in After Effects. Compound Blur uses the pixels from one layer to control how much to blur another layer. But the trick is that it uses the pixels before any effects of transformations. So you need a pre-comp where you reposition and possibly even animate the cloud layer. Here's how to set it up:

1. Create a Cloud Anim comp that features just the semi-transparent cloud with whatever animation you create.

2. Bring the Cloud Anim comp into a Cloud Over Bridge comp, and stack it on top of the bridge photo.

3. Because Compound Blur cannot directly use this layer's alpha channel as its blur layer (it uses Luminance of RGB), duplicate the Cloud Anim layer and apply Shift Channels, setting Alpha to Full On and Red, Green, and Blue to Alpha.

4. Because Compound Blur needs to see the pixels of a layer before any effects, pre-compose this layer (choosing the Move All Attributes option from the dialog), and name the pre-comp Cloud Blur Map.

5. Because Cloud Blur Map is used only to drive the Compound Blur, you can turn its visibility off in Cloud Over Bridge.

6. In Cloud Over Bridge, create a new adjustment layer between the cloud and the bridge and apply the Compound Blur effect. Choose Cloud Blur Map from the Blur Layer pull-down menu.

7. Adjust both the Maximum Blur and the Opacity of the adjustment layer to dial in the effect to match your reference.

If all goes well, your Flowchart view should look something like **Figure 15.9**. Now, if you move or even replace your cloud layer in the Cloud Anim comp, the rest of the comp will reflect those changes automatically.

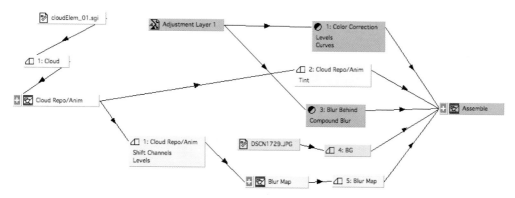

Figure 15.9 Take a look at the bridge composite in Flowchart view.

Integration

In compositing, we talk about *integration* of elements. Yes, this means color correction, matching black levels, and tracking in the right motion, but the more advanced tricks of integration usually can be filed under the general idea of "everything in the scene affects everything else in the scene." Much of the reference you collect will yield revelations along these lines.

Check out **Figure 15.10**. Imagine it's your job to add an annoying CG alien next to this handsome guy. The 3D artist has lit the alien to match, but dropping him in A over B leaves the shot looking sad.

Take a closer look at the guy by extracting him from the shot (**Figure 15.11**).

Figure 15.10 What a handsome guy.

Figure 15.11 Isolate Handsome from his scene.

When you isolate him from the scene, it becomes very clear that he has a lot of contamination from the bright background behind him. Your eye can cancel this out in the same way it can allow you to see that the green tomato is really yellow, but when you isolate the guy you prevent your brain from "knowing" that it's right for the dude to look washed out if he's against a bright sky.

That CG alien is going to need more than just color correction, he's going to need *light wrap,* or a simulation of this contamination. This is a popular effect that is available as a plug-in and tempting to overuse. Because of the order of operations in After Effects layers, however, it's also very easy to use light wrap effect plug-ins incorrectly. For example, if you apply light wrap to a foreground layer and you tell it to wrap to the background, it will grab the pixels of the background before any color correction you may have done to it, which is not good. In the interest of becoming more mighty, create a light wrap effect from scratch using only layer blend modes and the Fast Blur effect, using the process detailed back in Chapter 12, "Working with Light." Here it is in brief:

1. Create a pre-comp with your background and foreground elements.

2. Set the foreground to the Silhouette Alpha blend mode. This punches a hole in the background.

3. Add an adjustment layer at the top, and apply Fast Blur.

4. Turn Repeat Edge Pixels on, and crank up Blurriness until you really can see it.

5. Duplicate the foreground layer, move the copy to the top, and switch this new top layer to the Stencil Alpha blend mode. You are left with a halo of background color that matches the shape of the foreground.

And that's your light wrap element. Create a new comp that has this light wrap pre-comp on top of the foreground on top of your color-corrected background. As with the last example, it's both the blur size and the opacity of the layer that you use to dial in this effect. Generally you will use big blurs and small opacities, but there are times where you might use just the opposite. And you can play with various blend modes for the light wrap layer; Normal, Screen, Lighten, and Add are all good options.

Sometimes a photo will suggest a cool technique like this. Other times it will simply help you dial in the look of an effect. When I was asked to create the most dreaded of all compositing effects, a lens flare, for a shot in *Star Wars, Episode One: The Phantom Menace*, I asked John Knoll to shoot some reference the next time he was on the motion control stage. In between explosions and lightsaber sparks, John had the crew shoot a series of flare reference passes with various lenses. We picked the one we liked, and I spent three days (and about 17 nested After Effects comps) matching it exactly.

Emotional Truth

Photographic reference can help you get the facts straight in your shot. The highlights on your stompy robot look just like the ones on the live action car he's about to step on—no one can argue with the realism of that. But photos can also help us with another, far more nebulous concern.

Our clients are making movies, and movies are designed to do one thing: elicit an emotional reaction from the

TIP

Fast Blur and Gaussian Blur are the same (at Best quality), except that Gaussian Blur has no Repeat Edge Pixels option. So you might as well throw Gaussian Blur away.

audience. Even though our clients know that they are using technical tools to achieve this goal, they are still reacting emotionally to the images we show them. This is true whether you're working for a first time indie auteur or James Cameron. Clients react from the gut—as well they should. But here's the catch: They critique in technical terms.

This is a problem that I suspect jazz musicians do not have. When they are jamming and creating a new tune, I bet they are totally comfortable talking in emotional terms about their work. "Dude, this just isn't reminding me enough about the ills of society. We need to get more *strife* into this track!" OK, clearly I know as much about jazz as I know about running an oil refinery. The point is that our clients are not comfortable saying things like "This shot isn't scary enough," or "This shot just needs more umph!" That may well be their reaction, but rather than simply saying that, they feel compelled to suggest possible solutions. "Make his teeth more wet," or "Throw a lens flare in there."

At The Orphanage, we once had a very tech-savvy client who was obsessed with a shot that he felt was falling way short on photorealism. Every time it would come up, this client would explode with reasons why it was not realistic-looking. This contact shadow isn't right. There's not enough detail here. These particles are too bright. We looked at shots that had finaled already and saw what our shot was missing. We made it darker, more blue, and we added contrast. The shot finaled. We addressed the emotional shortcomings of the shot and the technical problems, legitimate as they may have been, magically went away.

The lesson here is: Don't be afraid to make your shots beautiful. And your photography should help you. Chances are you've taken a hundred sunset shots that look like you shot them with a camera phone. Sunsets are hard, especially with digital cameras. But I bet you've got one sunset shot that you just nailed. It's a thing of beauty. Well, compare it to your hundred crappy sunsets and analyze the differences. And when the time comes to create a dusk shot of the enemy base, eyedropper the color palette straight out of your good one.

The matte paintings of Cloud City in the original *The Empire Strikes Back* are perfect examples of this. These paintings by

Ralph McQuarrie are not very photoreal. But it so does not matter. You know why? Because they are purple and orange. They are beautiful, and they strike an emotional chord in the viewer. Have a smooth Colt 45 and watch your precious laserdiscs of the original *Star Wars* movies, because you truly belong here with us among the clouds.

If you take enough boring pictures of your car (**Figure 15.12**), one of them will eventually look decent (**Figure 15.13**).

Figure 15.12 A boring photo of a non-boring car.

The emotional resonance of a shot can also be linked to a common technical mistake. One of the biggest sins of visual effects shots that are built up from scratch is that they tend to contain no overexposed or underexposed elements. Skies are often a good example of this. Show me a shot with a perfectly exposed blue sky with no blown-out detail, and I'll show you a visual effect. The reason that the notorious car comp, in which the view out the window of a vehicle shot on a green-screen stage is replaced with moving scenery, usually looks wrong is often that the artist failed to slightly overexpose the exterior. **Figure 15.14** shows the kind of reference that can help you nail your next car comp.

Figure 15.13 Those are speed fangs.

Night exteriors are the worst culprits. In the middle of a sequence of inky black night shots set off by artificial but highly cinematic rim lighting, you can smell the matte painting coming from a mile away. It's the only shot where you can clearly see everything *except* where the light is coming from!

The eyedropper, the Info palette, and our friends Copy and Paste can help make tangible the intangible reasons why some images pop and some go thud. You are not just a technician assembling elements. You are a salesperson, trying to get the audience to buy the shot, warts and all. Use your reference and your dirty tricks, and close that deal.

Figure 15.14 Dare to overexpose the stuff you comp out the window.

Rolling Thine Own

When you use these techniques to start seeing the world, and then begin implementing your profound insights in your comps, you will begin to see the importance of this last point: It is almost always better to create effects from the basic toolkit of After Effects than to resort to an off-the-shelf, canned effect.

"Default" is a dirty word. Remember that weeklong effort to re-create a photoreal lens flare? It's worth noting that this effort was supported fully by the guy whose name is synonymous with digital lens artifacts. But even John Knoll knew that to appear unflinchingly huge on the big screen, his schwings were going to need some nuancing.

I hope you do have Knoll Light Factory(Red Giant Software; a demo is on the CD-ROM) because its documentation is an excellent treatise on the importance of good reference. John points out some of the vital design aspects of flares that he noticed when scrutinizing the real thing.

In **Figure 15.15**'s real-life flare, the little septagonal reflections that slice through the center of the frame have seven sides because the camera's aperture has seven blades. The star-shaped core of the flare has 14 points (not counting the purplish CCD smear), each pair perpendicular to the edge of one of these blades. This is because the star is an artifact of light grazing off the edge of the aperture blades. This also means that if you were to defocus an element in this shot, you should use a five-sided camera blur shape for the proper boke effect for this lens.

Figure 15.15 I'm directly below the Earth's sun…now!

Now, if you start throwing out terms like "boke" in dailies, even Dennis Muren will be impressed.

Most effects we use in After Effects are built up of smaller, simple filtering operations that themselves exist as effects. There's nothing about the built-in Glow effect, for example, that you cannot easily create on your own. You could wrestle with Glow all day long and never match the reference you shot of an F-18 afterburner, but with your homebrew glow not only will you have finer control, but you will have a better understanding of how glows work (**Figure 15.16**).

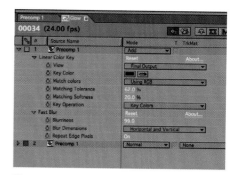

Figure 15.16 This simple glow outperforms the default.

After Effects ships with hundreds of effects. Apple's Shake ships with far fewer nodes but is viewed as "high end." Although some would say that the decision to eschew canned effects is one you arrive at after becoming an expert, I propose that the opposite is true: Skipping the all-in-one plug-ins and developing your own looks from scratch will propel you toward expert status.

Not a Conclusion

This chapter is not composed of conclusions. It is a dog-eared page in the lifelong process of one visual effects supervisor. We will all struggle with the answer to the Ultimate Question with each new shot. Keep taking pictures, remember your cures for Familiarity Disorder, and beg those close to you for forgiveness—for you are a compositor for life.

Index

What's on the CD?

Professional tools produce professional results, and the *Adobe After Effects 6.5 Studio Techniques* CD-ROM has what you need to add new dimension to your work. The disc includes demos of more than a dozen plug-ins and programs, including After Effects itself. Not simply glorified ads, these are test-drivable versions that let you experiment with your own footage. Check out what you get:

▶ **After Effects 6.5** (*Adobe*): Shows you what you've been missing with earlier versions.

▶ **SynthEyes** (*Andersson Technologies*) Provides fully automatic, as well as user-controlled match moving for single or batch-processed shots; a stand-alone program that exports to After Effects.

▶ **eLin** (*Red Giant Software*): Converts clips between linear color space and either video or film color space, enabling you to work with the linear color model in After Effects to produce more photorealistic effects and lighting.

▶ **Particular** (*Trapcode*): Designs 3D particle systems that simulate air resistance, gravity, and turbulence; provides real-time preview, as well as controls so you can freeze time and manipulate a camera in the scene.

▶ **Lenscare** (*Frischluft*): Includes two plug-ins: Depth of Field produces depth-of-field effects using a depth buffer; Out of Focus creates a blur with a constant radius over the complete image.

- **Knoll Light Factory** (*Red Giant Software*): Includes such pre-built lighting effects as lens flares, sparkles, glows, and more; also provides individual lens components so you can create your own custom effects.

- **Primatte Keyer** (*Red Giant Software*): Extracts keys from any background and includes controls to handle uneven lighting, difficult shadows, light spill, and more.

- **Lux** (*Trapcode*): Simulates light reflection, using After Effects' built-in lights to create visible light that corresponds to your layers' lighting schemes.

- **Shine** (*Trapcode*): Produces a 2D light-ray effect that closely resembles volumetric light; includes controls for coloring and shimmering lights.

- **Composite Wizard** (*Red Giant Software*): Optimizes composites and automates color correction, blurring or feathering of edges, artifact removal, and more.

- **Magic Bullet Suite** (*Red Giant Software*): Manipulates digital video to look like film with tools for 24p conversion, mimicking film artifacts and damage, creating film-like cross dissolves, removing DV compression artifacts, and more.

- **3D Stroke** (*Trapcode*): Creates organic shapes using paths from masks and renders volumetric strokes that you can manipulate in 3D space.

- **Starglow** (*Trapcode*): Produces an eight-pointed star-shaped glow around a source's highlights; enables you to assign each direction of the star an individual color map and streak length.

- **Sound Keys** (*Trapcode*): Generates keyframes from audio energy; enables you to select a range in an audio waveform, then converts the frequencies into a stream of keyframes.

You'll also find stock footage from Artbeats that you can use to practice your techniques.

Finally, because sometimes the best way to understand something is to see it, the CD-ROM includes example clips and images for many of the techniques discussed in this book, including light wrap, relighting, morphing, and more.